W0246835

Madan Mohan Malaviya and the Indian Freedom Movement

Madan Mohan Malaviya and the Indian Freedom Movement

Jagannath Prasad Misra

Indian Council of Historical Research

OXFORD
UNIVERSITY PRESS

Oxford University Press is a department of the University of Oxford.
It furthers the University's objective of excellence in research, scholarship,
and education by publishing worldwide. Oxford is a registered trademark of
Oxford University Press in the UK and in certain other countries

Published in India by
Oxford University Press
22 workspace, 2nd Floor, 1/22 Asaf Ali Road, New Delhi 110002

© Indian Council of Historical Research 2016

The moral rights of the author have been asserted

First Edition published in 2016

All rights reserved. No part of this publication may be reproduced, stored in
a retrieval system, or transmitted, in any form or by any means, without the
prior permission in writing of Oxford University Press, or as expressly permitted
by law, by licence, or under terms agreed with the appropriate reprographics
rights organization. Enquiries concerning reproduction outside the scope of the
above should be sent to the Rights Department, Oxford University Press, at the
address above

You must not circulate this work in any other form
and you must impose this same condition on any acquirer

ISBN-13: 978-0-19-946375-6
ISBN-10: 0-19-946375-1   .

Typeset in Bembo Std 10.5/13
by Tranistics Data Technologies, New Delhi 110 044
Printed in India by Repro India Limited

Table of Contents

Abbreviations

AICC	All India Congress Committee
BHU	Banaras Hindu University
C.V.R. Papers	C.Vijayaraghavachariar Papers
CWC	Congress Working Committee
CWMG	*Collected Works of Mahatma Gandhi*
CWLR	*Collected Works of Lala Lajpat Rai*
GAD	General Administration (Uttar Pradesh State Archives)
ICS	Indian Civil Services
NAI	National Archives of India
NMML	Nehru Memorial Museum and Library
SWMN	*Selected Works of Motilal Nehru*
SWJN	*Selected Works of Jawaharlal Nehru*
UP	United Provinces
UPSA	Uttar Pradesh State Archives

Preface

This work aims at providing an integrated analysis of Madan Mohan Malaviya's long-term involvement in Indian nationalist politics. It takes Malaviya as its focus but becomes, of necessity, an investigation into the changing nature of India's nationalist struggle. It traces, from new and authentic source material, precisely what Malaviya did, whom he relied on for support, what his relations were with the established political leaders of the country, and how he saw his own actions and role in Indian public life. It asks whether Malaviya's career generated certain changes in Indian politics and, if so, in what directions, or whether it exploited existing forces of change in politics and society. It attempts to trace various stages of Malaviya's leadership and his ability to retain and wield authority.

The study concentrates much more on the relationship between Malaviya and his followers, between Malaviya and the Congress leadership, and between Malaviya and various leaders and workers of the Muslim League, the Hindu Mahasabha, the Sikh leaders, and those belonging to various other organizations or institutions. It investigates the means of communication between them, the barriers and contradictions, and tries to assess the way they influenced one another. An attempt is also made to explain the continuity of his long-term involvement in the Indian nationalist struggle in terms of not only the changing constitutional structure but also the organizational base of his leadership. The study examines how the method and manner of Malaviya's nationalist propaganda and some of the campaigns launched by him tended to affect the different communities.

Information about Malaviya is particularly difficult to find because he was not in the habit of entering into regular correspondence with his contemporaries. We have information that he made no effort to preserve his letters, telegrams, or other communications. Unfortunately, even after his death, no efforts were made to collect, preserve, or publish his papers. This has made the task of later researchers far more difficult than in the case of other nationalist leaders. As a result, we have to go through various scattered sources to locate his letters, correspondence, and statements, without which any investigation of his role would not be very convincing.

As most of the authors writing on Malaviya made no serious effort to consult various original sources and as Malaviya's private papers are not available, it became absolutely necessary for me to go through source material available for consultation at the National Archives of India, New Delhi; Nehru Memorial Museum and Library, New Delhi; the Uttar Pradesh State Archives, Lucknow; and various other research centres, institutions, and libraries located in different cities. These are included in the select bibliography.

This study is primarily based on the proceeding volumes and files of the Home–Political Department, Government of India (cited as Home Poll); the microfilm collections of the private papers of the viceroys and governors of United Provinces (UP; now Uttar Pradesh); and the documents available for consultation at the Uttar Pradesh State Archives (UPSA), Lucknow. Because of the unavailability of Malaviya's papers, the letters and telegrams addressed to him and some of the replies received from him, available in the private papers of other leading nationalists of the time, help us to understand how he thought and acted at a given time or in a given situation. These private papers throw much light on Malaviya's role and are authentic records of his contemporaries. These papers become all the more valuable as the letters available in these series were often written either immediately before or soon after a major event, meeting, or gathering, and the immediate reaction of the nationalist leaders often assumes great significance. This study has been undertaken with a detailed review of the contemporary newspapers, both in English and Hindi. I have made special efforts to consult the newspapers and journals founded and patronized by Malaviya. The microfilms of *Abhudaya*, the *Leader*, and the *Hindustan Times* were consulted with a view to examining his major interests during the period.

I am thankful to the authorities and the staff of the National Archives of India, New Delhi; the Uttar Pradesh State Archives, Lucknow; the

Nehru Memorial Museum and Library, New Delhi; the Nagri Pracharni Sabha, Varanasi; the Theosophical Society Library, Varanasi; and the Central Library, Banaras Hindu University, for providing me facilities and help. I am obliged to Sri B.M. Birla for providing me photocopies of several letters and other correspondence of Sri G.D. Birla.

I recall with pleasure the warmth and affection extended to me by my son, Awadhesh, sons-in-law, Ramesh and Anurag, and daughters, Sandhya and Seema. Madhavan, Mukul, Sarthak, Roli, Suhasni, and Shristi have made my life a great deal more interesting and rewarding than it would have otherwise been. My wife, Padma, has constantly been by my side in this endeavour, always offering encouragement and support.

I acknowledge with gratitude and thanks the cooperation extended to me by Professor Anand Shankar Singh and my former colleagues at the Department of History, Banaras Hindu University.

I am deeply obliged to the Chairman and the Member-Secretary of the Indian Council of Historical Research, New Delhi, for their decision to publish this book.

I alone am responsible for the deficiencies that remain and the opinions expressed.

Jagannath Prasad Misra

1 Transformation

Indian nationalism was a direct outcome of the establishment of the British imperial authority and colonial economy in our country and the slow but inevitable transformation of our traditional economy by the late nineteenth century. Western education and learning, and all that flowed and followed from it, were only corollaries to the colonial imperial policy followed by the British. This gave rise to an English-educated and professional elite, which helped and expedited the process of significant social change in the urban life of the country. This new class and the process of change in which it was involved gave birth to nationalism in India.[1]

During the last quarter of the nineteenth century, the idea of Indian nationalism was still in its early stages of construction. Indian leaders were defining the concept in different ways depending on their own background and perspective. In various localities and provinces, two broad patterns were slowly emerging. There was an influential secular and political strain along with strong community concerns emerging side by side in various urban centres of UP, particularly at Allahabad. Since English-educated men continued to identify with their respective castes and communities, they often belonged to organizations of both types, one based on socio-cultural-religious persuasions and the other on political persuasions. What connected them was that each type of association penetrated the membership of the other.[2] Malaviya played the two roles side by side and provided the linkage between the two types of associations at Allahabad.

In the early stages of its development, the vision of a national movement in India was substantially different from what was seen after 1920.

During this stage, India and the emerging nation were conceived as a collection of communities, each with its own history and culture and its own special contribution to the common nationality.[3] Thus the communities together constituted the nation and service to community implied service to country. Terms such as 'nation' and 'community' were being commonly used by politicians by the turn of the century and the widespread notion was that India was one country and its people a nation. Malaviya's range of activities during the earlier part of his career, both at the local and national levels, were largely influenced as well as determined by such concerns.

The Indian National Congress grew out of the secular associations and the social reform movements of the later decades of the nineteenth century. It was significant not only because it began to work at the all-India level right from the time it was founded, but also because it provided a link with organizations and leaderships at the regional, district, and local levels of politics. It was through this linking effect that the Congress encouraged the local leaders to play an active role at the subcontinental level as well.

THE LOCAL AND REGIONAL POLITICAL RESPONSE

The Indian National Congress, in the first two decades of its existence, was an amorphous annual gathering of English-educated, middle-class, professional men interested in questions of public affairs in India. It had no continuous executive body and did not have a uniform structure of organization in all parts of India. By the very nature of circumstances of its establishment and the type of persons who were attracted to the Congress, it was impossible for the party to develop as a centralized institution. Virtually anyone could gain admission to its ranks leading to an enormous potential for diversity within the Congress Party. Such inclusiveness inevitably opened it up to varied and contradictory doctrinal interpretations, both by its followers and its opponents. It also meant that as the Congress took root in India as the premier nationalist political organization, its decentralized mode became apparent.

The capture of the Congress at the local level by many of the same elements of the emerging middle class that were promoting the integration of the Hindu community around the theme of cultural reconstruction and self assertion was the most significant reason for political mobilization in UP. This requires detailed attention. What happened, of course, was that as a political organization, the Congress needed financial support and an expanding membership. It could not, therefore, ignore the issues, forces, and actors at play in urban politics. As the prime sources of both manpower and money were the local merchants, bankers, professionals, and religious figures, the Congress had to make the concerns of these social categories its own concerns. Both membership and leadership in various cities of UP heavily overlapped those of the explicitly casteist, communalist, and political organizations within a decade of the establishment of the Congress in 1885.[4]

This interlocking nature of the Congress support was largely due to the 'rich commercial men' who were funding both Congress and revivalist organizations. They directly or indirectly helped to strengthen the forces of Hindu cultural revivalism within the emerging nationalist movement.[5]

EARLY CAREER

Madan Mohan Malaviya came from a family of devoted priests who had settled in Allahabad and were engaged in the exposition of the Puranas and other religious texts. His father, Brij Nath, an erudite pandit reputed for the exposition of ancient lore, was the author of several books in Sanskrit and earned his livelihood by reciting the Ramayana and Bhagwat Gita. The earning thus acquired by him was far too meagre for the family.[6] Born on 25 December 1861, Malaviya was brought up in this traditional cultural atmosphere, which remained a decisive influence on him all through his life. Though he commenced his schooling in a Sanskrit school, he was later sent to a local Government High School. As a child from an orthodox family, Malaviya had to adjust to the discipline of a school which had recently been started functioning under a European headmaster. It, however, helped him immensely in gaining proficiency in the English language.[7]

The Muir College of Allahabad, where Malaviya sought admission for higher education, was the premier educational institution of the province. His stay in the college for five years, from 1879 to 1883, proved very fruitful and momentous in the full development of his personality and talents. His tenure as a student at Muir College opened up before him the vast treasure house of western learning. English education helped him considerably to broaden his vision and encouraged him to take up social and political issues in a spirit of sympathy and accommodation.[8] While he was still at college, he started writing on public issues in local journals and took part in the activities of the Prayag Hindu Samaj. This was largely due to the inspiration of Aditya Ram Bhattacharya, the Sanskrit professor of the college, who patronized and guided the young Malaviya and encouraged him to play an active part in socio-political awakening.[9] Malaviya remained in close touch with Professor Bhattacharya, drew inspiration from him, and constantly sought his guidance and advice.[10]

After obtaining his BA degree in 1884, Malaviya was forced to suspend his studies due to the financial hardships that his family was facing.[11] He joined as a teacher in the local Government High School. But that did not dishearten him and he waited for a suitable opportunity to prove his mettle. Such an opportunity came his way at the time of the second session of the Congress.

THE SOCIO–POLITICAL SETTING AT ALLAHABAD

That Malaviya grew up in Allahabad is a fact of considerable significance since the city provided the setting in which he could rise to his full potential in the semi-political organizations and in the local Hindu society. It has been pointed out that the 1880s saw the emergence of such leaders in Allahabad 'who appear to have employed fairly indiscrimately "traditional" and "modern" idioms of propaganda and were connected both with new public associations and with older forms of social power'.[12] It reflected the response of the local Hindu society to the challenges posed by the activities of the provincial government. It is through the examination of the distinctive socio-cultural features of Allahabad, and indeed of the North-Western Provinces (as Uttar Pradesh was then known) as a whole in the last quarter of the nineteenth century, that we can analyse the early role of Malaviya in local and regional politics.

Following in the footsteps of his preceptor, Aditya Ram Bhattacharya, Malaviya was involved with associations professing socio-religious activities in Allahabad. He joined the newly established Hindu Samaj while pursuing his studies as an undergraduate student at Muir College. When the Samaj was later reoriented as a provincial organization and renamed the Madhya Hindu Samaj, Malaviya became actively associated with it. Even though the purpose of the Hindu Samaj was the uplift of Hindus and to push through Hindu interests, the newly established local organization was also involved in a wide range of other activities in the city. It played an effective role in the management of the Magh Mela, a fair held every year near Allahabad at the confluence of the Ganga and Yamuna Rivers, and encouraged its members to help the local administration.[13] The Madhya Hindu Samaj was one of the recognized political bodies through which delegates were elected to attend the annual session of the Indian National Congress. Malaviya attended the second Congress session at Calcutta in 1886 as one of the representatives of the Madhya Hindu Samaj.

The socio-political conditions of the region reflected the emergence and growth of revivalism together with the consolidation of political awakening in UP. It should, however, be pointed out here that Malaviya 'was never amongst the most zealous'[14] campaigners of the cow-protection movement of the period.

EDITORSHIP OF THE *HINDUSTAN*

Malaviya's teaching career spanned only a short period, and he shifted to journalism soon after the Calcutta Congress session of 1886. While attending the session, Ram Pal Singh, the raja of Kalakankar, was so impressed by Malaviya's oratory and talents that he immediately offered him the editorship of a Hindi daily newspaper, *Hindustan*, which was already in circulation under his ownership—a challenging task to be assigned to a young Malaviya who was, at the time only twenty-six years old.[15] He lost no time in picking his own team of young Hindi scholars, guided them in writing on social and political issues, and most ably conducted the newspaper by giving it a new orientation. The *Hindustan* gained in circulation and was adjudged the 'best edited' newspaper.[16] Even though Malaviya was able to steer the newspaper onto a new course, his association with it did not last long. He severed his connection with the newspaper in as dramatic a fashion as he had joined it. That Malaviya left the job in this way speaks volumes about his strength of character. He resigned from the post at a time when he had no other alternative source of income. But that did not deter him from compromising on the principles which were dearer to him.[17] He was not willing to accept the patronage of anyone, howsoever wealthy and mighty he might have been. The raja proved equally magnanimous and continued to pay Malaviya the salary he was drawing as an editor and maintained the best of relations with him.[18]

After severing his connections with the *Hindustan*, Malaviya decided to qualify himself for the bar. He passed the pleadership examination in 1891, and after obtaining his law degree from the University of Allahabad in 1892, started practice at the district court and later at the high court. Within a few years, he established himself as a lawyer of distinction, earned both fame and fortune, and quickly rose to eminence in the profession.[19] He stayed in the legal profession for as long as it was absolutely necessary for him to be able to provide a suitable financial foundation for his family. No sooner that he realized that he had fulfilled this responsibility, he bid goodbye to his legal career. Malaviya had no ambition to amass money and had his eyes set for higher and nobler vocations. He gave up his legal practice in 1911 and began to concentrate on his lifelong work, the establishment of a university at Banaras.[20]

MAKING HIS MARK AT THE EARLY CONGRESS SESSIONS

Malaviya's superb performance during the second session of the Indian National Congress at Calcutta held in 1886 proved to be a turning point in his life and political career. For a young man who had graduated only two years earlier and worked as a school teacher in a Government High School at Allahabad, it required considerable courage and talent to make his maiden speech in this august body. For Malaviya, this proved to be a fitting occasion to exhibit his rare qualities of the head and the heart. His speech in support of the resolution demanding the extension of popular representation in legislative councils made a lasting impression on the audience. A.O. Hume, the founder of the Indian National Congress, was deeply impressed by the speech and wrote about it in terms of high appreciation in his official report of the session, where the following passage occurs:

> But perhaps the speech that was most enthusiastically received was one by Pandit Madan Mohan Malaviya, a high caste Brahmin, whose fair

complexion and delicately chiselled features, instinct and intellectuality at once impressed every eye and who suddenly jumping up on a chair beside the president poured forth a manifestly impromptu speech with an energy and eloquence that carried everyone before him.[21]

Malaviya's participation in the third session of the Congress, held in Madras, was equally significant. He again supported the resolution on the subject of the admission of people's representatives in the legislative councils, arguing that 'the country stands badly in need of this reform and the entire nation prays for it'.[22] A.O. Hume was so much impressed by Malaviya's speech that he gave it wide coverage in his report. He wrote: 'It was the only single speech during the whole Congress to the tone of which even the hostile critics could possibly take no objection.'[23] A.O. Hume's open support to Malaviya went a long way in encouraging the latter to play an effective role in popularizing the Congress in UP. The opportunity soon came his way when the decision was taken to hold the fourth Congress session at Allahabad.

PARTICIPATION IN THE CONGRESS SESSIONS AT ALLAHABAD

The decision taken by the organizers of the Congress to hold the fourth session at Allahabad was both an opportunity and a challenge for the local leaders, including Malaviya. Under the leadership of Ajudhianath, a Reception Committee was formed in 1888, with Raja Ram Pal Singh of Kalakankar as secretary and Malaviya as joint secretary.[24] Its aim was to enlist the sympathies of the people, collect subscriptions, and to meet the expenses for the Congress session at Allahabad. The Provincial Congress Committee decided to depute some persons to different towns and villages to explain the aims and objectives of the Congress to the masses at public meetings.[25] The need for propaganda was greater that year as a result of the opposition to the Congress openly voiced by the UP governor, Auckland Colvin, Sir Syed Ahmed Khan, Raja Shiv Prasad, and a few other Awadh *taluqdars*.[26] With a view to counteract their criticisms against the Congress, Raja Ram Pal Singh and Malaviya went around to several towns in UP. Between October and November 1888, they addressed Congress-sponsored meetings in various cities, sought popular support for the party, and impressed upon people the need to come forward in large numbers in

support of the nationalist endeavour. Malaviya and the raja explained
to people the need and justification of a political body to voice their
demands. Thus the two Allahabad leaders heralded a new political
campaign in the province.[27] Similar public meetings followed year
after year particularly on the eve of annual Congress sessions.

The wide publicity which the Allahabad Congress achieved during
1888 was linked to the peculiar circumstances of the local organizations and society. The accounts of public meetings at Allahabad suggest
that even though the Hindu leaders of the city were prominent in
campaigning, they were well aware that 'the lines of political division
should not harden along lines of religious distinction'.[28] Malaviya and
his associates always kept this objective before themselves. Another factor affecting the local politics was that the merchants and bankers who
supported the Allahabad Congress session were as much the supporters of the Hindu Samaj as the Congress. The link between religious
philanthrophists and the Congress was 'indistinguishable' during the
early stages of the nationalist activities in Allahabad. Inevitably, this
led Malaviya to play his role in local politics in accordance with the
demand of the social situation in which he was placed in the city and
the region.[29]

The Congress session of 1888 marked a milestone in the propaganda effort of Indian nationalism. The methods employed to arouse
political activity in different cities and regions were followed over the
next decades. The willingness of the raja of Kalakankar and Malaviya
to participate in semi-political movements of religious revival was
noted by local officials.[30] This was in sharp contrast to the secular and
non-communal propaganda campaign and the speeches made by the
Congress orators. Since the opponents of the Congress were attacking
it on communal grounds, it became almost inevitable for Malaviya and
various other Congress leaders to rely on local politics. This deepened
sectarian politics in the city as well as in the province.[31]

The decision of the Congress to hold another session at Allahabad
in 1892 was taken largely due to the initiative of Ajudhianath. His sudden death in the middle of the year posed unforeseen challenges to the
local leaders who pulled together under the leadership of Bishambhar
Nath, geared up the Congress machinery, and prepared an extensive
schedule of public meetings at various urban centres of the province.
Since Bishambhar Nath himself was physically incapable of bearing

the exertion of travel and public speaking, Malaviya took upon himself the responsibility of addressing public meetings to convey the message of the Congress to the people. He undertook whirlwind tours to different cities and made a great impression on the audience by his persuasive reasoning and charming style of speaking. Malaviya's personal approaches, appeals, and lectures yielded fruit and sufficient funds were raised for the eighth session of the Congress. Any effort as great as that which was required to provide a suitable welcome to the Congress session raised the stature of Malaviya in popular estimation and earned him a permanent place in the national organization.[32]

GROWING FAITH IN REPRESENTATIVE INSTITUTIONS

The assumption that British rule in India rested upon liberal principles and that the statesmen who controlled the destiny of the British empire would respond positively to the growth of national consciousness in the country went a long way in shaping the attitude of Malaviya. The moderate strategy to which he subscribed during these years rested upon far too flattering an appreciation of the strength of liberal principles. Malaviya voiced these principles almost continuously in the Congress sessions and looked forward to a package of reforms by the British rulers. His most favourite theme was people's representation in the legislative councils. He was never tired of voicing this demand in the Congress sessions. In the sixth Congress session held at Calcutta, Malaviya pressed his demand in the following words: 'The sole privilege which we are praying for is to be allowed to choose our own counsel to represent our case and condition fully before the Government.'[33] He referred to this demand of popular representation in the Councils in Congress sessions as well.[34]

Since his first participation in the Congress session of 1886, Malaviya was never tired of expressing concern over the limited functions of the legislative councils, the restricted nature of their membership, and the total absence of popular representatives in them. He attached so much importance to the functioning of these legislative councils because he felt that they would provide a suitable platform to him and to others to effectively voice the grievances of the people. He also demanded a general increase in the size of the Councils, insisting that at least one half of its members must be elected.[35]

ORGANIZATION OF PUBLIC MEETINGS

In addition to voicing these demands at various Congress sessions, Malaviya mobilized public meetings on certain specific issues from time to time. One of the sustained demands for which he evinced keen interest was the question of holding simultaneous examinations for the Indian Civil Services (ICS) in India and in England.[36] Since this examination was held only in England, there was an impression in India that this was an obstructive device employed to keep Indians out of the top civil service positions in the country. This issue suddenly assumed importance in June 1893, when the House of Commons adopted a resolution calling upon the Government of India to initiate measures for simultaneous examinations for the ICS in India and Britain. The nationalist leaders hailed the resolution in the House of Commons,[37] and lost no time in organizing public meetings demanding immediate implementation of the resolution. Malaviya addressed one such meeting at the Kayasth Pathshala Hall, Allahabad, on 13 August 1894, during which a resolution was adopted condemning attempts to obstruct the implementation of the resolution of the House of Commons. Malaviya expressed his fear that the powerful British officials were out to defeat the proposal.[38] During the last week of September 1894, he set out for a series of meetings at Moradabad, Agra, Lucknow, and Kanpur with Raja Rampal Singh to impress upon the people the need to remain vigilant.[39]

HINDI–URDU CONTROVERSY

The British language policy in UP and several other parts of northern India showed contradictions, inconsistencies, and confusion, which led to the Hindi–Urdu controversy in the last quarter of the nineteenth century and persisted even thereafter. The confusion of language and script began in 1858 with the government's decision to make Urdu the official language of the courts and revenue services of the North-Western Provinces. The convenient existence of Urdu was maintained and the language thrived with official support.[40] Because of this, Hindi suffered a serious setback as the increasing importance of Urdu meant a corresponding diminution in the attention paid to Hindi as a formal style of expression. The reaction to this decision gave birth to a Hindi movement which gained momentum as the years rolled on. The language issue gradually gained new national and political dimensions.[41]

The cause of Hindi was taken up by the newly emerging middle class representing its own social and cultural interests. Most of them were the Hindi elite concentrated in the cities of Allahabad and Banaras, with links to other urban centres of northern India. They repeatedly brought forward the idea of the 'inner life of a nation' in an effort to mobilize the masses.[42] From the 1860s, the protagonists of the Hindi movement began to make serious, sincere, and consistent efforts to convince the British authorities of the necessity and urgency of giving Hindi the same status that Urdu was enjoying. It required great skill and persuasion, besides marshalling of facts and public support for the cause of Hindi.

With this background it would be convenient to examine how and with what motives Malaviya got associated with the Hindi movement. His involvement began in 1884 with the formation of the Hindi Uddarni Sabha at Allahabad as the cultural counterpart of Madhya Hindu Samaj. The editor of the *Hindi Pradeep*, Bal Krishna Batt, and Malaviya began to take part in the meetings of the sabha, developed close links with the local writers and journalists, and discussed measures to popularize Hindi.[43] During his stay at Kalakankar, Malaviya's enthusiasm for Hindi received a greater fillip. He got in touch with several leading writers and journalists, and was able to get first-hand knowledge of the Hindi–Urdu controversy. This helped him in outlining his future course of action.[44]

The establishment of the Nagri Pracharni Sabha at Banaras in 1893 was an effort to provide an organizational base for propagating the cause of Hindi. Malaviya joined the sabha since its very inception, took active part in its proceedings, and encouraged its members to make it a significant channel of communication between the promoters of Hindi and the government.[45] He welcomed the arrival of Antony MacDonnell as the new lieutenant governor of the province in 1895 and impressed upon his supporters the necessity of utilizing the opportunity to their advantage. Since the new lieutenant governor had earlier supported the cause of Hindi during his stay in Bihar, his arrival in the North-Western Provinces and Oudh gave a new hope to Malaviya and other champions of Hindi.[46]

Hopeful of a favourable response from the new lieutenant governor, Malaviya decided to bring out an exhaustive memorandum entitled 'Court Character and Primary Education in N. W. Provinces and Oudh', making a case for the substitution of Urdu in the Persian script, which was then in use in the law courts and revenue services, with Hindi in the Nagri script.[47] He was fully engaged in the preparation of the memorandum for two to three years, and instead of devoting himself to legal practice, was seen 'surrounded by piles of books of reference and standard journals' in the High Court Library of Allahabad.[48] In the memorandum, which ran into almost 100 pages, he dealt with the historical background of the linguistic situation in the North-Western Provinces and Oudh, discussed in-depth the merits of the Nagri and the defects of the Urdu script, and outlined the impact of the official language and script on education. Malaviya appended various documents, official reports, and opinions of experts in the memorandum with a view to strengthen his presentation. Malaviya's effort was to win over the support of the lieutenant governor through this well-written, persuasive, and thoroughly documented work.[49]

For Malaviya the preparation of documentary evidence in support of the Hindi claim was only the beginning of the campaign.[50] The matter demanded much wider public support in favour of Hindi to bring round the provincial government. He succeeded in enlisting the support of several eminent persons and leading taluqdars. With their support, a strong deputation comprising Raja Pratap Narayan Singh of Ayodhya, Raja Balwant Singh of Awagarh, Raja Ram Pratap Singh of Manda, Sundar Lal, member, UP Council, and Malaviya waited upon Antony MacDonnell, Lieutenant Governor of the North-Western Provinces and Oudh.[51] The latter's reply was quite encouraging. MacDonnell openly said that he was willing to consider the demand of the deputationists, taking into account the growing popularity of Hindi in the province.[52]

For nearly two years the lieutenant governor discussed the language question with various officials, thought seriously over the various options, and ultimately announced his decision in April 1900. An official resolution was issued purporting to give Hindi in Nagri medium a status equal to Urdu on the ground that 'the measure provided the merest justice to 90 per cent of the people of the provinces'.[53] Thus Hindi gained a similar official recognition that Urdu had enjoyed up to that time. The provincial government ordered the permissive use of Hindi in Nagri script in courts and revenue services without affecting the status of Urdu in any way. The concession, limited in scope, was only symbolic. It was, however, enthusiastically welcomed by Malaviya and various other Hindi supporters.

Less than a month after the promulgation of the new regulations, a leading UP newspaper reported 'considerable dissatisfaction in the ranks of the Muhammadan community'[54] and elaborate arrangements were made to hold a mammoth meeting of Muslims in north India to protest against the Hindi circular. An Urdu Defence Association was formed and under its auspices, pamphlets were issued, funds collected, and leading Muslims were chosen as delegates. The meeting took place in Lucknow in August 1900 under the presidentship of Mohsin-ul-Mulk.[55]

The Urdu Defence Association raised several objections against the Nagri resolution and condemned Malaviya's activities.[56] The moves of the association led the lieutenant governor to take a firmer stand on the issue. He invited Malaviya for a meeting in the Government House to convey to him his determination to ignore the Muslim outcry.[57] The meeting was also an indirect message to Malaviya's critics that the provincial government stood entirely in support of Malaviya's efforts. However, it was unfortunate that in spite of the most laudable motives expressed by Malaviya, the provincial government's declaration proved to be a major cause of bitterness between the two communities, and the supporters and opponents of the two languages began to look at the issue from the viewpoint of their own religious and historical traditions.[58]

From the date of the issuance of the Nagri resolution, Malaviya continued to insist on the absolute need for harmony between the supporters of Hindi and Urdu, and conveyed the message from different platforms that he held no ill will against Urdu. He was convinced that any attempt to harm the on-flow and growth of Urdu would be like harming the growth of Hindi.[59] His constant effort was to bring Urdu closer to Hindi. Malaviya's services to Hindi are too well known to be recounted in detail. Presiding over the inaugural session of the Hindi Sahitya Sammelan at Banaras in 1910, Malaviya appealed for reconciliation. In his presidential speech at the Delhi Congress session of 1918, he referred to the need for evolving consensus in favour of making Hindi the national language of the country. The theme of his next major speech, delivered in 1939, was a warning against the attempt to distort Hindi in the name of national language. Malaviya opposed any state patronage to the new concept of evolving a Hindustani language. Thus Malaviya spelt out his views on the language issue keeping in mind its likely impact on Hindu–Muslim relations.

NOTES

1. Niharranjan Ray, *Nationalism in India* (Aligarh, 1973), p. 10.
2. Anil Seal, *The Emergence of Indian Nationalism* (Cambridge, 1968), p. 15.
3. Gyanendra Pandey, *The Construction of Communalism in Colonial North India* (Delhi, 2010), p. 210.
4. C.A. Bayly, *The Local Roots of Indian Politics, Allahabad 1880–1920* (Oxford, 1975), pp. 10–14.
5. Bayly, *Local Roots of Indian Politics*, pp. 75–9.
6. Sita Ram Chaturvedi, *Pandit Madan Mohan Malaviya* (New Delhi, 1992), pp. 1–6.
7. Giridhar Malaviya, *Madan Mohan Malaviya: Ek Jiwan Parichaya* (Varanasi, 2007), pp. 14–18.
8. G. Malaviya, *Madan Mohan Malaviya*, pp. 14–18.
9. Venkatesh Narain Tiwari, *Mahamana Madan Mohan Malviya Ki Jiwani* (Varanasi, 1962), pp. 10–11.
10. Tiwari, *Mahamana Madan Mohan Malviya*, p. 11.
11. Tiwari, *Mahamana Madan Mohan Malviya*, p. 17.
12. Bayly, *Local Roots of Indian Politics*, p. 120.
13. Chaturvedi, *Pandit Madan Mohan Malaviya*, p. 28.
14. Bayly, *Local Roots of Indian Politics*, p. 113.
15. Ram Naresh Tripathi, *Tees Din Malaviyaji Ke Sath* (Sasta Sahitya Mandal, Delhi, 1942), p. 7.
16. *Bharat Jiwan*, 4 January, 1891.
17. Tiwari, *Mahamana Madan Mohan Malviya*, p. 27.
18. Tiwari, *Mahamana Madan Mohan Malviya*, p. 18.
19. Malaviya, *Madan Mohan Malaviya*, p. 32.
20. Malaviya, *Madan Mohan Malaviya*, p. 35.
21. A.N. Zaidi and S.G. Zaidi, eds, *The Encyclopedia of the Indian National Congress* (New Delhi, 1976), pp. 80–1.
22. Zaidi and Zaidi, *Encyclopedia of the Indian National Congress*, p. 90.
23. Zaidi and Zaidi, *Encyclopedia of the Indian National Congress*, p. 96.
24. G.L. Verma, *Party Politics in U.P.* (Delhi, 1978), p. 16.
25. *Bharat Jiwan*, 11 October 1888.
26. M.L. Bhargawa, *First Martyr to Constitutional Freedom* (Allahabad, 1978), pp. 36–7; a *taluqdar* is a proprietor of a *taluqa* or regional sub-division, holder of a right to property in land who engaged to pay revenue to the government.

27. Bhargawa, *First Martyr*, pp. 36–7.
28. Bayly, *Local Roots of Indian Politics*, p. 128.
29. Bayly, *Local Roots of Indian Politics*, p. 132.
30. Collector of Banaras's letter to Chief Secretary, North-Western Provinces, Lansdowne Papers.
31. Bayly, *Local Roots of Indian Politics*, pp. 139–41.
32. Verma, *Party Politics in U.P.*, pp. 102–4.
33. Speeches of the Hon. Pandit Madan Mohan Malaviya (Ganesh & Co., Madras, 1918), Nehru Memorial Museum and Library, New Delhi (henceforth NMML), p. 116.
34. Speeches of the Hon. M.M. Malaviya, pp. 120–126.
35. Speeches of the Hon. M.M. Malaviya, pp. 128–131.
36. Surendra Nath Banerjea, *A Nation in Making* (London, 1925), p. 54.
37. *Hindustan*, 23 August 1893, Selections from Vernacular Newspapers of NWFP and Oudh, 1885–1901, Allahabad, p. 339.
38. Home Public–B Proceedings, October 1893, 211–22.
39. Home Public–A Proceedings, June 1894, 191–2.
40. Paul R. Brass, *Language, Religion and Politics in North India* (London, 1974), pp. 128–9.
41. Brass, *Language, Religion and Politics*, pp. 130–1.
42. Bayly, *Local Roots of Indian Politics*, p. 149.
43. Tiwari, *Mahamana Madan Mohan Malviya*, p. 36.
44. Tiwari, *Mahamana Madan Mohan Malviya*, pp. 25–6.
45. C.R. King, *One Language Two Scripts* (New Delhi, 1996), p. 78.
46. King, *One Language Two Scripts*, p. 78.
47. Brass, *Language, Religion and Politics*, p. 131.
48. *Bharat Jiwan*, 7 January, 1893.
49. Brass, *Language, Religion and Politics*, pp. 131–2.
50. Rafiq Zakaria, *The Rise of Muslims in Indian Politics*, pp. 202–3.
51. Verma, *Party Politics in U.P.*, p. 35.
52. MacDonnell to Curzon, 24 April 1900, Curzon Papers, no. 22.
53. Uttar Pradesh State Archives (henceforth UPSA), General Administration (henceforth GAD), October 1900, no. 105.
54. *Pioneer*, 12 May 1900.
55. Zakaria, *The Rise of Muslims*, p. 305.
56. Zakaria, *The Rise of Muslims*, p. 307.
57. Verma, *Party Politics in U.P.*, p. 35.
58. King, *One Language Two Scripts*, p. 16.
59. Padmakant Malaviya, *Mahamana Malaviya Ke Lekh* (Delhi, 1962), p. 126–36.

2 Moderate Politics (1905–16)

The assumption that British rule in India rested upon liberal principles and that the statesmen who controlled the destiny of the British Empire would respond positively to the growth of national consciousness in the country went a long way in shaping the attitudes of men like Malaviya who had adopted a moderate position within the Congress. During the two early decades of the twentieth century, the Moderate leaders controlled the Congress and maintained their supremacy over it; their ideas and ideals were largely accepted throughout the country. Disappointed with the cool official response to their prayers, petitions, and protests, the Congress leaders, including Malaviya, often tended to concentrate all hopes on the British politicians, who, however, turned a deaf ear to their modest and reasonable demands. The failure of the established moderate leaders to secure any substantial concessions from the British encouraged younger nationalists to become increasingly critical of them, their ideals, and their methods of agitation and organization. The controversy over ideals and methods that began within the Congress by 1905 was indicative of a deeper schism within the nationalist movement. The need for new and more determined methods of agitation came to be widely felt. The rebels within the Congress styled themselves as the 'New Party' in order to distinguish themselves from the old organization. They called themselves 'Nationalists' as opposed to old loyalist Congressmen. Their critics nicknamed them 'Extremists' and this term gained currency as the years rolled on. Malaviya thought it prudent to be in the company of the established moderate leadership and firmly resolved to follow its line in the years following the partition of Bengal.

The Congress had, so far, devoted itself to demanding isolated reforms and redress of particular grievances; it believed that the continuance of British rule was an indispensable condition of India's progress and prosperity and had faith in the liberality and sense of justice of the British people. The Extremists dismissed these ideals as impractical and visionary. They believed that any foreign rule, however just, was a curse. The Extremists demanded radical changes in the system of government and put forward the view that political freedom was the essential preliminary to India's progress.

The three Congress sessions of 1905, 1906, and 1907 witnessed the trial of strength between the emerging New Party and the Moderates. The latter got alarmed at the growing strength of the rival faction within the party. During these years, the established leaders hesitated to take any drastic steps. They were anxious to avoid any open split within the Congress and were fully conscious of the likely consequences of such a course. The rival factions could not ultimately evolve an agreed formula because of the growing suspicion between their top leadership. In such a confusing political situation, Malaviya's continuous effort was to impress upon the contending factions to evolve a middle course which could appeal to both sides.

BANARAS CONGRESS SESSION OF 1905

In the Banaras Congress session of 1905, sharp differences were voiced over the proposal of Bal Gangadhar Tilak and B.C. Pal that a countrywide boycott of foreign goods and all forms of association with the government be started as a mark of protest against the partition of Bengal. The Moderates, led by Gopal Krishna Gokhale, the president of the session, felt that the boycott was really a 'political weapon', an 'extreme measure to be reserved for extreme occasions' for it tended to excite angry passions. At this point, Malaviya came to the rescue of the two opposing factions by proposing a compromise resolution which was finally adopted by the Congress. While moving his resolution, Malaviya said:

> It would be wrong to the country and to the best interests of the people to mix up the two, to confuse the Swadeshi movement wth Boycott.

Speaking for myself I do not want to keep up boycott of foreign goods. What is desirable so far as the Swadeshi movement is concerned is quite another matter. That has gone on and will go on.[1]

Malaviya's contention was that the Swadeshi movement appealed to everyone and was the need of the hour, while the boycott could be resorted to in Bengal for a limited period only and need not be implemented across the country. The official report of the Congress, paying a handsome tribute to Malaviya, stated:

Differences of opinion were overcome and complete unanimity attained by the exercise of that sweet reasonableness which is one of the best known characteristic of Hon. Mr. Malaviya. He moved the resolution in an able and persuasive speech and his exposition of the peculiar need of boycott at the juncture at which it was used and its differentiation from Swadeshi proper was particularly happy.[2]

Giving an account of the Banaras Congress session nearly two decades later, Lajpat Rai wrote that Malaviya's 'indefatigable exertions had materially contributed to the sucess of the arrangements made' at that time.[3]

CALCUTTA CONGRESS SESSION, 1906

During the next Congress session at Calcutta, efforts were made to win over the Extremists by means of persuasion. The major resolutions adopted during the session indicate that large concessions were made to the Extremists. The latter desired that a boycott be staged throughout the country and were keen to seek the approval of the 1906 Congress to this effect.[4] Gokhale and Malaviya were unwilling to concede such a demand and proposed that the boycott be resorted to only in Bengal. This view ultimately prevailed and the final resolution adopted on this occasion was fully supported by all the UP delegates attending the session. This was a clear sign of Malaviya's influence over them.[5] Once more, he made an eloquent plea for Swadeshi at the session, calling upon every Indian to work in this direction and save the masses from starvation. An open rupture between the Moderates and the Extremists was averted at the Calcutta Congress session of 1906. However, the tensions between the two sections of the Congress persisted during the ensuing year.

REVITALIZATION OF PROVINCIAL AND LOCAL POLITICS

The Extremist movement revitalized local and provincial politics as well. This was particularly noticeable in a province like UP which was described, in the official Congress Report of 1905, as 'backward, having little political and social activity in Oudh, the people were wedded to old order and averse to new education'. The report considered Banaras as an intensely conservative city.[6] Compared to this, greater political activity was seen in Allahabad, which prompted the leaders of both the Moderate and the Extremist groups to visit the city in the early weeks of 1907 in an effort to develop closer links with the local leaders. Bal Gangadhar Tilak came over to the city 'to see whether the province was not really ready to accept the boycott'.[7] He was keen to discuss the issue with Malaviya and Ganga Prasad Varma. The former, however, distanced himself from Tilak and the two leaders did not meet at Allahabad. Malaviya was closely aligned to the Moderate camp and was, at that time, looking forward to Gokhale's visit to Allahabad and other cities of UP.[8]

Gokhale ultimately visited in the first week of February, and it soon became clear that his major objective was to win over as many city leaders to his side as possible. He spoke on 'the work before us' and 'Swadeshi', explained the Moderate ideology, and gave a call to his supporters to organize at the regional level.[9] Malaviya's strategy paid dividends and the Moderates seemed firmly entrenched in the province. They further consolidated their position by organizing yearly UP provincial conferences on the model of the Indian National Congress. The first such conference was held at Allahabad on 29 March 1907 and was presided over by Motilal Nehru. The next UP Provincial Conference met in Lucknow in 1908 under the chairmanship of Malaviya. The unanimity between Malaviya and Motilal Nehru consolidated their hold over UP politics. So long as the two Allahabad leaders shared their faith in the moderate ideology of the Congress, they found no difficulty in working together.

CHANGE IN VENUE OF THE 1907 SESSION

The Moderate leaders' anxiety and apprehension worsened as the year rolled by. They had decided to hold the next Congress session at Nagpur as it was considered a quiet and politically backward centre.

But the quarrel between the two wings of the City Congress Committee gradually came to the fore in the composition and working of the Reception Committee. The local Moderate leaders realized that the Extremists were putting forward impossible preconditions for their cooperation in holding the Congress session at Nagpur. This led to the suggestion of changing the venue for the session from Nagpur to Surat. Malaviya was invited to attend the All India Congress Committee (AICC) meeting at Bombay which was convened to finally decide upon the question. He did 'not think it absolutely necessary to attend the meeting', and conveyed his 'humble opinion' to Gokhale on the eve of the AICC meeting. Malaviya considered it 'extremely impolitic to abandon Nagpur as it would show that the Extremists have acquired more power and influence than they really have'.[10] He further added: 'To my mind it is a deplorable weakness of a few of prominent men [sic] among the Moderates at Nagpur which really stands in the way.'[11]

Malaviya later made another attempt to convince Gokhale that shifting the venue of the 1907 Congress session from Nagpur to Surat would give wrong signals to his supporters. But his advice did not find favour with the members of the Central Standing Committee, which, acting on Gokhale's advice, announced its resolve to shift the venue to Surat. Malaviya did not take part in the deliberations at Bombay since he feared that most members of the committee favoured the change of venue. His alternative suggestion to hold the 1907 Congress session at Madras was also turned down, causing him deep disappointment. Even after the rebuff, he did not lose heart, chose to abide by the final decision, and participated in the Surat Congress session with full enthusiasm.[12]

In early 1907 Malaviya launched the Hindi weekly *Abhudaya* from Allahabad to expound and defend the ideology and programme of the Moderates. In its columns, he attacked the Extremists for converting the Congress from a 'deliberative body' into a 'Kurukshetra'[13] and deplored the abuses hurled upon the senior leaders by the Extremists as 'the height of impertinence'.[14] He was particularly hurt by the speeches made by these leaders at Allahabad and shocked by the 'open defiance' of the students of the Hindu Boarding House. He dissociated himself from those who were 'misguiding' the youth and were speaking of severing all connections with the British.[15]

TRIAL OF STRENGTH AT SURAT

Long before the Congress assembled at Surat, there were signs that there was going to be a trial of strength between the Moderates and the Extremists at the session, and the possibility of disorder and division could not be ruled out. Many leading Moderate politicians made no secret of their dislike of the four Calcutta resolutions, particularly the one relating to boycott. Some of them even desired and advocated a rectification of the 'mistake' committed in 1906.[16] All this aroused Extremist suspicions about the Moderate leaders' designs. These suspicions were reinforced by the omission of the Calcutta resolutions from the list of subjects of discussion at the ensuing Congress at Surat. Both parties tried to muster strong at Surat. The conflict between the Moderates and the Extremists was irrepressible and, therefore, the split at Surat became inevitable.[17]

Malaviya was so shocked at the disorderly and ugly scenes witnessed on the second day of the Surat Congress session of 1907 that, for quite some time, he did not move away from the scene; he was in tears at the behaviour of his compatriots and was finally persuaded to leave the *pandal* (marquee) by his friends with great difficulty.[18] He put all the blame for the Surat debacle on the Extremists, especially Bal Gangadhar Tilak.[19] Soon after this 'saddest event' in the history of the Congress,[20] Moderate leaders swung into action. P.M. Mehta, D.E. Wacha, R.B. Ghosh, V.K. Iyer, Malaviya, and others met in private and gave a call to hold a National Convention at Surat on 28 December 1907.[21] Only those delegates who subscribed to the ideal of self-government for India on the colonial model and its attainment by strictly constitutional means were asked to attend the convention. Thus the doors of the Congress were closed to the Extremists. Nearly 900 delegates out of 1600 met the next day at Surat and appointed a committee to draw up a constitution for the Congress at a later date.[22] In accordance with this decision, the Convention Committee held its sittings at Allahabad. Malaviya, Motilal Nehru, and some other UP leaders had the opportunity to participate and influence the recommendations of the Committee. It drafted and adopted a new constitution for the Congress on 18–19 April 1908 and laid down a set of rules for the conduct of its business. The new creed of the Congress required every delegate to express, in writing, his faith in the objectives of the Congress. It was announced, in no uncertain terms, that 'no compromise of any kind was admissible with the Extremist Party ... which was persisting with their wild propaganda'.[23] C.Y. Chintamani, a close associate of Malaviya, recalled later that 'the disgrace of Surat was naturally before the mind's eye of those who met at Allahabad in 1908'.[24] Malaviya largely agreed with the strategy adopted at Allahabad as he thought that this was the only course left to save the Congress.

MORLEY–MINTO REFORM ACT OF 1909

Expectations were aroused in India that with the Liberal Party in the saddle in England and with John Morley as the secretary of state for India, a real advance would be made in the direction of constitutional reform. Morley's speeches in England and Minto's utterances in India raised hopes of constitutional changes in India in the period following the partition of Bengal. Moderates in India, whose sentiments Malaviya voiced in 1908 and 1909, pinned their hopes on the British response to their longstanding demands. What they got instead was a constitutional scheme which suffered from several fatal flaws. The reform scheme failed to recognize the strength of the nationalist sentiment in India, and it drew upon the most conservative classes in Indian society which could be relied upon to counterbalance the nationalism of the professional classes. Together with these serious defects, the Indian Councils Act of 1909 introduced the separate electorate system in India with the intention of playing up the differences between Hindus and Muslims.[25]

Like other Moderate leaders, Malaviya set much store by Morley's desire and ability to inaugurate a new chapter in India's relations with Britain. However, the publication of the reform proposals in November 1908 came as an anti-climax. The image of Morley as a friend of India suffered a severe jolt and led to widespread gloom all over the country.

Even though Malaviya welcomed the reform proposals in the initial stages, expressing 'lasting gratitude for the statesmanlike wisdom and courage which they (the viceroy and Lord Morley) have shown in formulating the scheme,'[26] he soon began to have second thoughts about the real intentions of the viceroy and the secretary of state. Malaviya voiced his scepticism in February 1908 while delivering the extempore presidential address at the Second United Provinces Conference held in Lucknow. He minced no words in asserting that the avowed object of the reform proposals was to destroy the influence of the educated classess:

It is, therefore, most surprising and disappointing that the Reform proposals of the Government are intiated by an unmistakable and deplorable exhibition of hostility towards the educated class.... The change of attitude towards the educated class is neither just nor wise. And it cannot be too much regretted that the proposals for reform are based upon and start with a desire to create a counterpoise to the influence of that class. Proposals conceived in such a spirit cannot but be radically unsound and defective.[27]

To Malaviya, the constitutional proposals constituted a repudiation of the liberal promises which had been held out to the political classes in India. He argued that the proposals 'had been vitiated by wrong underlying considerations', which led the Government 'to introduce [*sic*] race, class and religious representation in the Councils in place of territorial representation which had hitherto worked with success'. At the end of the address, Malaviya warned that 'a policy of partiality to one class and prejudice against another will be unwise and unsafe'.[28] At this stage Malaviya could not visualize the obvious contradictions of the British policy in India. The British policymakers were as keen as ever to keep intact the imperial hold over India and had no intention of giving any thought to even ramotely slackening their hold over the country in spite of the pronouncements of faith in liberal principles. The viceroy insisted that the 'ulimate executive responsibility in India would remain with them as far as they could see ahead'.[29] In the House of Lords, John Morley declared: 'If I were attempting to set up a parliamentary system in India or if it could be said that this chapter of reforms led directly or necessarily up to the establishment of a parliamentary system in India I for one would have nothing to do with it.'[30] The consititutional proposals of 1909 must be seen against this backdrop of the British unwillingness to recognize, much less to encourage, the growth of any sort of representative system in India.

The separate Muslim electorate which the Government of India actually introduced under the Act of 1909 was designed to exclude the Hindus from any share in the election of a Muslim representative. The object was to see that all Muslims were obliged to act together as part of a distinct religious and political community. To secure their interests fully, Muslims were further given the benefit of double voting. They voted along with others in general electorates, which, in addition to non-Muslims, also returned Muslim representatives. These were to be filled exclusively by them either through election, or in consultation with their associations, or through nominations as required by the circumstances of each province.[31] These provisions in the Act of 1909 came as a great surprise to Malaviya, who voiced his criticism of these features of the act both in private correspondence and on public platforms. On 4 March 1909, he wrote to Gokhale:

> Now that the Mohammedans have successfully pressed their claim for separate electorates their representatives will owe no responsibility to non-Muslim voters. We should protest against their being given a number of seats in excess to what they would be entitled to by reason of their proportion to total population. We apprehend that if we will remain silent, a very much larger number of seats will be allotted to them. This will be a wrong to other communities and it will, besides being a source of discord between Hindus and Mohammedans, give rise to a feeling of resentment and discontent as far as the Government is concerned. Indeed the promise of exceptional treatment of Mohammedans which has been made by Lord Morley has already aroused dissatisfaction among Hindus which is likely to deepen into discontent. We fear that our Provinces will suffer most heavily from this policy.[32]

Malaviya's fears were, to a large extent, shared by Gokhale, who referred to the likely fallout of the constitutional measure in the following words: 'The situation is further complicated by the fierce antagonism between Hindus and Mohammedans that has been rekindled by the open partiality which the Hindus generally believe, has been shown by the Government to the Mohammedans in working out the details of the Reform scheme.' Gokhale conceded further that 'the concessions to the Mohammedans and the manner in which they have been obtained by them—have already cooled the enthusiasm of many for the Reforms.'[33]

The reforms of 1909 brought India not peace, but discord—both by extending the system of representative government in the country and by the manner in which it was done. They heightened the latent tensions in Indian society, particularly between officials and non-officials, between Hindus and Muslims, and between the professional classes and the landed gentry.[34]

PRESIDENTSHIP OF 1909 CONGRESS

When Malaviya was called upon, at short notice, to fulfil the high office of the president of the Congress in December 1909, he chose to deal at length with the regulations announced sometime earlier by the Government of India. His enthusiasm for the scheme, like that of other

Congress leaders, had been greatly dampened by this time. Therefore, he made it a point to make a detailed reference to these regulations in his presidential speech in the following words:

> The regulations framed to give effect to them have unfortunately de parted, and widely too, from the spirit of those proposals and are illiberal and retrogressive to a degree. Educated Indians have been compelled to condemn them. They have done so more in sorrow than in anger. Let the Government modify these regulations to bring them into harmony with Lord Morley's proposals and in the name of the Congress and I venture to say, on behalf of my educated countrymen generally, I beg to assure the Government that they will meet with a grateful reception.[35]

Referring to the effect of these regulations in his own province, UP, Malaviya observed:

> The result has been that in addition to the four seats specially reserved to the Mohammedans they have won two more seats in the United Provinces and these with the nominations made by the Government have given them eight seats out of a total of 26 non-official seats in the legislature of the Province, where they form one-sixth of the population.[36]

After providing these details, Malaviya said: 'This is protecting the interests of the minority with a vengeance. It looks more like a case of allowing the majority to the driven to corner [sic] by a minority.' Malaviya cautioned the government that these regulations would lead to estrangement between the two communities:

> Under the influence of this feeling some of my Hindu brothers have been led to think and to advocate that Hindus should abandon the hope of building up a common national life and should promote the interests of their own community.[37]

The viceroy and the secretary of state offered similar comments on the Reform Act of 1909. When the viceroy referred to 'the excess of representation granted to Mohammedans',[38] Morley's answer was: 'It was your early speech about their extra claims that started the Muslim hare.' The viceroy later took comfort by saying: 'It passes the wit of a man to frame plans that will please Hindus without offending the Mohammedans and we shall be lucky if we don't offend both.'[39]

Gokhale's assessment of the likely fallout of the Act of 1909 was not much different from that of Malaviya. He wrote to Wedderburn, one of the founding fathers of the Indian National Congress, in June 1910:

The feeling has no doubt been rapidly spreading in the Hindu community since last year that the Congress has done no good to it, that it bore the brunt of the struggle all these years, the Mahommedans have walked away with the greater part of the spoils and it is necessary for the Hindus now, first and foremost to look after their own interests as distinguished from the Mahommedans.[40]

By this time Malaviya had come to understand that Morley's effort was to persuade those who hoped for 'autonomy or self government of the colonial pattern in India to give up their dream and be content with admission to cooperation with the British administration'.[41] The eyes of Moderates like Malaviya and Gokhale were now fixed towards the future and, despite the assertions of British statesmen to the contrary, they continued to assert that the reforms of 1909 were an advance towards parliamentary democracy. Malaviya, who stood for cooperation with the British administration, did not consider the Act of 1909 as an end in itself. As was to be expected, he began persuading the British government to accept his vision of the future as their own. In July 1910, Malaviya wrote that the political evolution that Indian reformers looked forward to was 'representative Government on democratic basis' and declared 'that the first requisite of improved relations between Englishmen and Indians was a determination to help forward the growth of representative institutions in India'.[42] The immediate reaction of the British government to such pleadings was a more emphatic reiteration of the dogma of perpetuity of the British hold over India. Like other Moderate leaders, Malaviya was, however, not disheartened and had no desire to reconsider his abiding faith in the good intentions of the British government. He found no other way except to show his willingness to extend a helping hand to the Government of India.

He demonstrated in every possible way his willingness to meet the British more than halfway in ensuring orderly progress in the country after the Surat Split. To give the reform scheme a fair trial, Malaviya called for 'active loyalty' to the British administration with which the Congress leaders were to be responsibly associated in the Central Legislature.[43]

PARTICIPATION IN UP LEGISLATIVE COUNCIL

As a member of the UP Legislative Council from 1902 to 1912 and the Supreme Legislative Council first from 1910 to 1919 and then from

1923 to 1930, Malaviya devoted considerable time and energy to legislative activities. During his long association with both the Provincial
Council as well as the Central Legislative Council, Malaviya made the
best of the very limited opportunities that these councils provided by
taking active part in their proceedings. The available statistics show that
the UP legislature met for two days in 1904, 1906, and 1908, three
days in 1905 and 1909, and for five days in 1909.[44] The fact that the
Council, on an average, met only for two-and-half days in a year is
sufficient indication of the limited opportunities that were available to
its members for scrutinizing the functions of the provincial administration. Malaviya's constant endeavour under these circumstances was to
make full use of the opportunities provided to him, and this he did to
the best of his ability. His speeches cover one-sixth of the total proceedings of the UP Legislative Council for the years 1904–09. He was
present in fifteen of the seventeen sittings of the UP legislative body.
These details speak volumes about the importance Malaviya attached
to the legislative business.[45]

Malaviya's speeches in the Provincial Council were invariably based
on historical and statistical data. He was untiring in the pursuit of
highlighting the economic hardships which the rural population of the
province was facing. His maiden speech on 19 January 1903, opposing
the Bundelkhand Land Alienation Bill, speaks volumes of his sound
preparation, full grasp over the problem, and the ability to present his
arguments in a convincing style. Malaviya asserted that the poverty and
indebtedness of the peasants of Bundelkhand were due to causes other
than those enunciated by the government. The proposed legislation,
he pointed out, would diminish the value of the land and curtail the
credit of the landowner:

> The value of the land will be reduced not merely as a security but also
> as a transferable property even when it should be transferred with the
> sanction of the Collector.... The result will be that people will not be
> encouraged to invest their capital in land and considering that land has
> already suffered from want of capital in land in that part of the country,
> that will be a serious misfortune.[46]

Malaviya argued that since the need for borrowing and, in the long
run, alienating landed property arose from heavy assessment and rigid
collection of land revenue, the proper remedy was to reduce the land
revenue demand and to rationalize the system of collection rather than

to restrict the right to sell land. In April 1904 he made a comprehensive speech in the council on the economic condition and needs of the province.

Malaviya spoke regularly in the Provincial Council on the budgets, moved resolutions on subjects of public importance, and impressed upon the provincial government the need to respond to the demands of the people. He particularly referred to the backward condition of agriculture, industry, education, public health, and local self-government. He pleaded for large budgetary grants, reduction in land revenue, extension of irrigation facilities, and extension of protection to the sugar industry.[47]

ACTIVE ROLE IN THE IMPERIAL LEGISLATIVE COUNCIL

At the time of joining the Imperial Legislative Council in 1910, Malaviya was aware of the limited opportunities provided by the Indian Councils Act of 1909 to non-official members like him. He knew that under the provisions of the act, the official majority in the council was intact and the viceroy still enjoyed extraordinary powers to control the working of the Central Legislature. This, however, did not dissuade Malaviya and various other nationalist leaders like him to play effective roles in the council. As a member of the Central Legislature, he voiced a deep commitment to democratic ideals, represented the aspirations of the people in the council, cautioned the government against adopting harsh measures, and constantly put forward the high ideals of the representative system.[48]

No sooner did the first sitting of the reformed Central Legislature begin in the early months of 1910 that Malaviya faced a very delicate situation with the introduction of the press bill by the newly appointed sole Indian member of the viceroy's Executive Council, Satyendra Nath Sinha. Though Gokhale did not approve of the provisions of the proposed bill, he decided not to vote against it because he did not think this was the right occasion to embarrass the Indian member of the viceroy's council and advised Malaviya to follow suit.[49] In a normal situation, the latter would have only been too happy to go by Gokhale's advice. But Malaviya's commitment to the freedom of press was so strong that he felt bound to respond to the call of his conscience rather than follow Gokhale's suggestion. Malaviya explained later that he 'did what [he] believed to be the rightful thing to do in an unfortunate position'.[50] In fact he exhibited considerable courage of conviction by voicing his strong opposition to any attempts to muzzle the press.

In his forceful and spirited speech in the Imperial Legislative Council on 4 April 1910, he pleaded for due deliberation for the measure as he saw that there was no need to decide the issue in a hurry:

> There is very little justification for introducing and passing the measure that is now before the council. If it cannot be abandoned I submit there should be at any rate time allowed for further consideration of this measure.... There is a real danger felt that the provisions of the Bill as it stands, will seriously affect the legitimate liberty of the Press. Those provisions are unnecessarily wide and drastic.

In his speech, Malaviya made a pointed reference to the Vernacular Press Act of 1878 and observed that in certain respects, the proposed bill was even harsher than the earlier one. He saw real danger in arming the executive with extraordinary powers and opposed the process of taking the press offences out of the purview of the regular courts of justice. Malaviya stressed this point in the following words:

> When the Press is left at the mercy of the Local Government, when it is left to the Local Governments by merely issuing a notice to demand a security, I submit that the freedom with which these newspapers have expressed their criticisms of the acts of omissions of the Government, is very much likely to suffer.[51]

In spite of Malaviya's objections the Press Act of 1910 was passed and the provincial governments lost no time in taking repressive actions against various journals and newspapers. Malaviya's fears largely came true, as within a year of its enactment, the new press law brought an end to the publication of nine major Indian newspapers, while confiscating the security money deposited by the tenth newspaper.[52]

The harsh enforcement of the Press Act led Malaviya to re-evaluate his position. Rising in the council on 6 August to speak out against the Seditious Meetings Bill of 1910, he reminded the viceroy that the earlier legislation had been facilitated because the non-official members had no desire to add to the difficulties and anxieties that the government was confronting at the time. Yet, since the act had been passed, 'a regular sedition-hunt has been going on in some of the provinces. Hardly a day now passes without some obscure sheet or pamphlet or old book being dragged forth from oblivion and notified first by one provincial government and then by another as forfeit by the authorities.'[53]

Public assembly had received its first blow in 1907 with the hasty passage of the Seditious Meetings Act. It was designed as a three-year emergency measure. This act was brought before the council for a five-month extension, which Malaviya feared was only the prelude to the government's intention to permanently empower the police to break up any public meeting. He pointed out that such legislation was 'intolerable', especially in an era of reform and responsible association:

> The policy of conciliation is in these circumstances the only safe and wise policy, that it should be steadily and earnestly pursued, that unless some overpowering causes intervene, nothing should be done which is likely to interfere with the success of this policy.[54]

When the bill was passed despite opposition by Malaviya, Gokhale, and various other nationalists, the former commented:

> The Government of India have no doubt carried the measure by their standing official majority but the moral victory will be ours and I hope this will be recognised soon in England.[55]

Malaviya further suggested that the speeches should be 'reprinted in pamphlet form and circulated largely in England as well as in India,' and hoped that these denouncements 'afforded great consolation to all thoughtful people'.[56] In March 1911, a new Seditious Meetings Bill was introduced and rudely awakened Malaviya to the inpossibility of a doctrinaire stand of active cooperation in dealing with an irresponsible administration.[57]

While participating in the budget speech of 1910, Malaviya laid great stress on the advisability of a better financial arrangement between the Govertnment of India and the provincial governments so that the latter could spend more on public works. He argued that 'the Imperial Government was shearing the provincial sheep and leaving it shivering in the cold'.[58] In his next budget speech, Malaviya made out a strong case for just apportionment of the charges on the British troops stationed in India between the British government and the Government of India. He pleaded that the amount so liberated should be spent on the development of education in India. He regretted that the army and the police had received twenty-five times more money than education during the previous twelve years.[59]

Malaviya concentrated his efforts in the council on using to the utmost the newly granted right to non-official members of introducing resolutions. Due to this privilege, granted under the Act of 1909, the annual Congress resolutions could now be voiced directly before the highest legislative body in the country which, to a certain extent, became an extension of the Congress Subjects Committee. Malaviya used this right to press his favourite idea: that the budgetary surplus be spent on promoting the welfare of the people in areas such as education, medical relief, and sanitation. He also moved resolutions on effecting reduction on the expenditure of various departments, such as stationery and printing, railways, mint, salt, police, and so on. Malaviya was very keen on promoting indigenous industries. He moved a resolution on 9 March 1911 recommending that the duty on imported sugar be so raised as to make it possible for the indigenous sugar industry to survive the competition to which it was exposed.[60]

During this period, negotiations regarding the establishment of the Banaras Hindu University got underway, and Malaviya and his associates were keenly looking forward to win the favour of the Government of India. Malaviya was, therefore, shocked and surprised to learn in his meeting with the viceroy on 10 October 1911 that 'his attitude to Government had on certain occasions given an impression of hostility and distrust'.[61] The viceroy conveyed his displeasure to Malaviya frankly, asking him, indirectly, to mend his ways before seeking the support of the Government of India.[62]

Malaviya took the hint soon enough and gradually toned down his opposition to the government's proposals in the Legislative Council. This was as much due to his anxiety to win over the viceroy's support for his dream project, the establishment of Banaras Hindu University, as because of his experience of the workings of the council. Time and again, Malaviya had realized the futility of voicing criticisms of the government in the council at a time when the non-official members were working in opposition to each other and the government had no difficulty in carrying its proposals through as and when it desired.[63] In 1915, he cooperated with the government in its efforts to seek an early passage of the Defence of India Act. Malaviya's appointment as a member of the Industrial Commission in the following year was a signal that the Government of India was equally keen to keep Malaviya in good humour.

REUNION OF THE MODERATES AND EXTREMISTS

While the top Moderate Congress leaders were engaged in discussions within the reformed council, they were fully alive to the consistent demand for reunion with their old colleagues who had stayed away from the Congress largely because of their objections to certain clauses of the Congress constitution adopted by the Allahabad Convention of 1908. It was apparent for some time that this Congress constitution stood in need of considerable modification, in the direction of a relaxation of the restrictive rules framed in 1908 under the circumstances which had changed within a span of three to four years. By the time the Congress met at Calcutta in 1911, the confusion and chaos in the Moderate camp had grown enormously. The Congress organization was in virtual disarray and the top Moderate leaders were finding it difficult to evolve an agreed-upon formula to modify the Congress constitution. Some of the Moderates, notably Gokhale, S.N. Banerjea, and Malaviya, realized the advantage of making a compromise with the Extremists both in order to put themselves in the right with the Indian public and to infuse new life into the Congress movement and organization. Supporting such a stand, Malaviya stated that the Congress's rules needed to be revised and its doors should be opened to all 'lovers of the country' who wished to work for the amelioration of its condition along constitutional lines.[64]

Under the leadership of Malaviya and G.P.Varma, the UP Congress Committee suggested 'a compromise amendment' which recommended that only such public meetings as were convened by the Congress committees should be allowed to elect delegates to the Congress.[65] The amendment adopted by the Bankipur Congress of 1912, however, failed to satisfy the Extremists who continued to stay away from the party.[66] The popularity of the Moderates and the Congress that they controlled had been on the decline, and the Bankipur Congress had provided proof of this. In the next few years, the Moderates realized the urgent need of responding more favourably than they had hitherto done to the growing demand of a rapprochement between the two wings of the national movement.

With the release of Tilak from jail and his early statements, Gokhale was encouraged to feel that 'the prospects for compromise for Congress reunification were on the whole fair'.[67] For some time, there was optimism in the air as Mrs Annie Besant and some other intermediaries attempted to work out a compromise formula. But they could not persuade Bal Gangadhar Tilak to dilute his demand for self-government within the Empire. This unnerved Gokhale and the events of 1907 loomed in his memory. He wrote a long letter to B.N. Basu who was to preside over the 1914 Congress session at Madras:

> When Pandit Madan Mohan Malaviya and I and others urged at Calcutta three years ago that the right of electing delegates should be restored to public meetings … we were under the impression that our Extremist friends in different provinces had by that time seen the error of their ways and had come to realize that the only political work possible in the existing circumstances of the country was on the lines of the Congress.[68]

In another letter, Gokhale summed up his own position and that of Malaviya in the following words:

> I am in favour of anything that is reasonable being done to bring back the seceders of the Congress by present methods. If, however, they want to revive the struggle of 1906 and 1907 I am firmly opposed to any changes that would facilitate their return.[69]

In view of such a stand taken by Gokhale, Malaviya retraced his steps, realizing clearly that at least for some time, there was little hope of bringing back the Extremists to the Congress fold.

With Gokhale's death in February 1915 and the sudden passing away of Pherozeshah Mehta by the end of the year, the last human obstacles to the Extremists' re-entry were, in effect, removed from the Indian scene. In the following year, Tilak and Mrs Annie Besant put further pressure on the Congress by establishing Home Rule Leagues. Malaviya and other Moderate leaders could clearly see that the only course open to them under the circumstances was not to resist any further moves to bring about unity within the Congress.[70] The union came in the United Provinces in the year 1916. For the first time in nine years, Tilak attended the Congress session and the delegates of the two wings of the Congress sat together in the same pandal.

THE LUCKNOW PACT

A far more significant decision taken by the Lucknow Congress of 1916 was the rapprochment between the Congress and the Muslim League. The Lucknow Pact, successfully negotiated during the session, indicated that the leading figures of the Congress and the Muslim League were willing to rethink their own positions and the positions taken by the political bodies in order to find a workable solution. Both the Congress and the League postulated complete self-government as India's goal and their joint scheme demanded, as the first step to that goal, an elected majority in the central and provincial legislatures. Their other major demands were the control of India's internal affairs by these legislatures through the power of the purse and half of the positions in the viceroy's and governor's executive councilss to be drawn from the legislative councils.

Throughout the year, the chosen representatives of the Congress and the Muslim League had carried on negotiations for drawing up a constitutional scheme. These representatives held joint meetings during the final stages of hammering out the pact in the last two months of the year. The key issue during their joint sittings was the incorporation of the principle of separate representation, and for long, there was the fear that such a proposal would be unacceptable to a large section of the Congress. Ultimately, M.A. Jinnah successfully prevailed upon the Congress leaders to accept it in order to realize Congress-League unity. Both Mrs Besant and Tilak showed readiness to accommodate Muslims.[71] As a member of these committees, Malaviya took active part in the discussions held at Calcutta. Since he had consistently opposed separate representation for Muslims up to this time, all the participants were keeping a careful watch on his utterances. It was with considerable difficulty that he was ultimately persuaded to accept a separate electorate for Muslims in the central as well as provincial legislatures. Tilak played an important part in prevailing upon Malaviya and other participants to acquiesce to the final terms of the Pact.[72]

However, though this is largely true, there were several other factors affecting Malaviya's decision. He was well aware that the dominance of the Moderates was now over and the need of the hour was to make adjustments with Mrs Besant and Tilak together with their associates. With a change in the political situation following the Lucknow Congress session, Malaviya and various other Congress leaders of his thinking were called upon to rethink their future strategy. Besides this, the uppermost question in Malaviya's mind was the demand for self-government. He knew very well that the support of the Muslim League was likely to strengthen his stand during his negotiations with the government. This influenced his decision to accept the proposals of the Lucknow Pact.

Once the Congress had accepted the principle of separate representation, the next point at issue between the representatives of the two communities was the proportion of weightage for Muslims in each provincial legislature. It was clear to the participants at the Calcutta meeting that weightage could only be successfully negotiated by agreeing upon the percentage of total representatives in each province that would be elected separately by Muslims. Representatives met separately to sort out the actual percentage of seats to be fixed for Muslims in their provinces.

At Calcutta the committees had recommended 33 per cent representation to UP Muslims. When the issue was placed before the Lucknow Congress session for its final approval, Malaviya and C.Y. Chintamani opposed the recommendation made at Calcutta session. The two leaders desired that the Muslim representation in the UP legislature should not be more than 28 per cent.[73] The Muslim representatives, however, stuck to their guns and it was only after long deliberations between 25 and 28 December 1916 and on the urgings of Mrs Besant, Tilak, and B.N. Basu, that M.A. Jinnah and Wazir Hasan were able to induce the other U.P. Muslims to accept the offer of 30 per cent by the peacemakers. The negotiations indicated that even though Malaviya accepted the need of Muslim cooperation in the nationalist struggle,s he was not happy with the weightage granted to Muslims in U.P. under the Pact.[74]

That the Lucknow Pact was achieved in the face of great obstacles demonstrated that the leaders of the Congress and the Muslim League could exert the determination and energy required to prevail upon others and bring them around successfully to their point of view. During the talks leading to the finalization of the pact, Malaviya agreed to reconsider the principles which had appealed to him so far and accepted the compromise for achieving larger national interests.

With regard to the reaction of the Hindu Mahasabha to the Lucknow Pact, it should be pointed out that up to 1915, the Hindu Mahasabha did not criticize Muslims or their constitutional demands.

While presiding over the 1915 session of the sabha, Malaviya stressed the need for unity among the Hindus and made no reference to the Muslim demands. In 1916, the Hindu Mahasabha, in its session held at Lucknow, expressed its strong opposition to separate representation, particularly to the weightage. Malaviya did not take any prominent part in the 1916 proceedings of the Mahasabha and concerned himself more with the negotiations of the pact as a member of the AICC.[75] Obviously, he distanced himself deliberately from the activities of the Mahasabha as much as possible in 1916 as in the next few years.

Commenting upon the Lucknow Congress session, James Meston, the lieutenant governor of UP, informed the viceroy that 'the Extremists and Moderates have again joined hands and have achieved the remarkable feat of capturing the advanced Mahommedans...'. He added further:

> What we have undoubtedly got to face is that the British public and the House of Commons will be told, with every appearance of veracity that at last the whole political opinion of India—both wings of Hindus and all that is vital and progressive among Mahommedans—presents a united front in its demand for reforms.... The situation is thus one of considerable seriousness.[76]

In the qualitatively changed political situation in India after the Lucknow Congress, Malaviya went around the country and delivered powerful speeches in support of the proposals of the Lucknow Congress demanding a substantial measure of constitutional advancement in India. Malaviya now became more active than before and emphasized united action by all sections of society. Addressing the second session of the UP Political Conference at Lucknow, his message was:

> Let us organize without any further loss of time and arrange to preach the great Mantra, the humane religion of self-government or Swaraj or home rule in every home, in all parts of our country. Let us teach every brother and sister, Hindu and Mussalman, Parsi or Christian, young and old, humble as well as high, to understand the meaning of self-government.[77]

In accordance with Malaviya's suggestion, a joint meeting of the AICC and the council of Muslim League was held in Bombay on 28 and 29 July 1917. Seventy members were present on the occasion and it was decided to make a representation to the secretary of state and the viceroy to implement the proposals of the Congress–League

Scheme as early as possible. Malaviya was one of the persons appointed to draft the representation and was included in the deputation that was asked to present the case before the Government of India and the British government.

NOTES

1. S.R. Bakshi, *Madan Mohan Malaviya: The Man and His Ideology* (New Delhi: Anmol Publication, 1991), pp. 62–3.
2. Zaidi and Zaidi, *Encyclopedia of the Indian National Congress*, vol. IV, p. 675.
3. B.R. Nanda, ed., *The Collected Works of Lajpat Rai*, vol. XI (New Delhi: Manohar, 2008), p. 95.
4. Nanda, *Collected Works of Lajpat Rai*, p. 684.
5. Rama Kant Malaviya to Gokhale, 9 January 1907, Gokhale Papers.
6. Zaidi and Zaidi, *Encyclopedia of the Indian National Congress,* p. 67.
7. Rama Kant Malaviya to Gokhale, 9 January 1907, Gokhale Papers.
8. Malaviya to Gokhale, 23 January, 1907, Gokhale Papers.
9. Motilal Nehru to Jawaharlal Nehru, 7 February 1907, Motilal Nehru Papers.
10. Malaviya to Gokhale, 8 November 1907, Gokhale Papers.
11. Malaviya to Gokhale, 8 November 1907, Gokhale Papers.
12. Malaviya to Gokhale, 8 November 1907, Gokhale Papers.
13. *Abhudaya*, 16 March 1907.
14. *Abhudaya*, 17 March, 1907.
15. Ravinder Kumar and D.N. Panigrahi, eds, *Selected Works of Motilal Nehru*, vol. 1 (New Delhi, 1982), p. 118.
16. Stanley Wolpert, *Tilak and Gokhale* (New Delhi: Oxford Univeristy Press, 1989), p. 199.
17. Wolpert, *Tilak and Gokhale*, pp. 200–2.
18. *Abhudaya*, 7 January 1908.
19. Tripathi, *Tees Din Malaviyaji Ke Sath*, p. 249.
20. Annie Besant, *How India Wrought for Freedom: The Story of the National Congress Told from Official Records* (Madras, 1915), p. 131.
21. P. Malaviya, *Mahamana Malaviya Ke Lekh*, pp. 59–60.
22. Report of the Twenty-third Indian National Congress, 1908, p. 17.
23. Kumar and Panigrahi, *SWMN*, vol. I, p. 138.
24. *Leader*, 26 October 1911.
25. Wolpert, *Tilak and Gokhale*, pp. 228–9.
26. *Indian Review*, March 1908.
27. Malaviya's presidential address at the Second United Provinces Political Conference, 29 February 1908, in *The Hon. Pandit Madan Mohan Malviya: His Life and Speeches* (Madras: Ganesh and Co., 1979), pp. 121–2.

28. Malaviya's presidential address at Second United Provinces Political Conference, 29 February 1908.

29. P. Hardy, *The Muslims of British India* (Cambridge, 1972), p. 163.

30. Hardy, *Muslims of British India*, p. 163.

31. Hardy, *Muslims of British India*, pp. 162–3.

32. Malaviya to Gokhale, 4 March 1909, Gokhale Papers.

33. G.K. Gokhale to W. Wedderburn, 24 September 1909, Gokhale Papers.

34. B.B. Misra, *The Indian Political Parties* (New Delhi: Oxford University Press, 1976), pp. 160–1.

35. Malaviya's presidential address, 28 December 1909.

36. Zaidi and Zaidi, *Encyclopedia of the Indian National Congress* vol. IV, p. 675.

37. Zaidi and Zaidi, *Encyclopedia of the Indian National Congress*, vol. IV, p. 675.

38. Minto to Morley, 11 November 1909, in Stanley Wolpert, *Jinnah of Pakistan* (New Delhi, 1985).

39. Morley to Minto, 6 December 1909, in Wolpert, *Jinnah of Pakistan*.

40. Gokhale to Wedderburn, 30 June 1910, Gokhale Papers.

41. S.R. Mehrotra, *India and the Commonwealth, 1885–1929* (London, 1965), p. 58.

42. Malaviya to Wedderburn, 16 July 1910, Gokhale Papers.

43. G.L. Verma, *Party Politics in U.P.* (Delhi, 1978), pp. 77–9.

44. S.L. Gupta, *Pandit Madan Mohan Malaviya: A Socio-Political Study* (Allahabad, 1978), p. 179.

45. Gupta, *Pandit Madan Mohan Malaviya*, p. 181.

46. Madan Mohan Malaviya, *Speeches and Writings of Pandit Madan Mohan Malaviya* (Madras: G.A. Natesan & Co., 1920), p. 267.

47. Gupta, *Pandit Madan Mohan Malaviya*, pp. 154–5.

48. Verma, *Party Politics in U.P.*, pp. 85–99.

49. B.R. Nanda, *Gokhale: The Indian Moderates and the Raj* (Delhi, 1977), pp. 75–8.

50. Malaviya to C. Vijayaraghavachariar, 5 March 1910, C. Vijayaraghavachariar Papers (henceforth C.V.R. Papers).

51. Malaviya's speech at the Imperial Legislative Council, 4 April 1910, in Malaviya, *Speeches and Writings*, pp. 307–22.

52. *Leader*, 5 November 1910.

53 Manoranjan Jha, *Role of Central Legislature in the Freedom Struggle*, (New Delhi, 1972), p. 36.

54. Malaviya's speech at the Imperial Legislative Council, 4 April 1910, in Malaviya, *Speeches and Writings*, pp. 307–22.

55. Malaviya to Gokhale, 7 September 1910, Gokhale Papers.

56. Malaviya to Gokhale, 7 September 1910, Gokhale Papers.

57. Wolpert, *Tilak and Gokhale*, pp. 236–7.

58. Jha, *Role of Central Legislature*, p. 16.
59. Jha, *Role of Central Legislature*, pp. 17–19.
60. Jha, *Role of Central Legislature*, pp. 24–6.
61. Hardinge's note (he had taken over as viceroy only a few months prior), 10 October 1911, Education–A Proceedings, March 1912, pp. 54–9.
62. Hardinge's note, 10 October 1911, Education–A Proceedings, March 1912, 54–9.
63. Jha, *Role of Central Legislature*, p. 27.
64. Malaviya to C.Vijayaraghavachariar, 8 March 1910, C.V.R. Papers.
65. *Leader*, 30 December 1912.
66. *Leader*, 30 December 1912.
67. Nanda, *Gokhale*, p. 107.
68. Gokhale to Basu, 14 December 1914, Gokhale Papers.
69. Gokhale to Basu, 25 December 1914, Gokhale Papers.
70. *Abhudaya*, 16 August 1916.
71. Misra, *The Indian Political Parties*, p. 229.
72. Mushirul Hasan, *Nationalism and Communal Politics in India* (New Delhi: Manohar, 1979), p. 76.
73. UPSA, GAD, 140/1917.
74. *Leader*, 29 December 1916.
75. *Leader*, 6 January 1917.
76. James Meston to Chelmsford, 11 January 1917, Meston Papers.
77. Malaviya, *Speeches and Writings*, pp. 156–7.

3 The Foundation of the Banaras Hindu University

The most prominent example of the importance of education in India during the early decades of the twentieth century was the consistent and widespread effort championed by Malaviya to establish the Banaras Hindu University. Malaviya wanted to set up the university because the five universities then existing in India—Calcutta, Bombay, Madras, Lahore, and Allahabad—were mainly examining universities, and he felt that the Hindu community needed a residential and teaching institution. He thought that Muslim, Christian, and Sikh efforts to found their own respective universities made the need of a Hindu university even more necessary.[1] During that period, the Arya Samaj, the Servants of India Society, and the Theosophical Society were also engaged, in their own ways, in uplifting the Hindus, and Malaviya's tireless promotion of the Hindu university was a significant effort in the same direction. All these efforts were oriented towards strengthening and improving the Hindu community materially, physically, and intellectually so that it could reverse a perceived sense of decline and ultimately assume its rightful place in the hierarchy of races and nations. It was, in fact, a type of constructive nationalism based on many ostensibly non-political activities that were imbued with the spirit of self-help, and it had education at its core.

EARLY EFFORTS

Malaviya proposed the establishment of a residential Hindu University at a meeting arranged at the Mint House at Banaras, which was presided over by the maharaja of Banaras. At this meeting Malaviya proposed, for the first time, the idea of a Hindu University. Thereafter, Malaviya reduced to writing the greater portion of the prospectus of the proposed university with a view to garner support of the Indian National Congress, which was holding the annual session at Banaras. The Congress gave its formal support to the establishment of a Hindu University.

A separate meeting was held later on 31 December 1905 at the Town Hall in Banaras, at which, besides selected Congress delegates, many eminent educationists were present. They considered and approved the prospectus of the proposed Hindu university.[2] Soon after this, the scheme was laid before the Sanatan Dharm Sabha which met at Allahabad during the Kumbh Mela from 20 to 29 January 1906. It was here that Malaviya took a resolve to devote his life to the realization of his project.[3]

THE PROSPECTUS OF 1905

The prospectus of the proposed Hindu university, published in 1905, is an important document. Malaviya explained that the proposed university aimed at the 'promotion of Scientific, Technical and Artistic Education' combined with 'Religious Instruction and Classical Culture', and, quoting a phrase from a Sanskrit scripture, laid down 'that it is religion which ensures temporal prosperity and eternal bliss'.[4]

The prospectus stressed that the proposed university was not intended to be an ivory tower isolated from society. From the very outset, it was intended to be an institution that would be strongly tied into the community to maximize its usefulness. Clearly, the university was to be a functional and practical vehicle to help improve and uplift the Hindu community. But it was also important as a powerful symbol of what Hindus could do together—a prominent and visible example of public work and public service.

The prospectus of 1905 began with an analysis of India's situation. It compared India's present situation with her past and with the contemporary situation in Europe. It pointed out that the per capita income of an average Indian was one-twentieth of that of an Englishman and was still sinking. Regarding education, the prospectus enumerated that 94 per cent of the people in India were illiterate; in UP the figure was 97 per cent, compared to 5 per cent in Great Britain and 1 per cent in

Germany. Millions of people died every decade in India due to famines and diseases. It emphasized the need to study the causes of this misery. Several Indian and foreign critics blamed India's social system for her misery. They said the cause was too much religion, and according to the missionaries, 'the wrong religion'. Malaviya gave an altogether different answer: not too much religion but too little of it was the cause of India's downfall. He refuted the view that Hinduism hampered modern development by favouring mysticism. Malaviya took it for granted that values laid down in the Hindu scriptures would be useful for laying the foundation of a modern technical civilization in India.[5]

Notions such as Hindus 'lagging far behind' and 'not keeping pace with the times' were an important part of the ideology and discourse of the prospectus.[6] It supported the widespread feeling of that time that Hindus had slid close to the bottom of the supposed 'scale of nations', and that if they did not begin to revitalize their community, the march of progress would forever pass them by. Newspapers in north India were filled with comments which documented this mentality. The Allahabad daily *Leader*, chastized Indians for lacking in character and asked, 'Who prevents us from infusing into the masses the spirit of manliness, self-reliance, and self-respect?'[7] Other periodicals referred to Hindus as 'a lifeless community'[8] belonging to a 'lethargic race', 'cowards', and 'lacking in courage'.[9]

Pre-existing Hindu anxieties about the community's decline were clearly reflected in the 1905 prospectus of the proposed university. There was widespread concern about the miserable position of the Hindus. The establishment of the Banaras Hindu University and the expansion of education in general were seen by Malaviya as remedies for the situation.

There was a broad consensus that Indians had to take the control of management of educational institutions into their own hands. Highlighting the importance of Hindu history and promoting Hindi as a national language were some of the ways in which educational institutions could create an awareness of a strong and unifying Hindu culture. Malaviya showed that Hindus had a great historical tradition of educational enterprise at the university level and claimed that universities existed in India 'ages before the idea of a university dawned on the minds of men in Europe and so far as history records prove, in any part of the world.'[10] Several years later, in 1919, this theme was still in Malaviya's mind when he spoke of Banaras as an ancient seat of learning and of the university as a national institution to record and preserve history and culture.[11]

Malaviya took the earliest opportunity to despatch the prospectus for the consideration of the UP government. He pointed out that 'the promoters of the scheme have taken it up as a purely educational scheme and are sincerely anxious that it should be judged as such and not suffer by reason of any misapprehension that it has anything to do with any political movement.'[12] He was referring to the demand of 'national education' made by the Extremists in the post-Bengal-partition era and was keen to convince the provincial government that his proposals for a Hindu university were in no way inspired by their ideology. There was no response from the provincial government as the UP governor, John Hewett, was opposed to Malaviya's proposal. In a letter to the Government of India, the official communication stated: 'In so far as the university would be a teaching university Sir John Hewett's opinion is that there is no room for a teaching university in India. In so far as it would be Hindu denominational university his opinion was, and still is, that the creation of such a university is most undesirable.'[13] In view of such a stand of the provincial government, no progress towards the establishment of the university could be made before 1910.

MRS BESANT'S 'NATIONAL UNIVERSITY' SCHEME

Meanwhile, in 1907, Mrs Annie Besant launched her scheme of establishing a University of India that would represent all religions. In July 1910, she submitted to the viceroy her petition for a Royal Charter, which was signed not only by Hindus, but also by several Muslims, one Buddhist, one Sikh, and one Christian. The university was to be located in Banaras with powers to affiliate colleges throughout the country.[14] Contrary to Mrs Besant's expectations, the viceroy did not immediately forward her petition to the secretary of state before holding detailed consultations with his colleagues and the provincial governments.[15]

The Government of India was unwilling to support Mrs Besant's scheme due to several reasons. In the first place, it viewed with dismay 'the effort to establish a University, such as proposed, independent of Government control', emphasized that 'it must control University education', and expressed the view that 'the Charter asked for by Mrs Besant and others would undo the work of at least sixty years.'[16] The second objection of the Government was that Mrs Besant's views and her writings on national education were not consistent with the assurances that her university would not be in opposition to the Government. There was a strong fear that the new University would become 'a political organization promoting ends disapproved by Government.'[17] The third objection of the government was against the Central Hindu College. It observed that 'the Hindu College, Banaras, is reported to be the worst college in the jurisdiction of the University of Allahabad from the point of view of teaching.... We also know that the college is very short of funds and has no means to improve matters.' Fourth, it noted with concern that, in Mrs Besant's scheme, the viceroy was not assigned any position in the management of the university. Due to these considerations, the Government of India 'strongly disapproved'[18] of Mrs Besant's scheme and later conveyed its objections to her proposal to the secretary of state.

LINKAGES WITH ALIGARH MUSLIM UNIVERSITY PROJECT

During the early decade of the twentieth century, the campaigns for the Banaras Hindu University and the Aligarh Muslim University developed simultaneously in a spirit of cordial, though sometimes outright, competition. Soon after a discussion of the proposal for a Muslim University at the Mohammedan Education Conference in 1904, Malaviya proposed, for the first time, his scheme for the establishment of a university at Banaras. Welcoming Malaviya's proposal, Aga Khan issued the following statement:

> Most Muslims I think would most gladly welcome a Hindu University at Banaras. We would gladly welcome another at Poona a third in Bengal and Madras. But because there is evidently no desire on their part to have a sectarian university with a Brahmanical atmosphere, it is absurd to deny us a university at Aligarh with affiliated Colleges all over India.[19]

Aga Khan's open support to the establishment of a 'sectarian university with a Brahmanical atmosphere' at Banaras indicated that the promoters of the two universities were prepared to work together from the very beginning. He sent a message to the organizers of the Congress at Banaras conveying his support to the proposal of the Hindu university and promising a donation of five thousand rupees as a token of support to Malaviya's project. Welcoming Aga Khan's support Malaviya wrote to Gokhale,

> I have written to His Highness today to thank him for his generous sympathy and offer of a handsome donation and I request you also to kindly thank him on my behalf. I hope to write to you about the University soon.[20]

RENEWED EFFORTS AFTER 1910

Early in 1910, there were renewed efforts to establish a Muslim university at Aligarh. At the Muhammedan Educational Conference held at Nagpur in December, Aga Khan issued a 'now or never' appeal and threw himself in a whirlwind campaign far surpassing the efforts of previous twelve years. A Muslim Univeristy Foundation Committee was formed under his presidentship with a wide network of provincial committees. Choosing Shaukat Ali to accompany him, Aga Khan went around the country collecting funds for the university.[21] Their speeches repeatedly stressed that the Muslim university would affiliate colleges on the Aligarh model all over India. This promise helped him immensely to raise money. In August 1911, the amount pledged was twenty-five lakhs and the amount collected was four lakhs.[22]

The viceroy took note of Aga Khan's 'very energetic efforts in collecting money'[23] and began to think over the desirablity of establishing denominational universities in India. Harcourt Butler's comment on this occasion that 'I told Aga Khan at Calcutta—why do you come with a pistol at my head of 20 lakhs'[24] shows that the Government of India had come to realize that it was time to take a final decision in this sensitive matter.

At a different level Annie Besant was also publicizing her project for a University of India to include all religions and regions and be free from government patronage. In January 1910, she wrote to the Secretary, Mahammedan Anglo-Oriental College, calling for his support by writing, 'I am aware that Aligarh may be raised to the work of a University for Islam but even then the granting of the Charter asked for would render the granting of other petitions more likely.'

Regarding her own petition, Mrs Besant wrote, 'H.E. the Viceroy has promised to present the petition to the Secretary of State and has expressed his approval of it.'[25] The Aligarh College authorities refused to cooperate with Mrs Besant on the ground that Muslims desired to have their own university. Her three chief Muslim supporters withdrew their signatures from her petition.[26]

The withdrawal of Muslim representatives made Mrs Besant's project of a 'University of India' obsolete and aroused a strong desire among the Hindus to have their own university. According to Mrs Besant's own version, 'friends on both side counselled Hon'ble Pandit and myself to blend our schemes.' Negotiations between Malaviya and Mrs Besant took place in Calcutta in March 1911 and both of them agreed to join together. While informing the viceroy about her intentions to alter her original petition, Mrs Besant wrote:

> The movement for a Muslim University has led to some modifications of my more sweeping scheme and to my consenting to make the petition one for a Hindu University. The only really important changes are the immediate establishment of a residential University, giving a predominantly Hindu tone to it, the inclusion of His Excellency the Viceroy, the Governors and Lt. Governors as Governors of the Univeresity.[27]

Mrs Besant did not give up her proposal for the 'University of India' altogether. She only 'consented' to submit the petition for a 'Hindu University' along with Malaviya.[28] A detailed and well-thought out proposal could not be worked out immediately as Mrs Besant left India on 22 April for six months to stay in Britain.

Malaviya's agreement with Mrs Besant to amalgamate their plans on the lines indicated above soon came under pressure from his own orthodox supporters. They resisted such a joint venture out of resentment against recent developments within the Theosophical Society of India and the new ideas propogated by Mrs Besant. Giving his own version of the new situation emerging after Mrs Besant's departure, Malaviya informed her: 'During the last three months there has been quite a flood of criticism of your views regarding the coming of a great World-Teacher and of the predominance of Theosophy in the affairs of the Central Hindu School.'[29] Malaviya was referring to the discovery of the 'future Messia': the 'coming of Christ' in an eleven-year-old boy named J. Krishnamurthy. This was the beginning of the J. Krishnamurthy cult within the Theosophical Society. Annie Besant began to propagate J. Krishnamurthy as a coming World-teacher, being an incarnation of the Buddha and Christ.

In 1910–11, a small group was formed, mainly consisting of Central Hindu School teachers and students, who pledged loyalty to Mrs Besant. The main opponents of these developments within the Theosophical Society and the Central Hindu College were Bhagwan Das and his brother Govind Das. Bhagwan Das resigned as secretary of Theosophical Society. Bhagwan Das's break with Annie Besant over the J. Krishnamurthy cult was to have a decisive influence over the developments of the Central Hindu College and its future incorporation into the Banaras Hindu University.[30] Attacks against Mrs Besant began in March 1911 by the Bharat Dharm Mahamandal as well. The Mahamandal was working under the patronage of the maharaja of Darbhanga who put forward his own plans of a Hindu university and expressed concern at Mrs Besant's plans of projecting theosophy in the minds of the students of a new university at Banaras.[31] Similar fears arose in the minds of Malaviya's orthodox supporters. This put Malaviya in an awkward position as he had, on the one hand, to honour the support extended to Mrs Besant and, on the other hand, to satisfy the orthodox section of the Hindus. Malaviya explained the new situation to Mrs Besant in the following words: 'Since the proposal to amalgamate the scheme of the University of India with the Hindu University was published it has met with warm suport from one party and with uncompromising opposition from the other. When you left for England the opposition had not become half so loud and strong as it has become since.'[32]

Malaviya had detailed discussions with leading members of the Central Hindu College Committee on 10 July and informed Mrs Besant that

> the majority desire or expect that the University will be a distinctively Hindu University. The most judicially minded among these consider that the proposals which have been put forward in your letter of the 11th April last, do not ensure that it will be so and that if an amalgamation is brought about on the basis of the proposals contained in that letter, the University will fail in a large measure to enlist the sympathy and support of the Hindu Community.[33]

Malaviya issued a statement in the *Leader* on 15 July 1911 stating that Annie Besant's petition and rules of management, even with the

changes proposed on 11April, do not meet the requirements of a
teaching university and asserted that 'on close examination it becomes
evident that what both parties really want is that the Hindu University
should be, both in name and in reality a distinctively and genuinely
Hindu institution, the governing body of which should be Hindu.'[34]

COLLECTION CAMPAIGNS

Malaviya decided that no further time should be lost in starting
the collection of funds for the proposed univeristy. On 15 July 1911,
he issued an appeal for the collection of a crore of rupees—a sum he
declared was 'the minimum amount required to establish and maintain
a fairly good residential and teaching Hindu University at Benaras.'[35]
He exhorted the Indian princes and the Hindu public to contribute
liberally to make this venture a success. At the same time Malaviya put
forward a revised scheme indicating the lines on which he intended to
build the university.

In the revised scheme, Malaviya made considerable concessions to
win the favour of the government. The main difference between his
old prospectus of 1905 and the new one was that now the medium of
instruction was to be English, priority was to be given to science and
technology, and the interests of the government were to be respected
as far as necessary. The past and present situation of the Hindu religion that he had described in the 1905 prospectus was reduced to a
fifth in the revised scheme. Malaviya's new plan was economical as he
suggested building on existing institutions. The Government Sanskrit
College was to be incorporated in the new Hindu university, the
Central Hindu College was to be new College of Arts and Literature,
and only a College of Science and Technology remained to be immediately founded. The Colleges of Agriculture, Commerce, and Medical
were to be founded later.[36]

Malaviya emphasized that the success of a large scheme like this
depended 'upon the approval and support of (1) the Government
(2) the Ruling Princes and (3) the Hindu public'. He left no one in doubt
that his plan was to aproach the government for a Royal Charter for the
University as 'it is only when an institution receives the Royal approval
and authority to confer degrees that it attains the full status and dignity of
a University and enters upon a career of unlimited usefulness.'[37]

Nothing was more urgently and immediately necessary than funds for realizing the objective for such an institution. Malaviya, therefore, took upon himself the responsibility of the fundraising campaign and was ably assisted by several prominent persons like Raja Rampal Singh of Kurri Siddhauli, Ganga Prasad Varma, Gokaran Nath Misra, Iqbal Narain Gurtu, Shiva Prasad Gupta, Mangala Prasad, and several others who joined the collection campaign either at particiular places or for a shorter period. It may, however, be mentioned that in spite of Malaviya's best efforts, Sundar Lal and the maharaja of Darbhanga did not join Malaviya's first collection campaign from July to October 1911 as they were still waiting and watching the government's reaction to Malaviya's efforts. There were several other leading figures who were similarly sitting on the fence throughout the year.[38]

During this period, the delegation led by Malaviya visited Faizabad, Jaunpur, Gorakhpur, Kanpur, Muzaffarpur, Darbhanga, Bhagalpur, Jabalpur, Lucknow, Calcutta, Rawalpindi, Lahore, and Amritsar. The collection campaign aroused widespred support at all these places; big public meetings were organized to explain the need for and necessity of a Hindu university and great enthusiasm was witnessed everywhere. Malaviya's strategy was to collecting money first and approach the government for favours later. In his speeches during the three-month-long fundraising campaign, Malaviya repeatedly asserted that the Government of India was not opposed to the idea of a Hindu university at Banaras. Malaviya thus put the Government of India in a difficult position. It could not say that it was opposed to Malaviya's plans as that would make it appear that the government was 'unfriendly to the Hindus'. The government could not postpone the decision on the university for much longer as it considered that it would be difficult to oust Malaviya later.[39] This explains as to why the Government of India was ultimately called upon to announce its decision of establishing the university in October 1911.

Urging Hindus to contribute and support his efforts in founding the university, Malaviya asked them to emulate Muslims: 'Our Mahomedan fellow subjects have waked up and have, it is said, raised nearly 25 lakhs to lay the foundation of a Muslim University at Aligarh. Shall Hindus remain asleep? Is not their sense of duty to their own community strong enough to rouse them to action?'[40] The fundraising campaigns for the two universities attracted the attention of the UP government.

It was informed that government officials were participating in the actual collection of subscriptions. There were several instances of Muslim officials collecting subscriptions for the establishment of the Muslim university. When the Hindu officers followed suit and desired to take part in the fundraising campaign for the Hindu university, the provincial government got alarmed. It issued orders in May 1911 that as 'neither the Hindu nor Muhammadan university scheme had been recognized by the Government as an object worthy of official support, the government officials should neither attend meetings regarding them nor participate in the actual collection of subscriptions.'[41] The Hindu officers were sore about the treatment meted out to them. Reporting about their feelings, the District Collector of Faizabad wrote:

> Somehow or the other these orders are a burden to the Hindus and are bitterly resented—rightly or wrongly they say such orders were not issued when the Mohammedan University scheme was is progress. In short there is an impression that the Government has not been impartial in this matter.[42]

The observations of the Commissioner, Faizabad Division, on this occasion were on the similar lines:

> I understand the feeling of the Hindus on the subject for the Confidential letter No. 20633 did not issue till 26 May 1911 and it was in April I think that Muhammadan Deputy Collectors and other Government servants attended meetings in support of Muhammadan University scheme without any objection being taken.[43]

The confidential correspondence of the senior British officials of Faizabad is self-explanatory. They acknowledged that even though local Muslim officers were earlier permitted to take part in the collection campaign for Aligarh Muslim University, the same facility was not granted to Hindu officers during the collection campaign for the Hindu university. Under these circumstances, the local Hindu officers regarded the new government orders to be discrimiratory. When Malaviya was visiting Faizabad on 8 November 1911 in connection with his fundraising campaign where he was also scheduled to address a public meeting in the city, the issue came to the surface again. On the eve of his visit, the District Collector wrote: 'I think it is politic to permit attendance but orders are orders ... in my opinion it would be wise to allow attendance than to prevent officials from attending.'[44]

The chief secretary of the UP government ultimately decided to take a lenient view on the subject, and stated:

> I do not see how Government officials can be prevented from subscrib-
> ing if they wish. The foundation of neither University can be called a
> political movement. They are quasi-political movements, their institu-
> tion is fraught with political consequences and they have a political as-
> pect but it will be a straining of words to call it a political movement. In
> these circumstances I suggest that government officials can be allowed
> to subscribe to the proposed universities.[45]

Rejecting the views of various British officers that both the university campaigns were political in nature, the chief secretary ultimately
allowed to government officials the right to subscribe to the two
universities as and when they thought fit.

To a large extent, the chief secretary was influenced by the signs
of growing enthusiasm among the Hindus in favour of the Hindu
university. The provincial government could not disregard for long
the reports submitted by its own officials. The district collector of
Ghazipur informed the commissioner of the Banaras Division on
2 September 1911:

> The Hindus are getting rather excited over the proposed visit of Madan
> Mohan Malaviya for the Hindu University. They do not at all relish, how-
> ever, the prospect of being bled. I was asked to preside. But that was
> merely a matter of form.... There can be no doubt that the announcement
> in regard to the Muhammedan University has helped him enormously
> and it seems quite possible that he really will get a sum sufficient to enable
> him and his co-adjustors to come up for a charter.... The general expecta-
> tion here is that once the sufficient funds are collected there willl be no
> difficulty in arranging matters with Government.[46]

The Commissioner, Banaras Division, H.V. Lovett, who had close
relations with several leading figures in the city, kept a close watch
on Malaviya's moves. His assessment in early September was that 'the
whole movement was going very strong indeed. There could be no
question about the enthusiasm it evoked. The success in Bengal had
been remarkable and the meeting at Lucknow had been a great gathering.' He acknowledged that 'the idea of a University was now spreading fast among the Hindus and they would very soon raise sufficient
funds'. He added, 'Babu Moti Chand informs me that his relative Sheo
Prasad Gupta is travelling with Malaviya on the University crusade

and that the movement is spreading with great force "bari zor se". The difficulties with the Central Hindu College are temporary. Mrs. Besant is "bari politic" and will be back early in October when all come right [*sic*].'[47]

The official reports of Malaviya's successful fundraising campaigns ultimately led the Government of India to seriously ponder over the wisdom of giving the green signal for the establishment of the Banaras Hindu University. In the last week of August 1911, Butler wrote: 'There is danger in awaiting development that Pandit Madan Mohan Malaviya is meanwhile collecting money. He says, Darbhanga tells me, that Government are not opposed to his scheme, that he is doing what Aga Khan did, collecting money and framing a scheme afterwards.'[48] Butler's main worry was that 'it will be very difficult to oust him (Malaviya) later unless there is a rival scheme to swamp him. There is this danger in showing our hand that we may appear unfriendly to Hindus. We cannot say openly that we distrust Madan Mohan Malaviya.'[49]

Malaviya's collection campaign in Bihar and Bengal further confirmed that people were responding to his appeal with open hearts, that local leaders were cooperating with his delegation, and that, on several occasions, senior British officials presided over such public meetings. Malaviya's assertions that 'his scheme had the support of the Government'[50] had the desired effect and an impression gained ground that the government was likely to announce its acceptance of the scheme for the vniversity.[51]

Giving a detailed account of Malaviya's collection campaign to Harcourt Butler, the maharaja of Darbhanga impressed upon him the need to announce the intentions of the government without any further delay:

> I have already given you the history of the meetings at Darbhanga, Mozaffarpur and Barkipore. I am told at Bhagalpur they have had an equally encouraging response. The action of the local authorities makes it now impossible for anyone to convince people that Malaviya's scheme has not the sanction and the approval of the local Government. I am told that when the Commissioner of Tirhut and Collector of Darbhanga preside and other high officials attend local meetings my refusal to join the movement can only be due to the fact that I do not want to part with my money or to some equally ignoble reason.[52]

The Maharaja was obviously nervous as it was becoming difficult for him to explain why he was keeping away from Malaviya's campaign. Yet he did not fail to impress upon Butler that 'the Hindu movement has now gone too far to permit of differential treatment between the two great communities.'[53] The repeated pleadings of the maharaja at last moved the Government of India. The viceroy asked Butler on 11 September 1911 to 'prepare a scheme for the Hindu University which would be acceptable to Government.'[54] It was now evident that Malaviya's campaign had at last led the government into early action. It accepted the need for making its intentions clear on the foundation of the university at Banaras.

On 10 October, the viceroy ultimately allowed Butler to inform the maharaja of Darbhanga 'the general lines on which the Government of India would agree to the creation of a Hindu University.'[55] The next day the official letter was issued informing the maharaja of the conditions on which the Government of India would consider the establishment of the university.

Thus, the Government of India gave a green signal for the Hindu university after a long consideration that lasted eight months. In fact, this was a pawn in a larger political game. The real concern of the British government and the Government of India at this time was to satisfy the Muslim community. A Muslim university was one of the boons by which Muslims were to be dealt with and saved from alienation by the Raj. Once the Muslim university was granted, a Hindu university could not be denied. Thus the broad principle of establishing the two denominational universities was ultimately decided upon at the political level.

The viceroy repeatedly stressed that he was opposed, in principle, to the establishment of denominational universities in India. His colleagues and advisors were similarly opposed to the foundation of any such university. Yet the viceroy conceded to the demand of establishing denominational universities in India because of certain compelling circumstances. He explained:

> I do not like these denominational universities. I think they are a mistake. But at the same time I think it would be extremely dangerous to discourage the Muslim undertaking which has been received with great enthusiasm by the Muslim community all over India.[56]

The viceroy repeated the same argument again within a fortnight, indicating that this consideration was uppermost in his mind:

Although we are opposed to the principle of denominational universities it would be a very dangerous step to show active opposition to the idea. We should have the whole of Musalmans of India against us.[57]

The viceroy was well aware that the likely fallout of this policy would be the demand for the establishment of the Hindu university:

> The establishment of a Muslim University, I fear, will be immediately followed by propaganda for the Hindu University. If this movement is started we shall be able to apply to the Hindu University the same conditions of control as we intend to obtain for the Muslim University.[58]

Under these circumstances the foundation of the two universities was linked. The government of India knew that immediately after its decision in favour of establishing a Muslim university at Aligarh was made known, the demand for the foundation of a Hindu university at Banaras would gain momentum. Throughout 1911, there was growing demand in favour of establishing the Hindu university at Banaras, Malaviya's fundraising campaign received widespread popular support, and the Government of India ultimately decided to give consent to establish the university.

The viceroy was still not fully convinced of the wisdom of establishing denominational universities in India and expressed his doubts in the following words:

> A good deal of pressure is being brought to bear on me to give Government support to the proposal for a Hindu University. I am still hoping that the Mohammedan University may fall through owing to lack of funds which do not seem to be pouring in as I dislike the denominational universities the chief tendency of which will be to perpetuate strife between Mohammedan and Hindu communities. Butler is rather enthusiastic on the subject and I am making him go slow as I do not want to hurry the pace.[59]

Once the Government of India had conceded the demand of establishing the two denominational universities, it lost no time in deciding upon imposing strict conditions on which these universities were to be established. The viceroy outlined his policy in the following words:

> If we are able to obtain a really effective control and impose stringent conditions on the Moslem University it would be a good precedent for applying the same restrictions and conditions on the Hindu University.[60]

As it turned out, the process was almost reversed in case of the two universities. While the promoters of the Aligarh Muslim University refused to accept the conditions laid down by the government to establish the institution, in August 1912, the organizers of the Banaras Hindu University promptly accepted all the conditions conveyed to them.[61] The result was that the Government of India decided in favour of accepting the demand for establishing the Banaras Hindu University and postponed its consideration for the foundation of a Muslim University at Aligarh.

THE GOVERNMENT'S LURKING FEAR OF MALAVIYA'S MOTIVES

For the Government of India, the question now was who could be accepted to channel the Hindu university movement. It did not regard Malaviya as sufficiently trustworthy. From the very beginning, the viceroy, his colleagues, and the lieutenant governor of UP were suspicious of Malaviya's motives. They were prejudiced against him and desired to keep him out of the whole campaign of the foundation the Hindu university at Banaras. This was first reflected in the following communication by the viceroy:

> What makes me shy of it is the fact that the chief promoter—a member of my Legislative Council—is very hostile, very fanatical and anti-British is his views.[62]

The viceroy was in no mood to allow Malaviya to lead the Hindu university campaign as the latter's speeches against the officially sponsored Press Act of 1910 were still fresh in his mind. He was similarly unhappy with Malaviya's other speeches delivered during the period. The viceroy noted:

> I cannot say that I feel much confidence in the chief promoter, Pandit Malaviya.... Maharaja of Bikaner and his brother chiefs will keep the Pandit straight.... I see no reason to encourage his scheme.[63]

The members of the governor general's council fully endorsed the views of the viceroy and argued against allowing Malaviya a prominent role in the university campaign. Harcourt Butler's observation was that Malaviya 'has been crying in the wilderness ... he is not liked or trusted personally'.[64] Another member of the council argued that 'the Pandit's presence as the chief promoter of the Hindu University is not a happy augury. If the movement can be dissociated from him by the inclusion of Native Chiefs I would not mind their coming in.'[65] The lieutenant governor of UP, J.P. Hewett, was similarly against Malaviya and demanded that he should be kept out of the movement:

> So long as Madan Mohan Malaviya retains his position of influence in respect of the project it is most unlikely that this will ever be done. He is not practical. He is very slippery and there can be no doubt that the real object at the back of his mind is a political one. He is not liked and is man of little influence.[66]

The Home Member, J.L. Jenkins, also demanded that 'Pandit Madan Mohan Malaviya should not be permitted to become the fungleman of the Hindus.'[67]

At the end of August 1911, the Government of India laid down the following four principles with regard to the foundation of the proposed Hindu University: '(a) that we must have the strictest Government control, (b) that it is desirable to associate the Ruling Chiefs, (c) that we should have nothing to do with Pandit Madan Mohan Malaviya's scheme and (d) that given a satisfactory basis we should try to get Hindus of good repute to take it up.'[68] At this point of time, Butler asked, 'How should we proceed? Either we can await developments or we can show our hand.' Elaborating further, he noted that 'there is this danger of awaiting developments that Pandit Madan Mohan Malaviya is meanwhile collecting money.... It will be very difficult to oust him later.'[69] Butler, however, admitted that it was not possible to say openly that 'we distrusted Madan Mohan Malaviya' as 'we may appear to be unfriendly to the Hindus.'[70] In such a situation, Butler supported the policy of sidelining Malaviya and encouraging others to take up the responsibility of leading the university movement. As shall be explained later, on being informed of such intentions of the government, Malaviya did not lose his patience, kept his cool, and thought it prudent to act in accordance with the wishes of the Government of India.

Once Malaviya had collected subscriptions for the proposed Hindu university, which exceeded the amount stipulated by the government in the case of the Aligarh Muslim University as a condition for considering the grant of a charter, he proceeded to Shimla to ascertain the wishes of the Government of India. He had no idea that in the mean time, the viceroy and the members of his council had decided upon a policy of keeping him out of the whole project and to pass on the responsibility to some other 'respectable Hindus' of their liking. Malaviya was therefore shocked and disappointed as a result of his interview with the viceroy on 10 October 1911. The viceroy put on record his version of the interview in the following words:

> I told him [Malaviya] that from what Government had heard of his proposals, they seemed to be more of a political than of an educational character and although government never object to criticism of their actions, his attitude towards Government had on certain occasions given an impression of hostility and distrust. This had tended also to prejudice Government against the movement that he was leading and Government would, therefore, before giving support to any scheme for a University, required to be assured that it would not be utilized for political ends and that there should be sufficient Government Control.[71]

Referring indirectly to Malaviya's recent speeches in and out of the Imperial Legislative Council, the viceroy told him frankly that these gave 'an impression of hostility and distrust'. Coming from the viceroy himself, this was a very strong indictment of Malaviya's actions. The viceroy told Malaviya honestly what was passing in his mind at that time and gave him a clear hint to be ready to take a backseat in the university movement. Malaviya wisely decided to keep out of the movement, for some time, in accordance with the wishes of the viceroy. The latter noted:

> The Pandit assured me at some length of his loyalty to the British Government and admitting that he had used on certain occasions unnecessarily hard words, expressed his regret for having done so. He was, he said, quite ready to remove himself from the movement if his personality was unwelcome on the Committee although he had the idea of the University greatly at heart and that he or the Committee would be willing to accept any scheme that the Government might propose. He asked for an assurance that the Government would not oppose the creation of a Hindu University.[72]

The viceroy told Malaviya that the 'Government would certainly not offer opposition to a scheme on sound lines on [the] conditions approved by them and that the Hindu University would be treated on terms of equality with the Mohammedan University.'[73]

As a result of his interview with the viceroy, Malaviya got first-hand information of the viceroy's line of thinking about the conditions under which he was willing to grant permission for the establishment of the university. He had no other alternative except to obey his instructions. Therefore, he lost no time in bowing to the viceroy's wishes to fulfil his lifelong ambition of laying the foundation of the Hindu university at Banaras.

Only two days after the Malaviya–Hardinge meeting, Butler formally handed over a letter to the maharaja of Darbhanga spelling out the terms and conditions under which the Government of India was willing to recognize the movement for the establishment of a Hindu University. These were

1. The Hindus should approach Government as a body as the Muhammadans did.
2. A strong, efficient and financially sound college with an adequate European staff should be the basis of the scheme.
3. The University should be a modern University.
4. The movement should be entirely educational.
5. There should be same measure of Government supervision and opportunity to give advice as in the case of the proposed University at Aligarh.[74]

Thus we find that the government, in the person of Harcourt Butler on the one side and Malaviya on the other, were looking for intermediaries who could be acceptable to both. The two intermediaries were the maharajah of Darbhanga and Sundar Lal. The former was already involved with the movement of the foundation of the university, had close and intimate links with the government, and represented the landed aristocracy. The other intermediary was Sundar Lal who, as the former vice chancellor of Allahabad University, had won the confidence of the government. He had, however, refused to associate himself with the Hindu University Society founded by Malaviya. He accepted the secretaryship of the society after Butler appealed to him 'to stand forth on this great occasion, so pregnant with good, if only rightly guided, to your community and to the government.'[75]

RESPONSE OF THE RULING CHIEFS

Winning over the favour of the government was crucial to Malaviya for another reason. The ruling chiefs were not prepared to help him in raising funds for the university without the government's blessing. The maharajas of Bikaner, Banaras, and Darbhanga conveyed their intentions in this regard to Malaviya in no uncertain terms. When Malaviya got in touch with the maharaja of Bikaner in May 1911, asking him to become the patron of the proposed University, the latter turned down his request saying that 'he could support the movement only if it received the approval of the Government'.[76] The maharaja reiterated his stand two months later, informing Malaviya that 'I cannot have anything to do with any scheme that has not got the approval of the Government and I cannot move in the matter until you have obtained that approval.'[77] The maharaja of Bikaner frankly told Malaviya that he was totally unwilling to be associated with the Hindu university movement unless and until the Government of India's approval had been sought. The chief secretary to the maharaja of Banaras wrote to Malaviya along similar lines:

> I am desired by His Highness the Maharaja to say that he is very sorry in being quite unable to associate his name with the project or subscribe anything towards it until he is fully satisfied on the following points:
>
> 1. That the Government has approved of the scheme and are likely to sanction the proposal.
> 2. You have got sufficient money in hand to carry on the project.
>
> Unless and until you get any sort of assurance from the Government that they are likely to sanction the scheme and unless and until you succeed in securing at least 30 lakhs of rupees His Highness is totally unable to consider the proposal seriously. If you succeed in the two above named points the Maharaja will be most glad to do all that he possibly can in this respect.[78]

The curt language used by the maharaja of Banaras in his communication alarmed Malaviya particulary because of his fear that the maharaja was acting on the advice of the Commissioner, Benaras Division. The following report of the senior British official reveals that Malaviya's impression was largely correct:

> His Highness's Chief Secretary visited me and said that His Highness was being worried by Pandit Madan Mohan Malaviya. I asked if the Maharaja had in any way changed his views in the matter. Colonel Vindeshwari Prasad replied in the negative but gave me the impression that His Highness was somewhat perplexed. He informed me that the

Pandit had said to him that he supposed that the draft of His Highness's
letter had been approved by me.[79]

Another report by the commissioner refers to his influence on the
Maharaja of Banaras:

> My visitor went on to say that the Pandit had revisited Benaras to in-
> terview His Highness. If, as was probable, I should be now consulted, he
> hoped I would advice His Highness to send a reply more in consonance
> with his position and interests.'[80]

All through the year 1911, the maharaja of Darbhanga wanted to
keep the best of terms with both the government and Malaviya. His
letter to Butler speaks of the conflict in his mind:

> Mr. Malaviya was not at all pleased with the letter I had sent him from
> Simla in accordance of His Excellency's instructions to me.... He said
> he was very sorry I was not helping the movement and asked me to
> give him five lakhs at least. I replied that I could not help any scheme
> that had not Government's approval.... He warned me as a friend that
> my inaction would be construed in a most unfavourable manner by the
> entire Hindu community.[81]

In the following month, the official announcement granting recognition to the Hindu university movement came as a big relief to the
ruling chiefs, as they were now free to play their role in the establishment of the university as they wished. By now the tables had urned and
instead of imposing conditions, the Government of India was encouraging the ruling chiefs to come to the rescue of the university in a big
way. Their financial and moral support helped Malaviya immensely not
only in pushing forward his dream project but also in consolidating his
position as the central figure of the university campaign.[82]

At the close of 1911, Malaviya founded the Hindu University
Society 'to collect funds, to acquire and hold property and move the
Government for enactment of such legislation, as may be necessary,
for establishing a Hindu University at Benaras.'[83] For the management
of the affairs of the society, a 61-member committee was constituted,
comprising very eminent persons from different parts of the country.
The maharaja of Darbhanga took over as the president of the society
and Sundar Lal assumed charge as its secretary. The maharaja, Sundar Lal,
and Malaviya carried out negotiations with the government for almost
four years, discussed various important issues relating to the establish-

ment of the university with the representatives of the Government of India and the provincial government, and continued to correspond with them in detail. Even though the maharaja and Sundar Lal were in the forefront during the early years, they were always careful to seek the advice and help of Malaviya on all important issues. The trio worked perfectly as a team, respected each other immensely, regularly consulted each other, and never resorted to any uncompromising postures. As the years rolled on, Malaviya's pre-eminent position was recognized at various levels.

In his revised scheme of the proposed university outlined in July 1911, Malaviya informed the Hindus that one crore rupees would be collected in the next few years to meet its initial cost.[84] During the first fundraising campaign, Malaviya collected Rs 25 lakhs, which was considered a good beginning. He launched the second and the third collection campaigns in the following two years. During this period, Malaviya visited several towns in which huge public meetings were organized. People listened to his speeches as well as the speeches of his prominent supporters with rapt attention and liberally contributed to the funds of the proposed university. The collection campaigns moved the Hindus into action, encouraged them to feel as a community, and led them to believe that organized action was the need of the hour. These collection campaigns raised Malaviya's stature as a public figure in the eyes of the government.[85] By March 1913, he was able to convince the Government of India that Rs 58 lakhs had been collected to meet the initial cost of the foundation of the university. The Government of India took it as only the first step and put forward further conditions as precedent to its final approval.[86]

AMALGAMATION OF THE CENTRAL HINDU COLLEGE WITH THE UNIVERSITY

It has been explained earlier that since the middle of 1911, Malaviya was pleading for the amalgamation of the Central Hindu College with the proposed Hindu university on the ground that it was an 'avowedly Hindu institution and had been built up largely by the donations of the Hindus.'[87] In the same year, Mrs Besant agreed to work jointly with Malaviya and expressed her readiness to support Malaviya's plans of future incorporation of the college in the university.

The formal negotiations about the transfer of the college to the proposed university, however, ran into difficulties in 1913 as Mrs Besant desired the absorption of most of the Theosophist professors in the university. She also wanted all the trustees of the Central Hindu College to be the members of the Hindu University Court at the time that it was constituted.[88] But Malaviya was under heavy pressure not to concede to Mrs Besant's demands. Echoing the government's policy, the maharaja of Darbhanga proposed to Malaviya that 'we should clear the College of Mrs Besant's elements and we should bring it to a proper level.'[89] The majaraja suggested that this was the right occasion for bringing the college in line with the ideals and objectives of the proposed Hindu university.

Malaviya's task was made easier as Mrs Besant was facing problems due to a split in the Theosophical Society and the continuing financial crisis in the college. Under these circumstances, she called a meeting of the trustees of the college 'to consider the position of the C.H. College and to arrange for carrying it on until it is taken over by the proposed Hindu University.'[90]

However, this meeting of the trustees of the college was postponed twice and adjourned once during March–April 1913 at the behest of Mrs Besant. She was perhaps finding it difficult to bow to the inevitable. When Mrs Besant did not attend the meeting of the Board of Trustees, scheduled on 4 May 1913, and submitted her resignation from the presidentship of the board, its members, present on the occasion at Allahabad, decided to take up the question of the management of the college in her absence. The Board accepted Malaviya's suggestion that it was 'desirable to arrange as far as possible that the management of the Central Hindu College be taken over by the Hindu University Society',[91] that a subcommittee be appointed to recommend further steps to implement the decision, and requested Mrs Besant to continue as president until the college was handed over to the Hindu university.[92]

On 14 May, Mrs Besant wrote a letter to the members of the Board of Trustees and sent it for publication in the *Leader* and various other newspapers. Along with this, she also published various other letters and communications relating to the Central Hindu College and its relations with the Hindu university giving 'a further lease of life to the controversy.'[93] The following passages occur in her letter:

1. I will continue in office as you wish till the Hindu University takes over the College—action which, I hope, will not be delayed; for the change of policy which was followed on the promised transfer of the College to the University is to my mind, fatal to the ideals for the spread of which the College was founded and by which it has flourished. Intolerance has now replaced tolerance and nearly all the honorary members of the staff, whose labours have made the College what it is, have been driven away.

2. I have withdrawn from the Hindu University Committee as it is evident that Theosophists are not wanted in this body by Pt. M.M. Malaviya. The CHC was built up chiefly by Theosophists and with their money. It is taken over by a curious alliance of very orthodox Hindus and free thinkers and both hate the middle way of Theosophy.

3. The Allahabad group now rules the College and has brought about the present catastrophe. Until it got rid of the Theosophical element in the staff it would not move a finger to help the College financially.[94]

Sundar Lal was shocked at the publication of the letter and wrote, in a confidential note, that 'the undercurrent of Mrs Besant's letter is one of undisguised hostility to her colleagues of the Board of Trustees of the CHC and the Hindu University Society.... That the observations are based upon utter misapprehensions, if not upon actual misrepresentations, will be evident from a moment's consideration of the situation.'[95]

The Allahabad daily, *Leader*, lamented that

it has been impossible for us even to attempt to deal with all the astounding mis-statements of which the communications are sickeningly full. Whether one turns to the most unworthy and untruthful accusations and insinuations made with a too light sense of responsibility or in a spirit of mad rage against the Hon. Pandit Madan Mohan Malaviya and the Hon. Dr. Tej Bahadur Sapru[,] most straight forward and unoffending among men[,] or to the bitterness against Babu Bhagwan Das.

The paper also added: 'After the communications she has addressed to the press Mrs Besant has no right to expect anybody to think of her with greater respect or to show her greater consideration than she has done in the case of numerous good men whom she has gratutously vilified.'[96]

In spite of such wild accusations against Mrs Besant, the Hindu University Society went ahead with its programme of taking over the management and control of the Central Hindu College and the

Central Hindu Boys School. The formalities were completed with the signing of the certificate of taking over charge on 27 November 1914 by Sundar Lal as the secretary of the Hindu University Society. Mrs Besant was left with no option but to bow to the inevitable.[97]

At the time of the amalgation of the Central Hindu College with the Banaras Hindu University, there was an understanding that ten of the college trustees, including Mrs Besant, would be members of the University Court when it was formed. By the time the first meeting of the University Court was held in August 1916, no firm announcement could be made in this regard. It was decided to give effect to this understanding during the first meeting of the court as laid down in the relevant clause of the University Act. Explaining the reasons for the delay, Sundar Lal wrote a letter to Mrs Besant in an effort to convince her about the actual process to be followed during the meeting of the Court.[98] While replying to this letter, Mrs Besant wrote that she was 'much surprised' and 'much pained', which shows that she was still nursing considerable misgivings regarding the transfer of the Central Hindu College to the university and the promises made regarding her membership and that of her colleagues in the University Court. She insisted that 'we should have been the original members of the Court. As it is we cannot be there as members of the Court on its opening, a great historical occasion.'[99]

The issue was finally resolved when ten members of the Board of Trustees including Mrs Besant, were elected to the University Court in the first meeting in accordance with the resolution proposed by Malaviya. Sundar Lal later explained to the lieutenant governor as to why such a step was taken in the University Court:

> We must, however, to keep our obligation elect her at least for this once. It is also proposed to put her name on the Senate. Since the time when the bill was passed Mrs. Annie Besant's activities have brought her to the notice of the Government of India in more ways than one. It is only because we cannot omit her name by reason of the understanding on which the college was taken over by us that her name has been proposed. The University will have nothing to do with current politics of the day and she cannot take any part being only one of the many members of the Court and the Senate in the work of the University.[100]

Obviously Mrs Besant and her colleagues found their place in the university bodies as Malaviya had no intention of keeping her out of the newly established institution only because the government favoured such a course.[101]

LOCATION OF THE UNIVERSITY

Regarding the selection of the site for the university, a myth persists that the land was given as a gift to Malaviya by the maharaja of Banaras, Prabhu Narayan Singh. Giving credence to the view, a recent writer goes to the extent of saying that 'it would be easy to suspect that the records did not reveal fully the nature of the transaction.' The author refers to the official history of the university which, it has been pointed out, does not give 'a full description of the process whereby the land came under the possession of the University.'[102] Thus, it becomes necessary to analyse the role of the maharaja of Banaras in the acquisition of land for the university and to examine various steps taken in this long-drawn process from 1911 to 1917. The contemporary official records convincingly show that there was no ambiguity in the acquisition of the site by the university; the land was acquired by it under the Land Acquisition Act and full compensation was paid by the university as per the cost of the land fixed by the collector of Banaras.

According to the available evidence, Malaviya had several meetings with the Maharaja of Banaras during the early years of the establishment of the University. There is no doubt that he requested the maharaja to extend suitable financial help to the university scheme and to make a land grant available for tit. But the maharaja did not give Malaviya an encouraging answer. There was a conflict in the maharaja's mind. On the one hand, he was sympathetic towards Malaviya and desired to support him in his effort with regard to the uplift of the Hindus, and on the other, he wanted to keep the best of relations with the government. The maharaja could not muster courage to act against the advice of the divisional commissioner. During these years, the government was pressurizing the ruling chiefs to keep away from Malaviya's project. Therefore, the chief secretary to the maharaja wrote a hard-hitting letter to Malaviya on 9 August 1911 informing him that the Maharaja was 'totally unable to consider his proposal' till certain

conditions were fulfilled.[103] Referring to this letter, we have explained
earlier that Malaviya did not believe that this represented exactly the
views of the maharaja and thought that it was written due to the influence exercised by H. V. Lovett, the Commissioner, Banaras Division.[104]

The Maharaja of Darbhanga's letter of 17 June 1912 further confirms that the maharaja of Banaras was unwilling to help Malaviya
at this time. He wrote: 'I have received an unsatisfactory reply from
Banaras. But nothing need surprise us as His Highness simply repeats
what he had said to Malaviya about paying his subscriptions in five
years. I am afraid that Malaviya's statements that we were to expect
a large landed grant from the Maharaja was very deceptive.'[105] The
maharaja of Darbhanga informed Sundar Lal again that 'Banaras will
not give the site and we need not build castles in the air.'[106] Since the
chief promoters knew that the maharaja of Banaras was not prepared
to make any land available for the university, the only option open to
them at that time was to find a suitable site on their own.

The executive council of the Banaras Hindu Society appointed a
subcommittee comprising Malaviya, Sundar Lal, Ganga Prasad Varma,
Bhagwan Das, Moti Chand, and Gokaran Nath Misra to select the site.
The subcommittee found three sites at Nagwa, Sarnath, and Harahua
suitable and also estimated the cost for each piece of land. The members
were well aware of Malaviya's vision of a spacious university: a campus
spread over at least two square miles with a tank and a temple at the
centre.[107] The final selection of the site was made after Harcourt Butler's
visit to Banaras on 27 July 1914. It was finally decided to have the Nagwa
lands for the location of the university buildings. Harcourt Butler noted:

> Meston, the Maharaja of Darbhanga, Sharp and myself went over to
> the sites today and we met Madan Mohan Malaviya there. There can
> be no doubt that the site opposite Ramnagar is the only possible site.
> They say it will cost 4½ lakhs but even if it will cost 10 lakhs it will be
> worth having it.[108]

Since the final choice of the Nagwa land was taken with the
approval of the senior functionaries of the Government of India and
the lieutenant governor of UP, their continued support went a long
way in helping Malaviya and his supporters in acquiring the site. Soon
after his visit to Banaras, the lieutenant governor of UP, James Meston,
gave the following instructions to the chief secretary:

In connection with the proposed site for the Hindu University at Nagwa, opposite Ramnagar Palace, please have the Collector asked to prepare a rough estimate of the cost of acquisition. The Maharaja of Darbhanga has sent me his private estimates.... The Collector may be able to get a map of the proposed site from Babu Moti Chand or from Hon'ble Pandit Madan Mohan Malaviya.[109]

Some months later, the Maharaja of Darbhanga requested the lieutenant governor that 'all preliminaries in regard to the acquisition of the Nagwa site be settled with the land acquition authorities.'[110] On 30 June 1915, Sundar Lal wrote to the chief secretary of the UP government: 'Would you kindly oblige by letting me know the exact amount estimated by the Collector of Benaras as the cost of the acquisition of site for the Banaras Hindu University and the probable time it will take to acquire it under the Land Acquisition Act?'[111] Sundar Lal was informed that 'the Collector has estimated the cost of acquiring the site for Hindu University at Nagwa, opposite the Ramnagar palace, at Rs. 5,23,662. This estimate was originally prepared by the Land Acquisition Kanungo but subsequently the Land Acquisition Officer was requested to examine it and he has reported that it was fair and reasonable.'[112]

The official correspondence quoted above shows that the actual proceedings of acquiring the Nagwa land for the university went on for three to four years and the Collector of Banaras was involved in the transactions all along. He got the map of the area prepared, decided the cost of the land to be paid by the university, and worked under the instructions of the provincial governor. The correspondence between Harcourt Butler and the provincial governor also bears this out in ample measure. Butler wrote on 18 October 1915: 'I sent you a copy of a note of a meeting I had at Benaras this morning. Hopkins advised me that the sooner the orders were issued on the acquisition of land the better and if you could see it through you would be conferring a great boon on the University Committee.'[113] Butler put on record: 'I discussed the question of the Hindu University with Sir James Meston. He said there would be no difficulty about the site and the acquisition proceedings had already begun.'[114]

Giving an account of 'how matters stand in regard to the acquisition of land for the Banaras Hindu University' the Chief Secretary, UP Government, informed the Government of India that in accordance

with the particular provision of the Land Acquisition Act, 'some portion, however small, of the cost is to be met out of Government funds'
and added further:

> This has been pointed out to Dr. Sundar Lal who has practically guar-
> anteed that the Committee will be allowed to utilize a portion of the
> Government of India's grant to pay part of the cost of the acquisition
> of land. Accordingly we are working on the assumption that this will be
> permitted and the Collector of Banaras is preparing a draft notification
> showing the land required. When this is received a notification under
> section 6 will be published in the United Provinces Gazette.[115]

It was further pointed out that 'the land is being taken up for a public
purpose as contemplated under paragraph II of the Act'.[116] The Deputy
Secretary, UP, Government, finally informed Sundar Lal on 17 November
1915 that 'a notification, acquiring 1,165 acres 1 rood and 21 poles of land
will be published in this week's Gazettee.'[117] The area of land acquired
by the university was notified and it gradually took over its possession in
due course. The tenants were formally dispossessed of the particular land
in pursuance with the provisions of the act in the next few years.

It has been explained earlier that the university authorities were well
aware that they would be required to bear the cost of acquiring the site
as per the directions of the collector of Banaras who had been authorized to prepare an estimate of the cost of land under the provisions
of the Land Acquisition Act. The collector informed the university in
August 1916 that he was 'now in a position to proceed with the payment of compensation to the land holders and tenants' and asked that
'at present a sum of three laks of rupees' be placed at his disposal. The
university was told that 'further sums will be asked for as the awards
are prepared'.[118] The university deposited Rs 140,000 soon after and
requested the Government of India that the grant of one lakh rupees
be paid to it, as promised, at an early date. The Finance Member of the
viceroy's council noted that 'we might help the University as far as possible by giving the money now'.[119] The Government of India was keen
to 'show their goodwill towards the University' and was willing to sanction the payment of the grant this year for the acquisition of land.[120]
For the payment of the remaining sum, negotiations were carried out
with the local bank which agreed to permit the university to take an
overdraft of Rs 600,000. The money was deposited into the treasury at
Banaras and the possession of land was given to the university on 18

February 1917. Sundar Lal informed the lieutenant governor of UP on 3 July 1917: 'We have already paid this year 6 lacs to the Government for the acquisition of site at Nagwa [about 1,250 acres of land].'[121]

Another point regarding the land acquisition proceedings was related to the provision of sites required for new houses for the dispossessed tenants. The chief secretary of the UP government observed: 'The persons to be ejected have clearly a claim on the university and His Honour in fact understood from Pandit Madan Mohan Malaviya to be the full intention of the University authorities to find new sites for the dispossessed residents.'[122] The chief secretary stated that 'Sundar Lal himself is prepared to be very reasonable.' In view of the fairly close relationship between the provincial and district officials and the university, the issue was amicably resolved causing as little hardship as possible to the dispossessed tenants.[123]

FRAMING OF STATUTES AND REGULATIONS

In the middle of the year 1914, the Government of India indicated the lines on which the constitution of the university was to be drawn. These lines meant a number of powers of control and intervention for the government in the university administration.[124] The contents of the letter were received with utmost reservation. Public opinion was generally against the acceptance of such conditions. Some commentators even went to the extent of suggesting the rejection of the conditions and giving up of the plan for the university altogether.[125] Taking note of various strong reactions voiced through the press and in public meetings, the Government of India immediately held consultations with the lieutenant governor of UP with a view to chalk out further course of action. His assessment of the situation was as follows:

> I do not think the Hindus will seriously object to the arrangement though they would certainly prefer the Viceroy on many grounds and particularly in accord with the universal tendency to fly as far possible which is incidental to one of the most persistent and insidious features of the nationalist programme.... The all-India concept is for the moment really stronger. Still when all is said and done they are all so anxious for a settlement now and they will welcome a complete and, as far as possible, a final statement of Government's requirements, however, much there may be in what they dislike.[126]

Whereas Malaviya and his supporters insisted on having the governor general as the chancellor of the university, the Government of India came forward with the proposal that the lieutenant governor of UP would be its chancellor. This came as a bolt from the blue to Malaviya. He found it difficult to ask his supporters to swallow this suggestion. When the viceroy realized that there was 'strong opposition' to the government proposals, he decided to open a dialogue with the Hindu University Society at Allahabad. The viceroy pointed out:

> I have sent Butler to discuss the whole subject with the promoters of the University. He will have a difficult task but with the assistance of Darbhanga who is the head of the committee I am in hopes that our views may obtain a fair amount of support.[127]

Under instructions from the viceroy, Harcourt Butler and James Meston met the maharaja of Darbhanga, Sundar Lal, and Malaviya on 27 July 1914 at Allahabad. Reporting about the proceedings of the meeting, Butler stated:

> Malaviya was more reasonable than I expected. Sundar Lal was rather upset because we had not followed his draft but I explained that we had to deal with a public which was hostile to the University as well as a public which was favourable to it and that we could not wrap up and conceal our meaning in legal phraseology. It was absolutely necessary to be frank and to explain what sort of control we wanted.[128]

The lieutenant governor of UP was hopeful that Malaviya and his supporters would ultimately give in: 'I had a couple of days over with them with Harcourt at Allahabad. The Hindus will kick, but will come in, Darbhanga and Malaviya have been talking too big to afford to let the thing drop and they will accept the terms.'[129]

One month later, Butler tried to assuage agitated emotions by arguing that the powers of intervention were emergency powers, only to be used by the governor general.[130]

Butler had a better understanding of the situation after his meeting with Malaviya in the first week of October. Giving the following account of the meeting, he asked the lieutenant governor of UP to suggest a way out:

> Pandit Madan Mohan Malaviya came to see me yesterday and handed me a copy of the proceedings of the Hindu University Committee. He told me that while Darbhanga, Sundar Lal and himself were prepared to

accept any terms, the majority of the subscribers would not and unless Government gave way on the point of Chancellorship he thought the movement would fall through.... I shall be glad to know what you think of the whole situation now.[131]

To find a way out, Butler visited Allahabad again in November 1914 and discussed various alterative suggestions with the provincial governor, the maharaja of Darbhanga, Sundar Lal, and Malaviya. Ultimately a compromise formula was evolved. It was now agreed upon that the university was to elect its own chancellor, the viceroy was to be the patron, and the lieutenant governor was to be the ex-officio visitor to the university. It was further agreed upon that the visitor was to have all the ordinary powers and the Government of India was to exercise emergency powers.[132]

The viceroy requested the secretary of state to accord his consent to the 'compromise proposals of the promoters of the University' with the following remark:

It will have a great effect in this country amongst the Hindus and it is very desirable to placate them as far as possible during the course of the present War.[133]

In December 1914, the final decision of the government based on the terms of the compromise formula was transmitted in Butler's letter to the university.[134] The viceroy noted with satisfaction that the 'end of wearsome negotiation is in sight' and conveyed his feelings on this occasion to the secretary of state in the following words:

The Hindu University scheme will now go through. I am glad of it as I regard it of some importance and it will be regarded by the Hindus as a triumph. We will have a bill in Council and I hope you will assist us as much as possible to pass in this session. The Hindus trust Butler and me to push it through and I think it is important to get it fixed up before Butler goes.[135]

For the next few months Malaviya, Sundar Lal, and the members of the Hindu University Society were busy pondering over various provisions of the bill to be introduced in the Supreme Legislative Council. Giving a detailed account of the meetings he had with the secretary of the Department of Education, Malaviya made special reference to two clauses in the draft bill which would 'give rise to apprehensions of undue interference' of the government in university affairs. He added

'I suspect that Mr. Sharp has an idea that he would under this provision be able to put stiff Statues and Regulations and that we shall have to submit to them helplessly.' Malaviya further conceded that he was 'so apprehensive on this that I would rather delay the passing (not introduction) of the Bill till September to secure that the Statues and Regulations should be settled before the Act is passed'.[136] Malaviya's representations had the desired effect and certain sections of the proposed bill were redrafted and the exact wordings of the regulations were suitably amended.

MALAVIYA'S SPEECHES ON THE DRAFT BILL

As a member of the Imperial Legislative Council, Malaviya spoke on 22 March 1915 at the time of the introduction of the Banaras Hindu University Bill and on 1 October when the bill was finally passed by the central legislature. During the first speech, his major task was to respond to the criticism voiced in the Imperial Legislative Council that the proposed university would be a sectarian university and would foster or strengthen separatist tendencies. Malaviya's contention was that the 'University will be a denominational institution but not a sectarian one. It will not promote narrow sectarianism but a broad liberation of mind and a religious spirit which will promote brotherly feeling between man and man.' He went on to say: 'I believe instruction in the truths of religion, whether it would be Hindus or Muslims, whether it is imparted to the students of the Banaras Hindu University or of the Aligarh Moslem University, will tend to produce men who, if they are true to their religion, will be true to their God, their King and their country.'[137]

Referring to the objections against the provision for compulsary religious education in the proposed university, Malaviya said that 'to remove this provision would be like cutting the heart out of the scheme'. He further added, 'It is regretted that some people are afraid of the influence of religion. I regret I cannot share their views. That influence is ever ennobling. I believe that where the true religious spirit is inculcated there must be elevating feeling of humility. And where there is love of God there will be greater love and less hatred of man.'[138]

During the second speech delivered in the Imperial Legislative Council on 1 October 1915 Malaviya minced no words in expressing the need for gaining full favour and confidence of the government: 'The movement has from the start been worked in the conviction, the deliberate conviction, that it is essential for the success of the University that it should secure the goodwill and sympathy of the Government and that it should always retain that sympathy.'[139] This was a candid admission of the larger effort of the university movement so far and his plan of action in carrying forward the development of the university in the years to come. The bill was passed on the same day and received the governor general's assent on the 18th of the same month.

By this time Malaviya had learnt his lessons well. He had come to realize that sympathy and support of the government was vital as much for the establishment of the university as for its proper functioning, particularly during its early years. The government's blessings were similarly needed for winning over the ruling princes in support of the university. Malaviya, therefore, went around several Indian states to personally invite the ruling chiefs to attend the foundation-stone-laying ceremony. He issued instructions that all those ruling chiefs who were entitled to a salute were to be invited.[140] With regard to his motives, Malaviya wrote, 'But if we invite them all even those who do not come will be pleased with the compliment and will probably be led by circumstances to take an interest in the University and will possibly be more inclined to listen to an appeal for subscription when we approach them.'[141] Malaviya's policy of reaching out to the ruling chiefs paid rich dividends in the years to come.

THE FOUNDATION–STONE–LAYING CEREMONY

The foundation-stone-laying ceremony of the university, held on 4 February 1916, turned out to be an official show where 'loyalty was the keynote of the function.' Apart from the viceroy and several provincial governors and senior government officials, about fourteen ruling chiefs were also present on this occasion. Giving an account of the function, the viceroy remarked:

> The ceremony at Benaras was a wonderful success and I have seldom seen a more enthusiastic gathering. After the big Durbar of 1911 it was the finest Durbar that I have seen in India. The arrangements were perfect

and the whole scene most picturesque. My speech was received with great
enthusiasm and altogether the whole function was a great success.[142]

The viceroy gave the following assessment of the future of the
university to Butler:

It is very satisfactory to feel that this new venture in Indian education
for whose birth you and I are chiefly responsible, has been successfully
launched and it now remains for the Hindus themselves to make it a
complete success. Should it prove to be a failure, as some carping critics
seem to think it will, we cannot help it but in my opinion the Ruling
Chiefs will take very good care that the whole institution is properly
conducted and does not become a home for sedition and mere examining University [*sic*].[143]

It was a great tribute to Malaviya's patience and integrity of purpose
that he could finally win over the viceroy who had used the most
derogatory words against him in 1911 and was, for several years, sceptical of his moves to establish the university.

No one was surprised at the absence of the nationalist leaders at
the foundation-stone-laying ceremony. Malaviya had purposely kept
his university movement away from the political currents of the time
and did not seek Congress support for his university campaign. As
such, only Mrs Annie Besant was present at the opening ceremony
and Gandhi appeared on the scene two days later. Mrs Besant was
studiously kept in the background and not offered a seat on the dais
as the organizers knew that official opinion was against her. The lieutenant governor noted that 'she was a particularly bad influence in
Benaras'.[144]

In the following days, several lectures were delivered, and one of the
speakers was Gandhi. He had returned from South Africa in the previous year and on Gokhale's advice had abstained from public utterances.
He used the Banaras celebrations to break his public silence. Gandhi's
lecture turned out to be highly controversial particularly because he
chose to hit out directly at the ruling chiefs and indirectly at the viceroy and also because the tenor and tone of his speech was unusual. He
criticized the ruling princes for their exhibition of pomp and show:
'There is no salvation for India unless you strip yourselves of this jew-
ellery and hold it in trust for your countrymen in India.' Speaking
about the security measures for the viceroy, Gandhi asked, 'Why is

this distrust? Is it not better that Lord Hardinge should die than live a living death?'[145] Other subjects of his speech referred to the spiritual life in the university, the use of Hindi, anarchism, and the behaviour of British civil servants. Gandhi could not finish his speech as the princes left the hall 'in a body'. He was interrupted earlier by Mrs Besant but had continued with the permission of the chairman who happened to be the maharaja of Darbhanga. Malaviya tried to explain Gandhi's speech in an apologizing manner but could not prevent the complete break-up of the meeting. The maharaja of Alwar, who was present at the occasion, observed, 'Gandhi exceeded the limits of prudence and good judgement' and expressed his 'unhesitating repugnance and disapproval' of Gandhi's lecture.[146] When Malaviya heard that the Commissioner, Banaras Division, was about to issue orders for Gandhi to leave the town the next day, he found himself in a difficult situation. It was embarrassing for Malaviya to appear on the side of the authorities against Gandhi and it was expected that Gandhi would not obey the order. Malaviya found a solution. He persuaded Gandhi to leave the city voluntarily, which he did.[147] The UP lieutenant governor's remark on Gandhi that 'there does not seem to be malice in his speech but it was all so unnecessary'[148] was a correct assessment of the situation.

From the very beginning, Malaviya was careful to shape the newly established university as an all-India institution. He was very keen to combat the notion that the 'proposed University was a more or less local affair of our provinces.'[149] He thought of offering the post of the first vice chancellor of the university to Gurudas Bannerji. But the suggestion did not find favour with Harcourt Butler who threw his entire weight in favour of Sundar Lal and asked him to shoulder the responsibility:

> I have already recorded my opinion which cannot be altered that you are unquestionably the right man to be the first Vice-Chancellor of the University. The University Bill has been passed and I think some years will elapse before the buildings are ready and the University housed and set going. At any rate, in the preliminary stage it seems quite necessary that you should be Vice-Chancellor.[150]

Sundar Lal quietly bowed to Butler's suggestion and wrote to the latter: 'I am willing to lean to your decision. I only wrote to you what I considered my duty in the interests of the University.'[151] Sundar Lal was referring to Malaviya's desire to offer the post to Gurudas Bannerji and his willingness to act upon Malaviya's advice. Butler's firm opinion turned the table and Sundar Lal and Malaviya thought it best to act according to his advice. The appointment of Sundar Lal as the first vice chancellor of the university was a clear instance of the manner in which the university authorities sought to work with the cooperation of the government. There was no difficulty in organizing the governing bodies of the university—the court, the council, and the senate.

There were no further difficulties in initiating measures for organizing the administrative set up of the university. While making suggestions to the government for the appointment of the chancellor, the pro-chancellor, and vice patron of the university, the two major considerations in Malaviya's mind were obtaining funds for the university and the strengthening of the Hindu sentiment. With these ends in view, he canvassed for the appointment of the maharaja of Mysore as the chancellor, the maharaja of Gwalior as the pro-chancellor, and the maharaja of Darbhanga as the vice patron. The government accepted these suggestions as it always desired that the ruling princes be assigned prominent roles in the proper functioning of the university.

GIVING AN EARLY START TO THE UNIVERSITY

In March 1916, Malaviya proceeded to Delhi to settle preliminaries and obtain the Government of India's permission for an early start for the university. He considered this necessary in order to keep alive popular enthusiasm without which the huge funds needed could not be raised. Giving an account of the his visit, Malaviya conveyed the following details to Sundar Lal:

> I have informed to them all why we want to have the Act put into force at once and they are quite willing to do so.... I have fully explained to Sir Edward Maclegan and W. Sharp—as also to Sir Shankaran Niar—the necessity and advantages of starting the University in the present premises. I believe I have impressed them.[152]

The main objection of the Government of India to allow the university to start functiong was the want of accommodation in the Central Hindu College. Malaviya, therefore, decided to remove the school department in the Central Hindu College premises to another building in an effort to convince the government that 'we shall have accommodation for up to one thousand students of the University in our present premises.'[153] Thus Malaviya had his plans ready in as early as March 1916 for an early start to the teaching work of the university at the Central Hindu College premises.

As a visitor of the university, the lieutenant governor of UP was reluctant to recommend this proposal for quite some time as he had his own doubts of the wisdom of allowing the university to start functioning from the Central Hindu College. However, he agreed to accept the proposal after one year, giving the following explanation to the viceroy:

> The determination of the Brahman clique who now control the University to secure their ascendancy without delay, has beaten us. They have laid themselves out at all costs to consolidate their position before the inevitable enquiry into our university system imperils it. We have no statutory powers to check them and persuasion is useless.[154]

The lieutenant governor assured the viceroy that the promoters of the University were getting ready to make full use of the Nagwa site as early as possible:

> To do them justice Malaviya and his followers ... are desperately anxious to push forward but are equally full of the idea of imposing buildings and a worthy employment of the site on which the foundation was laid.[155]

It was with considerable diffidence that the government of India at last agreed to declare the Central Hindu College as a college maintained by the university with effect from 1917.

At the time, it had certain other considerations in mind of according permission to the university to start work at Central Hindu College in October 1917. H. Sharp, Educational Advisor to the Government of India, noted: 'Meantime Sir Sundar Lal's three years' term of office is half way through. Plots are afoot to prevent his reappointment as Vice-Chancellor and it would be deplorable if Sir Sundar Lal's reputation were to be injured in the public eye by apparent failure to do anything and if the university is to commence under auspices other than his.'[156] Writing further on 'the present unsatisfactory state of affairs in the University', H. Sharp observed:

> There are two factions in the University. One is represented by Sir Sundar Lal and the other by the brothers Babus Bhagwan Das and Govinda Das and Sheo Prasad Gupta. This party is allied to Mrs. Besant....
> I understand that Sir Sundar Lal is backed by Dr. Tej Bahadur Sapru

and to some extent by Pandit Madan Mohan Malaviya who, however, inclines, I imagine first to the one side, then to the other, clings to his idea of an enormous University springing up in a day with thousands of students but at the same time is always apt to be antagonised by any scheme likely to play into the hands of Mrs. Besant.[157]

The official assessement of the emergence of the two factions in the newly established university conceded that Malaviya did not openly support one or the other group. In fact, his effort was to bridge the gulf between them and bring about an amicable settlement acceptable to all the well-wishers of the university.

It was unfortunate that Bhagwan Das and Shiva Prasad Gupta did not choose to raise their criticisms within the university bodies of which they had been members since the very beginning, but rather voiced their opinions in open letters to Sundar Lal. Between 19 August and 20 October 1917, three letters by Bhagwan Das were published in the *Leader* leading to considerable debate with regard to the contents and quality of education and the curricula.[158] Sundar Lal's attempts to offer satisfactory answers failed to satisfy Bhagwan Das.

While Malaviya favoured immediate construction of university buildings on the new site, Bhagwan Das was of the opinion that the old buildings of the Central Hindu College could be used for the time being. Bhagwan Das and Shiva Prasad Gupta's criticism developed into a real struggle for the leadership of the university. Since the issues raised by Bhagwan Das could not be resolved to his satisfaction, he decided to leave the university for good in December 1920.

NOTES

1.   Madan Mohan Malaviya, *The Banaras Hindu University—Why It is Wanted and What It Aims At*, edited by V.A. Sundaram (Banaras, 1945), pp. 25–64.

2.   S.L. Dar and S. Somskandan, *History of the Banaras Hindu University* (Varanasi, 1966), p. 48.

3.   Dar and Somskandan, *History of BHU*, p. 48.

4.   Dar and Somskandan, *History of BHU*, p. 86.

5.   Dar and Somskandan, *History of BHU*, pp. 49–74.

6.   Dar and Somskandan, *History of BHU*, p. 76.

7.   *Leader*, 24 June 1910.

8.   *Prem*, 24 December 1910, UP Native Newspapers Reports (henceforth UPNNR), 1910.

9. *Trishul*, 8 September 1910, UPNNR, 1910.
10. Dar and Somskandan, *History of BHU,* p. 61.
11. Dar and Somskandan, *History of BHU*, p. 357.
12. Malaviya's letter to Chief Secretary, UP Government, 26 September 1906, UPSA Judicial Public File, no. 2325.
13. Secretary, Government of UP to Secretary, Government of India, 28 March 1911, Education–A Proceedings, January 1911, 447.
14. Education–B Proceedings, February 1908, 23.
15. Education–B Proceedings, February 1908, 10–11.
16. Education–A Proceedings, January 1911, 76–7, note by Personal Secretary to Viceroy, 16 August 1910.
17. Director of Education's note, 5 October 1910, Education–A Proceedings, January 1911, 76–7.
18. Director of Education's note, 5 October 1910, Education–A Proceedings, January 1911, 76–7.
19. Dar and Somskandan, *History of BHU*, p. 44.
20. Malaviya to Gokhale, 20 February 1906, Gokhale Papers.
21. Note by H.V. Lovett, 15 April 1911, UPSA, Education–A Proceedings, May 1911, 14.
22. S.K. Bhatnagar, *History of the M.A.O. College, Aligarh* (Bombay, 1987), pp. 255–6.
23. Hardinge to Morley, 9 March 1911, Hardinge Papers, no. 24.
24. Harcourt Butler to Nawab of Rampur, 23 July 1912, Butler Collection, no. 3785.
25. Annie Besant to Hon. Secretary, Mahommedan Anglo-Oriental College, Aligarh, 4 January 1910, Education–A Proceedings, July 1911, 141–53.
26. Annie Besant to Personal Secretary to Viceroy, 13 April 1911, Education–A Proceedings, July 1911, 141–53, enclosure 12.
27. Annie Besant to Personal Secretary to Viceroy, 13 April 1911, Education–A Proceedings, July 1911, 141–53, enclosure 12.
28. Dar and Somskandan, *History of BHU*, p. 110.
29. Malaviya to Mrs A. Besant, 11 July 1911, Sundar Lal Papers, subject file no. 16.
30. Bhagwan Das, *The Central Hindu College and Mrs. Besant*, (Banaras, 1913), pp. 16–24.
31. Letter from O'Donnel, Secretary, Government of UP, to Secretary, Government of India, UPSA, Education–A Proceedings, 14.
32. Malaviya to Mrs A. Besant, 11 July 1911, Sundar Lal Papers, subject file no. 16.
33. Malaviya to Mrs A. Besant, 11 July 1911, Sundar Lal Papers, subject file no. 16.

34.   Malaviya's statement in *Leader*, 15 November 1911.

35.   Dar and Somskandan, *History of BHU*, p. 157.

36.   Bhai Parmanand, *Mahamana Madan Mohan Malaviya*, vol. I (Varanasi, 1985), p. 218.

37.   *New India*, 6 November 1906.

38.   Gupta, *Pandit Madan Mohan Malaviya*, p. 337.

39.   Harcourt Butler's note, 24 Agugust 1911, Education–A Proceedings, March 1912, 54–9.

40.   Malaviya to Gokhale, 20 February 1906, Gokhale Papers.

41.   UPSA, GAD, 271/1911.

42.   District Collector, Faizabad, to the Commissioner, Faizabad Division, 30 October 1911, UPSA, GAD, 271/1911.

43.   Commissioner, Faizabad Division, to District Collector, Faizabad, 8 November 1911, UPSA, GAD, 271/1911.

44.   District Collector, Faizabad, to Commissioner, Faizabad Division, 30 October 1911, UPSA, GAD, 271/1911.

45.   L. Stuart's note, 10 September 1911, UPSA, GAD, 271/1911.

46.   Collector of Ghazipur to Commissioner, Benaras Division, 2 September 1911, Education–A Proceedings, March 1912, 54–59.

47.   H.V. Lovett to H.C. Hose, 6 September 1911, Education–A Proceedings, March 1912, nos 54–9.

48.   H. Butler's note, 29 August 1911, Education–A-1 Proceedings, March 1912, 40–6.

49.   H. Butler's note, 29 August 1911, Education–A-1 Proceedings, March 1912, 40–6.

50.   Maharajah of Darbhanga to H. Butler, 28 August 1911, Education–A Proceedings, March 1912, 54–9.

51.   H. Butler to the Personal Assistant to the Viceroy, 31 August 1911, Education–A Proceedings, March 1912, 54–9.

52.   Maharaja of Darbhanga to H. Butler, 7 September 1911, Education–A Proceedings, March 1912, 54–9.

53.   Maharaja of Darbhanga to H. Butler, 7 September 1911, Education–A Proceedings, March 1912, 54–9.

54.   H. Butler's Note, 11 September 1911, Education–A Proceedings, March 1912, 54–9.

55.   Hardinge's Note, 11 October1911, Education–A Proceedings, March 1912, 54–9.

56.   Hardinge to Morley, 19 March 1911, 24, Hardinge Papers.

57.   Hardinge to Morley, 29 March 1911, Morley Papers.

58.   Hardinge to Morley, 29 March 1911, Morley Papers.

59.   Hardinge to Crew, 10 August 1911, Hardinge Papers, no. 53, roll 5.

60. Hardinge to Morley, 9 March 1911, Hardinge Papers, no. 24.

61. Hardinge to Morley, 29 March 1911, Hardinge Papers, no. 24.

62. Hardinge to Crew, 10 August 1911, Hardinge Papers, roll 9.

63. Viceroy's note, 29 July 1911, Education–A Proceedings, March 1912, 54–9.

64. Harcourt Butler's note, 4 August 1911, Education–A Proceedings, March 1912, 54–9.

65. S.A. Imam's note, 22 August 1911, Education–A Proceedings, March 1912, 40–6.

66. J.P. Hewett's note 15 August 1911, Education–A Proceedings, March 1912, 40–6.

67. J.L. Jenkins' note, Education–A Proceedings, March 1912, 40–6.

68. H. Butler to Maharaja of Darbhanga, 30 August 1911, Education–A Proceedings, March 1912, 40–6.

69. H. Butler's note, 24 August 1911, Education–A Proceedings, March 1912, 40–6.

70. H. Butler's note, 24 August 1911, Education–A Proceedings, March 1912, 40–6.

71. Hardinge's note, 10 October 1911, Education–A Proceedings, March 1912, 54.

72. Hardinge's note, 10 October 1911, Education–A Proceedings, March 1912, 54–9.

73. Hardinge's note, 10 October 1911, Education–A Proceedings, March 1912, 54–9.

74. H. Butler to Maharaja of Darbhanga, 12 October 1911, Education–A Proceedings, March 1912, 56–9.

75. H. Butler to Sundar Lal, 12 October 1911, Sundar Lal Papers, file no. 18.

76. Maharaja Ganga Singh to Butler, 9 May 1911, Education–A Proceedings, March 1912, 56–9.

77. Maharaja of Bikaner to Malaviya, 31 August 1911, Education–A Proceedings, March 1912, 56–9.

78. Vindeshwari Prasad to Malaviya, 9 August 1911, Education–A Proceedings, March 1912, 54–7.

79. Commissioner of Benaras Division's fortnightly letter, 21 August 1911, Education–A Proceedings, March 1912, 56–9.

80. Commissioner of Benaras Division's fortnightly letter, 21 August 1911, Education–A Proceedings, March 1912, 56–9.

81. Maharaja Rameshwar Prasad of Darbhanga to Butler, 4 September 1911, Education–A, March 1912, 56–9.

82. Parmanand, *Mahamana Madan Mohan. Malaviya*, p. 224.

83. Dar and Somskandan, *History of BHU*, p. 195.

84.   Parmanand, *Mahamana Madan Mohan. Malaviya*, p. 220.

85.   Parmanand, *Mahamana Madan Mohan. Malaviya*, p. 222.

86.   Harcourt Butler to Maharaja of Darbhanga, 14 March 1913, Education–A Proceedings, 40–6.

87.   Malaviya's statement in the *Leader*, 18 June 1911.

88.   Bhagwan Das, *The Central Hindu College and Mrs. Besant*, (Benaras, 1913), pp. 46–8.

89.   Maharaja of Darbhanga to Malaviya, 14 June 1912, Sundar Lal Papers, file no. 16.

90.   Minutes of the meeting of the Board of Trustees, Central Hindu College, 4 May 1913, Sundar Lal Papers, 13.

91.   Minutes of the meeting of the Board of Trustees, Central Hindu College, 4 May 1913, Sundar Lal Papers, 13.

92.   Minutes of the meeting of the Board of Trustees, Central Hindu College, 4 May 1913, Sundar Lal Papers, 13.

93.   *Leader*, 15 May 1913.

94.   Annie Besant to the Trustees of Central Hindu College, 14 May 1913, Sundar Lal Papers, file no. 16.

95.   Sundar Lal's handwritten note, 18 May 1913, Sundar Lal Papers, file no. 16.

96.   *Leader*, 15 May 1913.

97.   Das, *The Central Hindu College and Mrs. Besant*, p. 46.

98.   Sundar Lal to Mrs Besant, 17 July 1916, Sundar Lal Papers, file no. 13.

99.   Mrs Besant to Sundar Lal, 29 July 1916, Sundar Lal Papers, file no. 13.

100.   Sundar Lal to James Meston, 16 July 1916, Sundar Lal Papers, file no. 16.

101.   Parmanand, *Mahamana Madan Mohan Malaviya*, p. 96.

102.   Leah Renold, *A Hindu Education: Early Years of the Benaras Hindu University* (New Delhi: Oxford University Press, 2006), p. 74.

103.   Colonel Vindeshwari Prasad to Malaviya, 9 August 1911, Education–A Proceedings, 54–9.

104.   Fotnightly report of the Commissioner of Banaras Division, 21 August 1911, Education–A Proceedings, 54–9.

105.   Maharaja of Darbhanga to Sundar Lal, 17 June 1912, Sundar Lal Papers.

106.   Maharaja of Darbhanga to Sundar Lal, 25 June 1912, Sundar Lal Papers.

107.   Harcourt Butler to James Du Boulay, 27 July 1914, Education–A Proceedings, July 1915, 56–7.

108.   Harcourt Butler to James Du Boulay, 27 July 1914, Education–A Proceedings, July 1915, 56–7.

109.   J. Meston's note 29 August 1914, UPSA, Education file no. 39/1921.

110.   Maharaja of Darbhanga to Lieutenant Governor, UP, 15 December 1914, UPSA, Education Proceedings, file no. 39/1921.

111. Sundar Lal to S.P. O'Donnell, 30 June 1915, UPSA, Education Proceedings, file no. 39/1921.

112. S.P. O'Donell to Sundar Lal, 4 July 1915, UPSA, Education Proceedings, file no. 39/1921.

113. Harcourt Butler to James Meston, 18 October 1915, Education–A Proceedings, June 1916, nos 25–38.

114. Butler's Note, 10 October 1915, Education–A Proceedings, June 1916, nos 25–38.

115. Education–A Proceedings, June 1916, 25–38.

116. S.P. O'Donnell to H. Sharp, 13 November 1916, Education–A Proceedings, June 1916, 25–38.

117. J.N.G. Johnson to Sundar Lal, 17 November 1915, UPSA, Education Proceedings, file no. 39/1921.

118. G.B. Lambert to Sundar Lal, 18 August 1916, Education–A Proceedings, September 1916, 33.

119. Sundar Lal to Edward Maclegan, 20 August 1916, Education–A Proceedings, September 1916, 33.

120. Sundar Lal to James Meston, 3 July 1917, Sundar Lal Papers, 16.

121. G. Anderson's note, 25 August 1916, UPSA, Education Proceedings, file no. 39/1921.

122. Dar and Somskandan, *History of BHU*, p. 407.

123. S.P. O'Donnell to Sundar Lal, 13 April 1916, UPSA, Education Proceedings, file no. 39/1921.

124. Harcourt Butler to Maharaja of Darbhanga, 18 July 1914; Dar and Somskandan, *History of BHU*, pp. 248–51.

125. Dar and Somskandan, *History of BHU*, p. 152.

126. Meston to Butler, 2 May 1914, Meston Collection, no. 4253.

127. Hardinge to Crew, 30 July 1914, Hardinge Papers, no. 38.

128. Harcourt Butler to J. Du Boulay, 27 July 1914, Education–A Proceedings, July 1915, nos 56–7.

129. Meston to Craddock, 2 August 1914, Meston Collection, no. 4253.

130. Butler to Darbhanga, 26 August 1914, Meston Collection, no. 4253.

131. H. Butler to Meston, 7 October 1914, Education–A Proceedings, 156–7.

132. H. Sharp's note, 19 November 1914, Education–A Proceedings, 156–7.

133. Hardinge to Crew, 11 November 1916, Hardinge Papers, no. 58.

134. Dar and Somskandan, *History of BHU*, 264–7; Hardinge's note, 17 December 1916, Hardinge Papers, no. 58.

135. Hardinge to Crew, 6 January 1915, Hardinge Papers.

136. Malaviya to Sundar Lal, 13 January 1915, Sundar Lal Papers, 23.

137. Dar and Somskandan, *History of BHU*, pp. 281–4.

138. Dar and Somskandan, *History of BHU*, pp. 281–4.

139. For the full text of Malaviya's speech, see Dar and Somskandan, *History of BHU*, pp. 285–92.

140. Malaviya to Sundar Lal, 12 December 1915, Sundar Lal Papers.

141. Malaviya to Sundar Lal, 12 December 1915, Sundar Lal Papers.

142. Hardinge to Butler, 10 February 1916, Butler Collection, no. 3787.

143. Hardinge to Butler, 10 February 1916, Butler Collection, no. 3787.

144. James Meston to Chemsford, 11 August 1916, Chelmsford Papers, no. 189.

145. D.G. Tendulkar, *Mahatma*, vol. I (New Delhi, 1964), pp. 182–3.

146. Maharaja of Alwar to Malaviya, 8 February 1916, Sundar Lal Papers, 24.

147. Home Poll, 1 July 1916, no. 23.

148. James Meston to Sundar Lal, 10 February 1916, Sundar Lal Papers, 24.

149. Butler to Sundar Lal, 10 October 1915, Education–A Proceedings, March 1915.

150. Sundar Lal to Butler, 7 October 1915, Education–A Proceedings, March 1915, 31–3.

151. Sundar Lal to Harcourt Butler, 12 October 1915, Education–A Proceedings, March 1915, 31–3.

152. Malaviya to Sundar Lal, 3 March 1916, Sundar Lal Papers, 46.

153. Malaviya to Sundar Lal, 3 March 1916, Sundar Lal Papers, 46.

154. James Meston to Viceroy, 6 September 1917, Meston Papers.

155. James Meston to Viceroy, 6 September 1917, Meston Papers.

156. H. Sharp's note, 23 August 1917, Education–A Proceedings, nos 31–3.

157. H. Sharp's note, 23 August 1917, Education–A Proceedings, nos 31–3.

158. *Leader*, 19–20 October, 1917.

4 The Formative Phase

As Mrs Annie Besant successfully introduced the agitational style in Indian politics and established Home Rule Leagues in several parts of India from the middle of 1916 onwards to foster the demand for self-government, Malaviya played a waiting game and stayed aloof from the Home Rule movement in its early stages since he did not believe that there was a need for any organization other than the Congress, to launch a movement demanding major constitutional changes in Indian administration.

The popularity of the Home Rule Leagues showed strength in those areas where the Theosophical Societies were strong. The members of the leagues were largely drawn from these societies, and its several branches organized discussion groups, public meetings, and lectures in which students and women participated in large numbers. The press began to play an important role in popularizing the movement. Mrs Besant successfully launched a newspaper, *New India*, and the Home Rule Leagues organized popular demonstrations which demonstrated the growing influence of Mrs Besant, particularly in the southern and western parts of the country and in UP.

Such major developments in Mrs Besant's techniques of agitation forced the Government of India to consider how her methods should be dealt with. The government saw the movement as an effort to mount an all-India opposition which was united, organized, and strong. Instead of dictating any firm policy of his own, the viceroy allowed the provincial governors to deal with Mrs Besant's movement as they saw fit.[1] The provincial governors were given full freedom to suppress the movement, if they so desired, by resorting, within limits, to repression.[2] Thus the provincial governors became the focus of attention in deciding on the policy towards Mrs Besant and her Home Rule movement.

Since Mrs Besant's Home Rule League was the most effective in Madras, the provincial government's reactions to it assumed significance here. Its faith in the policy of repression was at first spelt out in late 1915 when it secretly but unsuccessfully proposed to the central government that she be deported.[3] Later, the Madras government confiscated the deposit of Mrs Besant's paper, *New India*, in 1916, thus indicating its resolve to deal with the Home Rule movement in the province with a heavy hand.

MALAVIYA'S OPEN SUPPORT TO MRS BESANT

It was at this point of time that Malaviya came to Mrs Besant's rescue and led an influential delegation to the viceroy on 5 March 1917 to appeal against the governor's efforts to stifle the movement.[4] In a letter to the editor of the *Leader* Malaviya expressed his determination to support Mrs Besant's Home Rule movement:

> I have had sharp differences with Mrs. Besant in the past. But I cannot but admire her and feel grateful to her for the splendid manner in which she has been sacrificing herself at her age in the cause of India's progress and reform. I hope she will be allowed to go on with her work.... If she is exposed to suffering in that cause, thousand of Indians who have not been able to see eye to eye with her on all things will think it their duty to follow her.[5]

The UP governor, James Meston, was quick to take note of Malaviya's letter. Drawing the viceroy's attention to it, he wrote:

> It indicates in moderate but unmistakable terms what is intended. It looks as if he [Malaviya] had some foreknowledge of Madras Government's action. Be that as it may, however, this leaves no doubt ... that a big outcry is being intended.[6]

The timing and the tone of Malaviya's announcement of open support to Mrs Besant's Home Rule campaign left no one in doubt about his intentions. Malaviya had seen the writing on the wall. He could easily observe that the governor of Madras was out to take stern action against Mrs Besant and thought that it was the right time to forewarn him.[7]

OPPOSITION TO MRS BESANT'S INTERNMENT

The governor of Madras, Lord Pentland, finally decided to silence Mrs Besant by issuing orders under the Defence of India rules, on 16 June 1917 for her internment along with two of her lieutenants. The news came as a bombshell to the nationalist leaders. Gandhi called it a 'big blunder'[8] and a young Jawaharlal Nehru opined that 'it is time we thought and acted like men'.[9]

During the week following Mrs Besant's internment, several Congress leaders of Allahabad including Motilal Nehru, T.B. Sapru, N.P. Asthana, and C.Y. Chintamani joined the local Home Rule League to voice their solidarity with Mrs Besant. Malaviya, however, did not fall in line. He explained: 'I am still quite unwilling to join the Home Rule League. But the presence of events is increasing.... I shall not join it in hurry.'[10]

Ten days after the issuance of the order of internment against Mrs Besant, Malaviya had a long interview at Simla with the viceroy, the home member, and the home secretary in order to ascertain the government's plan of action. He gave the following assessment of the views of the viceroy and his top advisers to V.S.S. Sastri:

> They do not show any inclination to interfere with the orders of internment. They supported them by much argument. I fear nothing will be done in this matter without the words in England. We should send a deputation at once to England if the submarines permit of our doing so.[11]

Now that Malaviya's hope of seeking the intervention of the viceroy against the governor of Madras were dashed, the only remedy he could think of was to send a deputation to England. This was not possible during the war. Malaviya's espousal of his stand on the Home Rule movement shows that he was still not prepared to move away from the moderate position. Elaborating his position to Sastri, he wrote:

> I am entirely with you as to the extreme undesirability of complicating the position by preaching a 'boycott' as part of our agitation. We shall put our foot down upon it.... It will be disastrous to our cause to take up such a wrong step. We shall not succeed now any more than we did last time. But we shall lose all our advantage which we have won by our contribution in men and money and goodwill to the cause of the Empire.... I have been hardpressed by several friends to agree to resign

our seats in Council—Provincial and Imperial. I am strongly against any such action.... We should do nothing in anger or in a spirit of antagonism except so far as our duty may compel us to do so.[12]

Even after asserting that there was no need to 'do anything in anger' Malaviya realized the need for immediate action in consultation with leaders of all shades of opinion spread out in various parts of the country. He wrote to V.S.S. Sastri:

> I am going to see every other Member of Council and after doing that to leave for Allahabad.... I intend to run up to Bombay to discuss the whole situation with you and other friends. We shall then lay out our plan of campaign and start work at the earliest date possible. I have made myself free now for this work ... from Bombay, I will subject to what we decide, go to Madras and then to Calcutta. We must move now, a few at least of us.[13]

Malaviya held consultations at various levels in several cities and with various nationalist leaders for organizing a protest against Mrs Besant's internment.[14] He was fully aware that the news of her internment had come as a shock to several nationalist leaders. Hearing the news, Gandhi wrote to the private secretary to the viceroy:

> In my humble opinion, the internments are a big blunder. Madras was absolutely calm before them. Now it is badly disturbed. India as a whole had not made common cause with Mrs. Besant, but now she is in fair way towards commanding India's identity with her methods. The Congress was trying to 'capture' Mrs. Besant; the latter was trying to capture the former. They have almost become one.[15]

Gandhi visited Allahabad to discuss the issue with Malaviya and stayed on in the city till the latter had come back to from Simla. The influential editor of the *Bombay Chronicle*, B.G. Horniman, informed Jawaharlal Nehru that in a telegram to M.A. Jinnah, Malaviya had suggested a joint session of the AICC and the Council of the Muslim League at Bombay on 8 July, and that he liked the idea and he himself 'would have gone to Allahabad for an earnest talk with Malaviya if it were not for the prospect of the latter being available in Bombay within a few days'.[16]

Speaking on Mrs Besant's internment in a public meeting at Bombay on 10 July 1917, Malaviya emphasized that the time for resolute action had come and the message of *swaraj* (self-rule) must be carried to every village, house, and cottage. From Bombay, he moved to several other cities in an effort to get in touch with regional and local politicians and impressed upon them the need to educate the people through lectures, writings, and tours, and also conveying to them the gross injustice meted out to Mrs Besant by the Madras government. Malaviya took the earliest opportunity to table a resolution in the Imperial Legislative Council urging her early release.[17]

Besant's internment certainly injected a spirit of radicalism, accelerated the popularity of the Home Rule movement, and led to the intensification of the movement in several new areas and provinces.[18] The campaign became popular in urban centres, more and more people were attracted to it, and an array of distinguished persons joined it.

The viceroy and the provincial governors were keeping a close watch over these developments. They were quick to initiate damage-control measures at different levels. James Meston, the lieutenant governor of UP, informed the viceroy on 20 June 1917 that he was 'going to try and appeal to the leaders in this province ... and will see group of them and speak to them with utmost frankness'. The lieutenant governor directed the commissioners of Allahabad and Lucknow to get in touch with the Congress leaders and various other politicians in order to convince them that 'the orders of the Madras Government were directed against the personal conduct of Mrs. Besant and not against the movement for self-government.'[19] The lieutenant governor reviewed the political situation in UP in the following words: 'The result has been that the agitators have, as a rule, been careful of their speech on and off their ground. The result has also been, I think, that there will be in this province a large number of intelligent men ready to discuss the problems of self-government in a reasonable way without bitterness.'[20] In view of these considerations, the lieutenant governor impressed upon the viceroy the urgent need for an early announcement of constitutional reforms.

Despite Wedderburn's advice to Malaviya to exercise patience in view of the assurance that an announcement on constitutional reforms was imminent, the latter did not slacken his efforts to put pressure on the government for Mrs Besant's release.[21] Malaviya's lecture at the mammoth public meeting at Allahabad under the auspices of the Home Rule League on 8 August 1917 attracted the attention of the provincial government. The UP chief secretary stated:

The Hon'ble Pandit M.M. Malaviya who is the mainspring of the movement here delivered a long speech ... while skillfully worded to keep within law was on the same lines as Mrs. Besant's speeches.... He argued that the mistake of Indians had been not to agitate sufficiently. Referring to the assistance given by Indians in the war he said if it had not been for them Paris would have been taken by the enemy and yet it was not proposed to give them any reward.[22]

While speaking on the occasion of the Special Provincial Congress session two days later at Lucknow, Malaviya referred to the Congress–League demand for self-government and condemned the policy of repression followed by the Madras government:

What I do say is that if she infringed the law in speaking or writing and if the infringement was serious enough to deserve action being taken upon, she should have been proceeded against according to the ordinary law of the land. I consider that in proceeding, as the Madras Government did against her they had abused the power possessed under the Defence of India Act.... The Act was clearly meant to be used against the enemies of the Government. I do not believe that Mrs. Besant is the enemy of the Government.[23]

The lieutenant governor of UP explained that he treated the Home Rule movement 'leniently' rather than 'strictly' because 'the time has passed when any Government in this country can stem a tumult by holding up its little finger' and argued that the temper of the people was evident. The movement would not be stopped by 'prohibiting a meeting here and suspending a newspaper there'. Nothing short of a 'general campaign of repression' would be of any avail.[24]

AUGUST DECLARATION WELCOMED

A collision between the nationalist leaders and the government was averted by an announcement in the British parliament by Edwin Montagu in August 1917 that an advance was to be made towards responsible government in India and that he was to visit the country at the end of the year. In a further attempt to lower the political temperature in India, Montagu persuaded the viceroy to release Mrs Besant a month later. Mrs Besant's release represented a decision to treat the Home Rule movement as a political and constitutional agitation rather than a revolutionary one.[25] It marked the beginning of a new tactical approach and the appeasement of politicians became a central tenet of the government's policy. Malaviya reacted favourably to the August declaration. Fresh political developments soon provided him new opportunities.

The August 1917 declaration specifying the initiation of a long-drawn process of democratization was bold enough to promise 'self-governing institutions' and a 'responsible government' for India, and cautious enough to qualify them with phrases like 'gradual development', 'progressive realization', and an 'integral part of the British empire'.[26] The announcement was a curious combination of liberal sincerity and imperial self-interest. It pledged the coveted goal of responsible government in India, but left its implementation to the discretion of the British government. The secretary of state decided to visit India to have on-the-spot consultations with the officials as well as the nationalist leaders. His arrival raised high hopes in India and led the Indian politicians to believe that 'something big ... something epoch-making was being envisaged.'[27]

Montagu desired that a constitutional party be built up in India in order to ensure favourable reception to the proposed constitutional reform scheme, especially so because the Home Rulers who had gained ascendancy in Indian politics were likely to take little interest in it.[28] The official view was that the very character of the Congress Party was a hindrance. Hence a split in the Congress was likely to help in the bureaucracy. Montagu's hope was that the secessionists would welcome the reform scheme. With this end in view, he requested the viceroy to foster a pro-government party to secure acceptance of the scheme.[29] The lesser Moderates like V.S.S. Sastri, T.B. Sapru, and C.Y. Chintamani took the hint, and in collaboration with several other Moderates of different provinces, began to discuss the steps which could be undertaken in that direction. They realized the need for securing the support of established national leaders such as S.N. Banerjea and M.M. Malaviya.[30] Their readiness was in complete contrast with the attitude of Malaviya who was cautious and sceptical of the official proposals from the very beginning and was not prepared to give in easily.

MONTAGU–MALAVIYA TALKS

Though Malaviya was much impressed by Montagu's sincerity and appreciated his resolve to visit India for discussions on constitutional reforms, he was cautious and full of misgivings about the outcome of the talks with him from the very beginning. Hence he demanded the following as the first instalment of reforms:

1. Abolition of communal electorates and of reservation of seats on communal lines
2. Grant of the power of the purse and control of the executive to the legislatures
3. Appointment of three Indian members in the Viceroy's Executive Council
4. Indianization of the civil and military services to the extent of 40 per cent[31]

There were at least three long meetings between Malaviya and Montagu between 27 November 1917 and 13 March 1918. Montagu's comments, recorded separately in his diary that was published later, provide the most authentic account of some of the major topics that came up before them. Some excerpts are given below:

> Malaviya assures me that if we did not give everything that they asked for ... there would be continued agitation. The power of the purse and the control of the Executive are essential at once. (27 November 1917)

> I had a long talk with Malaviya. He was very nice, very conciliatory, fully understanding that if India opposed our scheme we should never get it through. I assured him that we would be ready to consider any amendments but they must not be coupled with abuse of the civil service. (27 February 1918)

> Malaviya showed himself discontented with the scheme. He did not like the proportion, in the Council of State, of officials and reminded me of a more liberal recommendation of Minto's that it should be half and half. He also wanted three Indians in the Executive Council.[32] (13 March 1918)

Montagu's version of his meetings with Malaviya confirms the commonly held view that his constant pleadings had little effect on the visiting secretary of state who entirely depended on the advice given by the viceroy and his colleagues.[33] Under the circumstances the scheme of constitutional reforms, as it finally emerged, came as a rude shock to Malaviya.[34]

REACTION TO MONTFORD PROPOSALS

The joint Montagu–Chemsford report (also called the Montford Report) on constitutional reforms published in July 1918, which was the result of Montagu's consultations in India, was a disappointing document and had none of the grandeur which Montagu intended it to possess. It emphasized the backwardness of the vast majority of the Indian people, the social and communal barriers which divided them, and the essentially undemocratic character of the caste system and concluded that no important change could be made in the structure and functioning of the central government. The report, therefore, stressed the need for keeping the executive at the centre as independent of the control of the legislature as before.[35] Though the Montford Report contained the strongest condemnation of the communal electorates, it recommended not only their retention in the case of the Muslim community but also their extension to the Sikhs. The Report proposed to make an experiment of responsible government in the provinces but even there it refused to transfer complete responsibility to popular representatives. It proposed the introduction of dyarchy in the province.[36]

With the publication of the Montford Report, markedly different opinions were voiced by the Congress leaders belonging to the two schools of thought—the Extremists and the Moderates. On the day the report was published, Annie Besant remarked: 'The scheme is unworthy to be offered by England or to be accepted by India. It is petty where it should have been large and banal where it should have been striking.' Tilak was 'greatly disappointed' and declared that it was 'entirely unacceptable'[37]. The *Hindu* wrote that it was 'based upon unfounded and deeprooted distrust of the capacities and character of the country.'[38] In sharp contrast to these views, the Moderates lost no time in voicing their full support to the reform scheme. C.Y. Chintamani, T.B. Sapru and H.N. Kunzru, the three Allahabad-based Moderates, got in touch with Malaviya in order to win his favour. They did everything possible to bring Malaviya over to their side. H.N. Kunzru informed the leading Moderates of Madras: 'I have also suggested to Malaviya that it is not enough that he should recognize the merits of the scheme in a general way. The recognition must be wholehearted and he should dissociate himself in explicit terms from those who are seeking to wreck the scheme.'[39] As later developments confirmed, Malaviya, from the very outset, was not prepared to play the Moderates' game. He informed them about his stand in the following words:

> So far as the proposals go they constitute a large and liberal measure of reform which we should be grateful for but they do not go far enough to meet the requirements of the country. Have to suggest modification and expansion giving reasons therefore.[40]

Malaviya turned down the Moderates' suggestion that the reform scheme be accepted in its original form without insisting on certain alteration. Within a month of the publication of the official scheme, he offered his own detailed criticisms of the Montford Report running into fifty-three typed pages. Malaviya's note was published in the *Leader* between 4 and 7 August 1918, and was also issued in the form of a pamphlet.[41] At the very outset he pointed out that there were 'grave deficiencies' in the scheme 'which must be made up before the reforms could become adequate to the requirements of the country.' Malaviya regarded the chapter entitled 'The Conditions of the Problem' in the official scheme as 'bitter and derogatory to our self-respect' and explained, at length, that the arguments advanced against the 'rate of progress towards responsible government' in the scheme were uncalled for.[42] Some of the major recommendations made by Malaviya were as under:

1. To be laid down in the Statute that full self-government shall be conferred on India within 20 years.
2. Half of the higher appointments in the civil and military shall be given to Indians.
3. If the Council of State is created half of it should be elected by electorates in which Indians predominate.
4. Provincial councils to contain a member from each tehsil.
5. Ministers should be members of the Executive Council in provinces.
6. No reserved subjects and no grand committees.
7. Further increases of expenditure and necessary legislation should be controlled by the provincial council.[43]

Differences between Malaviya and the Moderates came to the surface after the publication of his note. The Moderates were nervous and feared that they 'shall be stigmatized as traitors.'[44]

SPECIAL CONGRESS SESSION AT BOMBAY

Soon after, the Moderates began to move in different directions. While some of them began to organize separate meetings, there were others who decided to carve for themselves an independent course of action, and even discussed the idea of deserting the Congress. D.E. Wacha and S.N. Banerjea organized separate meetings of the Moderates at Bombay and Calcutta in the middle of August 1918 and issued their statements in various newspapers.

The Congress had previously decided to hold a special session at Bombay in the last week of August 1918 to discuss the reform proposals. The Moderates were unwilling to wait for the Bombay Special Congress deliberations due to their fear that the Extremists would not allow them to put forward their views. Hence they began to entertain the idea of following an independent course of action.[45]

Since there were clear signs of the non-participation of most of the top Moderate leaders in the forthcoming Special Congress session, Malaviya decided to get in touch with some of them in order to avert such an unfortunate situation. He wrote a long letter to S.N. Banerjea expressing his regret that the publication of the proposal of constitutional reforms 'created serious differences of opinion among our public men' and emphasized that 'our duty to our country demands that we should meet together and try our utmost to come to conclusions which will express the sense of the bulk of the community.' Malaviya impressed upon Banerjea the need to attend the Special Congress session with the following words:

> In view of the opinion which Mr. Tilak and Mrs. Besant have published it seems to me that they will not move the rejection of the proposal and I believe that if we are there we shall be able to persuade them to fall in line with our views. In any event, I think, we owe it to the motherland that we should attend the Special Congress and thus plan [*sic*] all the knowledge and experience that we possess at the service of our countrymen who will assemble at the Congress.[46]

Stressing the need for the widest possible participation of the Congress leaders of all shades of opinion in the Special Congress session, Malaviya further observed:

> The weight that attaches to our views as public men is largely based upon the fact that we represent the sense of the bulk of the educated

community. If by keeping away from the Special Congress, and holding a separate conference and otherwise we ourselves demonstrate that public opinion does not stand behind us, our views will not carry the same weight which they have carried in the past. So long as we remain in public life it is our duty to do all we can to mould and guide public opinion according to our best light.[47]

Expressing deep commitment to democratic values, Malaviya's effort was to persuade S.N. Banerjea to participate in the Special Congress session. He sought not only to allay his own fears but also that of other leading Moderates who were apprehensive that the session was likely to be dominated by the Extremists. Motivated by the desire to bring the leading figures of the two wings of the Congress together, Malaviya issued an appeal on the eve of the session.[48] Since the Moderates did not pay much attention to Malaviya's overtures and seemed determined to keep aloof, he requested the Congress to postpone the opening of the session by a day. Malaviya made last-minute efforts to work upon an understanding with Wacha and some other Moderate leaders present in Bombay. He was let down by most of the Moderate leaders who boycotted the Special Congress session. But Malaviya was still not prepared to lose hope. He succeeded in getting the Special Congress to agree to the substance of the Moderates' demands on the Montford scheme. In the Subjects Committee meeting, he took an active part in the discussions aimed at bringing about ultimate unity. It was largely due to his efforts that the Extremists, including Tilak and Mrs Besant, agreed to accept the proposed reform scheme. They demanded responsible government in fifteen years and full provincial autonomy in six years. Thus Malaviya succeeded in moderating the views of the Extremists at the Special Congress session.[49] It was unfortunate that Malaviya's generous attitude did not evoke a favourable response in the Moderate camp and their leaders went ahead with their plans of organizing an all-India Moderate Conference at Bombay under the presidentship of S.N. Banerjee in September 1918. With the formation of the National Liberal League, and as a result of the horizontal split in the Congress, the chances of unity between the two wings of the party dimmed. Undaunted by his repeated failures, Malaviya continued the work of bringing the secessionists back to the Congress in its session of 1918.

PRESIDENTSHIP OF THE 1918 CONGRESS SESSION

In recognition of the unifying role he played in the Special Congress held at Bombay, Malaviya was invited to preside over the Delhi Congress session of 1918. His continued efforts to work as a bridge between various groups within the Congress led everyone to hope that he would provide the right leadership at this juncture. The following letter written by Malaviya appreciating the support extended to him amply bears this out:

> Long before Mrs. Besant and other friends in Madras and Bombay had very kindly proposed me for election. Sir Rashbihary Ghosh, Mr. Jinnah, Mr. Patel and other friends had pressed me to accept the Presidentship. Both Mr. Patel and Andrews wrote to me that Mr. Gandhi also was of the same opinion. The fact that Mrs. Besant along with other friends proposed my election created a little feeling in some quarters on this side also.[50]

In spite of the support extended to him from all quarters, Malaviya admitted that he was 'not all cheered by the thought that I shall have the great honour to preside over the Congress at Delhi',[51] largely because of the dissension and disunity in the Congress. In a public statement, he called for the cooperation of all those Moderate leaders who had stayed away from the Special Congress session. He reminded them that the Montford scheme had yet to obtain the sanction of the British Parliament and it was still open for modification. He further said that there was little chance of success in this direction unless the Congress pressed for changes in the Montford scheme with one voice. Malaviya wrote:

> I hope that our old friends and comrades among the moderates will revise their opinion and stand shoulder to shoulder with us to press for what is needed for the country ... we should do all we can to unite our forces.[52]

On the eve of the Delhi Congress Session, the president-elect was expecting much more from the British than they were inclined to offer as a 'prize' to India after the First World War:

> The end of the war means the birth of a new era for the civilized world. The liberalism of Great Britain has been rejuvenated by the baptism of fire through which it has passed during the last four years and the close association of Great Britain with France and America will strengthen

the forces of liberalism in England ... ought to arouse the most slothful and timid amongst us to realize the rare opportunity which lies before us for pressing for an adequate measure of responsible Government in our country.[53]

The Congress met on 26 December 1918 in Delhi under Malaviya's presidentship. It was attended by a record number of delegates. But apart from the actual number, its special feature was the presence of an unusually large number of *kisan* (agricultural worker or peasant) delegates who showed keen enthusiasm for the proceedings of the meeting. Malaviya had taken care to mobilize as large a number of peasants as possible for the purpose. His telegram to Mrs Annie Besant stated that it was 'extremely desirable that every taluka of Madras should send one peasant delegate to the Congress' shows his anxiety to open the doors of the Congress to the rural population of the country.[54]

Malaviya's presidential address was deliberately mild, soft, and full of reasonableness and persuasion. He referred at length to the Congress demand for 'self-determination' since its inception, explained its implications, and assured the colonial rulers that 'we still desire to remain subjects of British Crown'. Convinced that 'self-government' was the only remedy, Malaviya observed:

> If we Indians had an effective share in the administration of our affairs we should have managed things very differently. How we should have managed them is not a matter of conjecture but is clearly shown by the resolutions that we have passed during the last 32 years in regard to many questions of public interest....We ask for this opportunity of national self development.[55]

Like many of his contemporaries, Malaviya was still looking forward to a favourable response from Britain with regard to the constitutional proposals put forward by the Congress and suggested that 'there was a great need of sending a strong deputation to England so that our cause may not suffer for want of good and proper advocacy'.[56] In a separate letter, he emphasized the need for such a step again:

> The deputation should start about the middle of April. Unless our best and strongest men go to plead the Congress cause before the Parliament and the British public I fear that cause will suffer grievously.[57]

The Congress went ahead with its arrangement of sending a deputation of fifteen members to England, and Malaviya was keen to pick eminent representatives for the purpose. He pleaded that 'we should in the first instance select the best representative we can—men who command the respect and confidence of the country and who are best qualified to plead our cause in England with effect'.[58] The idea was later shelved because of the change in the political situation following the Rowlatt Satyagraha campaign.

CAMPAIGN AGAINST THE ROWLATT ACT

When the end of the First World War was in sight, the British carefully outlined a dual strategy to meet the challenge of nationalism in India. While the liberal face of imperialism was reflected in the constitutional proposals, the Government of India was, at the same time, preparing the ground for the enactment of a legislation which would greatly enhance its arbitrary powers.

The British insistence on rushing through the Rowlatt Act in the early months of 1919 and the strong wave of protest it generated indicated the widening gap between the expectations of Indian politicians and the efforts of a Government of India determined to rule with extraordinary powers.

The real intentions of the government were made known with the introduction of the two Rowlatt bills in the Imperial Legislative Council on 6 February 1919. The first bill sought to amend the Indian Penal Code to enable the executive wing of the government to restrict any activity deemed prejudicial to the security of the state. The second bill aimed at giving the Government of India discretionary powers to short-circuit the process of law in dealing with political crime.

The bills were singularly ill-timed, came as a bombshell, and were condemned by almost all sections of Indians. Public opposition to the bills had started even before they were introduced in the council. As the Congress president, Malaviya issued instructions that 'protest meetings against the said bills should be held as soon as possible throughout the country and resolutions wired to the Government of India'. He asked Congressmen to hold protest meetings in every district and impressed upon them that 'the matter is one of vital importance and affects the liberties of the people at large'.[59]

In accordance with Malaviya's instructions, public meetings were organized in different parts of the country to protest against the introduction of the proposed legislation in the Imperial Legislative Council. Malaviya presided over one such meeting held in Bombay on 3 February 1919 under the auspices of the Home Rule League.[60] In his hometown, Allahabad, people gathered in large numbers to lodge their protest against the efforts of the government to enact thislegislation.

Malaviya was appointed a member of the select committee to which the Rowlatt bills were referred by the Government of India. Along with two other non-official Indian members of the committee, he opposed the introduction of the bills in the central legislature on the grounds that such an effort was wrong in procedure and their provisions were drastic in nature.[61] The government, however, did not pay any heed to his objections and went ahead with its plans of moving the Rowlatt bills in the Legislative Council on 6 February 1919. During the heated debate that followed, Malaviya made an impassioned speech that lasted more than two hours. He criticized its provisions exhaustively, disavowed any sympathy with the anarchists, pointed out that any revolutionary crime was really the outcome of political and administrative stagnation, and maintained that the remedy lay not in the repression of political activities but in the removal of the standing grievances of the people.[62] Together with Malaviya, every other Indian member opposed the introduction of these bills. In the history of the council, this was the first occasion when all the non-official members voted one way. As a result of the united opposition of Malaviya and his associates, one of the proposed Rowlatt bills being introduced in the Imperial Legislative Council was waithdrawn and the other was amended.

Malaviya, however, was not convinced with these paltry concessions and repeated the demand that the other bill be also withdrawn. He was fully supported by all the other non-official elected members of the council. In spite of their opposition, the Government of India went ahead with its original plan of rushing through the Rowlatt bill as early as possible. It did not pay any attention to the objections raised by Malaviya and various other non-official members. The Government of India had to force the bill to pass in the council with its official majority on 21 March 1919.[63] As a finale to this, Malaviya tendered his resignation from the council as a mark of protest against the scant regard shown by the government to the united voice of the non-official members of the council. M.A. Jinnah, B.N. Sharma, and Nazharal Haque also resigned with him.[64]

Once the bill became law, verbal protests were rendered useless and the politicians' unity disintegrated. They were at a loss to decide upon the next step at a time when the government looked adamant. Their vision of limited politics had received a severe jolt and their hope of coming to a mutually acceptable agreement with the British on constitutional advance seemed a distant dream. Malaviya's proposal of sending a deputation to England to press for constitutional reforms was, therefore, abandoned.

In this uncertain political situation, Gandhi stepped forward to offer a novel form of campaigning against the Rowlatt Act. The remedy he proposed was *satyagraha*. The term 'satyagraha' means 'holding on to truth', 'adherence to truth', and 'insistence of truth'; Gandhi believed that observance of pure truth alone made man a *satyagrahi*. To provide organizational coherence to such a movement, Gandhi organized Satyagraha Sabhas in several cities, explained his doctrine and methods, and undertook journeys to rope in both established politicians and emerging leaders for the purpose. In its earlier phase of deliberation and preparation from February to the beginning of April, the heart of the movement was the cities of Bombay and Ahmedabad. Gandhi depended on his own resources and networks and made no attempt to involve the Congress in his Rowlatt Satyagraha movement.[65]

To provide organizational coherence to the Satyagraha movement, Gandhi encouraged the establishment of Satyagraha Sabhas in several cities. The creation of such a *sabha* (assembly) at Allahabad confronted the local Congress leaders, including Malaviya, with a dilemma. Malaviya had close links with Gandhi and the latter had supported his candidature for the presidentship of the 1918 Congress session. Despite all this, Malaviya kept away from the Allahabad Satyagraha Sabha as he was sceptical about the strategy proposed by Gandhi at this time.[66]

The second phase of the Satyagraha campaign began with Gandhi's decision to launch a *hartal* (strike) against the Rowlatt Act in various parts of the country. Owing to a mix up in communication, it was observed early on 30 March in Delhi. It led to police firing on the shopkeepers who had closed their shops and had collected together to voice their solidarity with the campaign. The incident at Delhi brought home to Gandhi the need for gaining Malaviya's support. He contacted Malaviya through a telegram saying, 'In view of what appears to be a slaughter of innocents at Delhi you cannot remain silent on it whether you join the movement or not.'[67]

Gandhi's message and the frightful happenings at Delhi led Malaviya to take a fresh look at the Rowlatt Satyagraha campaign. He was particularly shocked at the attempts made by the British officials to use force against unarmed people in Delhi. A fortnight later, the news of the Jallianwala Bagh massacre sent shockwaves of horror throughout the country. It was yet another piece of evidence that behind the liberal façade of the Raj lay a capacity for blind repression and brutal action which could surface at the slightest assertion of the will of the people.

Meanwhile, Malaviya had called for a common front on the 'Delhi outrage' and was present at a public meeting of about fifteen thousand men held at Allahabad on 10 April 1919. In this meeting, Malaviya 'described the meaning of Satyagraha and said that there was the least justification for the firing on the innocent population of Delhi and that the introduction of the Rowlatt bills was the beginning of the end of the present system of the Government of India, and ended by exhorting the audience to perpetuate Hindu–Muslim unity.'[68]

In response to the April violence in Punjab, Gandhi immediately called off his Satyagraha campaign. Surprisingly enough his reaction to the Punjab government's repressive actions was mild and restrained. Gandhi often looked indecisive and hesitant. When V.S.S. Sastri condemned some of the actions under martial law as 'barbarous',[69] Gandhi refused to offer any comments. His silence caused misunderstanding and, in the following few weeks, the Satyagraha movement lost its momentum.

MALAVIYA'S VISIT TO AMRITSAR

In contrast to Gandhi's response, Malaviya lost no time in lashing out at the Punjab authorities in various public meetings and was one of the first to rush to Punjab in the last week of June along with Motilal Nehru and Swami Shradhanand. He took upon himself the responsibility of providing relief to the people in distress, worked untiringly to boost their morale, and worked hard to ascertain facts with regard to the happenings in the province.[70] Since hundreds of persons had been rounded up all over the province and tried by summary courts set up under martial law, there was great need of outside help. The people, deprived of their leaders, were so terror-stricken that when Malaviya arrived at Amritsar, there was nobody to receive him and he had difficulty finding accommodation for his stay in the city.[71]

Malaviya and his companions stayed on in Punjab for several months, with intervals, braving all inconveniences and risks. Their presence helped the people regain their confidence. The official account reviewed Malaviya's role in the following words:

> Everyone admires Pandit's conduct in taking up the cause of the Punjabi victims of martial law.... Everyone who knows something which can be used to further the interest of the accused persons or can be utilized to expose the police or the authorities has voluntarily managed to communicate to the Pandit and his party. The relatives and friends, especially those from village, are hastening from all sides to see the party.[72]

Malaviya spared no efforts in providing relief to the sufferers and collected funds for the purpose at various places. Due to Malaviya's efforts, the entire Congress machinery was soon put in motion providing relief to panic-ridden people in different areas of Punjab. In his capacity as president of the Congress, he carried on a continuous battle against the excesses committed by the Punjab officers with great vigour. He brought the issue before the AICC meeting held on 21 April 1919. The Committee demanded a public inquiry into the happenings in Delhi, Punjab, Bombay, and Calcutta and brought the 'intense universal bitterness of opposition to the Rowlatt Act' to the notice of the secretary of state.[73] The AICC met again on 8 June and appointed its own subcommittee to arrange for an inquiry into the occurrences in Punjab, to initiate legal proceedings, and to collect funds for the purpose. In pursuance of this resolution, a nine-member committee was appointed under Malaviya's chairmanship. Malaviya and Motilal Nehru took charge of its proceedings in June 1919. Gandhi was co-opted in the committee at a later stage in mid-October. The Punjab government did not take kindly to the preliminary investigations undertaken by the subcommittee. It started finding fault with the Congress subcommittee's work, as is obvious from the following report by the deputy commissioner of Amritsar:

> I wish to remark that Pandit Madan Mohan Malaviya's inquiry was on a monstrously ex-parte nature. While he took the statements of relations of the killed and those convicted and received the visits of persons connected with those killed or arrested he made no attempt to obtain an opinion from citizens of influence and weight.[74]

The deputy commissioner of Amritsar was trying to refute some of the serious charges levelled by Malaviya. He denied the presence of any human corpses in the well in Jallianwala Bagh as reported by Malaviya. The latter was, however, accompanied by Motilal Nehru, who gave the following firsthand account of the visit:

> Malaviya arrived in Amritsar soon after I posted my letter of yesterday. We then visited the Jalianwala Bagh. It was a truly gruesome sight. In spite of the lapse of nearly 2½ months after the incident there were more than one corpses to be seen floating in the well in a decomposed state.[75]

This account is self-explanatory. It shows that the official report was nothing more than an attempt to cover up the misdeeds that occurred on that tragic day at Amritsar. The two contradictory versions of the investigation at the scene of the event at Amritsar are enough to show that the official machinery was fully geared to cover up as many details of the April 1919 events as possible. The official and unofficial enquiries into the events precipitated a confrontation between the Congress and the government.

Since the events in Punjab were to figure prominently in the Imperial Legislative Council due to meet in early September, the Congress leaders, led by Motilal Nehru, persuaded Malaviya to seek re-election to the central legislature. Motilal Nehru impressed upon Malaviya the need for his re-entry to the council in the following words:

> In view, however, of the grave crisis that has overtaken the country since you tendered your resignation, and the completely changed political situation and having regard to the arduous momentous nature of the work, especially in regard to the developments in the Punjab that lies immediately ahead for the leaders of the nation, we feel very strongly that so tried and trusted a representative of the people as yourself should once more take his place in the Imperial Council in order to protect and advance the interest of the nation.[76]

RE-ENTRY INTO THE IMPERIAL LEGISLATIVE COUNCIL

Soon after his re-election, Malaviya adopted a novel method of ventilating the grievances of the people of Punjab. He tabled seventy-five questions in the council seeking detailed information about the excesses, barbarities, and judicial tyrannies perpetrated in Punjab in the aftermath of the massacre at Amritsar. When the viceroy disallowed these questions for consideration in the council, Malaviya had them published in different newspapers. In this manner, 'some of the grossest cases of vindictive tyranny found their way to the English press.'[77]

The prospect of the announcement of a high-level inquiry into the events in Punjab produced considerable apprehension among officials. Therefore, the Government of India decided to protect officers whose conduct was to be investigated through the enactment of an Indemnity Act. This act provided that nobody could sue an official for actions carried out under martial law, nor could anyone imprisoned under martial law sue such officials for wrongful confinement.[78] Gandhi's reaction to the enactment of such a law was conciliatory. He thought that there was nothing objectionable to such a course. His attitude came as unpleasant surprise to most of the Congress leaders including Malaviya who, however, minced no words in attacking the government when the measure was brought forward before the Imperial Legislative Council. Malaviya's main indictment of the government was delivered in his memorable record-breaking four-hour-long speech, during which he had pointed out that the disturbances in Punjab were the inevitable consequence of the tactless treatment meted out to persons already exasperated by official harshness.[79] Malaviya's opposition, however, could not prevent the passage of the measures in the council, as it comprised an official majority. His services lay in denouncing the repression committed by the government and in exposing the high-handedness of the bureaucracy in Punjab.

HUNTER COMMITTEE

When the Hunter Committee was set up to investigate the actual occurrences in Punjab, the Congress laid down its own conditions for cooperating with the official inquiry. Its major demand was that prominent Punjab leaders, then in jail, should be released for the period of enquiry so that they could give evidence before the committee. Malaviya pointed out that this would be of great help 'in presenting people's case before the Hunter Committee and for heartening witnesses who were keeping back and for inspiring people with confidence in Government's good faith'.[80] With great reluctance, the Punjab government agreed that six leaders be freed on parole to give evidence. The Congress was willing to cooperate with the Hunter

Committee on the basis of this 'little concession' provided the principal leaders were permitted to attend various other sittings of the Hunter Committee as well. The provincial government did not accede to the their request. Malaviya felt that 'this was not fair to public or Punjab leaders whose political actions and career were under review.'[81] He explained to Montagu, the secretary of state, through a telegram, that the Congress had 'decided to abstain from cooperation with the Hunter Committee as it was unwilling to be party to proceedings where its Counsels are handicapped and placed under disadvantage for want of assistance from persons principally interested and most competent to instruct Congress Sub Committee.'[82]

CONGRESS INQUIRY REPORT

Once the Congress had refused to cooperate with the Hunter Committee, it had to do something positive at its own level. As the Congress president, Malaviya lost no time, on his own initiative, to appoint a committee 'to hold almost a parallel inquiry on behalf of the Congress.' The names of the committee members were also 'virtually' decided upon by Malaviya himself.[83] Motilal Nehru, C.R. Das, Abbas Tyabji, M.R. Jayakar, and Gandhi were asked to conduct its proceedings. The Congress Inquiry Committee went to several places in Punjab, held public meetings, invited the public to make statements before it, and examined about two thousand witnesses in total. Gandhi and M.R. Jayakar took upon themselves the responsibility of drafting the report. Both Gandhi and Jayakar affirmed that every care was taken to bring out the truth.[84]

The members of the Congress Inquiry Committee on Punjab, including Gandhi, Motilal Nehru, M.R. Jayakar and C.R. Das, decided to finalize the report in consultation with Malaviya. Jayakar wrote that 'technically Malaviya was not a member of the Committee but his voice was always respected and prevailed on the side of moderation and restraint. He generally agreed with Gandhi and to their joint effort must be attributed the recommendations of the Committee.'[85] The members of the committee visited Banaras and gave final shape to their findings after consulting Malaviya. This gave him abundant opportunity to offer his suggestions to the members of the committee.

Malaviya had announced at the Amritsar Congress session that Jallianwala Bagh had become the nation's property. He was instrumental in persuading the owners of the land on which Jallianwala Bagh stood to transfer the land to the nation on payment of Rs 500,000. A committee comprising Malaviya, Motilal Nehru, Swami Shraddhanand, and Gandhi was constituted to prepare a suitable national memorial at Jallianwala Bagh.[86]

By the time the annual session of the Congress was held at Amritsar in December 1919, the Reform Act had been passed. The new constitutional measure appeared 'unsatisfactory to everyone'.[87] The mood of most Congressmen was reflected in the resolution moved by C.R. Das and supported by stalwarts such as Lokmanya Tilak and Bipin Chandra Pal. It reiterated the previous year's declaration that India was fit for self-government, declared that the act was 'inadequate, unsatisfactory and disappointing',[88] and asked that early steps be taken by the British parliament towards the establishment of responsible government in India. This meant a rejection of the reforms. C.R. Das's resolution was not acceptable to Malaviya, Jinnah, and Gandhi who decided to propose an amendment to it in the open session of the Congress. These leaders proposed that the Congress should not call the reforms disappointing but respond to them positively, thanking Montagu for his work and calling upon Indians to cooperate in implementing the reforms despite their inadequacy. The differences from C.R. Das's resolution 'were so strong that the Congress came to the point of putting it to vote in the open session'.[89] For the first time in the thirty-four years of the life of the Congress, arrangements were set in motion for voting on the resolution. For almost five hours, speeches by Congress leaders holding different opinions went on. Meanwhile all the groups came to the conclusion that it would be better to have a compromise and dispense with the need to vote. If a compromise was ultimately reached and the resolution was passed with an amendment, it was largely due to the untiring, behind-the-scenes efforts by Malaviya.[90] Gandhi lauded his role by writing that he left 'no stone unturned to bridge the gulf' between the two factions.[91]

At Amritsar, Malaviya was the voice of caution and accommodation. The proceedings of the Congress made it clear that a cleavage was developing within the party. But the irony of the situation was that while C.R. Das was inclined towards obstruction and rejection of the Reform Act, Gandhi and Malaviya were there as the apostles of cooperation. In the following year, at the Nagpur Congress session, the cleavage became wider. But the position of groups led by Gandhi and C.R. Das was reversed at the Nagpur session of 1920 and Malaviya was at a loss to find his own position in the Congress.

The close alliance between Malaviya and Gandhi was a significant feature of the Amritsar Congress session. Gandhi eloquently writes about his proximity to him in the following words:

> Pandit Malaviya had harboured me in his own room. I had a glimpse of the simplicity of his life on the occasion of the foundation ceremony of the Hindu University; but on this occasion being in the same room with him, I was able to observe his daily routine in the closest detail and what I saw filled me with joyful surprise. His room presented the appearance of a free inn for all the poor. You could hardly come across from one end to the other. It was so crowded. It was accessible to all at all odd hours to chance visitors who had the licence to take as much of his time as they liked. In a corner of this crib lay my Charpai in all its dignity.... I was thus enabled to hold daily discussions with Malaviyaji who used lovingly to explain to me, like an elder brother, the various viewpoints of different parties.[92]

The growing intimate relationship between Malaviya and Gandhi was watched with considerable uneasiness by Motilal Nehru who wrote:

> Gandhiji's going to Delhi for a talk with Shastri, his constant association and general agreement with Malaviya are no good omens for our party.... As at present situated I have no right to quarrel with anybody for his political views much less with persons with the eminence of Gandhi and Malaviya. Any attempt to compromise with the authorities or the moderates is bound to result in disaster by whosoever made. This is my reading of the situation.[93]

Motilal Nehru's next letter was perhaps more specific: 'That Gandhiji is going to take up an attitude not in complete accord with the Congress resolutions is fairly clear. Our only grievance is that while he has taken Shastri and Malaviya into his confidence he has left us severely alone. However, we have to wait and watch.'[94]

Tilak also referred to the close links between the two leaders: 'I do not think we can do much unless Malaviya and Gandhi are prepared to help us. They are the men on the Punjab Committee who should have taken the work in the right earnest.'[95]

NOTES

1. Chemsford to Willingdon, 21 March 1917, Chelmsford Papers.
2. Viceroy to Secretary of State for India, 18 May 1917, Chelmsford Papers.
3. Home Poll, Deposit Proceedings, April 1916, no. 19.
4. Home Poll, B Proceedings, July 1916, nos 441–5.
5. Letter to the Editor, *Leader*, 18 June 1917.
6. James Meston to Chemsford, 16 June 1916, Chelmsford Papers.
7. Home, Poll, November 1915, nos 166–8.
8. Gandhi to Personal Secretary to the Viceroy, 10 July 1917, *Collected Works of Mahatma Gandhi* (henceforth *CWMG*), vol. 15, p. 144.
9. Jawaharlal Nehru's letter to the editor, *Leader*, 21 June 1917.
10. Malaviya to V.S.S. Sastri, 26 June 1917, V.S.S. Sastri Papers.
11. Malaviya to V.S.S. Sastri, 26 June 1917, V.S.S. Sastri Papers.
12. Malaviya to V.S.S. Sastri, 26 June 1917, V.S.S. Sastri Papers.
13. Malaviya to V.S.S. Sastri, 26 June 1917, V.S.S. Sastri Papers.
14. Parmanand, *Mahamana Madan Mohan Malaviya*, p. 317.
15. M. K. Gandhi to Private Secretary to Chelmsford, 10 July 1917, *CWMG*, vol. 15, p. 464.
16. B.G. Horniman to Jawaharlal Nehru, 1 July 1917, in Jawaharlal Nehru, ed., *A Bunch of Old Letters* (Bombay, 1958), pp. 1–2.
17. Jha, *Role of Central Legislature*, p. 67.
18. Hugh Dwen, *Indian Nationalist Movement* (Delhi, 1984), p. 147.
19. James Meston to Chelmsford, 20 June 1917, Meston Papers.
20. James Meston to Chelmsford, 20 June 1917, Meston Papers.
21. Wedderburn to Malaviya, 17 July 1917, Sundar Lal Papers.
22. Chief Secretary to Government of UP to Personal Assistant to the Viceroy, 17 August 1917, Home Poll, A Proceedings, 136/1917.
23. Malaviya's speech on 10 August 1917 at the Special Provincial Congress at Lucknow, in Madan Mohan Malaviya, *Speeches and Writings of Pandit Madan Mohan Malaviya* (Madras, 1920), pp. 144–7.
24. James Meston to Chelmsford, 20 August 1917, Meston Papers.
25. Edwin S. Montagu, *Report on Indian Constitutional Reforms*, (Calcutta, 1918), p. 16.
26. Montagu, *Constitutional Reforms*, p. 16.
27. Edwin S. Montagu, *An Indian Diary*, edited by Venetia Montagu (London, 1930), p. 8.
28. Montagu, *An Indian Diary*, p. 132.
29. Montagu to Chelmsford, 20 June 1917, Montagu Papers.
30. V.S.S. Sastri to S.G. Waze, 21 January 1918, V.S.S. Sastri Papers.
31. *New India*, 4 September 1917.
32. Montagu, *An Indian Diary* pp. 144–53.

33. Montagu, *An Indian Diary*, p. 18.
34. *Leader*, 15 March 1918.
35. B.N. Pande, ed., *A Centenary History of the Indian National Congress* (New Delhi, 1985), pp. 410–11.
36. Pande, *Centenary History of the Congress*, pp. 410–11.
37. Pattabhi Sitaramayya, *The History of Indian National Congress*, vol. I (Bombay, 1935), pp. 30–1.
38. Madan Mohan Malaviya, *A Criticism of the Montagu–Chelmsford Report* (Allahabad, 1918), pp. 1–18.
39. H.N. Kunzru to Vaze, 13 July 1918, V.S.S. Sastri Papers.
40. M.M. Malaviya to H.N. Kunzru, 13 July 1918, V.S.S. Sastri Papers.
41. H.N. Kunzru to V.S.S. Sastri, 31 July 1918, V.S.S. Sastri Papers.
42. H.N. Kunzru to V.S.S. Sastri, 31 July 1918, V.S.S. Sastri Papers.
43. H.N. Kunzru to V.S.S. Sastri, 31 July 1918, V.S.S. Sastri Papers.
44. H.N. Kunzru to V.S.S. Sastri, 31 July 1918, V.S.S. Sastri Papers.
45. *New India*, 10 August 1918.
46. Malaviya to S.N. Banerjea, 8 August 1918, V.S.S. Sastri Papers.
47. Malaviya to S.N. Banerjea, 8 August 1918, V.S.S. Sastri Papers.
48. *New India*, 21 August 1918.
49. Home Poll, B Proceedings, October 1918, 191–4.
50. Malaviya to C. Vijayraghavachariar, 14 November 1918, C.V.R. Papers.
51. Malaviya to C. Vijayaraghavachariar, 14 November 1918, C.V.R. Papers.
52. Malaviya's appeal for unity in *New India*, 16 December 1918.
53. Malaviya to C. Vijayaraghavachariar, 14 November, 1918, V.S.S. Sastri Papers.
54. Zaidi and Zaidi, *Encyclopedia of the Indian National Congress*, vol. IV, pp. 363–9.
55. Zaidi and Zaidi, *Encyclopedia of the Indian National Congress*, vol. VII, p. 39.
56. Zaidi and Zaidi, *Encyclopedia of the Indian National Congress,* p. 395.
57. Malaviya to C. Vijayaragavachariar, 24 January 1919, C.V.R. Papers.
58. Malaviya to C. Vijayaraghavachariar, 14 January 1919, C.V.R. Papers.
59. Circular letter from Secretary, AICC, to various provincial bodies, dated 1 February 1919, AICC (upplement), 18/1919–20.
60. *Leader*, 5 February 1919.
61. Jha, *Role of Central Legislature*, p. 35.
62. Jha, *Role of Central Legislature*, p. 37.
63. Sitaramayya, *History of the Congress*, p. 301.
64. Sitaramayya, *History of the Congress*, p. 302.
65. Judith M. Brown, *Gandhi's Rise to Power: Indian Politics 1915–1922* (Cambridge, 1972), p. 260.
66. Brown, *Gandhi's Rise to Power,* p. 262.
67. Gandhi to Malaviya, 3 April 1919, *CWMG*, vol. 17, p. 76.

68. Police report, 10 April 1919, UPSA, GAD, no. 262/1919.

69. V.S.S. Sastri's statement, 11 May 1919, V.S.S. Sastri Papers.

70. Hari Singh, *Gandhi, Rowlatt Satyagraha, and British Imperialism: Emergence of Mass Movements in Punjab and Delhi* (Delhi, 1990), p. 63.

71. Padmakant Malaviya, *Malaviyaji, Jivan Jhulkian* (Delhi, 1962) p. 52.

72. Punjab Fortnightly Report, vol. II, July 1919, National Archives of India (henceforth NAI).

73. Report of the General Secretaries of the Indian National Congress 1919, pp. 554–5.

74. Report of the Deputy Commissioner, Amritsar, 30 June 1919, Home Poll, October 1919, no. 63.

75. Motilal Nehru to Jawaharlal Nehru, 30 June 1919, *Selected Works of Jawaharlal Nehru* (henceforth *SWJN*), vol. II, p. 22.

76. Motilal Nehru to Malaviya, 4 June 1919, Motilal Nehru Papers, vol. II, p. 17.

77. Motilal Nehru to Jawaharlal Nehru, 16 September 1919, Motilal Nehru Papers, vol. II, p. 56.

78. Brown, *Gandhi's Rise to Power,* p. 233.

79. Jha, *Role of Central Legislature*, pp. 56–7.

80. Telegram from Malaviya to V.S.S. Sastri, 16 November 1919, V.S.S. Sastri Papers.

81. Malaviya to V.S.S. Sastri, 16 November 1919, V.S.S. Sastri Papers.

82. Telegram from Malaviya to Montagu, 17 November 1919, Montagu Papers.

83. M.K. Gandhi, *An Autobiography: The Story of My Experiments with Truth* (Ahmedabad, 1927), p. 362.

84. M.R. Jayakar, *The Story of My Life, Vol. I: 1873–1922* (Bombay, 1958), p. 167.

85. Jayakar, *Story of My Life*, vol. I, pp. 124 and 363.

86. *CWMG*, vol. 17, p. 55.

87. Gandhi, *An Autobiography*, p. 367.

88. Sitaramayya, *History of the Congress*, pp. 161–2.

89. *Young India*, 14 January 1920, *CWMG*, vol. 19, p. 61.

90. Sitaramayya, *History of the Congress*, p. 131.

91. Gandhi, *An Autobiography*, p. 368.

92. Gandhi, *An Autobiography*, p. 367.

93. Motilal Nehru to Jawaharlal Nehru, 27 February 1920, Motilal Nehru Papers, vol. II, p. 100.

94. Motilal Nehru to Jawaharlal Nehru, 29 February 1920, Motilal Nehru Papers, vol. II, p. 102.

95. B.G. Tilak to V.J. Patel, 26 June 1920, All India Congress Committee Papers (henceforth AICC Papers), file no. 9, 1920.

5   The Challenge of the Non-cooperation Movement (1920–22)

In the mid-1920s, Gandhi challenged the sterile form of nationalist struggle that had been followed by the Congress for so long. He was determined not just to right the Punjab and Khilafat 'wrongs' but also to advocate a direct confrontation with the British. The timing of Gandhi's decision was significant. Emotions ran high in India after the publication of the terms of the Treaty of Sèvres with Turkey in May 1920 and the Hunter Commission report in the same month. These reports represented the utter bankruptcy of the British government in India. Gandhi felt justified in appealing to people to adopt the path of satyagraha to rid themselves of a government which was 'satanic' in its total disregard of the conventions of civilized governance. Gandhi was determined at this juncture to rally the two communities of India—the Muslims and the Hindus—behind his programme of non-cooperation that exhorted people to withdraw support forthwith from the institutions of the British Raj. This meant that Gandhi needed to gain as much of the Congress's support as of the Muslim League's.

The evolution of Gandhi's programme of non-cooperation was intimately associated with his attempts to link the agitation over the Punjab issues with the Khilafat movement. Discussions began at a joint Hindu–Muslim Leaders' conference in March 1920. Ten Hindu and fifteen Muslim leaders met in Delhi. Among them were Gandhi, Malaviya, Lajpat Rai, Tilak, G.S. Khaperde, M.A. Ansari, Abul Kalam Azad, Abdul Bari, Hakim Ajmal Khan, and Shaukat Ali. Their main concern was united action in the future by both the communities. Malaviya voiced the Hindu anxiety that there was no proof that Muslims would support boycott and non-cooperation. The conference was inconclusive.

THE AICC MEETING AT BANARAS AND ITS AFTERMATH

Gandhi's non-cooperation proposals were further considered at the Banaras meeting of the AICC from 28 to 30 May 1920. Instead of taking any firm decision at that time, it was decided that the final decision would be taken at a special meeting of the Congress to be held in Calcutta in September 1920.[1] Malaviya expressed the general opinion that the Congress should do nothing about non-cooperation until the Muslims had decided upon a definite course of action. Soon after this AICC meeting, another Hindu–Muslim conference was held from 1 to 3 June at Allahabad. During this meeting, the Congress leaders did not offer any firm support to non-cooperation. T.B. Sapru, Mrs Besant, Motilal Nehru, and Malaviya were not convinced that non-cooperation was either necessary or practical and they wanted to leave the decision to the Special Congress.[2] Like most other Congress leaders, Motilal Nehru was not very hopeful of the acceptance of Gandhi's non-cooperation proposal by the Congress. He wote:

> As far as I can see it is not likely that the Congress as a Congress will bind itself to non-cooperation. It is too big an organization for this. The most that can happen is that it will approve the principle and leave members to follow their own inclinations.[3]

At this time elections to the legislative councils under the new Reform Act were round the corner and the two UP stalwarts, Malaviya and Motilal Nehru, had their eyes set on the elections rather than on the non-cooperation programme.

GANDHI'S UNILATERAL DECISION TO START THE CAMPAIGN

The reluctance of the Congress leaders to commit themselves to the non-cooperation strategy before discussion at the Special Congress in September made Gandhi act on his own authority. He now decided to begin the non-cooperation programme on 1 August 1920. Gandhi's announcement to launch the campaign before September was a deliberate move to garner support for himself at the forthcoming Special Congress where he expected opposition. Malaviya appealed to Gandhi to suspend the launching of the campaign till the Congress had pronounced upon it.[4] Gandhi remained unmoved and firmly turned down Malaviya's advice blaming the latter for his indecision:

> The advice which Panditji has given me only means that he has not formed a final opinion regarding non-cooperation. That I cannot accept his advice means that I have come to a firm decision.[5]

Despite the appeal of the 'Dharmatma', as Gandhi described Malaviya,[6] the former launched the non-cooperation campaign on his own initiative on 1 August 1920 and did not wait for the formal approval of the Congress which was due to give its verdict a month later.

SPECIAL SESSION OF THE CONGRESS AT CALCUTTA

By the first week of September, 1920, Gandhi had made full preparations to meet the challenge of the established leaders of the Congress. Before the Special Congress session began at Calcutta, his non-cooperation campaign was a reality. He had announced his intentions to carry on the struggle to the finish line. He pinned his hopes on the support of the Muslims who had already accepted his non-cooperation programme. The strong Muslim presence at the special session strengthened Gandhi's position.[7] He had also secured the support of several provincial Congress committees and had attempted to win the support of provincial leaders. Despite all these efforts, Gandhi described his own plight as 'pitiable indeed' and observed:

> I was absolutely at sea as to who would support the resolution and who would oppose it. Nor had I any idea as to the attitude that Lalaji would adopt. I only saw an imposing phalanx of veteran warriors assembled for the fray at Calcutta, Dr. Besant, Pt. Malaviya, Sjt. Vijayaraghavachari, Pandit Motilalji and the Deshabandhu being some of them.[8]

The non-cooperation resolution framed and moved by Gandhi was debated in a heated Subjects Committee meeting for three days and then accepted by a narrow margin of 12 votes with 144 members for and 132 against the resolution. At Calcutta, Gandhi was not swept to power on a wave of enthusiasm for his programme. The determining factor for the Congress was the large Muslim contingent. This was because, for the first time, Muslims came in significant numbers to the Congress.[9] In his closing presidential speech, Lajpat Rai referred pointedly to these Muslims, adding that he was 'a little sorry that Mr. Gandhi in his wisdom should have considered it necessary and proper in a way to tack the Indian National Congress to the Central Khilafat Committee.'[10] Few could have thought that Gandhi would carry the day and no one tried to counter Gandhi's elaborate preparations throughout July and August. Thus, on the eve of the Special Congress, Gandhi's preparations were complete while other Congress leaders remained prisoners of indecision. Leaders like Malaviya could not overcome their doubts about Gandhi and his proposal for satyagraha. Malaviya's indecision was echoed in the deliberations of the Special Congress session. A contemporary observer comments: 'Gandhi marched triumphant through the session in spite of the opposition offered by men like Das, Lajpat Rai and Malaviya.'[11]

Both Gandhi and Malaviya were deeply conscious of their relationships, the compulsions of the position they were taking at the Special Congress session, and the consequent fallout. While concluding his speech at the session, Gandhi made particular reference to Malaviya:

> I owe a great deal to Pandit Malaviya. The relations that subsist between him and me the country does not know. I would give my life to placate him, to please him and follow him at a respectable distance. But when it becomes a matter of duty and conviction I hold that he absolves me from any such decision of following him.[12]

Malaviya, for his part, explained that though he had the greatest regard and affection for Mr. Gandhi, it was his painful duty to differ from him entirely with regard to the resolution of the Congress on non-cooperation and that he had, therefore, determined to pursue a course of action different from that adopted by the Congress in September 1920.[13]

Despite these statements by Gandhi and Malaviya after the Calcutta Special Congress, the fact remains that the latter's hold over the Congress, both at the national and provincial level, weakened. Gandhi had come to understand that it was not easy to convince Malaviya and that he would often take an independent course of action. At the same time, the support extended to Gandhi by Motilal Nehru at the crucial moment of the session brought the two leaders closer to each other. Motilal's sudden change of sides in the Subjects Committee and his open support to the non-cooperation resolution significantly strengthened Gandhi's leadership.[14] This brought Motilal Nehru closer to Gandhi, enhanced his stature in the Congress, and swung the UP Provincial Congress to his side. Malaviya's relative position in his home province was adversely affected. The process of reassessment and realignment beginning from the Special Congress session continued for quite some time.

POST–CALCUTTA–SESSION POLITICS

Gandhi's victory at Calcutta did not mean that he had captured the Congress organization. Several established and senior leaders of the Congress, including Malaviya, still had strong a influence within the AICC and the Provincial Congress Committees and Gandhi was in no position to dictate his programme to the Congress. Under these circumstances, he had to take the path of least resistance. Soon after the Special Congress session, Gandhi went around to several places, addressed meetings, and explained his new gospel to politicians and the masses alike. His main task was to win over as many Congress leaders to his side as possible before the annual Congress session of December 1920.

From this time onwards, Gandhi was particularly careful about addressing the objections raised by Malaviya against the non-cooperation programme. With consummate skill, patience, and humility, he attempted to clarify Malaviya's reservations and, in spite of several ups and downs, attempted to maintain the best of relations with him. Malaviya was equally keen to keep the bond of affection and love with Gandhi intact. He did not challenge the necessity of non-cooperation in principle and based his opposition on expediency. In his opinion, this was not the right occasion to resort to the 'Brahmastra',[15] a weapon of the last resort, because sufficient preparation had not been made for launching such a campaign. Malaviya favoured a dialogue with the British government and did not think that any useful purpose would be served in hurling threats to the government.[16] Thus, he had his doubts about the efficacy and timing of the non-cooperation programme and did not mince words in voicing his views either at the Calcutta Special Congress session, the annual session at Nagpur, or at any other similar occasion.

Gandhi's call for the boycott of legislative councils was a sudden break in the continuity of local and regional political traditions and aspirations.[17] As late as 16 June 1920, these considerations were clearly still held by the two foremost political leaders of UP. Motilal Nehru wrote, 'I think Malaviya and I should make up our minds about the Council elections. It will be too late to do anything if we sit tight till the Special Congress has met.'[18]

The deliberations of the Calcutta Special Congress, however, led Motilal to reverse his earlier stand and, under his leadership, several UP Congressmen also declared themselves in favour of the boycott of the councils. This was openly reflected in the UP Provincial Political Conference held in Moradabad in October 1920 under the chairman-ship of Bhagwan Das.[19] A strong wave in support of the boycott of the councils was in the air, particularly among younger patriots including Sri Prakash, Sampurnanand, P.D. Tandon, and others, so much so that Malaviya thought it prudent to swim with the current rather than against it. He revised his earlier stance of opposition to the boycott of the councils and, in deference to Gandhi,s wishes, kept himself away from the November 1920 elections.[20]

MALAVIYA'S OPPOSITION TO GANDHI'S CALL OF BOYCOTT OF EDUCATION

The issue on which their differences were deepest was the boycott of education. Gandhi maintained that it was 'unmanly for us to con-tinue to receive grants for our education from a Government which we heartily dislike'.[21] He gave a call for the boycott of government-controlled schools and colleges. Malaviya firmly opposed Gandhi's proposal at the Special Congress and remained an 'uncompromising opponent'[22] of Gandhi's suggestions. If the situation did not give rise to feelings of jealousy between them, it was largely due to the 'splendid character of the leaders'[23]. Both Malaviya and Gandhi firmly stuck to their opposing positions and yet, they were able to maintain the best of relations.

The major theme of Malaviya's speeches and writings during this period was that the boycott of education was suicidal, that the funds with which the government maintained some educational institu-tions and gave grants to others were our own, and it was unwise to refuse the funds thus provided by the government. He argued that the existing educational institutions should be utilized until an adequate number of national institutions were established. Malaviya argued that the government did not stand to lose anything by the boycott of schools or colleges. However, such a step was likely to curtail the meagre facilities of education available to the Indian youth and would damage their interests. Gandhi acknowledged publicly that 'for the time being we differ on matters of great importance ... his diagnosis is different from mine'[24] and pointed out that the differences of opinion arose because Malaviya 'believes that there is an element of goodness in the Government. I feel that it is a sinful one.'[25] In various speeches and writings, Gandhi referred to his differences with Malaviya over the question of the boycott of educational institutions and sought to justify his stand.

While undertaking whirlwind tours after the Calcutta Special Congress, Gandhi visited Banaras with Malaviya's prior consent, stayed with him in the city for two days on 16 and 27 November 1920, and shared the same platform with him.[26] Gandhi 'had no apprehension of there being any bitterness'[27] with Malaviya which indicates the maturity of the relationship and deep understanding that existed between them. Both the leaders had differing opinions on the functioning and role of the newly established university at Banaras, firmly held to their positions, and were still willing to allow each other to put forward their respective views at both private and public meetings. In such a situation, it was only fair that both Gandhi and Malaviya together addressed the gathering of students within the Banaras Hindu University campus as well as outside it.

In his two major speeches before the gathering of the university students, Gandhi was cautions and careful and made it a point to pay rich tributes to Malaviya:

> I have come across no holier man than he; I see no living Indian who has served India more than he has done. What is our relation, Panditji and mine? I have revered him since I returned from South Africa. I have poured forth my troubles to him on innumerable occasions and received consolation from him. He is certainly an elder brother to me.[28]

In no uncertain terms, Gandhi told the students: 'If, however, you think it is a sin to continue your studies in this university you should leave it immediately and you will have Panditji's blessings in this.'[29] Gandhi did not mince words in inviting the students to discontinue their studies and join the non-cooperation movement.

Malaviya faced Gandhi's challenge calmly, boldly, and fearlessly. In his reply, Malaviya showed no signs of nervousness and said:

> I do not believe in keeping birds in a cage. Those whose minds have turned away from studies and those who have resolved to leave should surely go. I have no feeling of hostility. Those who wish to stay should study diligently and regard it as service to the country. Ask the Supreme God whether you are fit for serving the country. For you it is time for study. It is our duty to establish self-government; it is your duty as students to devote yourselves to study.[30]

The thrust of Malaviya's speech was on the idea that it was the duty of students to concentrate on studies rather than bothering about the problems facing the country. He asserted that this responsibility should be that of elders like himself. Even so, Malaviya did not ask the university students to stay on in the campus against their wishes. It was a testing time for the founder of the newly established university who exhibited exemplary courage in facing the situation. Nearly one-tenth of the students opted to leave the university and the crisis blew over soon after. Gandhi later wrote, 'I had a nice time in Banaras. What the outcome will be I do not know. The atmosphere is certainly clear and Malaviyaji is certainly calmer if not entirely calm.'[31]

Gandhi's whirlwind campaign following the Special Congress session made him so popular that no one could withstand him. His boldness in proclaiming the satyagraha doctrine staggered hesitating and doubtful leaders. In this atmosphere the Indian National Congress met at Nagpur. It was an eventful session because of the complete conquest that Gandhi staged here. He marched triumphant through the 1920 session.

NAGPUR CONGRESS SESSION

In fact, many top leaders who gathered at the session had, in the meanwhile, changed over to Gandhi's side. Owing to the change in public feeling in the intervening period, Gandhi had very much consolidated his position. It has rightly been pointed out that the temper of the session proved decisive: 'The fourteen thousand delegates had already made up their mind in the matter. They were not prepared to allow any moderation in the pace of the Congress and demanded the brakes put at Calcutta to be removed.'[32] The governor of Bombay reported to the viceroy:

> The situation politically may be described as stagnant, all are waiting for Nagpur, where I am afraid Gandhi will win simply because he will pack the Congress and the Moderates are too idle to do the same.[33]

Details of pre-Congress manoeuvres confirm that Gandhi's supporters had been active since early December and had gained a large majority in every province except Bengal. An influential Bombay daily reported:

> There is no manner of doubt that this is a Gandhi Congress, there might be varying shades of opposition to the Mahatma but the general opinion among delegates was that Gandhi would have his way.[34]

Against this background, the Congress met from 26 to 31 December 1920. A swing towards Gandhi among the prominent leaders became clear from the very first day and the trend was confirmed by the time the session came to an end. The president of the Congress session, C. Vijayaraghavachariar, who was, at the time, lukewarm towards the non-cooperation movement, cautiously cooperated with Gandhi. A similar change had taken place in the views of Lajpat Rai, B.C. Pal, K.R. Iyengar, Saifuddin Kitchlew, and Hakim Ajmal Khan. The change in the attitude of some of these leaders was further confirmed in the discussions in the Subjects Committee for the new Congress creed, which read, 'the object of the Indian National Congress is the attainment of Swarajya by the people of India by all legitimate and peaceful means.[35] Malaviya and M.A. Jinnah opposed the suggestion and were in favour of retaining in the creed the mention of the connection with Britain. Eventually a compromise was reached in the Subjects Committee.

There were rumours that Gandhi and C.R. Das were likely to reach a compromise on the question of the non-cooperation programme. On the closing day of the session, the Das–Gandhi pact came to the surface when C.R. Das moved the main resolution reaffirming the non-cooperation resolution adopted earlier at the Special Congress session. It was seconded by Gandhi and supported by Lajpat Rai and several other former opponents of the programme. The official explanation was that C.R. Das returned from the session 'an ardent convert to Mr. Gandhi's views and ... threw his lot with him while there was yet time.'[36]

In the face of this unexpected alliance, many of Gandhi's prominent opponents sat silently in the open session. Only Malaviya, unable to attend because he was ill, protested by sending a message opposing both the new creed of the Congress and the main non-cooperation resolution. Malaviya's message was read out by Gandhi in the following words: 'He [Malaviya] argues that we talk of bringing down the British Empire but that is beyond our power. How can India unarmed and weak bring down such a mighty empire?'[37] This question continued to haunt Malaviya and many other nationalist leaders for several years to come.

MALAVIYA ROLE AS A MEDIATOR

Malaviya's role during the non-cooperation campaign was that of a peacemaker. There were at least three occasions, between May 1921 and February 1922, when he attempted to bring Gandhi and the viceroy together, worked as a link between the two, and sought to bring about a settlement between them. His role as an intermediary was, of course, full of risks and invited adverse comments. Malaviya's contemporaries were often sceptical of his motives and watched his close relationship with Gandhi with serious misgivings. A contemporary writer has referred to 'a veil of secrecy over the talks between Gandhi and the Viceroy held in May 1921'.[38] However, with the help of official documents, recently made available, it is possible to probe the background of the high-level discussions held in Delhi and Simla and highlight the motives that prompted Malaviya to play the role of a mediator.

On his arrival in India in April 1921, the new viceroy, Lord Reading, realized that the non-cooperation movement was being carried out in the country 'with intense heat'. His assessment was that 'the danger is serious for I find the influence of the authority markedly impaired, on the one hand the extremists openly agitate against the Government and denounce it and defy it on the other. There is depression among the moderates and our officials at the spread of disaffection and failure to attempt to check it.'[39]

The viceroy was therefore anxious to explore 'reasonable means of arriving at some settlement of outstanding differences'.[40] He decided to get in touch with leading Indian politicians to know their views as well as to find out the possibility of any reasonable solution acceptable to the leaders of the non-cooperation movement and the government. Malaviya was among the first few leaders who were invited by the viceroy to meet him in early May 1921. During their talks, Malaviya came to know about the intention of the viceroy to prosecute the Ali brothers for their speeches pleading for possible Muslim assistance to the invading Afghan forces. Malaviya persuaded Reading not to proceed further in the matter before a discussion with Gandhi. When the viceroy agreed to do so, Malaviya sent urgent summons to Gandhi to reach Simla for the purpose.[41] Thus Malaviya took the iniative for the Gandhi–Reading talks and was confident that Gandhi would be willing to act upon his advice. Gandhi admitted later that he 'seized the opportunity of waiting upon His Excellency and assuring him that ours was a religious movement'.[42] Acting upon Malaviya's suggestion, Gandhi reached Simla for a meeting with the viceroy indicating his willingness to discuss issues relating to the non-cooperation movement with the latter. The talks between Gandhi and the viceroy held at Simla on 13 and 14 May 1921 were, however, not successful. Soon after meeting Gandhi, the viceroy reported that he was 'rather disappointed as Gandhi wishes to maintain the non-cooperation movement and strive to increase its power at any cost'.[43] The viceroy had no other option but to express his determination 'to fight this movement by doing the things that we consider right'.[44]

The 'only definite result'[45] of the Gandhi–Reading meeting was an apology by the Ali brothers for those parts of their speeches which appeared to incite violence and a promise not to advocate violence while they were associated with the non-cooperation movement. In return, the viceroy decided not to prosecute the Ali brothers. Gandhi later said publicly that the Alis had offered the apology not to the government but to their countrymen.[46] He also sent a telegram to Malaviya to that effect.[47] This put Malaviya in an embarrassing position as he could neither publicly support nor oppose Gandhi on this delicate issue. He decided to get in touch with the viceroy 'to express his great concern at the attitude Gandhi adopted in his publication and speeches respecting the apology of Mohammad Ali'.[48] Reporting about his next meeting with Malaviya, the viceroy wrote: 'Malaviya, who is aware of all that took place from his [Gandhi's] first interviews with me to the subsequent Gandhi interviews is shocked at the statement made by the latter and I think he [Malaviya] was little apprehensive that I might retort by a statement and publication of the material documents which would completely refute the statement of Gandhi.'[49] It was left to Gandhi to wriggle out of the difficult situation by saying that 'it is possible that we both have carried different impressions of various interviews'.[50] The 'apology' controversy was finally closed with the publication of an agreed statement between the viceroy and Gandhi on 4 August 1921.[51] Malaviya played a significant part in the preparation of the statement. The viceroy was deliberately 'mild' as he 'always [had] in mind that Gandhi is undoubtedly an enormous influence here and that it might be necessary or desirable at some time in the future to see him again and I do not want his sense of irritation at the result to him of those first interviews with me to be maintained [sic].'[52]

MALAVIYA'S DEMAND FOR SWARAJ

At this juncture, Malaviya did not share Gandhi's enthusiasm for the non-cooperation campaign. Nor did he entertain any hopes of what could be achieved by a frontal collision with the Government of India. He earnestly desired to build a bridge of understanding that would ensure India's elevation to the status of a self-governing community. Malaviya heavily relied on the viceroy in achieving his political goal, met him at regular intervals, and attempted to keep close and intimate relations with him. The viceroy wisely kept Malaviya in good humour, appreciated his moderate strategy, and encouraged him to play the role of a mediator between him and Gandhi. The viceroy conveyed to Montagu, the secretary of state, the following assessment of Malaviya's views:

> Although Malaviya is in sympathy with Gandhi on account of his social reform movement and carries weight with thoughtful Indians he is not quite a non-cooperator. To me he seems daily more inclined to advocate resort to more constitutional means of enforcing Swaraj and I am not certain that he may not eventually influence some of the chief supporters of Gandhi and possibly Gandhi himself to more moderate action.[53]

In another letter to Montagu, the viceroy informed him about Malaviya's insistance on a firm enunciation of the British policy on swaraj:

> Malaviya is evidently a person who thinks well ahead and he is much concerned in mind as to the period when complete Swaraj will be obtained. He urged me strongly to give some indication in a public statement of the date when complete Swaraj could be obtained be it 10, 15, 20 or even 25 years.[54]

The viceroy declined to give any assurance and told Malaviya that it was for the British parliament to decide on the question at an appropriate occasion. But Montagu's comment on Malaviya's demand was characteristic. He said:

> It is really astonishing to me that intelligent persons like Malaviya can still harp on their ambition to have a definite time-limit announced for Swaraj.[55]

Montagu's reply amply demonstrates the wide gap between the views of the British statesmen and the expectations of Malaviya on the crucial issue of the grant of swaraj to India in the forseeable future.

This confidential correspondence between the viceroy and the secretary of state on the request made by Malaviya about prescribing a time limit with regard to a difinite declaration on swaraj by the British authorities brings to light the 'pervasive dualism in the British stance towards India', which was at once 'longstanding and deliberate'.[56] This was largely because 'the British during the interwar years were always quite determined to do everything they could to hold on to the empire ... they had no intention of relinquishing it and with considerable assiduity and after steely resolve gave their minds to maintaining it'.[57]

It is difficult to understand how Malaviya was completely unaware of the basic tenets of the British policy in the post–First World War years. Even with a fair knowledge of the views of the British statesmen, he continued to nurse hopes of bringing about some change in the minds of the viceroy and the secretary of state. While nursing this fond hope, he maintained close links with the viceroy, met him repeatedly at short intervals, and was prepared to respond to the latter's wishes. The viceroy conveniently kept Malaviya by his side as he knew that at some later date he would need his help in bringing Gandhi around. He noted, 'Malaviya may in my opinion become an important factor with Gandhi at any time and he is, I consider, as thoughtful politician as he is.'[58]

EXTENDING SUPPORT TO THE PRINCE'S VISIT

In this broad context it would be possible to understand why Malaviya agreed to associate himself with the plans to welcome the Prince of Wales to India at a time when there was widespread enthusiasim all over the country to carry forward the non-cooperation movement. As soon as the preparations for the prince's visit were afoot, the viceroy

invited Malaviya to become the member of the top-level committee which was formed to make arrangements for the said purpose.
Malaviya 'expressed his readiness' to join the committee forthwith and
'promised to do all in his power to make the prince's visit most successful'.[59] The viceroy wrote to Montagu:

> In any event I attach great importance to associating Malaviya with
> Government in preparing a welcome to His Royal Highness. Of course
> I have emphasized to him that the Prince is not identified with party or
> politics and I am endeavouring to get this view carried through him to
> Gandhi and his associates.[60]

Thus the viceroy roped in Malaviya as soon as the prince's visit to
India was officially announced and he found the latter a willing partner
and supporter in his efforts. The viceroy, though doubtful about the
complete success of the prince's visit, hoped that it might wean the
masses away from the non-cooperation movement.[61] But public opinion in India was entirely against any such official move and gave ample
testimony of its feelings soon after the prince set foot in the country. In
fact, they had a deep suspicion that the visit was being arranged with
the object of eclipsing Gandhi. In an interview he gave to the press,
Malaviya gave his own disclaimer. His open support to the official plans
came as a shock in nationalist circles.

At the AICC meeting held in Bombay on 22 July 1921, Malaviya
'fought hard'[62] to tone down the Congress resolution which proposed
the boycott of the visit of the prince. It was because of his influence
that the apex body of the Congress called upon the people not to
observe a hartal on the day the prince was to land in Bombay but only
to abstain from the official celebrations.[63] The viceroy noted with satisfaction that 'Malaviya seems to have stood up well at the meeting'.[64]

As the prince's visit drew nearer, the viceroy received reports of
Gandhi's open opposition to the royal visit. Consequently, he began
to lose faith in the policy of conciliation towards the non-cooperation
movement and informed Montagu accordingly:

> I told him [Malaviya] that I had given conciliation a fair trial and that
> the more I did with this object the less success I have achieved and the
> more violent became Gandhi and his movement.[65]

The viceroy's worst fears largely came true. When the prince
landed in Bombay on 17 November, the non-cooperators abstained

from official ceremonies. Gandhi was in Bombay on this day and was present at a big meeting held in the city to make a huge bonfire of foreign cloth. Rioting broke out in the town on the same day on which Europeans, Parsis, and others who had participated in the reception of the prince were assaulted.[66] There were scenes of widespread violence in the town and the government resorted to coercive measures by arresting various eminent local and regional leaders.

In this politically tense atmosphere, the country witnessed the strange spectacle of Malaviya welcoming the Prince of Wales at Banaras Hindu University and honouring him with an honorary degree of Doctor of Laws while not only the city of Banaras but almost every city that the prince visited in India greeted him with boycott. Malaviya's action cannot be easily defended except on the ground that he had extended the invitation much before the arrival of the prince in India. Reading observed in as early as July that 'Malaviya is most anxious that the Prince should visit the University and I have pledged myself that the visit will take place if the satisfactory assurances are forthcoming'.[67] During the same month, the UP governor informed the viceroy, 'I have seen Pandit Malaviya who is very sanguine that he can assure a good reception.'[68] In any case Malaviya had sufficient time to reconsider his offer regarding the prince's visit to the university after the loud opposition voiced by the people of Bombay against him on 17 November. The temper of the Bombay mob was a clear sign that no one was willing to welcome the prince and there were clear signals that his visit would be boycotted in a similar manner in other cities. It is surprising that Malaviya did not reconsider his earlier proposal of honouring the Prince of Wales' visit to the university scheduled on 13 December 1921. The local influential daily, *Aaj*, had already warned him, a fortnight earlier, not to arrange a 'compulsive welcome' of the prince as it ultimately turned out to be.[69] Despite these warnings, Malaviya organized parades, receptions, and banquets in the prince's honour and no stones were left unturned to honour him on a grand scale at the university. However, the visitor did not fail to notice the 'empty streets, shuttered windows and brooding silence' in the city and expressed his displeasure at the efforts made for 'filling up empty students seats with High School boys' during the 'big ceremony' at Banaras Hindu University.[70] The provincial governor informed the viceroy, 'I am afraid that Madan Mohan Malaviya's influence failed at Banaras and practically no students turned up at University function.'[71]

HIGH-LEVEL PARLEYS FOR A CONFERENCE WITH THE VICEROY

The viceroy was feeling uneasy at the boycott of the public welcome for the prince. Every city he visited observed a hartal. 'The situation was going out of hand from the official point of view,' remarked Subhash Chandra Bose. The novelty of the tacticts employed by the Congress had left the government nonplussed.[72] The prince was due to arrive at Calcutta on 24 December 1921. The complete and peaceful nature of the hartal on 17 November in the city only reminded the viceroy of the spontaneity and organizing ability of its planners. He feared that arresting the leaders might not prevent the strike call of 24 December from disintegrating. So the viceroy began to think of coming to an understanding with the Congress before the prince's arrival in Calcutta and came down to the city to explore the prospects of negotiations with the Congress. He wrote:

> Something must be done to arrive at some basis of conference and truce for the time being. At the moment my main object is to arrive at a course which will enable the Prince's visit to take place without any demonstrations or arrests during his stay here.[73]

The viceroy impressed upon the provincial governors the need of a conference in the following words:

> The situation in Calcutta and elsewhere is developing very fast and the whole movement of non-cooperation is concentrated upon the Prince's visit on the 24th of December. Unfortunately large number of moderate and other opinion is either openly expressing dissatisfaction with Government policy described as repressive or is sulking in its tent. In Bengal Indian support of government policy is now difficult to find.... Suggestions are being made and strongly pressed that some arrangement should be arrived at temporarily and that a conference should be held. I have never been averse from holding a Conference provided it is made clear that in entering or calling it I am not in any way committed save to listen and discuss grievances or suggested changes.[74]

Mrs Annie Besant and T.B. Sapru were, in the meanwhile, making efforts behind the scenes for mediation between the government and the Congress. They got in touch with Malaviya at Allahabad and discussed with him the plan of winning Gandhi's favour. Mrs Besant informed the viceroy that

Malaviya will be at Calcutta before the 21st for the formal preliminary meeting. He assured us of Gandhi's cooperation. However, we have sent Jamnadas Dwarkadas and Pandit Kunzru to Ahmedabad to see Gandhi, either to bring him to Calcutta on the 21st or if he cannot come then to bring a note stating any point that he thinks should be discussed at the conference and stating conditions, if any, that he makes for taking part in the discussion.[75]

During the fortnight before the prince's arrival in Calcutta, Malaviya had three meetings with the viceroy. On the day of the first meeting, the viceroy frankly expressed the hope that 'Malaviya's arrival may help to a solution'. The meeting between the two went very well and Malaviya was willing to play the role of a mediator between the viceroy and Gandhi as he had done some six months previously. With regard to discussions with Malaviya, the viceroy reported:

> He at last asked whether we could not have a conference at which all the various parties including Gandhi were represented. He asserted definitely that Gandhi would attend if I asked him. I said vague talks of conferences had been going on ever since my arrival; if there was anything behind them, it must be put forward to me in a more precise form.... Malaviya said he would consider this with his friends and see if he could put forward a definite proposal.[76]

The viceroy was well aware that 'at present little good would result unless Gandhi takes his part. It may be that he will say he will only come on my invitation.'[77] In the late December 1921 parleys, all eyes were therefore focussed on Gandhi who was staying in Ahmedabad ahead of the annual Congress session in the city.

Malaviya set the ball rolling by despatching the following telegram to Gandhi on 16 December 1921:

> I am arranging deputation about seven to the Viceroy on twenty-first [*sic*] to press upon him necessity of Round Table Conference. Hence going to Calcutta. Jamnadas and Kunzru reach Sabarmati tomorrow to explain situation. Desire to have your authority to say that if Conference is accepted and Government stay hands and release leaders you will withdraw opposition to Prince's welcome and suspend Civil Disobedience till termination conference.[78]

Malaviya thought it necessary to discuss the proposal of a conference with C.R. Das and Abul Kalam Azad who were then serving a term there in the Presidency Jail.[79] The two leaders thought that the offer brought by Malaviya was worth considering. In a telegram to Gandhi, they urged him to accept Malaviya's proposal.[80] On his part, Malaviya also sent another telegram to Gandhi:

> If points mentioned in Das's telegram to you accepted and composition and date of Conference agreed upon we will call off Hartal and see that pending conclusion of proposed conference, Non-Cooperation activities … will be suspended and that real truce will be abserved on our side.[81]

Evidence is not lacking that Gandhi was initially inclined to join the round table conference. Jamnadas Dwarkadas communicated to Malaviya Gandhi's willingness to attend the conference 'called by Viceroy or anyone without imposing any previous conditions'.[82]

Gandhi's answer to Malaviya's telegram was as follows:

> Saw Jamnadas and Kunzru. Please do not worry over repression. Conference will be abortive unless Government truly penitent. Anxious to settle three things, Punjab, Khilafat and Swaraj.[83]

Gandhi's next telegram of the same date to C.R. Das and Abul Kalam Azad was, however, much different as Gandhi made his acceptance conditional on two assurances: that the date and composition of the Conference be settled in advance and that prisoners convicted in connection with the Khilafat agitation should be among the political prisoners to be released.[84]

Malaviya made a last-minute appeal to Gandhi a day before he was to lead a deputation to the viceroy requesting him to agree to the proposals conveyed by C.R. Das and Azad. Since Malaviya could not get any assurances from Gandhi he did not have much to offer to the viceroy at the crucial meeting held on 21 December 1921. The viceroy's response to the deputation led by Malaviya was marked by studied courtesy and often some biting comments. He explained his own compulsions, defended strong action against the non-cooperation movement, and cautioned Malaviya and his colleagues against the probable effect of the movement on the British parliament. Thus, the viceroy could not be pursuaded to call a conference and Malaviya's offer fell through.

There is considerable speculation on Malaviya's ultimate failure in calling a round table conference. This can be better explained by referring to the details provided in the viceroy's report of his meeting with Malaviya on 22 December. The viceroy wrote that as soon as the meeting started, Malaviya 'produced a document signed by C.R. Das and ten other leading non-cooperators in Calcutta proposing a Conference to be held in January'. He added, 'While I was discussing this document, which undoubtedly was a great advance by Das and others an Agency public telegram was brought to me containing observations of Gandhi couched in a tone and with conditions which made it impossible to consider the question.'[85] The viceroy was referring to the telegraphic reply sent by Gandhi to C.R. Das and others which has been referred to earlier. With regard to this telegram and the conditions specified in it by Gandhi, the viceroy said, 'When I read it to Malaviya he said—this makes discussion a waste of time.' The viceroy further stated:

> Malaviya was very downcast and really upset by it and said he could not understand it because of a telegram from Gandhi which he then produced to me. This would never have satisfied me as an assurance of his intentions to discontinue all non-cooperation activities regarded as unlawful by Government pending a conference and I so informed Malaviya. It was of course useless discussing further.[86]

The viceroy's report of his final interview with Malaviya confirms the view that he held back because he was not satisfied either by Gandhi's earlier telegram to Malaviya or by his later telegram of the same date to C.R. Das.

Undoubtedly Malaviya exaggerated the value of his interviews with the viceroy who was only manoeuvring for a tactical advantage at the time of the prince's visit and was prepared to negotiate with him and the other nationalist leaders on his own terms. Malaviya was disappointed by Gandhi's response who did not explicitly explain his stand to him.

Malaviya's disappointment over the failure of his efforts was noted by the governor of Bengal in the following words:

> The Pandit seemed to be tired and rather depressed and told me that he was leaving Calcutta that evening and that he intended to go to Ahmedabad. I asked him whether he would care to take a copy of the memorandum which I had just read to him with a view to placing before the leaders of the non-cooperation movement in Bengal. He told me that in view of his recent experience in discussing the situation with them he did not think anything would come of a further discussion.[87]

A controversy relating to the summoning of the late December 1921 conference at Calcutta erupted two years later when C.R. Das spoke about the episode in his speech of 21 December 1923. He said,

You [Gandhi] bungled it and mismanaged it.... The proudest Government did bend to you. The terms came to me and I forwarded them to the headquarters because at that time I was in jail. If I had not been in jail I would have forced the country to accept them. After they had been accepted you would have seen a different state of things.[88]

C.R. Das gave the following analysis of the situation which had prompted him and Azad to respond to Malaviya's call:

> Barely a fortnight was left and within this short period something had to be achieved in order to save the face of the Congress and fulfil the Mahatma's promise regarding Swaraj. If a settlement was made before 21st and all the political prisoners were released it should appear to the popular imagination as a great triumph of the Congress. The Round Table Conference might not be a success but if it failed and the Government refused to concede the popular demands the Congress would resume the fight at any time.[89]

This veiled condemnation of Gandhi created a furore in Congress circles. Various statements and counter-statements, some defending C.R. Das and Malaviya and others condemning them, filled several newspapers for many months.[90] An attempt has been made in the earlier pages to put the record straight regarding the role of the viceroy, Gandhi, and Malaviya in light of the confidential official correspondence. The controversy ended with a clarification by Malaviya who attempted not so much to justify himself as to defend Gandhi: 'We must not lightly blame Mr. Gandhi for it. Mr. Gandhi's opposition to the Prince's visit was based on a principle. He had consistently advocated it for two years.... The time was short, the distance great and the issues grave. However much I may deplore the result we must be fair to Mr. Gandhi.'[91] Malaviya's statement was in keeping with his reputation of an honest politician who attributed his failure to the prevailing circumstances, the shortness of time available for consultation, and the long distance separating the parties to be consulted.

AHMEDABAD CONGRESS SESSION

At the annual Congress session held in the last week of 1921 at Ahmedabad, there were two schools of thought trying to influence Congress policy. Malaviya wanted the Congress to pass a resolution calling for a round table conference. This was defeated at the session by

an overwhelming majority. The impatient elements within the party
showed indignation at the arrests of thousands of Congress workers,
and Hasrat Mohani wanted the Congress to change its creed and methods. Mohani put up a plucky fight for independence on the Congress
platform but was defeated. The delegates passed, by a huge majority, the
main resolution moved by Gandhi calling for aggressive civil disobedience to all government laws and institutions, for non–violence, continuance of public meetings throughout India despite the government
prohibition, and for all Indians to offer themselves peacefully for arrest
by joining the volunteer corps.[92]

LEADERS' MEET AT BOMBAY

Undeterred by the rejection of their proposal at the Ahmedabad
Congress, Malaviya and a few other leaders continued their efforts
for a round table conference as they were particularly against launching a mass civil disobedience movement. Malaviya, M.A. Jinnah, M.R.
Jayakar, and Mrs Annie Besant issued an invitation letter for holding
such a conference in response to which about 300 eminent Indian
leaders, representing all shades of political opinion outside the Congress
fold, met for a conference at Bombay on 14 January 1922.[93] Gandhi
attended in his individual capacity and not as a representative of the
Congress because he did not wish to commit the Congress beforehand
to the decisions that might be taken at the conference. Yet, Gandhi
was keen to 'persuade the Moderate friends to see eye to eye with the
Congress on the issue of freedom of speech and freedom of association'
and desired to 'utilize the services of neutral persons as intermediaries'[94] between the Congress and the government. With this end in
view, he came down personally to take part in the deliberations of the
Bombay Conference. Gandhi's significant assertion at this time was:
'I cannot desert Malaviyaji no matter where I find him for the time
being',[95] which shows that Gandhi was confident of winning Malaviya
back to his side sooner or later.

Malaviya and the other co-sponsors of the Bombay Conference
gave full weight to Gandhi's advice, demanded release of all political
prisoners at the earliest, asked the Government of India to immediately convene a round table conference, and requested the Congress
not to resort to civil disobedience till the viceroy had taken a final

decision on its proposals. Responding positively to the proposals of the Bombay Conference, the Congress suspended the launching of the civil disobedience movement for a fortnight. Gandhi described the conference as both a success and a failure: 'success in that it showed an earnest desire on the part of those who attended to secure a peaceful solution of the present trouble and that it brought together under one roof people possessing divergent views' and a failure because the 'gravity of the real issue did not seem to have been realized at all.' He further added:

> All the resolutions at the Conference can be said to be reasonable. They could have been more elaborate and stronger. If, however, the resolutions which have been passed are acted upon by the Government the foundation of a settlement will have been laid. But there is little hope that the Government will act upon the recommendations of the Conference.[96]

Gandhi's words came true. The resolutions of the Bombay Conference were forwarded to the viceroy on 18 January and a reminder was sent to him on 27 January. His much-awaited reply was not only cold but also disappointing. He informed the organizers of the Bombay Conference that the proposals submitted by them had not been found suitable for any further profitable discussion at the proposed round table conference.[97] It is difficult to avoid concluding that the conciliatory approach previously employed by the viceroy was mainly prompted by a desire to persuade the Congress to withdraw its boycott of the prince's visit and that after the Ahmedabad Congress session, he saw no need to placate it further. At this stage, the viceroy was in no mood to oblige Malaviya and various other Moderate leaders.[98] He noted with alarm Hasrat Mohani's speech which was 'directed to elimination of the doctrine of non-violence from the Congress resolution and that the declaration for complete independence and a Republic received a large amount of support at the Ahmedabad Congress'.[99] The viceroy noted that 'there is an opinion that under the guise of preaching non-violence Gandhi is really preparing eventually for a revolution by violence ... the worst that could be said about them [the non-cooperators] is that they desire to paralyse the Government and force upon a new constitution.'[100] In fact, the viceroy was under strong pressure from his colleagues and the provincial governors not to pay attention to any proposals of negotiations. The governor of Bombay was 'strongly opposed to any conference' and wanted an assurance from the viceroy that there would be 'no negotiations in the future for such a conference'.[101] In the changed political scenario after the Ahmedabad Congress, the Bombay Conference failed to make any impact on the viceroy or his advisors.

The failure of Malaviya's peace parleys, the large-scale arrests of Congress volunteers and leading non-cooperators, and the embargo on public meetings showed that 'matters were reaching a critical state' at this time.[102]

GANDHI'S CALL FOR A CIVIL DISOBEDIENCE CAMPAIGN

There was increasing pressure on Gandhi to give the green signal to launch a mass struggle. Gandhi was, however, cautious from the very beginning and advised his colleagues to move forward selectively and slowly. Instead of a countrywide campaign, he decided to start the civil disobedience movement in a small tehsil, Bardoli, in Surat district alone. Gandhi sent an ultimatum to the viceroy on 1 February informing him of his intention of starting the civil disobedience campaign in a week's time. It was a bold step that only a man like Gandhi could think of and he must have carefully weighed all the pros and cons of Bardoli's 'final and irrevocable choice' for beginning the campaign under his own responsibility.[103] In reply to Gandhi's letter, the viceroy issued a press statement rejecting his demands. He justified the repressive policy as being the result of the Bombay riots and the dangerous lawlessness that followed in various other places. On 7 February, Gandhi sent a rejoinder to the government giving a detailed account of the brutalities resorted to by the provincial governments in Lahore, Jullundur, Dehradun, and parts of UP and Bihar.[104]

Gandhi's ultimatum and rejoinder were sent from Bardoli where he had gone to lead the civil disobedience campaign. The whole country was looking forward to the impending struggle. But no one could foresee that the great battle for freedom planned with such fanfare would be lost before it had even begun. The morning papers on 8 February conveyed news of the tragic event of the massacre of twenty-two policemen at Chauri Chaura near Gorakhpur in UP, which was, for Gandhi, the last straw after all the ugly incidents taking place across the land, and 'on the spur of the moment he decided to scrap the plan of mass struggle'.[105]

Gandhi's decision to undertake a journey to Bombay at this critical juncture, on 8 February 1922, to meet Malaviya, M.R. Jayakar, and other organizers of the Bombay Conference speaks of the importance he attached to confer with them. In fact, the Bombay leaders had been in touch with Gandhi since 30 January and had asked him to postpone the Bardoli programme for at least three days. Gandhi therefore decided to postpone the publication of his ultimatum to the viceroy for three days with the remark that 'the more I think of it, the more clear it is to me that he [the viceroy] cannot call the conference but he can easily adopt my suggestion'.[106]

The secretaries of the Bombay Conference were as keen to discuss further strategy with Malaviya as with Gandhi. In fact, they simultaneously asked both of them to visit Bombay. Malaviya reached the city as per their summons on 7 February. However, in the meanwhile, the perspective of the Bombay Conference suddenly changed because of the Chauri Chaura tragedy. Soon after, Gandhi recorded:

> I am writing this on my way to Bombay. I am proceeding there on the invitation of Bharatbhusan Pandit Malaviya. The Working Committee meeting convened in Bardoli will take place on Saturday (11 February 1922). The reader will have this article in his hands on Sunday [12 February 1922]. As I do not wish to take upon myself the responsibility for suspending the mass civil disobedience I want to consult the Working Committee.[107]

Giving an eyewitness account of Gandhi's participation at the Bombay meeting on 9 February, M.R. Jayakar noted: 'Gandhi spent nearly [the] whole day in conference with us. The result of the Gorakhpur riot [Chauri Chaura] has brought down Gandhi from his high pedestal and we found him pliant and willing not only to postpone civil disobedience but also drop nearly all forms of provocative activities.'[108]

Gandhi has also provided an almost similar account of the nature of the talks held at Bombay:

> I went to Bombay at the instance of Panditji who, together with other friends of the Malaviya Conference, undoubtedly wished to plead with me for a suspension and who were agreeably surprised when I told them that as far as I was concerned my mind was made up but that I had kept it open so that I could discuss the point thoroughly with the members of the Working Committee.[109]

GANDHI'S DECISION TO POSTPONE THE PROPOSED CIVIL DISOBEDIENCE CAMPAIGN

Malaviya moved from Bombay to Bardoli on 11 February, on Gandhi's invitation, to take part in the discussions at the Congress Working Committee (CWC) meeting held there. The committee resolved to suspend indefinitely all forms of civil disobedience and advised people to concertrate on constructive programmes. Gandhi's abrupt and unilateral decision was resented by most of the Congress leaders who were behind bars and thus could not be consulted.

The sequence of events before and after the Chauri Chaura tragedy convincingly prove that Gandhi unilaterally decided to suspend the civil disobedience campaign at Bardoli, that this was entirely his own decision, and that he did not consult anyone as he was fully convinced that this was the only rightful course to be taken at that time. It needs to be emphasized that Gandhi undertook the journey from Bardoli to Bombay after he had made up his mind about the bold step. While doing so, he desired to seek an endorsement of his decision from Malaviya and various other nationalist leaders present in Bombay.

Thus, the opinion of a contemporary writer that 'they strongly urged Gandhi to suspend the civil disobedience movement and Gandhi agreed to do so'[110] does no justice either to the Mahatma or to Malaviya and his associates. There was, however, a lurking fear of Malaviya's role even at this time. This led Gandhi to clear the air with regard to Malaviya's role in the suspension of the civil disobedience campaign after the Chauri Chaura tragedy. In a forthright statement, Gandhi said:

> The charge against Pandit Malaviya has been levelled simply out of ignorance. Panditji had no hand at all in the suspension of civil disobedience. I resolved on it as soon as I heard in Bardoli about the Gorakhpur incident. I even wrote letters to that effect from Bardoli. I consulted colleagues and decided to convene a meeting of the Working Committee. Thereafter I went to Bombay. There is nothing surprising if Panditji also wants the same thing. But the decision was taken, independently of him, by the Working Committee and me.[111]

A few days later Gandhi made yet another effort to explain that Malaviya played no part in advising him to suspend the civil disobedience campaign:

I assure the public that Pandit Malaviyaji had absolutely no hand in shaping my decision. I have often yielded to Panditji and it is always a pleasure for me to yield to him whenever I can and always painful to differ from one who has an unrivalled record of public service and who is sacrifice personified. But so far as the decision of suspension is concerned I arrived at it on my reading the detailed report of the Chauri Chaura tragedy in the *Chronicle*. It was in Bardoli that telegrams were sent convening the Working Committee meeting and it was in Bardoli that I sent a letter to the members of the Working Committee advising them of my desire to suspend civil disobedience.[112]

Gandhi's statements with regard to the decision of the suspension of the civil disobedience at Bardoli and his all-out efforts to clear the misgivings raised about Malaviya's role were aimed at setting to rest the widespread rumours prevailing at that time. As the two leaders were in close touch with each other before and after the Working Committee meeting at Bardoli on 11–12 February, there was widespread speculation that at some stage or the other Malaviya successfully prevailed upon Gandhi to apply brakes on the proposed movement.

Soon after the news of the revocation of the civil disobedience movement reached the viceroy, he issued orders for Gandhi to be arrested. The viceroy was under heavy pressure for quite some time to take action against Gandhi. Montagu was asking him to arrest Gandhi and several provincial governors were also requesting the viceroy to take a similar step. But the viceroy was buying time and perhaps looking forward to the final decision taken by Gandhi regarding the civil disobedience movement. It was at this juncture that Malaviya requested an interview with the viceroy. His request was turned down as the viceroy wanted to avoid any discussion with Malaviya on Gandhi's imminent arrest. The viceroy wrote, 'A request was made by Malaviya for an interview to which my Private Secretary without reference to me but with knowledge of my views replied that I was overwhelmingly busy.'[113] The viceroy's refusal to meet Malaviya shows that in spite of all his desires to come to Gandhi's rescue, he was denied any opportunity to do so.

Gandhi was arrested at Sabarmati Ashram on 10 March; a trial was held eight days later at the Ahmedabad sessions court and, on the same day, he was sentenced to six years' imprisonment. Malaviya was with Gandhi at the time the sentence was announced and was shocked at the harsh treatment meted out to the great leader.

It is significant that Gandhi always thought that Malaviya's heart lay in the non-cooperation campaign. He observed in February 1922: 'I certainly feel that Pandit Malaviya has already come into the movement. It is not possible for him to keep away from the Congress or from danger.'[114] Reiterating similar views, he wrote, 'If Panditji is not in jail today it is not because he is afraid of it but because he is borne down with anxiety and torn asunder by an external conflict of duty.'[115] Gandhi had the same opinion in mind when he wrote to M.R. Jayakar that it was only 'for the time being' that Malaviya was not entirely in his camp.[116]

Thus, Malaviya maintained close relations with Gandhi all along the period of the non-cooperation movement. He was not directly involved in the campaign and yet could not keep himself away from it completely. In spite of his close committment to the Congress and to Gandhi, he was hesitant until the last moment and did not boldly plunge into the struggle. He was torn between his loyalty to the government and that to the Congress and missed the opportunity of boldly standing by Gandhi's side at this critical juncture. As a result of his indecision during these eventful years, Malaviya lost much of his influence in the nationalist organization, a postion from which he could never recover in the next few decades.

NOTES

1. *Leader*, 8 June 1920.
2. Home Poll, B Proceedings, July 1920, no. 109.
3. Motilal Nehru to Jawaharlal Nehru, 16 June 1920, *Selected Works of Motilal Nehru* (henceforth *SWMN*), vol. II, 156.
4. *CWMG*, vol. 18, p. 121.
5. *CWMG*, vol. 18, p. 123.
6. *CWMG*, vol. 18, p. 126.
7. *CWMG*, vol. 18, p. 126.
8. Gandhi, *An Autobiography*, p. 379.
9. *Bombay Chronicle*, 9 September 1920.
10. *Leader*, 17 September 1920.
11. Jayakar, *Story of My Life*, vol. I, p. 371.
12. *CWMG*, vol. 18, p. 255.
13. *CWMG*, vol. 18, p. 256.
14. Diary of G.S. Khaperde, 7 September 1920, Khaperde Papers.
15. *New India*, 10 September 1920.

16. *Aaj*, 12 September 1920.
17. Bayly, *Local Roots of Indian Politics* pp. 10–14, p. 256.
18. Motilal Nehru to Jawaharlal Nehru, 16 June 1920, Motilal Nehru Papers, vol. II, p. 156.
19. Malaviya's letters, *Leader*, 3, 6, 7 October 1920.
20. P.D. Reeves, B.D. Graham, and J.M. Goodman, eds, *A Handbook to Elections in Uttar Pradesh* (New Delhi, 1975), p. 16.
21. *CWMG*, vol. 19, p. 146.
22. *Harijan*, 22 September 1920.
23. Sitaramayya, *History of the Congress*, p. 318.
24. *Young India*, 27 October 1920.
25. *Nawajiwan*, 18 November 1920.
26. *CWMG*, vol. 19, p. 14.
27. *CWMG*, vol. 19, p. 41.
28. *CWMG*, vol. 19, p. 25.
29. *CWMG*, vol. 19, p. 26.
30. Sita Ram Chaturvedi, ed., *Mahamana Pandit Madan Mohan Malaviya*, (Varanasi, 1936), p. 317.
31. Gandhi to Sarla Devi Chowdharani, 28 November 1920, *CWMG*, vol. 19, p. 41.
32. Tendulkar, *Mahatma*, vol. II, p. 28.
33. Governor of Bombay to Chelmsford, 7 December 1920, Chelmsford Papers.
34. *Bombay Chronicle*, 25 December 1920.
35. *CWMG*, vol. 19, p. 241.
36. Report of the Nagpur session of 1920, AICC Papers, 226/1920.
37. *CWMG*, vol. 19, p. 165.
38. R.C. Majumdar, *History of the Freedom Movement in India*, vol. II (Calcutta, 1964), p. 117.
39. Telegram from Viceroy to Secretary of State, 28 April 1921, Reading Papers, no. 101.
40. Telegram from Viceroy to Secretary of State, 28 April 1921.
41. *CWMG*, vol. 20, p. 135.
42. Telegram from Reading to the Secretary of State, 14 May 1921, Reading Papers.
43. Telegram from Reading to the Secretary of State, 14 May 1921.
44. Reading to Ronaldshay, 15 June 1921, Reading Papers.
45. *CWMG*, vol. 20, p. 231.
46. *CWMG*, vol. 20, p. 231.
47. Telegram from Gandhi to Malaviya, 28 June 1921, *CWMG*, vol. 20, p. 232.
48. Telegram from Viceroy to Secretary of State, 23 June 1921, no. 533, Reading Papers.

49. Telegram from Viceroy to Secretary of State, 23 June 1921, no. 533, Reading Papers.
50. Gandhi's note, 29 June 1921, *CWMG*, vol. 20, p. 285.
51. *Young India*, 4 August 1921, *CWMG*, vol. 20, pp. 537–8.
52. Reading to Montagu, 14 July 1921, no. 15, Roll I, Reading Papers.
53. Telegram from Viceroy to Secretary of State, 6 July 1921, no. 581, Reading Papers.
54. Reading to Montagu, 9 June 1921, Reading Papers.
55. Montagu to Reading, 6 July 1921, no. 14, Reading Papers.
56. D.A. Low, *Britain and Indian Nationalism* (Cambridge, 1997), p. 35.
57. Low, *Britain and Indian Nationalism*, p. 17.
58. Telegram from Reading to Montagu, 6 July 1921, Reading Papers, no. 581.
59. Telegram from Reading to Montagu, 6 July 1921, Reading Papers, no. 581.
60. Telegram from Reading to Montagu 6 July 1921, Reading Papers, no. 581.
61. Telegram from Reading to Montagu 6 July 1921, Reading Papers, no. 581.
62. *Times of India*, 4 July 1921.
63. Reading to Montagu, 14 July 1921, Reading Papers, no. 15.
64. Reading to Montagu, 4 August 1921, Reading Papers, no. 11.
65. Telegram from Reading to Montagu, 14 November 1921, Reading Papers, no. 1148.
66. Telegram from the Viceroy to the Secretary of State, 14 November 1921, Reading Papers, no. 1148.
67. Reading to Harcourt Butler, 15 July 1921, Reading Papers, no. 186.
68. Harcourt Butler to Reading, 21 July 1921, Reading Papers.
69. *Aaj*, 28 November 1921.
70. S.D. Waley, *E.S. Montagu* (London, 1923), p. 263.
71. Harcourt Butler to Reading, 17 December 1921, Reading Papers, no. 721.
72. Subhash Chandra Bose, *The Indian Struggle 1920–1942* (Calcutta, 1964), p. 66.
73. Telegram from Reading to Montagu, 24 November 1921, Reading Papers, no. 1207.
74. Telegram from Reading to Provincial Governors, 19 December 1921, Reading Papers, no. 556.
75. Mrs Annie Besant to Reading, 17 December 1921, Reading Papers.
76. Telegram from Reading to Montagu, 14 November 1921, Reading Papers, no. 1148.
77. Telegram from Reading to Montagu, 24 November 1921, Reading Papers.
78. Malaviya to Gandhi, 16 December 1921, *CWMG*, vol. 21, p. 52.
79. Mrs Annie Besant to Reading, 17 December 1921, Reading Papers, no. 722.

80. Telegram from C.R. Das and A.K. Azad to Gandhi, 19 December 1921, *CWMG*, vol. 21, p. 55.

81. Jayakar, *Story of My Life*, vol. I, p. 507.

82. J. Dwarkadas to T.B. Sapru, 18 December 1921, Reading Papers.

83. Gandhi to Malaviya, 19 December 1921, *CWMG*, vol. 21, p. 54.

84. Gandhi to C.R. Das and A.K. Azad, 19 December 1921, *CWMG*, vol. 21, p. 55.

85. Telegram from the Viceroy to the Secretary of State, 24 December 1921, Reading Papers, no. 1401.

86. Telegram from the Viceroy to the Secretary of State, 24 December 1921, Reading Papers, no. 1401.

87. Ronaldshay to Reading, 26 December 1921, Reading Papers, no. 746(a).

88. *Leader*, 22 December 1923.

89. C.R. Das's speech, *Voice of India*, 16 June 1923, Madras edition

90. Jayakar, *Story of My Life*, vol. I, p. 509.

91. Sitaramayya, *History of the Congress*, p. 382.

92. Tendulkar, *Mahatma*, vol. I, p. 72.

93. Jayakar, *Story of My Life*, vol. I, p. 220.

94. Gandhi's article entitled 'Joint Conference', dated 21 February 1922, *CWMG*, vol. 22, pp. 232–3.

95. Gandhi to M.R. Jayakar, 15 January 1922, *CWMG*, vol. 22, p. 552.

96. Malaviya Conference, *CWMG*, vol. 22, p. 214.

97. Reading to Malaviya, 29 January 1922, Reading Papers.

98. Reading to Malaviya, 29 January 1922, Reading Papers.

99. Reading to Montagu, 5 January 1922, Reading Papers, no. 1.

100. Reading to Montagu, 5 January 1922, Reading Papers, no. 1.

101. Reading to Montagu, 15 January 1922, Reading Papers, no. 1.

102. Jayakar, *Story of My Life*, vol. I, p. 552.

103. Gandhi to the Viceroy, 1 February 1920, vol. 22, p. 256.

104. *CWMG*, vol. 22, pp. 302–4.

105. Tendulkar, *Mahatma*, vol. I, p. 82.

106. Gandhi to M.R. Jayakar, 31 January 1922, in Jayakar, *Story of My Life*, vol. I, p. 554.

107. Gorakhpur Tragedy, 12 February 1922, *CWMG*, vol. 22, 386–7.

108. Jayakar, *Story of My Life*, vol. 1, p. 555.

109. 'My Notes', *Young India*, 23 February 1922, *CWMG*, vol. 22, p. 449.

110. R.C. Majumdar, *History of the Freedom Movement in India*, vol. III (Calcutta, 1969), p. 156.

111. 'What about Those in Jail', 19 February 1922, *Navajivan*, *CWMG*, vol. 22, pp. 428–9.

112. 'My Notes', *Young India*, 23 February 1922, *CWMG*, vol. 22, p. 449.

113.   Reading to Willingdon, 1 March 1922, Reading Papers.

114.   'My Notes', *Young India*, 23 February 1922, *CWMG*, vol. 22, pp. 445–8.

115.   'What about Those in Jail', 19 February 1922, *Navajivan*, *CWMG*,
vol. 22, pp. 428–9.

116.   Gandhi to M.R. Jayakar, 15 January 1922, *CWMG*, vol. 22, no. 79.

6 The Hindu Mahasabha

Malaviya's wide range of activities such as the establishment of major newspapers like the *Leader* and *Abhudaya*, his educational concerns reflected in the Hindu Boarding House at Allahabad and his life's work, the Banaras Hindu University, and his attempts to promote Hindi through the Nagri Pracharni Sabha and the Hindi Sahitya Sammelan in Prayag were deeply influenced by his belief that service to the community went together with service to the country. It reflected the existence of strong community concerns in his vision of Indian nationalism. Malaviya was deeply influenced by the Hindu resurgence of the late nineteenth century. The presence of Hindu imagery in his nationalist discourse provides strong evidence of the influence exerted by Hindu revivalist sensibility on his nationalist politics. As early as in the 1880s, Malaviya began to take interest in the activities of the newly established Hindu Samaj in Allahabad and explained that its purpose was to 'encourage the uplift of the Hindus to nurture their self-dependence and to present a strong face to their enemies'.[1] But his political vision was very much wider. He wrote in 1906:

> It is not the Hindus alone who live in Hindustan. Hindustan is no longer exclusively their country. Just as Hindustan is the beloved birth place of the Hindus so it is of the Muslims too. Both these communities now live here and will always live here.... To establish real affection and brotherly love among these communities and all the communities of India is the greatest duty before us all.[2]

Speaking in the Imperial Legislative Council on the introduction of the Banaras Hindu University Bill in March 1915, Malaviya declared in a similar vein that the university would be a denominational but not a sectarian institution. The broad parameters of his vision of Indian society and culture was shared by a wide variety of contemporary politicians.

Collective consciousness of the Hindu community took an organizational form when a number of Hindu bodies were formed in Punjab and UP, which prepared the ground for the formation of an all-India body—the Hindu Mahasabha.

ACTIVITIES OF THE HINDU SABHAS

In its initial phase the Hindu Sabha was a purely reactive phenomenon, an attempt to counter Muslim communal organization for the furtherance of Muslim interests, by means of Hindu self-organization for the defence of Hindu interests. The first major organization of the Hindus was formed in Punjab in December 1906 with the help of several provincial leaders including Lala Lajpat Rai, Harikrishan Lal, and R.R. Sahni. Within a few years, every district of Punjab had a Hindu Sabha affiliated with the provincial body. A deputation of prominent members of the Punjab Hindu Sabha met Lord Minto in 1909 to protest against the decision to introduce a separate electorate for Muslims under the Indian Councils Act of 1909. The first Provincial Hindu Conference was held at Lahore in October 1909 under the chairmanship of P.C. Chatterjee. The agenda of the conference and its deliberations highlighted the need for broad Hindu unity at the all-India level. The provincial Hindu conferences were further held in Multan, Amritsar, Delhi, and Ambala between 1910 and 1913.

During the Allahabad Congress session of 1910, a section of Congressmen felt the need to extend support to the demand for establishing a Hindu Sabha. Writing about the session, Motilal Nehru stated:

> Another new feature of the Congress week has been that it has given birth to an All India Hindu Sabha ... the great majority of the so called leaders in Upper India, especially those of the Punjab, had worked themselves to a high pitch and could not be made listen to reason.[3]

As Motilal Nehru's testimony confirms, this All-India Hindu Sabha was originally a forum comprising Congressmen. The Hindu politicians who founded the Hindu Sabha attempted to unite all sections of the community on a single platform in order to defend their interests. It did not make any headway in its endeavour. All these developments did not leave Malaviya unaffected. In various articles and editorials published in his weekly, *Abhudaya*, Malaviya lamented the government's policy of divide and rule, expressed his strong disapproval of the separate representation of Muslims, and cautioned Muslims against depending too much on the favours of the Government.[4] In his presidential address of the Congress session of 1909, he criticized the Hindu leaders who thought of severing connections with the Congress and had supported the idea of starting another organization on the ground that the Congress was ignoring Hindu interests.[5] With these ideas in mind, Malaviya kept away from any Hindu Sabha or a Hindu conference up to 1914.

Meanwhile the dream of a broader Hindu organization gradually found adherents in several parts of northern India and, ultimately, they were successful in forming an All-India Hindu Sabha at Haridwar in April 1915. The Hindu Sabha so organized, wanted to build up 'greater union and solidarity among all sections of the Hindu community', promote their education, ameliorate and improve their condition, and 'promote good feelings between Hindus and other communities of India'.[6] There was nothing in the goals of the Hindu Sabha Conference at this time that suggested a militant and anti-Congress approach that it would later go on to take.

MALAVIYA'S LINKS WITH THE MAHASABHA

Malaviya appeared for the first time on the platform of the Hindu Mahasabha in August 1916 at Banaras. The thrust of his speech was that the unity and amity among different communities could only be based on justice and fair play. It was therefore the responsibility not only of the Hindus but also of others to work for that unity in India.[7] An attempt in this direction was made in the famous Congress–League Pact of 1916, otherwise known as the Lucknow Pact. Malaviya was entirely opposed to the communal aspects of the pact but kept quiet largely because of the support extended to the measure by Tilak.[8] However, the Hindu Mahasabha was dismayed by the stand taken by the Congress in 1916. It argued that if Tilak could make such concessions, others might go even further in this direction in future. Opposition to the Lucknow Pact was particularly strong in Punjab. The Punjab Hindu Sabha raised a hue and cry against the provisions of the pact in several meetings all over the province. However, keeping in view the all-India interest of forging communal harmony between the Hindus and Muslims, they did not demand the rejection of the measure. Even so, the provincial Hindu leaders expressed their disappointment at the soft stand taken by Malaviya and other senior leaders at the Lucknow Congress session.[9] The 1918 session of the Hindu Mahasabha later made a symbolic protest against the pact.[10] When Gandhi decided to extend the support of the Congress to the Khilafat movement, Malaviya was in complete agreement with his move.[11] One of the highlights of the Khilafat agitation was that the pioneer of the Hindu Mahasabha, Swami Shraddhanand, spoke at Jama Masjid to the Muslims of Delhi in favour of the Khilafat cause.[12]

In its first phase, up to 1922, the Hindu Mahasabha was at best an inter-provincial organization linking Hindu movements in UP and Punjab. As its conferences were held in conjunction with the annual Congress sessions, it attracted casual support from other provinces. Predominnntly urban in character, it was concentrated in the larger trading cities of northern India. A small groups of professionals, mainly lawyers and the banking and landholding families, controlled the Mahasabha. The Hindu Mahasabha and the Congress had much in common as the same men who had been pioneers in the Congress also influenced the Mahasabha's activities. During the early period of its emergence and growth, Malaviya was sympathetic towards its demands and maintained contacts with some of the Mahasabha leaders. Beyond this, he did not play any significant role in its meetings. In fact, Malaviya kept himself away from the Mahasabha and did not take much interest in its activities.

IMPACT OF THE NON–COOPERATION MOVEMENT AND THE MOPLAH RIOTS

The most alarming development after the sudden suspension of the non-cooperation movement was the increasing communal distrust resulting in numerous Hindu–Muslim riots in different parts of the country. The Hindu–Muslim unity of the years of the non-cooperation movement was now a 'mere memory'; 'trust had given way to distrust' and 'there was a new bitterness in politics'.[13] This was a sad anti-climax to the spirit of fraternization so assidously built by Gandhi.

By bringing in the *ulama* (a body of Muslim scholars) and by overtly using a religious symbol, the Khilafat movement evoked religious emotions among the Muslim masses. Violent tendencies appeared in the Khilafat movement as the masses lost self-discipline and the leaders failed to control them. The worst case was the Moplah uprising in Malabar in August 1921 where the Moplah peasants, emboldened by the Khilafat spirit, rose against the Hindu landlords and the government. For months, the press in northern India was obsessed with detailed accounts of the forced conversions of Hindus in Malabar and with the means of reclaiming their lost brothers.

The question of forcible conversions was too sensitive an issue for those involved and the nationalist leaders sought to minimize the divisive effects of the Moplah rebellion on the Hindus. In spite of their efforts, the reports of the atrocities and forcible conversions, whether exaggerated or not, stirred fears of violence among the Hindus.[14] Thus the alliance between the Khilafat movement and the Congress proved artificial and short-lived. Furthermore, the alliance was responsible for the injection of an overdose of religion into politics. When the bubble of unity was burst—first by the Moplah atrocities in Malabar and then by the suspension of the non-cooperation movement by Gandhi—the two communities drifted apart and fell back to their old positions and whipped up old prejudices and fears with renewed vehemence. The result was that the Muslim League and the Hindu Mahasabha, whose activities were dormant during the days of non-cooperation, became more active with communalist politics.

The year 1922 was a turning point in the history of the Mahasabha, largely due to events which dramatized a Muslim threat to the Hindu community. During the observance of Muharram in September 1922, there was a riot in Multan. It started when Muslim gangs took revenge because they had information that stones were thrown at a *tazia* procession (taken out every year during the Muharram festival of the Muslims) from the roofs of the houses belonging to Hindu families. Their homes were looted, temples desecrated, and there were reports that a few Hindu women were ravished, injured, or killed.[15] At this time, Malaviya was in Punjab investigating the Akali Sikh troubles of Guru Ka Bagh. Along with Rajendra Prasad and Hakim Ajmal Khan, Malaviya visited Multan as a member of the subcommittee appointed by the Congress. He addressed largely attended public meetings in

Amritsar and Lahore and heard details of heart-rending incidents about
the riots. He criticized Hindus for their failure to organize their own
defence and proposed the formation of citizen guard units regardless of
religious affiliations. He impressed upon the Hindus the need for unity
with a view to resisisting attacks on their lives and property.[16]

The unfortunate result of the Moplah revolt in combination with
the Multan riots was the increasing communal distrust between the
two communities that led Malaviya to advise the Hindus to organize
and defend themselves. The riots that broke out in 1922 and 1923 led
to the revival the Hindu Mahasabha.

GAYA SESSION OF THE MAHASABHA

The Hindu Mahasabha held its important annual conference at the
Congress session grounds in Gaya in the last week of December 1922
with Rajendra Prasad as the chairman of the Reception Committee
and Malaviya as its President.[17] Malaviya set the tone of the session by
terming the level of degeneration of the Hindu community the worst
of any in India, as evidenced by the low birth rate, high death rate, lower
longevity, and cowardice in the face of attack. He blamed the Hindu
weakness for the poor state of Hindu–Muslim relations, claiming that
it invited assault by 'the bad elements among the Muslims'. Malaviya
maintained that the Hindu 'dharma' required that its followers be
non-agressive and show respect for all religious.[18] It also required that
they should give their lives, if necessary, in order to defend themselves
when under attack. He proposed the formation of Hindu Sabhas in
every village to promote Hindu unity and regeneration, which in turn
would eventually contribute to the improvement of inter-communal
relations. The resolutions adopted in the Mahasabha session echoed
Malaviya's speech and evidenced a more militant stance. One of these
called upon the Hindu religious leaders of Malabar to 'unhesitatingly
re-embrace all the converts and restore them to their former caste and
social status'. Another resolution called for an improved and extended
network of Hindu organizations 'for the fulfilment of the first essential
condition of attaining Swaraj viz. Hindu–Muslim unity as well as the
self-preservation and religious safety of the Hindu community'.[19]

In the first half of 1923, Hindu leaders were looking to the past
and the future in the course of reassessing their strategies and goals. A

general attitude becoming influential among Hindus that was cutting across political and religious lines was expressed in a newspaper editorial in the following words:

> Far-seeing Hindu leaders have for long fought against the communal spirit of the Mahommedans, but their efforts have been of no avail. The Mahommedans have, if anything, become more communal than ever before. Nothing is now left for the Hindus but to organise themselves certainly not with a view to encroach the legitimate rights of Musalmans but to protect their rights from beeing encroached upon by others. They must, as a community, inspire respect before they can have unity on reasonable and equal terms with the Muslims.[20]

BANARAS SESSION OF THE MAHASABHA

Contrary to earlier practice, the Hindu Mahasabha session held in Banaras in August 1923 did not coincide with the annual Congress session. In order to stimulate attendance, Malaviya published an appeal in which he referred to the 'lamentable condition of the Hindus', the 'inability of the community to defend itself', and held out the hope that 'the meeting at Benaras would consider the remedial measures as well as a series of important social and religious issues'.[21] An estimated 1,500 delegates attended the Mahasabha session at Banaras and there were 4,000 visitors in attendance, including representatives of the Jain, Buddhist, Parsi, and Sikh communities. A Sanskrit motto over the gateway of the pandal warned that by killing religion you are yourself killed and by protecting it you are yourself protected.[22] That may have indicated the spirit of the session, but giving shape to it in the deliberations, resolutions, and activities of the meeting proved to be a challenging task. Malaviya played a crucial role in moderating the views of diverse Hindu interests.

Defining the task before the conference, the chairman of the Reception Committee, Raja Moti Chand, pointed out that the Mahasabha's 'aim was to unite the different sects of Hindus in a bond of love'. A prominent participant, C.Y. Chintamani, desired that 'the result of the success of this movement would be not an increase in the differences between Hindus and Mahomedans but greater unification'.[23]

In his long address, Malaviya began with the review of the history of the Hindus from ancient times to the Muslim conquest and British rule, and noted that in the latter period the community had begun to suffer from many evils in its society. He stressed that strength and consolidation were the keys to repair the damage done to Hinduism and proposed a number of restoratives including celibacy, minimum age for marriage, female education, and dowry expenses. Rejecting the charge that in seeking to reconstruct the society, Hindus had any sinister motives or designs against the Muslims, he declared, 'I solemnly affirm before God that I never mean to hurt Muslims or desire supremacy of Hindus over Muslims. If that be my sentiment God may give me the greatest punishment.'[24] Nor was he prepared to agree that there was any valid reason for apprehensions regarding the fate and future of Hindu–Muslim unity in case the Hindu Mahasabha succeeded in its endeavours to breathe a new life and spirit into Hindu society. Malaviya repeatedly blamed a handful of bad elements for the Hindu–Muslim riots and called upon the Hindus to reorganize themselves against such elements in different parts of the country. He emphasized the need of harmonious communal relations between the two communities in the beginning as well as the concluding part of his presidential address.

He warned his supporters against insulting or showing any disrespect to other religions in the following words: 'Hindu–Muslim unity is an essential condition for the attainment of Swaraj. Therefore, look with reverence at places of worship of other religions' mosques and churches, speak with respect with followers of other religions, and give no cause of complaint in these respects.'[25]

The controversial issues before the conference were *shuddhi* (a process of 'purifying' certain Muslims and admitting them into the Hindu fold) and untouchability. As an arbiter behind the scenes, Malaviya attempted to assist the Sanatanists and the Arya Samajists to come to an agreement. Debate in the Subjects Committee over the wording of the untouchability resolution was so heated that, at one point, a group of Sanatanist pandits walked out. They returned only after Malaviya's intervention. To avoid an open split, the Mahasabha accepted a compromise resolution proposed by Swami Shraddhanand that acknowledged the need for making arrangements to allow untouchables to draw water, enter schools and temples, and sit in public places. The resolution was adopted largely due to Malaviya's efforts. The shuddhi question was subjected to a similar compromise.[26]

The Banaras session of the Mahasabha attracted attention all over India and various leading newspapers offered editorial comments. The *Daily Express* welcomed Malaviya's 'moving appeal',[27] the *Hindu* wrote that the 'solemn presidential address' and the 'declaration of the Sabha of inter-communal unity ... leaves no room for apprehension in the matter'.[28] The *Amrita Bazar Patrika* noted that there was 'great earnestness and enthusiasm' all along the session.[29] The *Indian Social Reformer* was happy that the 'first blow has been struck' by Malaviya against Hindu orthodoxy.[30] The *Justice* was of the view that 'it has to be gratefully acknowledged that Malaviya gave a right lead'.[31] These leading newspapers of the country desired that the Hindu Mahasabha fight against the prevailing social evils of the Hindu society. However, the Urdu press expressed hostility to Malaviya's efforts from the very beginning. The *Medina* wrote that his effort was to 'annihilate Islam from India'.[32]

Malaviya actively led the Mahasabha for five years from 1922 to 1927, attended its sessions, and was actively involved with its affairs. As one of its top-most leaders, Malaviya influenced the Mahasabha's decisions during these years. Therefore, it would be appropriate to probe his association with the Mahasabha during this period as well as his disenchantment from it thereafter. Since the membership of the Congress and the Mahasabha were not mutually exclusive, they often held their annual sessions together, with the result that a considerable number of Congressmen came under the influence of the Mahasabha.[33]

The Hindu Mahasabha revival of 1923 was the product of developments of events in Punjab and UP and was closely linked with the re-awakening of religious enthusiasm in reaction to Khilafat revivalism. Its emphasis upon religious issues, shuddhi, and reclamation of untouchables was a response to the quickening pace of social reform within Hindu society. The Mahasabha worked to unite a variety of movements and carried out various activities through the Arya Samaj, the Sanatan Dharma Sabha, the Hindu societies, and various caste associations. The Mahasabha was still a loose organization, essentially a platform for the Hindu unity movement in northern India. A prominent Hindi nationalist weekly, *Pratap*, editorially commented that the Mahasabha was the 'natural result' of the understanding of those Hindus who thought that 'it was necessary for the Hindus to organize themselves against the attacks of Muslims'. The paper conceded that such an organization would necessarily be 'reactive' and 'confrontationist' in nature.[34]

BELGAUM SESSION

The next session of the Mahasabha was held at Belgaum in December 1924 at the same time and place as the annual session of the Congress, which was presided over by Gandhi. It was attended by several leading Congress leaders including Gandhi, Motilal Nehru, Lajpat Rai, C.R. Das, Satyamurti, Swami Shraddhanand, and the Ali brothers. Malaviya dominated the proceedings and was delighted at the favourable response received from several provinces. Immediately after the Belgaum session, Malaviya gave the following account of the progress of the Mahasabha:

> There has been a very great change in favour of the Hindu Mahasabha movement since we talked of it at Gaya. The last session at Belgaum was a great success. Nearly all the prominent Hindu leaders have come round to the opinion that along with the Congress movement there must be the Hindu Mahasabha movement and that it should not confine itself to questions of socio-religious character but should deal with political questions also as far us they affect the Hindus.[35]

The Belgaum session of the Mahasabha marked an increased concern about the communal electorates in the anticipated constitutional reforms. A committee was appointed under the chairmanship of Lala Lajpat Rai 'to ascertain and formulate Hindu opinion on the subject of Hindu–Muslim problem'.[36] The other members of the committee were C.Y. Chintamani, Rajendra Prasad, B.S. Moonje, Narendra Nath, and Hans Raj. Malaviya explained the need for such an enquiry in the following words:

> The main question is whether representation in the Legislatures should be based upon the proportion of Hindus and Musalmans in the population or whether it should be on non-communal general qualifications and also whether the principle should be extended to local boards and the services.[37]

When the Congress organized an All Parties Conference in Delhi in January 1925 under the chairmanship of Gandhi, several political parties, groups, and interests took part in its deliberations. The Mahasabha was represented in the conference by the members of the committee appointed earlier under the chairmanship of Lala Lajpat Rai. The conference failed to arrive at any definite conclusions as several leaders were more interested in an 'unseemly selfish scramble for power and office' and 'Muslim representatives' appetite had grown by what it had fed on'. Malaviya urged Muslims to lay their cards on the table and explain what they wanted so that the Mahasabha could consult the Hindu community and arrive at conclusions.[38] The prevailing mood of suspicion between the Hindu and Muslim representatives led to the failure of this conference.

The regular session of the Mahasabha was held in Calcutta in April 1925. The Hindu–Muslim tragedy of Kohat and prohibition of playing music before the mosques by Hindus at Allahabad and other places created an atmosphere of bitterness. These issues were brought before the representatives of the session by Malaviya who recorded his protest against the policies of different provincial governments. Malaviya further demanded effective relief for those who were suffering after the Kohat tragedy. The Mahasabha also adopted a resolution opposing separate communal representation on the ground that it was 'harmful and detrimental' to the creation of national solidarity.[39]

Malaviya attempted to use the Mahasabha forum for social reforms such as the uplift of backward sections of society and improvement of the condition of women as he was fully aware of the fact that without undertaking these measures, Hindus were likely to remain backward and disunited. Foremost among Malaviya's activities were those that were against untouchability. He attached the highest importance to the problems of the people in these social groups in different Mahasabha sessions. In the Delhi session of the Mahasabha that was held in March 1926, serious differences emerged during discussions over the resolutions on various social reforms proposed by the organizers. Malaviya mediated between those who supported progressive measures and the orthodox section among the Hindus. It was with great difficulty and because of Malaviya's persuasion that the delegates agreed to the wording of the resolutions recommending social changes in the Hindu society.[40]

The ascendancy of the Arya Samajists in the Mahasabha was the result of local conditions in UP and Punjab and affected the new alignments that were to dominate the movement. The chief exponent of the shuddhi movement, Swami Shraddhanand, secured Malaviya's help in bringing back a large number of Malkhana Rajputs into the fold of Hinduism. When the Mahasabha adopted the shuddhi programme as its own, it led to considerable tensions between Hindus and Muslims.[41]

Although Malaviya was fully aware of the risks involved in the adoption of the shuddhi programme by the Mahasabha, he succumbed to the demand of the Arya Samajists.

THE MAHASABHA AND ELECTORAL POLITICS

Since 1926, the Mahasabha began to move towards becoming a more explicitly political organization. When it met in Delhi that year, Bhai Parmanand conducted an intensive campaign to convince delegates that the Mahasabha should become a political party so that Hindus would be sure to find condidates in the third election to the provincial legislative councils later that year. There were heated discussions on this proposal as several leading figures of the Mahasabha, including Malaviya and Lala Lajpat Rai, were unwilling to allow the Mahasabha to directly participate in the forthcoming elections. Ultimately, a compromise was reached authorizing the Provincial Hindu Sabhas to take all proper steps, which included putting forward or supporting its own candidates, for the next elections. The Mahasabha itself would not nominate candidates but its provincial branches could do so or could support candidates of other parties. The compromise was a victory for Malaviya as the old core of the Mahasabha from UP and Punjab wanted the oraganization to work for Hindu unity through a moderate political programme.

The Mahasabha's decision to enter the political arena came at a time when the Swaraj Party had gained complete control of the Congress. Even though the Swaraj Party kept its own identity intact, it had assumed full authority to take part in the next elections on behalf of the Congress as it thought fit and proper. Under the circumstances, Motilal Nehru began to guide the Congress as well as the Swaraj Party. In March 1926 he attended the Delhi session of the Mahasabha in an attempt to bring it under the Congress fold. The elder Nehru suggested that 'the true remedy lay in Hindusabha as a body joining the Indian National Congress and thereby influencing the whole programme of work in the councils'. In this appeal Motilal Nehru pointed out:

> There is no use concealing the fact that the Indian National Congress is predominantly a Hindu organization. It started and developed as such and whatever strength it received from the Musalmans from time to time is fast decreasing by the revival of independent Muslim Organizations.[42]

During the middle of 1926, Malaviya was busy in his negotiations with the Responsivists and the Swaraj Party. He discussed various proposals with them, had his eyes set on UP and Punjab, and with this end in view, desired to arrive at an understanding with the Swarajists as well. Motilal Nehru was, however, in no mood to oblige Malaviya and had his own plans to turn the tables on him. Throughout July and August he supported moves to capture the Bihar and UP Hindu Sabhas so as to win their support in favour of the Congress candidates for the membership of the provincial councils. Motilal outlined his plan of action in the following words:

> I cannot understand Malaviyaji's game and have not heard what he intends to do in the matter of U.P. elections. The Bihar Hindu Sabha has thrown him overboard and bodily adopted the whole list of nominations made by the Congress Executive. I am told a meeting of the U.P. section of the Hindu Sabha was to be held about the end of last month but it has not taken place. I am trying to get the U.P. section to follow the example of Bihar and there is every hope of success.[43]

Motilal Nehru intended to swamp the annual conference of the Agra Hindu Sabha in support of the anti-Malaviya faction. He deputed Sitla Sahai to execute the plan and he immediately went into action. Sahai reported to Motilal on 13 July that 'the election comes off on the 1 of August and Pandit Madan Mohan Malaviya will be present on the occasion. It is very probable that we may capture the Hindu Sabha. I am glad to inform you that the whole affair is quite confidential and the Hindu Mahasabha is unaware of our intentions.'[44] A week later he informed Motilal Nehru: 'We are trying our best to capture the Hindu Sabha and you will judge our effort by the result.'[45] On the eve of the election for the post of the president of the Provincial Hindu Sabha, a confident Sitla Sahai wrote again:

> The Hindu Sabha people are still unaware. Our men will remain solid. We will ask Anandi Prasad Dubey to announce his candidature for Presidentship. This is sure to create differences in the Hindu Sabha members for Raja Tirwa is the candidate of the orthodox section. We shall therefore have not much difficulty in winning the elections. Our policy is to create differences among the original members of the Hindu Sabha.[46]

As Motilal's representative, Sitla Sahai repeatedly emphasized that he was doing everything possible to 'create division in the original Hindu Sabha'. The gameplan was to weaken Malaviya's hold over the Agra

Hindu Sabha by removing his nominee from the post of president and getting Motilal Nehru's stooge elected in his place. Malaviya's camp was, however, vigilant on the election day and foiled all attempts by Motilal Nehru to get AP Dubey elected as the president of the Agra Hindu Sabha.[47]

The Agra Provincial Hindu Sabha formed an elections board in August 1926 to 'protect Hindu interests'.[48] A similar committee was organized by the Oudh Provincial Sabha that was to work in consultation with its counterpart in Agra. Malaviya now made a final attempt to come to terms with Motilal Nehru. When he failed to persuade the latter, Malaviya announced the formation of the Independent Congress Party in the first week of September. The leading members of the party were in fact the Mahasabha politicians and the executive committees of the Hindu Sabhas and the Independent Congress Party were practically identical.[49] Although the party was the electoral front of the Mahasabha, the party candidates did not represent various strands of the movement.

GROWING DIFFERENCES WITHIN THE MAHASABHA

The special session of the Hindu Mahasabha met at the Congress pandal in Madras on 29 December 1927 under the presidentship of Malaviya who made a fervent appeal to the Mahasabha leaders to adopt the following resolution:

> The Hindu Mahasabha, in association with the Indian National Congress and other bodies, calls upon the people to boycott the Simon Comission at every stage, in every manner.[50]

A section of the Mahasabha led by Bhai Parmanand and B.S. Moonje was unwilling to boycott the Simon Comission as they thought that they had an opportunity of securing advantages over Muslims or stalling concessions made to them. But their opposition proved to be of no avail. Malaviya, Lala Lajpat Rai, and M.R. Jayakar successfully prevailed upon the members present at the Mahasabha session to pass the resolution. Thus the Mahasabha finally decided to move forward with the Congress with regard to the Simon Commisson.[51]

The decision of the Mahasabha was endorsed by all its branches in the country except in Punjab. Bhai Parmanand persuaded the Punjab Hindu Sabha to oppose the resolution passed by the Madras session of the Mahasabha. In accordance with his wishes, the Punjab Hindu Sabha decided to cooperate with the Simon Commission and expected to gain certain benefits from the government by taking such a step. Contrary to the decision of the All-India Hindu Mahasabha, it presented a memorandum before the Simon Commission dealing with the exclusive rights of the Hindus. This led to 'a serious split in the ranks of the Congress'.[52] Bhai Parmanand later justified his step by arguing that 'M.M. Malaviya and Lajpat Rai were so incensed at the exclusion of Indians from the Commission that regardless of all other differences they went over to and joined forces with Motilal Nehru'.[53]

This was indicative of the emergence of a separate bloc in the Mahasabha working openly against Malaviya. The Patna session of the Hindu Mahasabha held in April 1927, further confirmed the trend. The new president of the sabha, B.S. Moonje, openly pleaded in favour of a swaraj scheme for the country in which Hindus would be supreme and dominant. This was contrary to Malaviya's views as he had repeatedly urged against making any attempts to establish Hindu Raj in India. He was totally opposed to any plans of spelling out any such policy from the Mahasabha platform. Under these circumstances, fundamental differences began to emerge between Malaviya and the newly emerging Mahasabha leadership.

The differences between Malaviya and certain other leaders of the Mahasabha again surfaced when M.A. Jinnah demanded the separation of Sindh from the Bombay Presidency and the reservation of seats for Muslims. Since the Congress and some other parties and groups were willing to accept the separation of Sindh from the Bombay Presidency, Malaviya was also prepared to accept this demand as a step to bring about a harmonious relationship between Hindus and Muslims. He thought that a broad understanding between the Congress and other political parties and groups was in the national interest. But the newly emerging Mahasabha leadership did not appreciate Malaviya's stand and accused him of being much too deep in the Congress camp. The viceroy gave the following assessment of the situation within the Mahasabha:

Hindu Mahasabha itself is not quite a happy family at present. A good many of them appear to look upon Malaviya and Lajpat Rai as too much in the pocket of the Congress. The Hindu Mahasabha people do not feel themselves committed to follow Lajpat Rai and Malaviya into the boycott camp.[54]

The viceroy was apparently referring to the growing rift within the Hindu Mahasabha that ultimately changed its course and character. Malaviya and Lajpat Rai, who were actively associated with the Congress, were deeply committed to carrying on the anti-imperialist struggle under its banner and were prepared to work with it within the broad nationalist framework of Hindu–Muslim unity. While presiding over the special session of the Hindu Mahasabha on 29 December 1927, Malaviya reiterated his views, explained the challenges before the Mahasabha, and defined its strategy for the years to come. He called upon the delegates 'to remember that this Hindu Mahasabha was never brought into existence as a communal organization to fight against any community'.[55] He further stressed that the prime objective before the Mahsabha should be to promote greater unity and solidarity among all sections of the Hindu community and to promote good feelings between Hindus and other communities. Malaviya used the opportunity to impress upon the delegates that 'ever since its inception upto date not a single resolution has been passed by this Sabha which any reasonable man who has any sense of nationalism in him can take exception to'.[56]

SUPPORT TO THE PREPARATION OF THE NEHRU REPORT

Malaviya cooperated with Motilal Nehru in his efforts to prepare a constitutional scheme as he was well aware that the support of various political parties and groups was necessary in this endeavour. The elder Nehru was keen to win over the support of the Mahasabha and laid down that 'the support of the Hindu Mahasabha is most essential as there is no knowing how the Muslim opinion will finally shape itself'.[57]

Motilal sought Malaviya's help in this direction and the latter worked behind the scenes to bring round the Hindu Mahasabha to Motilal's side. It was due to Malaviya's efforts that the Mahasabha agreed to take part in the committee's deliberations, its representatives were present in various committees which met for the purpose, and it did not put up unnecessary hurdles in the framing of the proposals.[58]

While the preparations for the swaraj scheme were underway, Malaviya extended full support to Motilal Nehru in various other ways as well. He stood by his side during various discussions, and worked in his own way to iron out differences among various leaders and groups. Malaviya's overriding concern was the framing of a constitutional scheme acceptable to everyone. Motilal Nehru looked to Malaviya for financial support as well. He reported to Gandhi, 'All that is needed is money which I hope will be forthcoming as Birla and Malaviyaji are interesting themselves in the work.'[59]

When the Nehru Report was presented for discussion at the All Parties Conference at Lucknow at the end of August 1928, Malaviya and Mrs Annie Besant supported the idea of dominion status for India and strongly appealed to various leaders gathered at the venue to help in reaching consensus in its favour on as many points as possible. However, a number of mutually contradictory amendments were proposed at Lucknow that were referred back to an enlarged Nehru Committee in which Mrs Annie Besant, Lajpat Rai, and Malaviya had been included. This enlarged Nehru Committee later issued a supplementary report.

The Nehru Report and the supplementary proposals were submitted for approval to an All Parties Convention at Calcutta at the end of December 1928. It soon became clear that the communal claims had no fixity. No sooner was an issue closed by one party or group than it was repoend by someone else. Gandhi wrote to Motilal on the eve of the meeting, 'You are having no end of difficulties with Musalman friends regarding your report.'[60] This observation came true with the three amendments proposed by M.A. Jinnah to the Nehru Report asking for one-third of seats in the central legislature for Muslims, reservation of seats for ten years for Muslims in Bengal and Punjab, and residuary powers for the provinces.

By the time the Calcutta convention met, the Hindu Mahasabha had openly declared that the 'final solution of the communal differences in respect of the drafting of the Swaraj constitution should not be reopened for revision but be accepted as such'. In view of the above declaration by the Mahasabha, M.R. Jayakar strongly rejected Jinnah's demands. His contention was that the very form of the Nehru Report would be altered once the modifications suggested by Jinnah were conceded. With the passing away of Lala Lajpat Rai, there was not much room left for Malaviya's intervention and he knew his limitations in influencing the newly emerging militant group within the Hindu Mahasabha very well. Malaviya endorsed the official stand of the Mahasabha at the Calcutta convention as he realized that there was not much chance left for the emergence of a broad consensus in favour of the Nehru Report. The following comment correctly summarizes the failure of the Calcutta Convention: 'The narowness and rigidity of the Hindus and Sikh politicians in these negotiations was bad enough but the fluidity of Muslim demands was worse. From 1906 to 1947 each communal "settlement" became the starting point for a better bargain until nothing was left to bargain about.'[61]

NOTES

1. Bayly, *Local Roots of Indian Politics*, p. 108.
2. P. Malaviya, *Mahamana Malaviya Ke Lekh*, p. 24.
3. Motilal Nehru to Jawaharlal Nehru, 6 January 1911, *SWMN*, p. 157.
4. S.R. Wasti, *Lord Minto and Indian National Movement, 1905–10* (Oxford, 1964), p. 160.
5. Malaviya's presidential address in Lahore, 1909, in Zaidi and Zaidi, *Encyclopedia of the Indian National Congress*, vol. IV, p. 176.
6. Chaturvedi, *Mahamana Pandit Madan Mohan Malaviya*, p. 53.
7. Gupta, *Pandit Madan Mohan Malaviya*, p. 261.
8. Wolpert, *Tilak and Gokhale*, p. 295.
9. Indraparakash, *A Review of the History and Work of the Hindu Mahasabha and the Hindu Sangathan Movement* (New Delhi, 1938), p. 11.
10. Indraparakash, *History and Work of the Hindu Mahasabha*, p. 13.
11. Brown, *Gandhi's Rise to Power*, p. 76.
12. Brown, *Gandhi's Rise to Power*, p. 77.
13. B.R. Nanda, *Mahatma Gandhi: A Biography* (Oxford and New Delhi, 2004), p. 256.
14. *Leader*, 10 October 1922.
15. *New India*, 22 October 1922.
16. Rajendra Prasad, *Autobiography* (Muzaffarpur, 1947), pp. 180–2.
17. Prasad, *Autobiography*, pp. 180–2.
18. O.P. Ralhan, ed., *Hindu Mahasabha* (New Delhi, 2004), pp. 58–9.
19. H.N. Mitra, ed., *Indian Annual Register, 1923*, vol. I (Calcutta, 1924), pp. 943–4.
20. *Leader*, 12 April 1923.
21. *Abhudaya*, 14 August 1923.
22. *Abhudaya*, 19 August 1923.
23. Ralhan, *Hindu Mahasabha*, pp. 61–2.
24. Ralhan, *Hindu Mahasabha*, p. 64.
25. Mitra, *Indian Annual Register, 1923*, vol. I, pp. 943–4.
26. *Leader*, 2 April 1923.

27. *Daily Express*, 22 August 1923, Madras edition.
28. *Hindu*, 23 August 1923, Madras edition.
29. *Amrita Bazar Patrika*, 25 August 1923, Calcutta edition.
30. *Indian Social Reformer*, 25 August 1923, Bombay edition.
31. *Justice*, 28 August 1923, Madras edition.
32. *Medina*, 26 August 1923.
33. Mukut Bihari Lal, *Mahamana Madan Mohan Malviya* (Varanasi, 1978), p. 219.
34. *Pratap*, 5 May 1924.
35. Malaviya to C.Vijayaraghavachariar, 30 December 1924, C.V.R. Papers.
36. Malaviya to C.Vijayaraghavachariar, 30 December 1924, C.V.R. Papers.
37. Malaviya to C.Vijayaraghavachariar, 30 December 1924, C.V.R. Papers.
38. Jayakar, *Story of My Life*, vol. I, p. 535.
39. Ralhan, *Hindu Mahasabha*, pp. 115–21.
40. Ralhan, *Hindu Mahasabha*, pp. 115–21.
41. *Leader*, 7 April 1925.
42. Motilal Nehru's speech, 15 March 1927, *SWMN*, vol. 5, pp. 407–9.
43. Motilal Nehru to Sri Prakash, 12 July 1926, *SWMN*, vol. 5, p. 95.
44. Sitla Sahai to Motilal Nehru, 13 July 1926, AICC Papers 13/Part II/1926.
45. Sitla Sahai to Motilal Nehru, 20 July 1926, AICC Papers, 13/Part II/1926.
46. Sitla Sahai to Motilal Nehru, 23 July 1926, AICC Papers, 13/Part II/1926.
47. Sitla Sahai's report, 2 August 1926, AICC Papers 13/Part II/1926.
48. A.K. Mishra, *Hindu Mahasabha, Ek Adhyan* (Lucknow, 2001), p. 102.
49. Indraparakash, *Hindu Mahasabha: Its Contribution to Indian Politics* (Delhi, 1966), p. 26.
50. H.N. Mitra, *Indian Annual Register, 1927* (Calcutta, 1928), vol. II, p. 99.
51. Home Poll 18/1/1928, Punjab Fortnightly Reports, vol. II, NAI.
52. Indraparakash, *Hindu Mahasabha*, p. 39.
53. Bhai Parmanand, *The Story of My Life* (New Delhi, 1996), p. 168.
54. Irwin to Birkenhead, 23 February 1928, Halifax Papers.
55. Proceedings of the Gauhati session, December 1927, in Ralhan, *Hindu Mahasabha*, pp. 127–31.
56. Proceedings of the Madras session of the Hindu Mahasabha, December 1927, in Ralhan, *Hindu Mahasabha*, pp. 175–8.
57. Motilal Nehru to M.S. Aney, 18 August 1918, M.S. Aney Papers.
58. Motilal Nehru to Purushotam Das Thakur Das, 29 September 1928, *SWMN*, vol. 5, p. 363.
59. Motilal Nehru to Mahatma Gandhi, 2 October 1928, *SWMN*, vol. 5, p. 368.
60. Gandhi to Motilal Nehru, 6 October 1928, *CWMG*.
61. B.R. Nanda, *Motilal Nehru* (New Delhi, 1998), p. 190.

7   Hindu–Muslim Relations

An ardent nationalist, Malaviya had always been conscious of his duties towards the Hindu community, mainly of the nature of social advancement and reforms; wherever Hindus faced problems they looked to him for help. Because of his association with the Hindu Mahasabha, efforts to organize Hindus, and his constant endeavour to voice their demands, he was dubbed by some of his contemporaries as communalist and the charge has often been repeated by a few of his later critics as well.[1] For a proper assessment of Malaviya's stand on communalism and nationalism, it would be useful to analyse his speeches at various Hindu conferences. These would show that he remained consistent in his attitude towards the Hindu–Muslim issue, that is, always remaining true to certain fundamentals, yet always willing to make adjustments in details. When Malaviya found it necessary to organize Hindus on a separate platform, he warned his supporters not to lose sight of the paramount need for a broad understanding between the two communities. As long as his voice prevailed in the Hindu Mahasabha, he insisted on the necessity of religious liberty for all communities and desired to keep the sabha's activities within proper bounds so that no further bitterness and communal conflicts were provoked. Malaviya attached the greatest importance to communal harmony. It is unfortunate that he has been condemned as a communalist without paying proper attention to his lifelong activities, public utterances, and participation in practically all the conferences organized for the purpose from 1916 to 1934.

He took good care that his work for his own community was carried on so as to make a wholesome contribution towards the bigger cause to which he had dedicated himself—that of liberation and of building a great Indian nation. Even for the furtherance of Hindu–Muslim unity, he thought that the work done through the Hindu Mahasabha was helpful and even necessary.

WAS MALAVIYA COMMUNAL?

When asked to comment upon the question 'Was he [Malaviya] communal in his approach?' J.B. Kriplani replied:

> No. Of course, he was orthodox in his ways but I would not call him communal in his approach. Certainly he did not want any injustice done to the Muslims. He followed his own religion but I don't think he was communal in the sense that he wanted the whole of India to be Hindu India in which the Muslims should have no place. He did accord an appropriate place to the Muslims in India. Only he faithfully followed his own religion and tried to propagate it and tried to educate the young men in Hindu religion and it was from that point of view that he started the Banaras Hindu University. If that is communalism then he was communal but otherwise in politics he wanted to have co-operation with the Muslims. He never wanted any injustice to be done to them. This is how I understood him.[2]

As the person who who was Malaviya's private secretary for a short period after 1918 and who had had several opportunities to watch his later activities closely, G.B. Kripalani's forthright assessment is significant in the sense that he stressed that Malaviya never lost sight of safeguarding the interests of Muslims. This testimony is equally important in another respect. It raises the question whether anyone is justified in calling Malaviya communal because of his lifelong commitment to Hinduism.

POST–KHILAFAT STRATEGY

How far did the Hindu–Muslim riots affect Malaviya's attitude? The happenings of the period 1922–24 deserve special consideration here as these led Malaviya to redefine his strategy and future course of action.

It is important to remember that the Hindu–Muslim problem was basically a question of a majority–minority relationship. The Muslims were generally apprehensive that they would be submerged by a Hindu majority and that their rights and interests would suffer in a free democratic constitution of the future. The Hindus strongly resented what they felt to be undue privileges and weightage granted to the Muslims by the government in provinces like Bengal and Punjab. The existence of a separate electorate since 1909 crystallized the antagonistic feelings of both communities. It is worth noting that agreements between Muslim leaders and the Congress materialized only twice—in the Lucknow Pact of 1916 and the non-cooperation movement of 1920–22. On both these occasions, Malaviya extended full support to these negotiations. This helped in bringing about political advance through regotiations and compromise.[3] When such agreements from the top did not materialize after 1922, the Congress appeared bereft of alternatives to resolve communal discord either at the elite or at the popular level.

Some of the factors which brought to the centre the communal riots of 1922–24 were themselves the outcome of the Khilafat agitation that was supported and directed by Gandhi. Like many others, Malaviya felt that that the Khilafat movement was wrongly handled and religion was given too much importance. He supported Muslims wholeheartedly in their Khilafat demands but could not keep quiet when some enthusiasts began to sing songs inviting Enver Pasha's hordes from Afghanistan to India.[4] Malaviya had his own apprehensions about certain measures the Khilafat leaders adopted or contemplated. The narrow and openly religious nature of the movement and its technique made the whole agitation suspect in his eyes.

It led Malaviya to doubt how far Khilafat would help in broadening the social base of the nationalist struggle. As to the popularity of this agitation among the Hindus, Sampurnanand pointed out that 'it was difficult for an ordinary Hindu to enthuse over it. What were the rights and wrongs of it? Normally the Hindu could not understand what it was all about.'[5] By its emphasis on Islam, the Khilafat movement made the Muslims conscious of their being Muslims and led some of them to look to their interests alone.[6] This was to prove the biggest blow to Hindu–Muslim unity. The unity of the Khilafat days has been described as 'artificial' and 'unreal', more formal than intimate, because it did not spring from any concrete or tangible interests but was built on a foundation of 'religious sentimentalism'.[7]

EFFECTS OF MOPLAH RIOTS

The outbreak of the Moplah rebellion in Malabar in August 1921, was marred by acts of violence and retaliation between the Hindu and Muslim communities. The Moplah peasants, emboldened by the

Khilafat spirit, rose against the Hindu landlords and the government.[8] They attacked the Hindus in large numbers, putting them to death as and when they desired. Arson and looting took place on a large scale and forcible conversions were reported from several areas. Malaviya toed the Congress line during this period, kept himself away from the controversies relating to the Moplah atrocities, and, on Gandhi's advice, arranged relief for the Moplahs.[9] The issue of forcible conversions in Malabar, however, did not escape Malaviya's notice and he voiced his support for those who desired to be readmitted to Hinduism, saying that they should be permitted to do so after a token expiation. Malaviya sent the following message to Gandhi:

> Please do not infer from the verse quoted by me that in my opinion all Moplahas have injured Hindus. But even assuming that all the Moplahs have done us an injury even then we must serve them in the hour of their need. In such conduct lies the beauty of our religion.[10]

COMMUNAL POLARIZATION

With the breakdown of the non-cooperation movement, the superimposed Congress–Khilafat unity broke into pieces and the rift widened as the masses were made aware of their communal identities. In September 1923 Abdul Bari urged Muslims 'to sacrifice cows without regard to Hindu feelings' and further added, 'We are determined to non-cooperate with every enemy of Islam whether, he is in Anatolia or Arabia or at Agra or Benaras.'[11] Such outbursts by the famous ulama and certain other Muslim leaders were most unfortunate as communalist politics of one community was bound to generate its counterpart in other communities, and the vicious circle widened with every favourable circumstance. The Hindu–Muslim unity of the Khilafat days was replaced by communal polarization after the suspension of the non-cooperation movement. Muslim leaders began to openly express anxiety for the defence of their interests and, as a result, the relations between the two communities became so greatly 'strained that each community had practically arrayed itself in an armed camp against each other'.[12] The talk of 'crystallising Hindu public opinion' and uniting all Hindus for shaping the 'destiny of Hindu nation' became quite frequent.[13] It was really tragic that the Hindu–Muslim unity achieved during the non-cooperation movement could not become a permanent feature of Indian politics.

From 1922 to 1928, there were communal clashes of a serious nature; Hindu–Muslim riots involving a large number of people took a heavier toll of human lives and left a permanent legacy of hatred in India. As many as 112 riots, which the government classified as 'serious communal disorders', were responsible for the loss of approximately 460 lives and major injuries to 450 persons during this period.[14] The distribution of these riots was remarkably wide but the main centres were Punjab, UP, and Bengal. The immediate triggers, though not the deeper causes, that sparked off communal outbreaks were music played in front of mosques, cow slaughter, and disputes connected with observance of religious festivals or ceremonies.[15]

The increasing incidence of communal violence throughout the country agitated the minds of the nationalist leaders and, unfortunately enough, divided them along communal lines. On the one hand, Hindu identity was strengthened, the Hindu Mahasabha was revived by Malaviya and a host of other leaders who enjoyed widespread support among the Hindus, while on the other hand, the Khilafat and Muslim League leaders called upon the Mulsims to separately organize themselves, which paved the way for subsequent growth of Muslim identity.

GANDHI'S STATEMENT ON HINDU–MUSLIM TENSIONS AND MALAVIYA'S ROLE

In this tense atmosphere, hopes were aroused with Gandhi's release in February 1924. He lost no time in entering into detailed discussions with several top leaders including Motilal Nehru, Hakim Ajmal Khan, and Malaviya. Gandhi held further consultations with M.A. Ansari and Mohammad Ali and issued a long statement entitled 'Hindu–Muslim Tension: Its Cause and Cure' on 29 May 1924.

In this statement, Gandhi stated, 'Musalman as a rule is a bully and the Hindu is a coward'. Even after asserting this Gandhi did not advise Hindus to 'organize the Hindu "goondas" in self-defence' as 'from the frying pan they will jump into the fire'.[16] He expressed frankly his views on cow slaughter, music in front of mosques, shuddhi and tabligh (propagation of the Muslim faith), and emphasized that the 'potent cause of tension is growing distrust among the best of us.' In this statement, he also stated that 'I have been warned against Pandit Madan Mohan Malaviyaji. He is suspected of secret motives. It is said that he is no friend of the

Musalmans. He is even credited with being jealous of my influence.'[17] In an effort to clear the air Gandhi came out strongly in support of Malaviya:

> I have the privilege of knowing him intimately ever since my return to India in 1915. I have had the privilege of closest communion with him. I regard him as one of the best among Hindus, who, though orthodox, holds most liberal views. He is no enemy of Mussalmans. He is incapable of jealousy of anyone. He has a heart large enough to accommodate even his enemies. He has never aimed at power. And what he has is due to a long period of unbroken service of the motherland, such as very few of us can boast.

Gandhi sought to further explain his relationship with Malaviya, saying:

> He and I are temperamentally different but love each other like brothers. There never has been even as much as a jar between us. Our ways being different there can be no question of rivalry, therefore, of jealousy either.[18]

The immediate reason for the Mahatma's strong public support of Malaviya was the criticism voiced against the latter by Mohammad Ali. He wrote the following to Jawaharlal Nehru after his meeting with Gandhi:

> I do not know whether my conversation with Bapu at Juhu had any effect at all in the matter of Hindu–Muslim relations.... In one respect, however, I am positive that I have failed to impress him [Gandhi] at all and that is the character of his 'worshipful brother' Pandit Madan Mohan Malaviya. He comes out of it the best of us all. And yet both Shaukat and I were under the impression that Bapu thought very differently of the noble Pandit. If Bapu believes all that he says about him and there can be little doubt of it—then I must despair of the near future at any rate.[19]

In these words Mohammad Ali challenged Gandhi's estimate of Malaviya, disapproved their close relationship, and hit out against Malaviya in the following words:

> Malaviyaji was out to defeat Gandhism and to become the leader of the Hindus only since he could not be the leader of Muslims as well as Hindus and that Hindu–Muslim unity was not his ideal.[20]

Mohammad Ali's outbursts against Malaviya, however, did not have any effect on the Mahatma as he knew very well that 'without Malaviyaji and Shraddanandji Hindu–Muslim unity will remain sheer impossibility'.[21] Gandhi firmly belived that full opportunity must be given to these leaders to play their part in bringing about Hindu–Muslim unity and sought their help in solving the communal impasse. The divergent views of the Ali brothers and Gandhi were further reflected, before the end of the year, during the Kohat riots.

UNITY CONFERENCES

Attempts were not wanting in the midst of these troubles to tackle the communal problem and reduce its intensity as much as possible. Prominent leaders of both the communities exercised their minds in the direction of permanent peace by attempting to draw up an agreement, pact, or covenant that would guide the future relations between Hindus and Muslims on the basis of joint action for the cause of freedom. A Unity Conference was convened at Delhi on 26 September 1924 to discuss the situation arising out of the tragic happenings in Kohat.

It was an impressive gathering attended by leaders of all shades of opinion including Mrs Annie Besant, the Ali brothers, M.A. Ansari, Swami Shraddhanand, and Malaviya. Though some pious resolutions were passed by the conference, the basic malady could not be cured. It has been pointed out that 'a solution could not be reached in the conference by a majority of votes but by virtual unanimity and this could not be achieved as there were extremists of various groups present whose idea of a solution was a complete submission to their views.[22] Another All-Parties Conference met in late January 1925. Its deliberations were again marred by mutual bickering. Jawaharlal Nehru recorded later that 'the discussions were painful to listen' to and thought that the time had not yet come for an agreement which satisfied all parties.[23] In this frustrating atmosphere, Malaviya was under attack from various quarters and all his energy was lost in explaining his links with the Congress and the Hindu Mahasabha. However, Gandhi kept a close watch over these negotiations and sought Malaviya's help by asking him to 'advise Hindus to accept the terms suggested' during the Unity Conference held in Delhi. When this conference could not resolve the differences between the two communities, Malaviya was disheartened and informed Gandhi telegraphically: 'Has been matter of deep pain that in our last two months discussion was not able to be any help to you.'[24]

With regard to Gandhi's suggestions on communal unity, Malaviya's dilemma was real. He very much desired to respond to Gandhi's call and yet could often not actually act according to his wishes as he had different views on Hindu–Muslim relations. In such a situation, the differences between Malaviya and Gandhi persisted. Gandhi was fully aware of what was passing in Malaviya's mind and did not slacken his efforts to win him over to his side.

Even though Gandhi knew that he could not 'join forces with Pujya Malaviyaji and Pujya Lalaji',[25] his constant effort was to seek an understanding with both leaders in an effort to find a solution to the Hindu–Muslim discord. Voicing this opinion, Gandhi pointed out: 'I know my views on Hindu–Muslim question do not accord with Malaviyaji, still there seems to be no alternative.'[26] Gandhi reaffirmed these views again in the following words: 'I want to function as a pathfinder. When the time for reconciliation arrives, consultation with Malaviya and others will become necessary.'[27]

THE BRITISH POLICY OF ENCOURAGING COMMUNAL DISCORD

During the post-non-cooperation period, the British played on the forces of separation with great vigour and used the weapon of 'divide and rule' to strengthen their own authority. They played the Hindus and the Muslims against each other to enliven the forces of communal discord. Outlining this well-thought-out policy, the viceroy informed his official chief:

> I have always placed my highest and most permanent hopes upon the eternity of the communal situation. The greater the political progress made by the Hindus the greater, in my judegment, will Moslem distrust and autogonism become. All the conferences in all the world cannot bridge over the unbridgeable and between these two communities lies a chasm which cannot be crossed by the resources of modern political engineering.[28]

Accordingly, the viceroy encouraged the provincial governors and the bureaucracy to extend preferential treatment to the Muslims. The UP Governor, one of the architects of disunity, endorsing the viceroy's views, observed:

> The only suggestion which seems worth passing on is that the Government should make a friendly signal to the Muslims. The suggestion is that we should take an opportunity of saying that whatever changes are made, now or hereafter, no British Government can possibly forget or fail in its obvious duty of seeing that all minority interests in India

are sufficiently protected against suppression by majorities.... I would I agree, do much to reasure the Muslims and to encourge them to try again to work out their own solution.[29]

The governor of UP further said that only the British could safe-guard and protect Muslim interests and firmly laid down that Muslims should look only to the British for safeguarding their interests and not to the Hindus. He insisted that 'the Hindus cannot honestly claim that they can be trusted to look after Muslims or Anglo-Indians'.[30] District officers were instructed to patronize Muslim organizations by allowing them to voice their demands and placing men recommended by them in public offices.

Thus, the fundamentals of the British policy were redefined, provincial governors and senior British officials were left in no doubt of their responsibility of winning over Muslims, and they were asked to carefully and continuously coordinate their efforts in implementing the policy.

KOHAT RIOTS

Of all the Hindu–Muslim riots of 1924, the most serious outbreak occurred at Kohat in the North-West Frontier Province in the middle of September 1924. It was sparked off by the publication of a poem which was considered by the local Muslims to be an outrageous insult to Islam. At Kohat, the Hindus formed a microscopic minority of 5 per cent. There was looting and burning for two days in the city in which 155 Hindus were killed, 145 were wounded, and property worth over Rs 900,000 was destroyed.[31]

There was an exodus of the entire Hindu population of Kohat—about 4,000 persons. They were forced to flee the city and take shelter in the nearby city of Rawalpindi.[32] The official historian of the Congress writes that the 'Kohat riots really broke the backbone of India ... a perusal of the reports on the Kohat outrages ... immediately after the riot sends a thril of horror through the reader'.[33] The Kohat riots grieved Gandhi so much that he went on a fast for twenty-one days beginning from 24 September 1924.[34]

Malaviya immediately rushed to Rawalpindi to organize help for the Kohat refugees, worked continuously for their resettlement and sought to put forward their plight before the people as well as the government. He worked hard to provide relief to the Hindus, arranged for their shelter and lodging, and desired to protect their interests in their hour of need. He was ably helped by Lala Lajpat Rai and various other Punjab leaders who reached Rawalpindi to extend as much support as possible to these unfortunate people. Gandhi was in constant touch with Malaviya during his efforts to provide help to the Kohat refugees.[35] Since the Government of India did not permit Gandhi to visit the region, he could not undertake the journey to Kohat for some time. In the mean time, Malaviya raised the Kohat issue in the Central Legislative Assembly demanding an immediate impartial inquiry into the riots. He drew the viceroy's attention to the matter soon after calling upon the latter to initiate measures to provide protection to the Kohat Hindu population. The viceroy, however, refused to intervene in the matter, held the Kohat Hindus responsible for inciting the Muslims, and did not speak a word to condemn the action of the majority population. He turned down Malaviya's request for an inquiry on the Kohat riots on the pretext that this 'would inevitably cause recurrence of bitter feeling between the two communities at Kohat and would postpone indefinitely the resumption of friendly relations between them'.[36] The viceroy acted on the advice of the local British officers and the Punjab governor rather than on the representations made to him by Malaviya, providing yet another proof of his utter disregard of the latter's requests made on such occasions.

While on a visit to various cities of Punjab, Gandhi conferred with Malaviya, Lala Lajpat Rai, and others on the plight of the Kohat refugees and advised them to return to the city 'only if the Frontier Muslims requested them to do so'.[37] However, this seemed to be a far cry considering the outbursts of senior Khilafat leaders against Malaviya, Lajpat Rai, and other Hindu leaders. They did not hesitate to criticize them openly in the public meeting held in Amritsar which was addressed by Gandhi on 6 December. This came as a rude shock to Gandhi who said that 'the remarks against Pandit Malaviyaji had greatly touched him and had broken his heart.' He could 'never believe that Malaviyaji was the enemy of the Mohammedans' and a block in the way of Hindu–Muslim unity and warned the Khilafat leaders that 'the reviling of Pandit Malaviya would not bring them nearer the solution'.[38]

During his visit to Punjab, Gandhi repeatedly emphasized that Hindu–Muslim unity could only be brought about in an atmosphere of mutual trust between the communities and not in one of mutual suspicion. He reminded the Muslim leaders of Punjab that no useful purpose would be served by disrespecting Malaviya and suspecting his motives and actions. He was of the firm view that winning over Malaviya's favour towards the cause of Hindu–Muslim unity was absolutely necessary. Gandhi asked the Muslim leaders of Punjab to similarly persuade Lala Lajpat Rai and other front-rank Hindu leaders to come to a conference table to find a way out of the growing communal conflicts in the region and in other parts of the country.

Gandhi and Shaukat Ali were asked by the Congress Working Committee to visit Kohat to inquire into the communal riots there and bring about peace. The work, however, did not proceed smoothly. When the two leaders visited Kohat in February 1925, 'Shaukat Ali tried to instruct the Muslim witnesses as to how they should give their evidence exonerating the Mulsims'. Expressing this view, J.B. Kripalani pointed out later that 'though Gandhi never talked of it, this disillusioned him completely'.[39] On 10 February 1925 Gandhi gave out the following 'heart-stirring disclosure' to his private secretary Mahadeva Desai: 'I am now in the position of a man who is shocked to find a snake under his quilt and gives it a thorough shaking and sweeps his whole room clean. I came to know amazing things about Kohat which I had never known before.'[40] Gandhi and Shaukat Ali differed on essential points and issued separate statements. Gandhi did not endorse Shaukat Ali's views and observed: 'During these days temples, including a Gurdwara, were damaged and idols broken. There were numerous forced conversions.... I fear the truth is bitterer than is put.'[41] Even after all these experiences, Gandhi tried to work with the Ali brothers so as to retrieve things to create conditions in which Kohat evacuees could return to their homes. The attempt proved a bitter disappointment. The way the Ali brothers reacted to the Kohat riots shocked and disappointed the Mahatma to such an extent that he chose not to play any effective role in the communal conflicts in the country for next few years.

THE MUSIC BEFORE MOSQUES CONTROVERSY

It has been explained earlier that the governor of UP, W. Marris, was one of the architects of disunity who continuously played the Hindus and the Muslims against each other to enliven the communal discord and undertook a policy to organize and coordinate Muslims in support of the government. He believed that the best way to check the growth of nationalism in India was to articulate the Muslims to the interests of the government and hence instructed the district officers to patronize Muslim organizations by meting out preferential treatment to them with regard to their demands and representation.[42] The nature of the communal problem, as it developed during the years 1923–26, reveal that owing to the increase in Hindu–Muslim antagonism, the question of music being played in front of mosques became more prominent during these years and led to communal riots in Akola, Ajmer, Aligarh, Lucknow, Allahabad, Calcutta, and several other parts of the country. Even though Malaviya was not directly involved in any of these communal riots, he kept a close watch over these occurences, attempted to find a solution to these clashes by appealing to the provincial governments as well as the Government of India to take preventive action, and keenly desired to find a solution to these unfortunate events. It is proposed to examine here the growing antagonism between Hindus and Muslims in Allahabad and Calcutta as Malaviya visited these two cities at one stage or another and his visits sometimes attracted adverse official comments. Malaviya's difficulty was that he could not properly assess the deep prejudices of the British officials who were totally unwilling to consider any of his suggestions. The following details would show that in the controversy surrounding music being played in front of mosques, the British administrators deliberately turned a deaf ear to Malaviya's proposals to provide facilities to Hindus to celebrate their festivals in the traditional manner without any government intervention.

The major Hindu festival of Ramlila, as celebrated on a grand scale at Allahabad, included a procession that traditionally played music without any obstruction even when passing through the streets close to the mosques. The rising tempo of communal politics disturbed this healthy tradition in the city and, in 1924, for the first time, Muslims objected to the playing of music in the vicinity of mosques at the time of prayer. This led to a communal riot in Allahabad during the year. A procession celebrating the birth of Lord Krishna was pelted with stones while passing in front of a mosque. A riot soon followed in which 9 persons were killed and 110 people were seriously injured. The district administration issued orders restricting processions in the city. Ramlila, which was to be celebrated a month later, was not celebrated in Allahabad as a mark of protest against the restrictions on processions imposed by the district administration.

The issue of playing music in front of mosques emerged again in Allahabad in 1925, as the local Hindu leaders demanded that the restrictions imposed the previous year on taking out a Ramlila procession during the Dussehra festival be withdrawn. A mass meeting held on 13 September protested against the district collector's orders under Section 144 'stopping music and cries of Jai with Ramdal procession in front of three mosques during Musim prayer'.[43] In a telegram sent to the viceroy, the chairman of the meeting asserted:

> Such music never stopped in the past from time immemorial and new official order prohibiting same is proof of local authorities' incompetence to give lawful protection to Hindu rights and perform their duty and creates precedent calculated to occasion Hindu–Muslim friction every day of year.[44]

The views expressed in the meeting and in the local newspapers[45] against the government intervention in Ramlila celebrations strongly indicated the intense feelings of the local Hindu population. But that did not have any effect on the district collector who brushed aside the suggestions put forward by the Hindu leaders, refused to reconsider his earlier order issued the previous year, and insisted that the organizers of Ramlila 'must agree to take out their processions punctually on the 26th and 27th so that everything will be over before dark. Then there will be no need to have an order about music at the time of evening prayer.'[46] He stated that 'if my order is cancelled there will be exactly the same trouble from the Mohemmadans as there is at present from the Hindus ... it is practically certain that their will be a big riot'. The tone and tenor of the district collector's letter reveals, in no uncertain terms, that he was playing one community against the other. He received ungrudging support from the commissioner of the Allahabad division. Giving an account of the meeting he had with a deputation of the Hindus on 17 August the latter reported:

> They wished to insist upon the right of the Hindus to play music without restriction and I made it clear to them that there was no possibility of Crosthwaite's order being withdrawn unless they would guarantee to get the processions past the mosque before sunset in accordance with what we believe to be the ancient custom.[47]

Both the district collector and the commissioner followed bullying tactics, adopted a rigid attitude, and decided to dictate terms under which the district administration was prepared to allow the Ramlila pocessions to pass through the streets of Allahabad. To add insult to injury, the two local officials asserted that their orders were based on 'ancient custom'. Obviously, as a result, no door was left open for negotiations as the officials insisted that their orders were final and the Hindu leaders were not prepared to observe the Ramlila festival on the dictates of the official intervention. The problem could not be resolved as the British officials were not prepared to accept that the issue of playing music in front of mosques was of recent origin. The impression that the local British officials were biased in favour of the Muslims made any compromise between the two communities even more difficult. It led the Hindus to adopt an equally hard line, particularly on the traditional rights of the Hindus to play music on the streets without any official intervention. The following exerpts from the commissioner's letter to the provincial government bears this out in ample measure. He wrote:

> You will see that the Hindus, as a whole are taking up an impossible attitude. Orders will have to be issued under section 144 Cr. P.C. to forbid music in the vicinity of the mosques at prayer time. Such orders will probably lead the Hindus refusing to take out the Ramlila processions. Considering their attitude no sympathy be wasted on them.[48]

A week later the Commissioner reported again:

> They may cancel the processions entirely. If they do, so much the better as feelings now are but if they do not cancel them I am convinced that a deliberate attempt will be made in front of the chief mosques to provoke the Mohammandans to violence. In this case there will be a worse outbreak than there was last year and it will require sterner repression.[49]

The entire effort of the local officials during August and September 1925 was to justify their orders imposing restrictions on taking out Dussehra processions on the pretext that any such effort would lead to communal flare-ups in the city. They desired to convince the provincial government that the danger of a communal conflict in the city was real and that, to avoid any such an eventuality, the only option before them was to impose suitable conditions on taking out Ramlila processions. With this argument they could easily win the provincial government over to their side.

While analysing Malaviya's role in this controversy, it is necessary to point out that he was not present in the city either in 1924 or in 1925 and, therefore, did not take any part in the developments at Allahabad. He arrived in the city in 1926 when his intervention was sought with a view to finding a solution to the ongoing dispute. However, some of his close associates and relatives holding prominent positions in Allahabad played leading roles in the controversy and met the local officials in this regard. They have been referred to as the 'Malaviyas', the 'Malaviya party', 'Malaviya's family', or his 'clan' in the official correspondence.

Since some recent historians have failed to make any distinction between the role played by M.M. Malaviya and the members of his family based in Allahabad, they have held the senior Malaviya responsible for all the actions of his relatives or their associates. Such a dictinction must be made when describing the participation of the senior Malaviya during the events in Allahabad from 1924 to 1926. M.M. Malaviya should not be held responsible for any actions of the members of his family. The local officials were in the habit of pointing an accusing finger towards Malaviya's family as they did not toe the official line on the taking out Ramlila processions in the city and were opposed to any official intervention in the Ramlila celebrations at Allahabad. The district collector's version that 'the Malaviya family have deliberately stirred up the Hindus and this has reacted on the Muslims'[50] was a deliberate attempt to hold the Hindus responsible for the occurrences in Allahabad at this time.

The district collector's prejudicial stand against the organizers of the Ramlila celebrations in Allahabad is further confirmed by the letter he wrote in August 1925 to Malaviya, who was at that time attending the Legislative Assembly session at Simla. The collector 'wrote a private appeal' to Malaviya asking him to come over to the city and help the district administation in finding a solution to the ongoing dispute. Referring to the communal riots of October 1924, the collector wrote that 'a mob deliberately made a noise during the time of the evening prayer outside the Shabrate Ka Masjid on the Dadhkando day.... Hindu dalals and khattris disguised themselves as Sadhus in order to create the noise.' The collector's version of events of the past year was that the Hindu mob 'deliberately' provoked the Muslims. Malaviya refuted the charges made by the British officer and observed: 'From my knowledge of them I think that if they wished to do so they would have done it without any disguise. But whosoever did it, if, as you say, they did it deliberately their action is entirely condemnable.'[51] Malaviya kept away from the Hindu–Muslim controversy as he did not think that it was the right occasion for him to intervene in the dispute and politely informed the district collector that he was at that time 'in very poor health and have been advised not to go down to the plains before the 20th September.'[52]

The stalemate could not, however, be resolved in September 1925 as the district administration persisted with its policy of allowing Ramlila procession only in accordance with specified restrictions. The organizers of Dussehra celebrations were totally opposed to accepting any government intervention in taking out Ramlila processions. This led to the abandonment of the Ramlila celebrations again. The local press was vociferous in condemning the action of the government and for several days the news of the abandonment of Ramlila celebrations made headlines.[53] The commissioner of the Allahabad division admitted that 'a lamentable feature is that of all the well-known public men and prominent politicians among the Hindu community of Allahabad not one has had the courage to stand up and point out the danger and folly of the attitude taken'.[54] The sad admission of the commissioner should have been an eye-opener to him and to other district officials. If no prominent city politicians were prepared to stand by their side, it was a clear sign that the officials had failed to win the hearts of the Hindus. The British officers showed no signs of arriving at a compromise with the supporters of the Ramlila celebrations and sought to impose their policy on them. As the Ramlila celebrations had been postponed for two years in succession in the city, there was a lurking fear that the stalemate could persist in the following year as well.

On his part, Malaviya was watching with deep concern the communal riots in Allahabad, Ajmer, Nagpur, and a few other places of the country. In an effort to find a solution to the controversy regarding music being played in front of mosques, he met the home secretary at Simla in September 1925. Malaviya asserted that this matter had 'only become important in the last few years and illustrated the intransigent attitude of the Muhammadans'.[55] The secretary had before him the official report of the Ajmer riots in which he was informed: 'Owing to uncompromising attitude of Muhammedans who demand absolute cessation at all times of music before all mosques negotiations between the two parties have broken off. This would amount to stopping all Hindu processions as there are one hundred mosques in the city and is against all precedents and previous orders.'[56] Even after receiving this report, the home secretary was unwilling to issue any 'general orders' and laid down that the 'cases must be dealt with by local authorities and past custom be the basis of their action'. He stressed the following principle about the controversy: 'My impression is that this is a matter purely of custom and where custom is established then it is allowed.'[57] The home secretary's note was very vague and it left many questions unanswered. The district officers often failed to convince the local Hindu population regarding the exact nature of the past custom and the need of imposing restrictions on playing music in front of mosques in a particular city.

OFFICIAL ESTIMATE OF MALAVIYA'S ROLE

At this stage, it would be useful to analyse the contemporary official estimate of Malaviya's role in the Hindu–Muslim dispute at Allahabad and other places. William Marris, the governor of UP, expressed the following views about him in August 1926:

> Since I have been Governor we have had no particular reason in this province to complain of the Pandit's activities. He has been mainly busy with his Benaras University and I believe is rather anxious to keep in with the Provincial Government with the hope of getting a grant from us. He has not figured prominently in Allahabad Hindu–Muslim controversy though some of the Malaviya clan have done so. He has doubtless been active in furthering Sangathan, but not in a way which would have brought him within the law. He has in fact avoided than courted the role of an inflammatory apostle of Hinduism inside the United Provinces.[58]

The Government of the United Provinces gave the following estimate of Malaviya's activities on similar lines:

> The Pandit, though undoubtedly a strong protagonist of Hinduism has ordinarily been careful at the same time to preach the cause of Hindu–Muslim unity. He has not personally been prominent in Hindu–Muslim disputes in Allahabad though some of the members of his clan undoutedly were. It is not possible to prove how far his influence stimulated them.... He has refrained from plunging into the fray on more than one occasion which might have tempted him.[59]

Some of the extracts from the confidential official correspondence quoted above and certain other passages from the official papers being referred to hereafter convincingly show that Malaviya kept away from the communal disputes and did not play any part in the dispute regarding the playing of music in front of mosques in Allahabad up to the middle of 1926. The extracts clearly make a distinction between Malaviya's role in the dispute and that of his 'clan'. We have noted above that Malaviya should not be held responsible for the activities of some of the members of his family which attracted adverse comments from the district officials. The official papers acknowledge frankly that Malaviya had 'not personally been prominent in the Hindu–Muslim dispute at Allahabad' in 1924 and 1925. The provincial government informed the Government of India on 8 October 1926 that the situation in Allahabad took 'a new turn with the open appearance, for the first time, on the scene, of Pandit Madan Mohan Malaviya as the protagonist of the Hindus of Allahabad'.[60] This is yet another piece of evidence that Malaviya's direct participation in the events in the city in October 1926 was noted with concern by the officiating governor of UP who very aptly discribed the step as his 'intervention' in the Ramlila dispute. He stated:

> The elections have been responsible for the intervention in the Allahabad Ramlila dispute of Pandit Madan Mohan Malaviya. I have known the Pandit for 25 years and there is no doubt that at heart he is a fanatical Hindu. Hitherto, however, he had in these provinces not often come into the open on communal issues. He took no part in the Ramlila dispute at Allahabad last year. But his party is bidding for the support in the elections of the Hindu Sabha and he evidently felt it was impossible to remain in the background any longer.[61]

MALAVIYA'S INVOLVEMENT IN THE DISPUTE OF 1926

Malaviya's prime consideration at this point of time was to find a solution to the ongoing controversy with regard to the Ramlila celebrations in Allahabad. As there were no signs of any resolution forthcoming from any responsible quarters, even for the third year in succession, the Allahabad Hindu leaders were getting nervous. In this desperate situation, they sought M.M. Malaviya's help and requested him to visit

Allahabad in order to persuade the district administration to revise the earlier orders and facilitate the holding of Ramlila celebrations in the city during that year. Malaviya responded positively to the call and arrived in the city on 4 October 1926. On that same afternoon, he addressed a huge public meeting which was called to protest against the orders of the district administration.

The public meeting held in Allahabad under Malaviya's chairman-ship communicated its resolutions to the provincial governor and the viceroy, requesting that the district authorities be instructed to issue a license allowing Ramlila processions without any restrictions or conditions in conformity with long-standing local customs. The government was further asked to provide all the facilities to the people 'to excercise their legal and customary rights without being deterred by the apprehension of violence on the part of rowdy elements in a section of community'. The officiating UP governor's comment that 'the Pandit's intervention is unfortunate and has given undesirable prominence to the question of music before mosques' expressed his displeasure at Malaviya's visit to Allahabad and showed no inclination to act upon his proposals. In accordance with his wishes, the provincial government rejected the proposals contained in Malaviya's telegram, pointing out that 'his demand was not supported by past practice, that restrictions imposed on Ramlila processions in Allahabad were justified, and that it was, therefore, unable to accede to his request of directing the local authorities to modify their orders.'[62]

Undaunted by this rebuff, Malaviya despatched a comprehen-sive letter to the provincial government asking that 'licences for the Ramlila processions should be issued without any new conditions laid down by the District Authorities as such restrictions constitute an unjustifiable encroachment on the rights of Hindu citizens to take out their religious and other processions through the public streets in a peaceable manner as they used to do from time immemorial'. Malaviya denied the correctness of the government's statement that there existed any custom to stop the playing of music in front of mosques in the city, stated that he heard about this for the first time in the previous year, and repudiated the existence of any such practice in the city. He asserted that 'it was not only probable but practically certain that no serious rioting will occur this year'.[63]

Putting forward the case of the Hindus, Malaviya further asserted:

What we say is essential is that Hindus should not be compelled to stop
their prayers, their religious songs and music, shouts of religious joy
because they happen to pass by a mosque inside which some of their
fellow subjects are saying their prayers in their own style and manner.
They have no thought of disturbing their fellow subjects in their prayer.
They only desire not to be compelled to stop theirs.[64]

Referring to the ongoing communal discrord in Allahabad since 1924,
Malaviya said:

Whether it is likely that the question of music before mosques will
be solved by humouring the new Muslim sentiment which does not
rest on any religious injunction by imposing unusual restrictions upon
Hindu processions, or by impartially and firmly upholding well recog-
nised rights and established local custom....After what has happened not
to permit Ramlila processions to be taken out here even this year will be
to allow resort to unlawful violence to gain its object to flout the Government and to inflict undeserved pain upon a hundred thousand law
abiding subjects of his Majesty in Allahabad and of millions outside it.[65]

Malaviya was well aware that time was running out and if the issuance of licences for permission to celebrate Ramlila was delayed further
by the district authorities, the celebrations would be postponed for the
third year in succession causing immense 'pain and mortification' to
the vast Hindu population of Allahabad. But the district collector was
not prepared to reconsider his stand; he was quick to get in touch
with the chief secretary and went all out to convince his superior that
there was no merit in Malaviya's plea, firmly putting forward arguments asking for the rejection of Malaviya's request. He forwarded an
exhaustive hand-written letter to the chief secretary on 10 October,
offering a reply to Malaviya's representation published in the local
English daily a day earlier. The collector brushed aside Malaviya's arguments for holding the Ramlila processions, arguing that it could lead to
another communal riot in the city. His letter contemptuously referred
to Malaviya's representation and the language and phrases he used were
full of ill-will against Malaviya and his colleagues:

All the Pandit's arguments about the duty of the Government to use
force in order that he may beat drums etc. in front of mosques apply
with equal force to leading cows through the streets on Id ul Zuha and
sacrifing them in places visible to Hindus. In fact they apply with more
force as the beating of drums before mosques during evening prayers is

not a duty prescribed by Hindu religion....Anyhow if the Pandit were given military and police support to annoy the Muslims the latter will demand similar help at next Bakrid to provoke the Hindus. In any case police or no police they will deliberately provoke them if Government gives way about music.[66]

The District Collector noted further:

Not 1 per cent of the Allahabad Hindus would enjoy a Ramlila procession which any moment might result in a riot and nobody would be less pleased than the Pandit and his Hindu Sabha colleagues if Government said 'Very good. Hold your Ramlila without any restrictions'. We cannot prevent a riot but we will use all the police and military available to stop the riot as far as possible. That is all that Government could guarantee.[67]

As a 'man on the spot' the district collector placed his cards before the chief secretary at the earliest opportunity and was finally successful in convincing the latter that Malaviya's request be turned down. The following reply sent to Malaviya was based on the feedback provided by the collector:

The Government have given to your letter their most careful consideration. They regret that it should have been necessary to impose any restrictions. They had hoped that the Hindus would voluntarily adopt an arrangement, in conformity with past practice, which would have obviated all controversy. But they adhere to their view and since they were unwilling to do so, the restrictions imposed were justified; and accordingly they are unable to alter the decision already conveyed to you.[68]

Sandwiched between the government's unkindness and Muslim demands, Malaviya could not bring any relief to the people of Allahabad. The provincial government remained as firm as ever and heaved a sigh of relief at the further postponement of the Ramlila procession in 1926. The Hindu leaders of the city were determined not to accept any restrictions and the stalemate continued for the next seventeen years.

The viceroy's comments on this occasion provide added proof that he entirely depended on the reports sent to him by the provincial government:

I am very glad that Ramlila passed off successfully despite the considerable agitation led by the Pandit in Allahabad. This is a regrettable tendency on the part of Malaviya, apparently of recent growth. Only in August last Sir W. Marris assured me that he had avoided the role of inflammatory apostle of Hinduism inside U.P. As you suggest this is another bad effect of the elections.[69]

In a period when the two communities were taking assertive postures in the defence of their rights, the question of whether or not music should be played before a mosque became a central problem. It has been pointed out that at least thirty-one of the serious riots of the 1923–28 period were occasioned by playing of music near a mosque.[70]

COMMUNAL RIOTS IN CALCUTTA

The Hindu–Muslim division was more than complete in 1926 in Bengal largely due to the inability or unwillingness of the British authorities to find an amicable solution to the controversy surrounding music being played in front of mosques.[71] The evils of the Khilafat agitation percolated to the lowest level. Muslim divines continued to hold important positions in political meetings and conferences and spread the doctrine of separatism among the members of the community. The Muslim press ceaselessly fomented communalism. Fazlul Haq, the editor, printer, and publisher of *Muhammadi*, was prosecuted for displaying a communal spirit during the April 1926 riots. A member of the governor's Executive Council reported that 'the state of tension was deliberately kept alive in Calcutta and spread in Bengal by the leaders'.[72] In 1924 and 1925, the issue of music in front of mosques had been the focal point of contention and, in anticipation of probable disturbances during 1926, the police were given special instructions to take precautions.[73]

Against this background, a major communal riot occurred in north Calcutta on 2 April 1926. In was the immediate consequence of the action of a single drummer in an Arya Samaj procession. His refusal to adopt silence provoked an altercation which grew, within minutes, into a pitched battle. Muslims began throwing bricks and fighting soon spread to other areas. Attacks were made on temples and mosques and troops had to be called out. The communal disturbances continued unabated for two weeks. Official casualty figures indicate that 328 Hindus and 238 Muslims were injured and 24 Hindus and 18 Muslims were killed.[74] The most unfortunate part of these riots was that communal tension persisted for several weeks. There was a resumption of rioting on 22 April, which could not be brought under control until 9 May. During the second phase of the Calcutta disorders, 67 were killed and 395 injured. A third phase of disturbances took place from 11 to 25 July 1926, as a *rath yatra* and a Raj Rajeshwari procession (taken out by Hindues as part of their celebrations every year) were attacked because of their refusal to stop playing music in front of mosques. In the ten days of rioting that followed, the official figures were 28 killed and 226 injured.[75]

Since Malaviya was on a visit to Calcutta during the last week of April in connection with a special meeting of the Hindu Mahasabha, he had the occasion to listen to first-hand accounts of the early phase of the communal conflicts in the city. He discussed the sensitive question with his close friends and colleagues and top British officials. He had the occasion to meet Lytton, the governor of Bengal, and offerered his detailed comments on 2 May 1926:

> The riots in Calcutta and the excesses which the Mohammadans are committing in Calcutta and several other places are a source of great pain and anxiety.... The Hindus at Calcutta were united because the Mohammadans attacked the Arya Samajists, the temples of Bengalees, the Gurdwares of Sikhs and other places belonging to the community as a whole. They also attacked all classes of Hindus, a spirit of retaliation has been aroused among Hindus and numerous Hindus and Mohammedans have been killed and many more wounded.[76]

Malaviya suggested that 'the only right solution is that Government should declare that music shall not be stopped before any mosques which obstructs a public pathway and punish those who may create any disturbance over it'. Even though Malaviya very much desired such a solution to the ongoing communal dispute in Calcutta and certain other parts of the country, he was aware that the British officials did not favour such a course of action. He had met the governor of Bengal only a few days earlier and was informed of his move to issue fresh orders prohibiting playing music in front of a Calcutta mosque. Reacting to the governor's proposals, Malaviya expressed his grave concern in the following words:

> If this is done it will be a fruitful source of frequent strifes between Hindus and Musalmans. But few among our own men realize how much trouble Hindus will have to face in the coming era if it is laid down that music must stop before a mosque at the time of the Namaz.

Who will fix the times of the Namaz five times every day? Who will stand before every mosque to see that the rule has been violated? It will strengthen the tendency which has been created among Moham-medans to object to any Hindu making any noise or repeating even a religious song as he may be passing along a mosque. We should make a representation to the Government of India and have this matter put on a satisfactory footing.[77]

In this letter, Malaviya referred to his plans to proceed to Simla with the hope that the new viceroy, Irwin, 'will do something to show his willingness to respect public opinion'.[78] Time and again, and in dif-ferent situations, Malaviya often depended on government interven-tion in resolving disputes among the two communities. Following the same course, he desired to find a solution to the music before mosques controversy by putting forward his proposals before the provincial gov-ernor or the viceroy. This made the task of the government easier as it could always explain its compulsions in following a particular course of action.

The Government of India and the provincial governments often asserted that their administrative action on the music in front of mosques controversy was based on customary practice in different places. However, in Calcutta, the official review of the situation which followed the 1926 riots revealed that there had been no single, city-wide customary pattern of action with regard to this dispute.[79]

Even though playing music in the vicinity of mosques had become a matter attracting general public attention, there had been some regular instances of playing music near mosques during times of worship and other instances of stopping music near mosques even at times other than those set for worship. Thus, customary practice had varied not only from one local situation to another but also from time to time.[80] In the absence of a generally specifiable customary practice up to the middle of 1926, the Bengal government authorized the commissioner of police to define in each licence issued the precise hours of public worship dur-ing which music in the vicinity of religious centres would be prohibited.

In addition to these orders, the Bengal government issued addi-tional restrictions in case of the Nakhoda Mosque, near which music was to be prohibited at all times. When the Bengal governor informed Malaviya about his intentions with regard to the new and rather unusal restrictions about this mosque, Malaviya was alarmed and expressed serious misgivings on the likely fallout of this order. Malaviya was not the only person who raised serious objections to this occasion. Serious apprehensions about the decision were also raised by several top British officials. Representing their views, the home secretary expressed his doubts on the wisdom of the Bengal government's decision in the following words:

> The point which seems doubtful and which will probably give rise to widespread criticism by Hindus is the ruling about the Nakhoda mosque. This appears to be a new restriction not based on custom. As it has no clear basis it will probably be claimed by the Mohammedans that it establishes the principle that no music should be played at any time before mosques of special importance. Such claims will very likely be put forward on the basis of this decision in other provinces.[81]

The home member, however, looked to the Bengal government's decision from the political angle and overruled the suggestion made by the home secretary stating:

> It is clear that the regulating orders of this kind by the Government or its officers will become a more and more frequent necessity and it is equally clear that such orders cannot be made without exciting criticism or some of their contents being cited as precedents.[82]

The home member considered it 'impolitic to interfere with the considered conclusion of the Government of Bengal in the important case of the Nakhoda Mosque'. This advocacy of localism, illustrated in the exchanges between the Home Department of the Government of India and the Government of Bengal, in connection with the music before mosques controversy and the Calcutta riots demonstrates the 'hands off' policy advocated by the Government of India. During this time the Hindu Mahasabha was preparing a campaign to demand legislation to determine rights on the subject. The Government of India laid down that 'it is really impossible to make any general pronouncement on such a subject as music before mosques ... which is not really capable of being dealt with in this way'.[83]

The controversy over playing music near mosques continued in Bengal during the rest of 1926 and in 1927. It was fanned by detailed coverage of events in the popular press in Bengal. The provincial government's use of the principle of local customs was seriously debated. It was pointed out that the administrative decisions were based on unreasonable principles and designed merely to create problems by showing favouritism to one or the other community.

BENGAL GOVERNMENT'S MOVE TO BAN MALAVIYA'S ENTRY

The Bengal government's next move demonstrated its strong bias against Malaviya. At the time it received information that Malaviya, along with Moonje, intended to visit Calcutta at the beginning of August 1926, the communal disturbances that had occurred in the city had died down and there were no immediate signs of tension or excitement between the two communities.[84] Even so, the provincial government took the unusual step of issuing a direction to both leaders to abstain from visiting Calcutta. On an application moved by the commissioner of police, the chief presidency magistrate issued an order on 2 August banning the entry of Malaviya and Moonje to the city for a period of two months on the ground that during his earlier visit to the city, Malaviya had addressed, on 30 June, a gathering of *durbans* and *jamadars* (junior personal assistants employed by merchants to safeguard their establishments) 'urging them to practice martial exercises and be prepared to scrifice their lives for religions' sake'.[85] The provincial government took the hasty step with the full knowledge that it had no authentic version of Malaviya's speech, that the said speech was reported in different ways in various newspapers, and that it was difficult to ascertain the actual contents of the speech for which legal action against Malaviya was being contemplated after a two months had passed.

If the provincial government thought that Malaviya would quietly submit to its directive to keep away from Calcutta, it was sadly mistaken. Malaviya decided to defy the ban and reached Calcutta according to his original schedule on 6 August, posing an open challenge to the Government of Bengal. On its part, the provincial government lost no time in taking further legal action against Malaviya and promptly initiated legal proceedings against him in a local court which fixed the hearing of the case on 23 August 1926. Serious differences soon emerged between the Bengal government and the Government of India over the wisdom of filing an appeal against Malaviya in the Calcutta court.

The provincial government's contention that Malaviya's 'arrival would provide an immediate riot and that his presence would be accompanied by action likely to cause riot hereafter',[86] however, cut no ice with the Government of India. The home secretary disapproved 'the ill-considered action'[87] of the provincial government and wrote that 'the point of practical importance lies in the present conduct and utterances of Malaviya and not those of previous one'. He pointed out that the Bengal government's decision to initiate legal action against Malaviya on the basis of a speech delivered by him almost two months ago was a mistake.

Meanwhile, the officiating governor of Bengal got in touch with the viceroy in an effort to convince the latter that there was an immediate need to prosecute Malaviya. His letter was an attempt to discredit Malaviya and clearly reflected his strong prejudices against him. The governor desired:

> that we should do something to show that the Government is not content to let wirepullers use the inflammable material to further their political ends or revenge. This is the history of the proposals that my Government have just sent up and this is the history of the order against Malaviya and Moonje.

He further added:

> With regard to Malaviya there is and will be a great agitation. He has had plenty of rope here; he has been allowed to spend a large part of his time in Bengal since the beginning of April and so far as politics and his Sangathan are concerned, he has no grievance. But his real activities are not on the platform, but in daily meetings and intercourse; we have not the slightest doubt that he is definitely against the restoration of peace until the Hindu has his foot on the neck of the Mahomedan.... We have little doubt that his object in coming back to Calcutta was to prevent reconciliation and to encourage Marwaris and the Arya Samajists to hold out. That being our opinion we felt we were justified in preventing his coming.[88]

While justifying his action against Malaviya, the governor played Hindus against Muslims:

> We realised the possible effect of our action in embittering the Hindus. I have only had the papers to go on so far but my reading of them is that there is a feeling that our view was right but that it is a tremendous

triumph for the Mahomedans and therefore not to be borne; if we had been able to deal with a Mahomedan at the same time the opposition would have decreased by at least half.[89]

The governor's letter reflected his deep-rooted contempt for Malaviya. He sought to draw comfort by arguing that such a step would win Muslims over to the side of the government as they would regard it as a 'tremendous triumph'.[90]

The governor of Bengal, however, failed to make any impression on the viceroy who noted:

I confess that the Bengal Government seemed to have bungled the matter badly. It is difficult to see what sufficient grounds the Magistrate could have had for passing the original order under section 144, unless he was relying on confidential police reports which could not, in any circumstances, have been produced in Court as evidence. The question is how to get out of the mess. I dislike the idea of overruling the Bengal Government but as things appear to me at present they have got to lose face in any event and on the whole I think that less harm will be done generally by withdrawing the prosecution than by proceeding with it and courting almost certain failure.[91]

It is significant that in the last week of August 1926, the viceroy, Lord Irwin, acknowledged frankly 'that the burning question of the last fortnight has been the Malaviya incident' and gave his assessment of the situation in a confidential letter to the Madras governor in the following words: 'The Bengal Government, I think, without doubt, acted hastily in issuing the original order under section 144 C.P.C. But once they got into the mess it was difficult to know how to extricate them without overruling the Local government.'[92] If the original mistake of the provincial government was to ban Malaviya's entry by order of the magistrate, it invited further trouble by filing a case in the Calcutta court to prosecute Malaviya for entering the city in spite of the magisterial order. Since the court had fixed 24 August for hearing the case, it was the Bengal government's responsibility to produce evidence against Malaviya on that date. The Government of India did not allow the Bengal government to proceed further in this direction as it considered that 'the embarrassment and risks of unsuccessful prosecution of Malaviya are obvious.'[93]

By now the viceroy had realized that the central government's earlier policy of giving a long rope to the provincial government was a mistake, that the time had come to overrule its stiputated action against

Malaviya, and that it must be informed, in no ambiguous words, that
its case against the latter was weak as little care had been taken before
seeking judicial remedy. The viceroy noted 'that the general opinion
was that if they proceeded with the prosecution they would be courting failure and that they were bound to lose face'. The viceroy, therefore, turned down the Bengal governor's suggestion of taking legal
action against Malaviya and asked him to withdraw legal proceedings
against him. In these circumstances the only course open to the Bengal
government was to drop the prosecution case against Malaviya.

The Government of India spelt out its objections to the Government
of Bengal in the following words:

> The aspect of the case to which fundamental importance is attached
> by the Government of India is the proposal to base the prosecution
> partly on Malaviya's activities in connection with the Hindu Sabha and
> Hindu communal organisations generally. This has most dangerous im-
> plications and could readily be represented as an attack, through one of
> its most prominent representative members, on the Hindu community
> as a whole. The Government of India desires to make it clear and in
> most express terms, that they cannot agree to any such extension of the
> grounds of the order and the prosecution. These must be limited strictly
> to Malaviya's personal activities in Calcutta.[94]

Thus the main point of departure was the Bengal government's
proposal to extend the grounds of the order and prosecute Malaviya
and its demand 'to produce evidence of his activities in Allahabad'.[95]
In its enthusiasm to prosecute Malaviya, the provincial government
was prepared to put forward certain official correspondence in the
Calcutta court. It was not allowed to do so as the viceroy was totally
against such a procedure. The viceroy was already in touch with the
governor of UP who did not share the Bengal governor's opinion.
The following extract from the UP governor's communication to the
viceroy confirms this to a large extent:

> The Bengal C.I.D. have asked our C.I.D. to help them with evidence
> as to Pandit Madan Mohan Malaviya's connection with the Sanghatan
> movement and his speeches in the Province. We, of course, realise our
> obligation to cooperate with another Government which asks for help.
> But we are decidedly reluctant that it should be made to appear that
> we ourselves regard the Pandit or the Sangathan movement as a public
> danger.... We shall therefore have to consider rather carefully what evi-
> dence we furnish to Bengal.[96]

The viceroy's comment that 'it was better to take the line which would give Malaviya the least chance of self-advertisement'[97] shows that he was well aware of the likely fallout of the Bengal Government's plans to prosecute Malaviya. However, Malaviya never intended to blow the provincial government's move out of proportion. His reaction on this occasion was mild, moderate, and dignified as is evident from the following account of his meeting with the governor of the Central Provinces:

> Incidentally Malaviya referred to the summons against him and said he had not made up his mind but thought he could answer it by pleader so as not to create any unnecessary excitement. He had no doubt about the illegality of the order. Thereafter he had it in mind to move you to take up the question of the use of Section 144 Criminal Procedure Code, as an all-India matter.[98]

While Malaviya was much in the news in August 1926, he was careful 'not to create unnecessary excitement' and looked forward to discussing the issue of the enforcement of section 144 of the Criminal Procedure Code with the viceroy. He never intended to follow a confrontational course at this time and was in constant touch with senior British administrators.

The governor of UP, W. Marris, who was now, in a way, an admirer of Malaviya, observed that he 'has in fact avoided than courted the role of an inflammatory apostle of Hinduism'.[99] It was a frank recognition of the reality that Malaviya never followed the line of a hardcore Hindu during these crucial years of Hindu–Muslim relations. He was a strong believer in Hindu–Muslim unity and was conscious, all along, of his responsibilties in bringing about a harmonious relationship between the two communities doing everything in his power to bridge the gulf between them. He could not, however, win the confidence of the Muslim leaders, particularly because of his links with the Hindu Mahasabha and the Arya Samaj. The provincial and the central governments also did not support him whenever he sought their help. During the Kohat riots, the viceroy did not appreciate his intervention in favour of the unfortunate Hindu population of the North-West Frontier Province city who had faced immense suffering during the communal riots. Similarly, both the central and provincial governments did not appreciate his suggestions of finding a solution to the Ramlila dispute in Allahabad. The hostility of the Bengal governor was very much obvious when he sought to prosecute him for defying his order banning his entry into Calcutta. The tragedy for Malaviya was that he constantly desired to find a solution to the communal problem with the help of the government and was never tired of seeking such support. Either he could not visualize that the British had no intention of coming to his rescue in his efforts in this direction or he failed to explore any other line of action. In the post-Khilafat era there was an intermixing of religion and politics. Gandhi asserted that 'the Muslim masses instinctively understood the religious issue and would feel brotherly towards non-Muslims who exposed their cause'.[100] But unfortunately, the 'minority community' could not get over their obsession of their religion being in constant danger among a hostile population despite the concessions—like the separate electorate, the prohibition of music in front of mosques, extra privileges such as reservation of employment in offices, and so forth—granted by the government. The bureaucracy seemed to enjoy the situation by 'continuously dangling before them [the Muslims] a carrot in the shape of greater privileges and concessions'.[101]

Due to a combination of all these factors, Malaviya watched the deteriorating relationship between the two communities with deep concern and yet he expected that their representatives would be able to find a way out of the malady in the years to come.

NOTES

1. Bipan Chandra, *India's Struggle for Freedom* (New Delhi, 1988), p. 436; Sumit Sarkar, *Modern India* (New Delhi, 1989), p. 230; Gyanendra Pandey, *The Ascendancy of the Congress in Uttar Pradesh* (Delhi, 1978), p. 118.
2. Oral history transcript of G.B. Kripalani, pp. 52–3, NMML.
3. Anita Inder Singh, *The Origin of the Partition in India* (Delhi, 1987), p. 107.
4. Reading to Montagu, 20 September 1920, Reading Papers.
5. Oral transcript of Sampurnanand, NMML, p. 22.
6. Moin Shakir, *Khilafat to Partition—A Study of Major Political Trends among Indian Muslims during 1919–1941* (New Delhi, 1983), p. 216.
7. M.R. Jayakar, *Story of My Life, Vol. II: 1922–1925* (Bombay, 1959), p. 76.
8. B.M. Taunk, *Non-Cooperation Movement in Indian Politics* (New Delhi, 1994), p. 211.
9. *CWMG*, vol. 24, p. 103.
10. *Leader*, 22 October 1921.

11. F. Robinson, *Seperatism among Muslims* (Cambridge, 1974), p. 339.

12. AICC Papers.

13. Pandey, *Ascendancy of the Congress*, p. 116.

14. G.R. Thursby, *Hindu–Muslim Relations in British India* (Leiden, 1975), p. 72.

15. Hasan, *Nationalism and Communal Politics in India*, pp. 230–40.

16. Gandhi's statement, 29 May 1926, *CWMG*, vol. 25, pp. 136–54.

17. Gandhi's statement, 29 May 1926, *CWMG*, vol. 25, pp. 136–54.

18. Gandhi's statement, 29 May 1926, *CWMG*, vol. 25, pp. 136–54.

19. Mohammed Ali to Jawaharlal Nehru, 15 June 1924, in Jawaharlal Nehru, *A Bunch of Old Letters*, pp. 39–41.

20. Mohammed Ali to Jawaharlal Nehru, 15 June 1924, in Jawaharlal Nehru, *A Bunch of Old Letters*, pp. 39–41.

21. Gandhi to G.D. Birla, 28 July 1925, G.D. Birla, *Bapu: A Unique Association* (Calcutta, 1998), p. 31.

22. Jawaharlal Nehru, *An Autobiography* (London, 1936), pp. 139–40.

23. Jawaharlal Nehru to Syed Mahmud, 3 February, 1925, in V.N. Datta and B.E. Cleghorn, eds, *A Nationalist Muslim and Indian Politics: Being the Selected Correspondence of the Late Dr. Syed Mahmud* (Delhi, 1974), p. 32.

24. Telegram from Malaviya to Gandhi, 6 September 1924, *CWMG*, vol. 25, p. 95.

25. Gandhi to G.D. Birla, 7 August 1925, in Birla, *Bapu: A Unique Association*, p. 33.

26. Gandhi to G.D. Birla, 10 August 1924, in Birla, *Bapu: A Unique Association*, p. 12.

27. Gandhi to G.D. Birla, 28 July 1925, in Birla, *Bapu: A Unique Association*, p. 31.

28. Reading to Birkenhead, 24 September 1925, Reading Papers, no. 25.

29. W. Marris to Reading, 21 December 1925, Reading Papers.

30. W. Marris to Reading, 21 December 1925, Reading Papers.

31. Mitra, *Indian Annual Register, 1926*, vol. II, pp. 25–32.

32. Tendulkar, *Mahatma*, vol. II, pp. 148–9.

33. Sitaramayya, *History of the Congress*, vol. I, p. 465.

34. Gandhi's statement on Kohat, *CWMG*, vol. 25, p. 327.

35. Mitra, *Indian Annual Register, 1924*, vol. II, pp. 176–9.

36. Telegram from the Personal Assistant to the Viceroy to Malaviya, 6 December 1924, Reading Papers, no. 436.

37. *CWMG*, vol. 25, p. 328.

38. Gandhi's speech at Khilafat Conference, Amritsar, 6 December 1924, *CWMG*, vol. 25, pp. 402–3.

39. Oral transcript of J.B. Kripalani, NMML.

40. Mahadev Desai, *Day to Day with Gandhi*, vol. V (Ahmedabad, 2001), p. 264.

41. *Mitra, Indian Annual Register, 1925*, vol. I, pp. 97–106.

42. W. Marris to Reading, 21 December 1925, Reading Papers, no. 617, roll 11.

43. Home Poll, Proceedings, no. 333/1925.

44. Telegram from Kapil Deo Malaviya to Viceroy, 14 September 1925, Home Poll, Proceedings, no. 333/1925.

45. *Leader*, 14 September, 1925 and *Abhudaya*, 20 September, 1925.

46. H.S. Crosthwaite, Collector of Allahabad, to Commissioner, Allahabad Division, 14 September, 1925, UPSA, GAD file no. 680/1925.

47. J.C. Smith, Commissioner, Allahabad Division, to C.L. Alexander, Chief Secretary to UP government, 21 September 1925, UPSA, GAD, 680/1925.

48. J.C. Smith to C.L. Alexander, 7 September 1925, UPSA, GAD, 650/1925.

49. J.C. Smith to C.L. Alexander, 14 September 1925, UPSA, GAD, 650/1925.

50. H.S. Crosthwaite to J.C. Smith, 14 September 1925, UPSA, GAD, 650/1925.

51. Malaviya to H.S. Crosthwaite, 14 September 1925.

52. Malaviya to H.S. Crosthwaite, 14 September 1925.

53. *Leader* and *Abhudaya*, 5 to 18 September 1925.

54. Commissioner, Allahabad Division, to Chief Secretary, UP, 19 September 1925.

55. H.G. Haig's note, 21 September 1925, Home Poll, 368/1925.

56. Telegram from Agent to the Governor General in Rajputana, Ajmer, to the Secretary, Home Department, Government of India, 3 August 1923, Home Poll, 368/1925.

57. H.G. Haig's note, 21 September 1925, Home Poll, 368/1925.

58. W. Marris to Irwin, 12 August 1926, Halifax Papers, no. 203.

59. Telegram from the Government of United Provinces, 17 August 1926, Home Poll, 187/1926.

60. Telegram from the Government of United Provinces to the Government of India, 8 October 1926, UPSA, GAD, 613/1926, no. 230.

61. S. O'Donnell to Irwin, 14 October 1926, Halifax Papers.

62. Telegram from the Government of the United Provinces to Malaviya, 7 October 1926, UPSA, GAD, file no. 613/1926.

63. Malaviya to G.B. Lambert, Chief Secretary to the Government of the United Provinces, 9 October 1926, UPSA, GAD, file no. 613/1926.

64. Malaviya to Lambert, 9 October 1926, UPSA, GAD, file no. 613/1926.

65. Malaviya to Lambert, 9 October, 1926, UPSA, GAD, file no. 613/1926.

66. H.S. Crosthwaite to G.B. Lambert, Chief Secretary to the Government of the United Provinces, 10 October 1926, UPSA, GAD 613/1926.

67. H.S. Crosthwaite to G.B. Lambert, 10 October 1926, UPSA, GAD 613/1926.

68. G.B. Lambert to Malaviya, 12 October 1926, UPSA, GAD, 613/1926.
69. Irwin to S. O'Donell, 14 November 1926, Halifax Papers, roll no. 10.
70. Thursby, *Hindu–Muslim Relations in British India*, p. 175.
71. Home Poll, 112/IV/1926.
72. Home Poll, 187/1926.
73. Chief Secretary of Bengal to Home Department, 16 April 1926, Home Poll, 11/VII/1926.
74. Chief Secretary of Bengal to Home Department, 16 April 1926, Home Poll, II/VII/1926.
75. Arya Mitra's comments on the absence of Lord Lytton from Calcutta, Home Poll, 112/IV/1926.
76. Malaviya to C.Vijayaraghavachariar, 2 May 1926, C.V.R. Papers.
77. Malaviya to C.Vijayaraghavachariar, 2 May 1926, C.V.R. Papers.
78. Malaviya to C.Vijayaraghavachariar, 2 May 1926, C.V.R. Papers.
79. Chief Secretary, Government of Bengal, to Home Department, 17 April 1926, Home Poll, II/VII/1926.
80. Chief Secretary, Government of Bengal, to Home Department, 10 May 1926, Home Poll, II/XXV/1926.
81. J. Crerar's note, 4 June 1926, Home Poll 1–12/1926, II/XXV/1926.
82. J. Crerar's note, 4 June 1926, Home Poll 1–12/1926, II/XXV/1926.
83. Haig to Chief Secretary, Government of Bengal, 8 March 1927, Home Poll, 166/1/1927.
84. Telegram from Government of Bengal, 18 August 1926, Home Poll, 187/1926.
85. Telegram from the Government of Bengal, 18 August 1926, Home Poll, 187/1926.
86. Telegram from Government of India to Secretary of State, 15 August 1926, Home Poll, 187/1926.
87. J. Crerar's note, 9 August 1926, Home Poll, 187/1926.
88. Hugh Stephenson to Irwin, 9 August 1926, Halifax Papers, no. 197, roll no. 10.
89. Hugh Stephenson to Irwin, 9 August 1926, Halifax Papers, no. 197, roll no. 10.
90. Hugh Stephenson to Irwin, 9 August 1926, Halifax Papers, no. 197, roll no. 10.
91. Irwin to Montagu Butler, 18 August 1926, Halifax Papers, no. 211, roll no. 10.
92. Irwin to Goschan, Governor of Madras, 24 August 1926, Halifax Papers, no. 221, roll no. 10.
93. Home Poll, Proceedings, Telegram to the Government of Bengal, 15 August 1926, 187/1926.

94. Home Poll, Proceedings, Government of India to the Government of Bengal, 15 August 1926, 187/1926.
95. Home Poll, Proceedings, J. Crerar's note, 9 August 1926, 187/1926.
96. W. Marris to Irwin, 12 August 1926, Halifax Papers.
97. Irwin to Goschen, 24 August 1926, Halifax Papers, no. 221, roll 10.
98. Montagu Butler, Governor of Central Provinces, to Irwin, 12 August 1926, Halifax Papers, no. 202, roll 10.
99. W. Marris to Irwin, 12 August 1926, Halifax Papers.
100. Durga Das, *India from Curzon to Nehru and After* (New Delhi, 1971), p. 86.
101. Das, *India from Curzon to Nehru and After*, p. 151.

8 Constitutional Politics (1922–29)

The suspension of the non-cooperation movement led to a reorienta-
tion of the Congress strategy. The pendulum swung back to constitutional politics and the Swaraj Party was formed within the Congress
with the twofold line of action of entering the councils and wrecking
the Reform Act of 1919 from within. Obviously, Malaviya's place
should have been in the party whose main objective was entry into the
councils. But that was not to be. From the very beginning, Malaviya
had sharp differences with the founding fathers of the Swaraj Party over
the programme and policies to be pursued in the councils. He stood
for entry into the councils not for the sole and avowed purpose of
wrecking them but for the purpose of using them for national advancement—obstructing their activities where necessary and extending
cooperation when beneficial. These differences were, no doubt, more
in the details than in the fundamentals. But these considerations were
important to Malaviya. Hence he kept away from the Swaraj Party
since its very inception. Malaviya was apprehensive that there would
be lesser freedom of expression and action and more clashes within the
new party. However, he was confident that substantial unity could yet
be forged among various leaders and groups willing to work in favour
of the constitutional programme of contesting elections and carrying
on the fight for swaraj within the councils.[1]

THE ELECTIONS OF 1923

At the time of the elections of 1923, Malaviya was under no obligation
to support the Swaraj Party candidates against the candidates of other

parties. In fact, he had proposed that all leaders, whether Swarajists or Independents or Liberals, should arrive at a mutual arrangement by which they could avoid opposing each other and, instead, offer a united opposition to those who were either not believers in swaraj or were not prepared to do everything in their power to win it. Malaviya urged the desirability of the best of men, irrespective of party affiliations, being returned to the legislatures and was not in favour of confining his support to Swarajist candidates alone. Elaborating this strategy, he wrote to Lajpat Rai:

> I am really glad you have adopted a broad-minded policy in this important matter, a policy which is calculated to unite all workers in the country's cause who are earnest and sincere, though their points of view may at times not coincide with those of the Congress party. I hope the electors will appreciate the wisdom of your action.[2]

Malaviya's proposal did not, however, appeal to the Swarajist leadership, which decided to fight the 1923 elections on party lines. Undeterred by this lack of response, Malaviya entered the fray in accordance with his original plans. He was elected unopposed to the Legislative Assembly and did his utmost to extend support to some eminent liberal leaders like Iswar Saran, Hridaya Nath Kunzru, and H.T.Telang. While supporting the candidature of Iswar Saran, he publicly explained his position and asserted that the former's election to the Legislative Assembly 'will be a distinct public gain and his being set aside in favour of any three younger candidates will be regrettable in public interest'.[3] Malaviya did not hesitate to oppose the candidature of the veteran journalist C.Y. Chintamani as during his tenure as a minister, the Chintamani had worked in close collaboration with the provincial government and had supported its repressive policy. It was largely due to Malaviya's opposition that Chintamani lost the election. In the Legislative Assembly, Malaviya was instrumental in the formation of a coalition between the Swarajists, Moderates, and Independents.

PARTICIPATION IN THE SECOND LEGISLATIVE ASSEMBLY

The newly elected Legislative Assembly, which met for the first time in January 1924, had 140 members, 104 of whom were elected. Malaviya helped the formation of the Independent Party in the Central

Legislature consisting of the members belonging to his own group and that of M.A. Jinnah. Malaviya was so keen about the formation of this party of 25 members within the assembly that he facilitated Jinnah's leadership and agreed to work as deputy leader of the newly formed party, in spite of his seniority in age and experience compared to the latter.[4] He was then in a position to reach out to Motilal Nehru and C.R. Das, offering to merge his party with the Swarajist Party, which had 32 members in the assembly. A new Nationalist Party was thus formed within the assembly which could challenge thirty-six official members in the central legislature whenever it wanted to do so. The powerful Indian bloc of elected representatives, committed to achieving dominion status and full responsible government, thus came into existence.

The tone of the nationalist demand for constitutional reform was set in the very first session of the assembly. A resolution was moved demanding that necessary steps for revising the Act of 1919 be immediately taken so as to secure full self-governing dominion status for India, and a suggestion was put forward that, if necessary, a Royal Commission be appointed for the purpose. While speaking for the motion, Malaviya came down heavily on the mismanagement of law and order during the last two years:

> We believe that it is a convention which has gone like steel into our hearts that the British bureaucracy in this country will not even take the measures that are necessary to enable the Indians to get actual responsible government in this country as long as they are in power and we ask that they should cease to be in power.[5]

M.A. Jinnah, R.K.S. Chetty, P. Thakurdas and several other members of the central assembly strongly supported the motion which was finally carried by 64 votes to 48. This was a great victory for the nationalists against the government. The viceroy wrote to the secretary of state: 'I am rather surprised at the practical unanimity among Indians of all shades of description.... Their attitude is of such doubt of our intentions as to amount almost to mistrust. They think I am too slow, too cautious and have been restrained by public opinion in England. I confess I am not happy about it. I do not like the mistrust of Government's intentions which seems to be spreading.'[6] The viceroy further informed his superior that the general tenor of the debate in the assembly was 'in favour of definite advance on constitutional advance of a much more extensive character than had been contemplated in the discussion between you and me'.[7]

The viceroy's letter was a frank admission of the actual 'constitutional advance of a much more extensive character' envisaged by Malaviya and most other members of the central legislature, and their distrust of the motives of the viceroy. In an apparent effort to minimize the damage to his reputation, the viceroy appointed a committee under Alexander Muddiman to inquire into the working of the Act of 1919. The terms of reference of the committee were very circumscribed as it was only asked to enquire into the difficulties arising from the working of the act and investigate the feasibility and desirability of securing remedies. The Muddiman Committee could not come to any unanimous conclusions. As such, there were two reports—the majority report signed by official members and the minority report signed by four Indian members.[8] When the home member moved a resolution in the assembly on 7 September 1925 recommending the acceptance of the majority report, it was opposed by the Swarajists and the Independents. Malaviya demanded extensive changes in the constitutional machinery and administration of India and reiterated his proposals made earlier in the assembly in February 1924. While taking part in the long debate in the assembly, several other members supported Malaviya and impressed upon the government the need for extensive and fundamental changes in the Reform Act of 1919. It was in this atmosphere of compromise and threat that the debate on the Muddiman Committee was conducted. When the resolution moved by elected Indian members was put to vote, it was carried by 72 to 45 votes in the Legislative Assembly, giving out a clear message that the Indian representatives had grave doubts about the government's actual intentions with regard to constitutional changes in India.[9]

Soon after the end of the Assembly session, the viceroy got in touch with Malaviya and several other legislators in an effort to win them over to the government side or at least to neutralize their opposition to the official stand on constitutional reforms. Giving a detailed account of the 'long talk' he had with Malaviya in September 1925, the viceroy reported that the members of the assembly 'acted very unintelligently for reasons which rather amazed me and that so far from advancing

India's cause, if they proceeded on present lines, they would retard it'.[10] He further stated::

> When I suggested to Malaviya that they might have been more wisely advised if they had grasped the hand which you and I had generously extended to them he asked whether it was now too late and whether I would advise them of some means or procedure whereby they could do it.[11]

The viceroy's version of his meeting with Malaviya indicates that the latter was willing to work in close cooperation with him in the hope of securing constitutional reforms. Malaviya's faith in the good intentions of the British was still intact.

By this time the Nationalist Party, which had worked successfully in the assembly during the first session, began to show signs of crumbling. The unity between the Swarajists and the Independents was short-lived in the absence of a broad common ideological basis. The demand for granting immediate constitutional progress as a precondition for cooperating with official measures of national importance was too limited a goal to hold together men of intelligence and independent thinking like Malaviya and M.A. Jinnah who had their own misgivings about the actual strategy of the Swaraj Party.[12]

The independents, led by M.A. Jinnah, were especially opposed to resorting to wrecking and destruction within the assembly and were the first to announce their separation from the Swarajists. Soon after, in September 1925, Malaviya also started having second thoughts about the usefulness of working together with Motilal Nehru. It was singularly unfortunate that the fragile nature of the solidarity between the Indian members of the assembly came to the surface within a short period of one year.

In October, the Swaraj Party was faced with a revolt within its own ranks. In the Central Provinces—the only province where the Swarajists had an absolute majority—S.B. Tambe, the Swarajist leader, accepted a seat in the governor's Executive Council. Motilal Nehru's condemnation of Tambe's action accelerated the pace of the rift among the Swarajists. N.C. Kelkar and M.R. Jayakar openly began to advocate that the Swarajists should abandon 'the role of wreckers' and instead adopt an attitude of 'responsive cooperation' towards the government. Malaviya and Lajpat Rai were also prepared to extend support to them.[13]

THE KANPUR CONGRESS SESSION AND AFTER

Meanwhile, fresh developments of great significance were taking place within the Congress which decisively influenced Malaviya's position. Soon after his release from jail in August 1924, Gandhi wrote a 'very confidential' letter to Motilal Nehru, informing him that he was prepared to facilitate his securing the Congress machinery and would actually assist him in doing so.[14] The Mahatma explained that he preferred 'to support Pandit Motilalji and the Swaraj Party because they were at least nearer to his line of thinking and it precludes his personal involvement with them'.[15] What has been termed as Gandhi's 'surrender' was completed in the Kanpur Congress session of 1925. It was entirely due to his influence that the Congress machinery came under the control of the Swaraj Party. The Swarajists thus had the entire Congress prestige, machinery, and funds at their disposal. The Congress now accepted the responsibility of whatever the Swarajists did as a parliamentary party. The surrender completed, Gandhi retired to Sabarmati announcing his intention to keep away from the council politics.

Gandhi, however, could not prevent an open tug of war at the Kanpur Congress. When Motilal Nehru moved a resolution calling upon the Swarajist members to withdraw from the Legislative Assembly in the event of the government being unwilling to accept their national demand, Malaviya moved an amendment to it proposing 'cooperation being given when it may be necessary to advance the national cause and obstruction resorted to when that may be necessary'.[16] Malaviya was supported by M.R. Jayakar and various other leaders from Maharashtra. Motilal Nehru brushed aside Malaviya's amendment to his resolution with humiliating comments. This did not augur well for the future of the Congress, as it signified a widening rift between the believers of the two ideologies within the party. There were growing signs of a 'perpetual fight for the sake of fight' after the Kanpur Congress session.[17]

DEMAND FOR RESPONSIVE COOPERATION

The cult of responsive cooperation was definitely in the air at the time the Responsivists held a conference with the leaders of the other parties in April 1926 in Bombay, and the result was the formation of an Indian

National Party to prepare for and accelerate the demand for swaraj based on the dominion-status model by all possible means. Malaviya was, however, not fully satisfied with the decisions of the meeting and felt that 'the golden opportunity was not fully utilized at Bombay'.[18] Malaviya moved to Sabarmati in order to persuade Gandhi to use his influence to bring about a compromise between the Swarajists and the Responsivists. The leaders of the two wings of the Congress later met at Sabarmati, on 20 April 1926, in an attempt to explore the ways of bringing about a reunion between them. Those present included Sarojini Naidu, Motilal Nehru, Jayakar, Kelkar, Moonje, and Gandhi. Since Malaviya was unable to attend the Sabarmati meeting, he telegraphically offered his suggestions for consideration by all those leaders who were taking part in it. As a result of these talks, the Sabarmati Pact was signed conceding the demand for the acceptance of office under specific conditions.

FAILURE OF TALKS WITH MOTILAL NEHRU

From the time of the signing of the Sabarmati Pact to the final preparations for the council elections, Malaviya left no stone unturned to arrive at an understanding with Motilal Nehru. He noted: 'If Motilal will honestly decide to re-unite Congressmen and share responsibility and power with a few select Congressmen the results we desire will follow.'[19] Such a response, however, remained a distant dream for Malaviya as the elder Nehru repudiated the Sabarmati Pact within a month of signing it. With the annulment of the pact, Malaviya's hopes of reaching a settlement with Motilal Nehru suffered a serious setback. Malaviya analysed the new political situation emerging after the end of the Sabarmati Pact in the following words:

> Where we desired unity a fight has become inevitable. There are only two parties in the field. The hope of a reunited Congress must for the present be abandoned. With it must drop all ideas of utilizing the existing Executive of the Congress for educating the electorate.[20]

Malaviya's disappointment in the middle of 1926 was largely due to his failure to reach an agreement with Motilal Nehru. His speeches and writings until this period are a clear testimony of his earnest desire to fight the November 1926 elections together with the Swarajists and not separately. However, until early May 1926, there were no signs of any compromise between the Responsivists and the Swarajists. Malaviya was, therefore, forced to define his strategy in the following manner:

> The only practical course left open to us is to join hands with the Indian National plus Responsive Cooperation Party and to help to see the right kind of candidates elected so far as it lies in our power.[21]

MALAVIYA'S PROPOSALS FOR EDUCATING VOTERS

While making preparations for the November 1926 elections, Malaviya laid down detailed proposals for educating the voters. He emphasized the 'great duty that lies upon you and me on the one side to make a proper use of the legislatures and on the other side, to educate the electors of their rights, responsibility, and power.' To this end he proposed 'to organize the preparation and publication of about a dozen pamphlets to educate the electors.' Malaviya desired that these pamphlets should deal with the 'most important national questions' which he outlined as under:

1. India's past, present and future or what we were, what we are, what we wish to be.
2. Swaraj and how to attain it i.e. the conditions of attaining and maintaining Swaraj.
3. Education of the citizens in patriotism, religious toleration and civic rights particularly.
4. Education for the Public Services.
5. Military Education or preparing the people for the defence of their country.
6. National Industrial development.
7. Banking facilities
8. Currency and Exchange
9. Railways and their administration
10. The condition of the cultivators. Agriculture and the agriculturist (The milk supply or dairy farming)
11. Industries and the Industrialist (Reduction of expenditure particularly)
12. Military Expenditure
13. Reduction of Taxation
14. Public Health and Hygiene

15. Rural and Urban sanitation
16. Nationalism versus Communalism, Democracy and Party system
17. Compulsory Elementary Education[22]

Referring to the slogan regarding the need to 'educate our masters'raised in England at the time of the passage of the Second Reform Act of 1867, Malaviya desired that similar efforts be made to educate the new voters in the country. He lamented that 'though the Act of 1919 has been passed no effort has been made by the Government or the people specially in the direction of "educating our masters"' and added, 'I personally think that public revenue should be voted not merely for establishing schools but also for educating the electors.'[23] With the larger view of strengthening democratic institutions in the country, Malaviya stressed the need for educating the people about their rights and responsibilities at the time of the November elections.

RENEWAL OF NEGOTIATIONS WITH MOTILAL NEHRU

Even after the failure of the Sabarmati Pact, Malaviya did not lose heart and continued making efforts to work out a compromise with Motilal Nehru in order to avoid a confrontation between the Responsivists and the Swarajists. Towards this end, Malaviya and G.D. Birla met the veteran nationalist leader, Bhagwan Das, on at least three occasions. Giving an account of their consultations, the latter informed Motilal Nehru that 'all that the non-Swarajists want is that they should be consulted before any matter is so declared to be an essential matter'.[24] Bhagwan Das further informed the elder Nehru that 'Malaviya was "agreeable" to the formation of a Board, consisting of five members, to manage the coming elections by mutual consultations.' He suggested that Motilal Nehru, Malaviya, Rampal Singh, and a representative of the Muslims could be included in such a board. Bhagwan Das wanted to convince Motilal Nehru that the board would help in the promotion of national interests as well as in the preservation of harmony of the private and personal relations between candidates, supporters, and all others concerned.[25] Unfortunately, Bhagwan Das's suggestion did not appeal to Motilal Nehru as he was not prepared 'to bear Malaviya's company on the road he has chosen'.[26] These consultations show that Motilal was prepared to fight the coming elections on his own.[27] He showed scant regard for any suggestions put forward by Malaviya and argued that the parties 'recently started under the name of "The Indian Cooperation Party" and the "Independent Congress Party" were not in any way connected with the Congress', and that 'they have come into existence with the avowed object of opposing the Congress candidates and defeating the Congress programme. Madan Mohan Malaviya has declared an open war against the Swaraj Party which means the Congress itself.'[28] Thus Motilal chose the 'party' line and did not show much willingness to have any truck with the 'other' party and its leaders. In such a situation Malaviya's attempts to bring the Swarajists and the non-Swarajists together failed and a head-on collision between them become inevitable.

As a last-minute effort, an 'informal conversation' was arranged between Malaviya and Lala Lajpat Rai on one side and Mrs Sarojini Naidu and Motilal Nehru on the other at Simla on 4 September 1926 'to explore the possibilities of an understanding to run the elections on a joint ticket'.[29] As expected, Malaviya repeated his demands for the acceptance of office after the elections and general revision of the list prepared for the Congress candidates so as to accommodate the nominees of the Responsivists. These negotiations failed again. Motilal Nehru announced that 'no compromise has been arrived at or is likely in the near future' and that 'no useful purpose could be served by continuing the conversation'.[30] The elder Nehru lost no time in asking 'all Congressmen to apply themselves to the work before them with usual energy and assiduity'.' With these words, Motilal closed the doors for the Congress and the Swaraj Party for any further dialogue with Malaviya and the Responsivists and engaged himself fully in the election propaganda.

FORMATION OF THE INDEPENDENT CONGRESS PARTY

In this political scenario a Responsivists' Conference met in Delhi on 12 September 1926 to take stock of the prevailing situation and decide upon the future course of action. In this conference, Malaviya announced the formation of the Independent Congress Party with the support of Lala Lajpat Rai, M.R. Jayakar, B.S. Moonje, N.C. Kelkar, and others with a view to organizing the various nationalist forces at work in the country on the basis of four cardinal principles, which were '(*a*) acceptance of Congress Creed, (*b*) Working the Council to the best possible advantage; (*c*) Acceptance of "Office" under the Crown; (*d*) leaving members free to vote as they liked on communal matters where differences between different communities could not be composed.'[31] The manifesto of the Independent Congress Party revealed that the party desired to use the provincial councils and the assembly for the establishment of full responsible government. The leaders of the Independent Congress Party not only refused to appeal to the voters in the name of the Hindu Mahasabha but also claimed to be as good Congressmen as those belonging to the Swaraj Party.

Thus the Independent Congress Party was formed by Malaviya with the help of dissident Congress elements, liberals, Hindu Mahasabhites, and Hindu Oudh landlords. It had, however, no real organization of its own and was able to use different Hindu Sabhas scattered all over UP, Punjab, and various other north-Indian provinces. He paraded quite an imposing line-up of speakers in various election meetings. They moved from one city to another, spoke about the Independent Congress Party and its programme, and helped boost the morale of the candidates selected by the party.

DISMAL PERFORMANCE OF THE SWARAJ PARTY IN THE ELECTIONS

It has been pointed out that 'since the basis of franchise was communal, communalism reached a peak in 1926, the election year.'[32] The constituencies where the elections were most fiercely contested in November 1926 were almost entirely 'non-Muhammadan'. The issue between the Swarajists and the Independent Congress Party centered on the most explosive issue of communal rights. It was not directly a fight between Hindus and Muslims; the point at issue was the Swarajists' readiness or otherwise to protect Hindu interests. The Independent Congress Party leaders alleged that the Swarajists were so concerned about securing Muslim support that they clung to a set of secular policies that, the former claimed, meant giving in to the Muslims and foregoing the legitimate rights and aspirations of the Hindus. Echoing these sentiments, Malaviya publicly asserted that the Swaraj Party was sacrificing Hindu interests.[33] The influencial Allahabad daily described 'Swarajism' as being synonymous with the 'the betrayal of legitimate Hindu interests'.[34] Such communal antagonism provided the worst possible setting for the electoral battle of November 1926.

Explaining the political scenario, Motilal wrote to his son:

> The political situation is almost hopeless ... the elections which it is now certain will be fought on communal lines. During my absence in the hills Malaviya has been hard at work and, by a free use of Birla's money, has won over many of our workers. The prospect in U.P. is very gloomy. With the exception of Rafi and Sitla Sahai there is not a man I can thoroughly rely upon.[35]

Motilal was being less than fair in pointing the accusing finger at Malaviya on the eve of the elections. Instead of owning responsibility for the 'hopeless' political situation at this time, he attempted to shift the entire burden on Malaviya and his associates. The sequence of events ahead of the 1926 elections, narrated earlier in this chapter, show that Malaviya was keen to fight the elections jointly with the Swarajists. He made several attempts in mid-1926 to get in touch with Motilal Nehru with the help of his well-wishers and friends. In spite of all these efforts, no compromise could be reached between them, either because Motilal Nehru had no desire to come to terms with Malaviya, or because he had already made up his mind to fight the coming elections alone. The sequence of events shows that, ultimately, no understanding could be reached between the two eminent leaders on the eve of the all-important council elections, due to the rigid stand taken by Motilal Nehru and not due to any lack of sincerity on Malaviya's part. The latter should, therefore, not be held responsible for the tussle witnessed between the Swarajists and the Independent Congress Party during the elections.

NOVEMBER 1926 ELECTIONS

The question has often been raised whether, during the elections, the real clash was between principles and policies or personalities. The differences in principles and policies have been explained earlier and these differences were by no means unreal or trival. However, the clash of personalities lent them an extra sharpness and precipitated matters.

The Swarajists did not spare even Lajpat Rai's seat and he was obliged to fight elections like any other leader. Similarly, the Independent Party put up a candidate against Ganesh Shankar Vidyarthi. There was a proposal that Malaviya should contest the same seat from where Motilal Nehru was expected to stand for the assembly elections. Lajpat Rai immediately intervened and asked Malaviya 'not to follow the advice of your friends in the matter as in my judgment the country needs both of you in the Legislative Assembly'.[36] The clash between the two leaders was averted. But it brought to surface the growing bitterness between the Swarajists and non-Swarajists during the elections.

Malaviya always tried to keep the fight clean and honourable even when he knew that mud was being slung at him. He did not attach an exaggerated importance to party labels. With regard to the notions of discipline within a political party, Malaviya was very different from the Swarajist chief.

Against this background, it would be useful to examine the 'personal political moves and countermoves'[37] of Motilal Nehru and Malaviya with regard to the Gorakhpur–Banaras assembly seat for which Sri Prakash very unwillingly fought the election against G.D. Birla. As early as 2 June, Bhagwan Das informed Motilal Nehru that it would be 'nothing short of a tragedy for Sri Prakash to be pitted in the coming elections against a man of Ghanshyam Das Birla's sterling worth, high patriotism public benefactions, supporter of many good causes'.[38] Motilal Nehru did not pay much attention to Bhagwan Das' viewpoint and, in order to win him over to his side, sought to convince him that Malaviya had 'purposely set up Birla against Sri Prakash'.[39] This silenced Bhagwan Das who left the issue to the judgment of his son, suggesting that he contest elections for the UP council rather than the central assembly. This was a way out for Sri Prakash to avoid a contest with Birla. The issue, however, dragged on for several months. Sri Prakash's letter to G.D. Birla aptly summarises his frame of mind:

> Believe me when I say that I had no wish to enter the Council and had, in fact, prayed Pandit Motilalji to spare me. Ever since your name appeared I have been feeling sore at the prospect of opposing you and have also been in communication with Pandit Motilalji on this subject. Father is so distressed over our contesting the same seat that I dare not broach the subject to him. I am myself in such a predicament that I cannot decide what to say or do.[40]

Motilal Nehru had made up his mind to put up Sri Prakash as a Swarajist candidate for the Gorakhpur–Banaras assembly seat and informed the latter about his decision in the following words:'We can rely upon our own and our worker's energy and whatever prestige Congress still enjoys.... If it comes to fight with Birla it is but fair that the Party should come to your assistance.'[41] Motilal knew, from the very outset, that Malaviya was equally keen to put up G.D. Birla for the same seat. It is unfortunate that the two top leaders could not find a way to avoid the contest. The communication gap between them on the eve of the elections unnecessarily led to bitterness between them as well as between their associates and followers.

Notwithstanding these developments, both Sri Prakash and G.D. Birla remained on friendly terms, fought the election with dignity, and carried on the election campaign without any bitterness. While on an election tour to Chunar, G.D. Birla paid a visit to Bhagwan Das who wrote to his son Sri Prakash, that 'the more I see Birla the more I like him.... He talked very nicely and far more reasonably than others.'[42] G.D. Birla not only won the heart of the veteran nationalist leader but his seat as well, which proved the correctness of Malaviya's faith in him.

The 1926 elections were fought less on issues of public importance than on such emotive issues as music in front of mosques and communal relations between the two communities. Never before had an election in India aroused such religious bitterness.

Taken as a whole, the Swaraj Party was weakened both in the councils as well as in the Legislative Assembly where it won 40 out of the 104 seats for which elections were held. The cleavage in political life was fully reflected in the Legislative Assembly. The Independent Congress Party and the Responsivists won 20 seats in the assembly. Thus Malaviya and Lajpat Rai had sufficient numbers to make their presence felt in the assembly.

In the provincial councils, the Swaraj Party scored a notable victory in Madras, capturing almost half the seats. In Bihar and Orissa it held its ground. In Bengal and Bombay it was worse off than before and in the Central Provinces, UP, and Punjab, it was almost routed.

Evidently, Motilal Nehru's election strategy had failed. One of the his close associates was led to comment that 'the whole of educated India was against him'.[43] Motilal himself admitted that 'I had hardly any workers worth the name in my own province'[44] and yet he attempted to put the entire blame on 'the kind of propaganda started against me under the auspices of Malaviya–Lala gang'.[45] He repeatedly referred to the 'onslaughts of Malaviya and Lalaji',[46] forgetting that the two leaders had time and again extended their hands in friendship to him before the November elections.

GAUHATI CONGRESS SESSION AND AFTER

Motilal Nehru was so keen to keep the Congress under his thumb that he expressed the imaginary fear, a few weeks before the Gauhati Congress session of 1926, that the 'Malaviya–Lala gang are busy at work with the aid of Birla's money to deliver a deadly assault on the Congress'.[47] He repeated his accusation again in the following words:

> The Malaviya–Lala gang aided by Birla's money are making frantic efforts to capture the Congress. They will probably succeed as no counter effort is possible from our side.[48]

Motilal deliberately used Malaviya's name so as to win the sympathy and support of Congressmen spread all over the country. Compared to Motilal's anxiety displayed ahead of the Gauhati Congress session, Malaviya was, as usual, composed and calm. He expressed no desire to persuade his friends or supporters to reach Gauhati in large numbers and was prepared to work with anyone to strengthen the Congress. He maintained that 'the Congress is yet a power and I wish it to become a greater power as it used to be by adopting a sound policy'.[49] In spite of these laudable motives, Malaviya could not make any impressive show at the Gauhati Congress session, as the majority of the delegates were on the opposite side.[50] His proposal for modifying the Swarajist policy of obstruction in such a way as to allow the acceptance of ministership was turned down. Malaviya could not carry the Congress with him. Reporting about the proceedings of the session to his son, Motilal was most uncharitable in his comments about Malaviya and his colleagues:

> Malaviya attended the Congress and, as usual, put in his plea for moderation and offices but was not taken seriously by anybody. Lajpat Rai, Jayakar and Kelkar did not attend. Aney and Moonje were silent spectators.[51]

Motilal's fears about the trial of strength at Gauhati proved groundless. There is no evidence that Malaviya or any of his associates had any plans to muster their forces at the session. Even so, Motilal wrote triumphantly:

> It is enough to say that the Gauhati Congress has been a greater success than expected. We have stood firm against all reactionaries and carried everything we wanted by overwhelming majorities.[52]

Notwithstanding Motilal's success at the Gauhati Congress, he no longer felt the optimism he had experienced in January 1924. By 1927, the political atmosphere had 'violently shifted',[53] the Swaraj Party had suffered a serious setback, the elections had left a bitter taste in his mouth, and he felt deeply despondent about his future role in the newly formed Legislative Assembly. Motilal wrote to Gandhi that 'I have already begun the process of slipping out of the Assembly. During the session I kept in the background as far as possible.'[54]

THE THIRD LEGISLATIVE ASSEMBLY

The atmosphere in the third Legislative Assembly, which met in January 1927, was very different from what it had been in the previous assembly, largely because of the reverses suffered by the Swaraj Party in the 1926 elections. It had only 40 seats of the total strength of 104 elected seats in the House. While the Swarajists were in a reduced strength in this assembly, Malaviya had a comparatively larger following in the house. He, however, did not fail to realize that the need of the hour was to arrive at an understanding with Motilal Nehru. Accordingly, 20 members of Malaviya's Nationalist Party and the members of the Swaraj Party decided to work together. The unity thus forged led the Swarajists to voice their views with greater force in the central legislature. The two stalwarts were quick to get over the bitter memories of the elections.

As the leader of the Nationalist Party in the central legislature, Malaviya made several notable speeches during the session, the first of which was in support of Motilal Nehru's resolution, moved on 3 February 1927, that the large number of political prisoners who were under preventive detention without trial for over twenty-seven months in Bengal should be released immediately. Supporting the resolution, Malaviya pointed out that the maintenance of law and order very much depended upon public opinion which was definitely in favour of justice for the political prisoners. He spoke at length on the Currency Bill which was introduced by the government during the same month, providing for raising the exchange value of the rupee from 16 to 18 pence per rupee. He traced the long history of currency in India and put his finger on the root of the currency problem by asserting that all the ills from which India suffered was due to the failure of the government to introduce a gold currency in India. The first great clash between the government and the Indian representatives in the assembly took place over the Steel Protection Bill. It was a clever device to secure British interests in India by offering a small bait of protection to the Indian steel industry. The preferential treatment, commonly known as Imperial Preference, was widely opposed by Malaviya. He was against the preferential rates of duty given to the British steel imported into India.

BOYCOTT OF THE SIMON COMMISSION

With the formal announcement of the appointment of the Statutory Commission, known commonly as the Simon Commission, on 2 November 1927, the issue of the future constitutional set-up of the country gained prominence. By providing a common platform against the government, the Simon Commission created an opportunity for various political parties and politicians not only to raise their voice against the imperial onslaught, but also to work together to find an answer to the questions which were to overshadow Indian politics for several decades to come.

Malaviya's reaction to the appointment of the Simon Commission was sharp, immediate, and vigorous. He published a pamphlet on this occasion in which he stated:

> I regret to say that I could not imagine a greater and more gratuitous insult to India at the hands of the British Government than is involved in the course which is decided by them.... Nor can I recall, in my mind, any document issued by the Government in England and India, which was a feebler apologia than the communique which has been published under the signatures of H.E. Lord Irwin.[55]

Together with Malaviya, the appointment of the commission was condemned by various other prominent political leaders including T.B. Sapru, Motilal Nehru, and M.A. Ansari. As a result a wave of protest swept over India. The Congress took over the issue in its annual session at Madras and declared that the Commission was appointed in utter disregard of India's right to self determination. It resolved that the only self-respecting course was to boycott the commission at every stage and in every form. Malaviya supported the motion and appealed for unity among the people as well as political parties. One of his close associates noted that Gandhi would be 'pleased to see how strong a view Malaviya had taken of the present situation'.[56]

The Simon Commission arrived in Bombay on 3 February 1928. The country's temper flared and demonstrations were organized practically in all the cities visited by it. In Bombay, the workers struck work and greeted the commission with the slogan 'Simon go back'. This had reverberations in the Legislative Assembly as well. On 16 February, Malaviya's Nationalist Party moved a resolution in the assembly, stressing that the constitution and scheme of the commission was wholly unacceptable to the house. Elaborating the views of his party, Malaviya claimed that India was entitled to self-government and asked the people to organize and carry out a complete boycott of the commission throughout India. Without denying the authority of the British parliament to take the final decision on the constitutional set-up in the country, he and his party wanted that the settlement of the Indian question must be approached 'in a spirit of mutual conciliation and mutual understanding of the interests of the two countries'.[57]

Malaviya addressed several public meetings in Allahabad and Banaras, encouraged people to voice their protest in an organized manner, and led demonstrations against the commission in these cities. When the commission reached Lahore on 30 October 1928, a black-flag demonstration under the leadership of Lajpat Rai was organized. Malaviya was by Lajpat Rai's side on this fateful day. The police came down heavily on the procession with lathi charges and Lajpat Rai was seriously injured. Malaviya was somehow spared and witnessed the happenings with deep indignation. When the issue relating to Lajpat Rai's death was brought before the assembly, Malaviya and Lala Hansraj described their own experiences of the events on that day at Lahore.

DRAFTING THE NEHRU REPORT

The Madras Congress of December 1927 considered the question of drafting a 'Swaraj' constitution and authorized its working committee to move forward in this direction. In an effort to prepare a universally acceptable constitution, the All Parties Conference met in Delhi in February 1928 and again in May 1928. Since the constitution-making was linked with the problem of communal settlement involving consultation with the Muslim League, the Hindu Mahasabha, and others, delays occurred in the laying down of the principles on which a new constitution was to be drafted. To expedite the matter, a committee consisting of representatives of various political groups and communities was appointed, which submitted its report, called the Nehru Report, in August. More than anyone else, Motilal Nehru was fully aware of the need for winning the support of various political leaders, representatives of the Hindu Mahasabha and the Muslim League, as well as the liberals for his constitutional scheme. He thought it was 'certainly the last effort to combine all parties in joint national front'.[58] He, therefore, engaged himself in winning them over. Motilal Nehru's task was considerably eased by the support extended to him by Malaviya. The latter did his best to exercise restraint over Hindu Mahasabha leaders, toned down their outbursts, and continuously attempted to bring them round in support of the Nehru Report. Motilal acknowledged that Malaviya 'really and truly feels for his country … and has no axes to grind'.[59] The estrangement between these two leaders had by this time been forgotten and they worked together to gain support for the Nehru Report from as many quarters as possible.

When the Nehru Report was placed before the All Parties Conference at Lucknow in late August, the initial discussions were encouraging. Motilal Nehru was happy with 'the brilliant victory achieved at Lucknow' and was appreciative of the support extended to him by Malaviya on this occasion.[60] However, the work of the Nehru Committee 'was at a standstill for want of funds'. Malaviya came to the rescue of Motilal Nehru at this juncture by arranging financial support for the propaganda efforts and extended full support to the elder Nehru in various other ways.[61] A vociferous section of the Muslim League lost no time in starting a vilifying campaign against some of the basic proposals of the All Parties Conference at Lucknow. Their attitude hardened as the year rolled on. There was every fear that, at a later stage, the Muslim League leaders would either propose amendments to the Nehru Report or submit their own proposals. Motilal Nehru was keen to dissuade them from any such venture during the forthcoming

Calcutta Convention of December 1928, which was likely to put the final seal on his constitutional blueprint. To counteract increasing opposition by certain Muslim leaders, Motilal Nehru opted in favour of a balancing game. He encouraged the Hindu Mahasabha leaders to voice their opposition to Muslim demands. He explained: 'Ultimately we agreed that the opposition to Muslim demands should continue and even stiffen up to the time the Calcutta convention was held. The object was to reduce the Mahommaden demands to an irreducible minimum and then to accept them at the Convention.'[62] Motilal Nehru and Lajpat Rai worked together in close alliance during this period and exchanged several letters on the strategy likely to be adopted at the Calcutta Convention. In accordance with the understanding arrived at between them, Lajpat Rai 'put up a strong opposition to every part of the Muslim demands' in his speech delivered on 27 October 1928 at Ettawah.[63] However, the sudden death of Lajpat Rai on 17 November 1928 upset Motilal Nehru's plans. Much against the elder Nehru's wishes, Lajpat Rai's Ettawah speech was considered as his last wish and considerably stiffened the Hindu Mahasahba attitude at the time. Motilal could not soften the reaction of the Hindu Mahasabha leaders. Under these circumstances, M.A. Jinnah's amendments to the Nehru Report proposed at the Calcutta Convention on 28 December were turned down. Speaking on behalf of the Hindu Mahasabha, M.R. Jayakar opposed Jinnah's suggestions and argued that if the modifications were conceded, the very form of the report would be altered. Malaviya was a silent spectator at the time and did not take part in the crucial discussion.[64] The Nehru Report was ultimately rejected as it failed to win the favour of a large section of Muslims.

MALAVIYA OPTS FOR DOMINION STATUS

Malaviya made dominion status for India the central theme of his constitutional proposals during the years 1927–29. He fully supported the proposals of the Nehru Report that the swaraj constitution should be based on the model of the self-governing dominions, making it clear that the attainment of dominion status was to be viewed not as a 'remote stage of our evolution but as the next immediate step'.[65] To young Congress leaders, this was an unacceptable retreat from the resolution demanding complete independence adopted by the 1927 Congress session.

When the Congress met at Calcutta in 1928, Gandhi's intervention was sought. He mediated between the old generation of nationalists and the young leaders. Through the efforts of the Mahatma, a compromise was reached granting 'a year of grace and polite ultimatum to the British Government'.[66] There was near unanimity among Indian nationalists that the immediate announcement of dominion status for India was the need of the hour. Representing their views, Malaviya informed the viceroy that 'it is only a few of us [that] can talk of Dominion Status at a public meeting without interruptions in favour of complete independence and without being exposed to ridicule'.[67] In such a situation, the only remedy Malaviya looked for was an announcement from the viceroy that dominion status was being seriously considered by the British government. Irwin's initiative seemed likely to win over the support of the liberal leaders and Congressmen of moderate views. The UP governor commented, 'It is clear that many of the older men in the Congress itself as well as the liberals would not be unwilling to find a temporary landing place in which they could rest a while and avoid being swept out into the stream of Independence and Young India politics.' The British officials felt that several senior Congress leaders were anxious to welcome such British initiative on constitutional changes to counteract the Youth Movement.[68]

By way of response to the proposals of the Congress came a statement issued by the viceroy on 31 October 1929, declaring that he had been authorized by the British government to state clearly that, in their judgement, it was implicit in the declaration of August 1917 that the natural outcome of India's constitutional progress was the attainment of dominion status.[69] The viceroy also announced a change in the procedure regarding the Simon Commission and suggested a round table conference of representatives of different parties and interests in India on constitutional reforms.

The top national leaders, including Malaviya, had received advance notice of the contents of the viceroy's declaration. This encouraged T.B. Sapru, V.J. Patel, and Malaviya to arrange a leaders' conference on 1 November, a day after the declaration, and to issue a joint manifesto welcoming the declaration under the signatures of Gandhi, Motilal, Malaviya, Sapru, Ansari, Patel, Jawaharlal Nehru, and others.

The viceroy's announcement, however, could not forge an emotional bridge between the Indian nationalists and the government largely due to the criticisms levelled against it both inside the British parliament and within British political circles. This gave further opportunity to Subhash Chandra Bose and Jawaharlal Nehru to voice their strong opposition to Irwin's declaration with greater vigour and compelled both Gandhi and Motilal Nehru to reconsider their earlier stand in favour of the declaration. Both of them realized the danger of alienating the younger section of the Congress and modified their strategy, losing no time in mollifying the two young leaders.

In the next few weeks, Sapru and Malaviya worked together to keep the doors open for a dialogue between the nationalist leaders and the viceroy. It was largely due to their efforts that a meeting took place between the viceroy and the five prominent political leaders, including Gandhi and Motilal Nehru, on 23 December 1929. Not unexpectedly, the meeting ended on a distinctly negative note since the viceroy was not willing to give an assurance that dominion status would form the basis of the deliberations of the proposed round table conference.

Writing on the next day, Irwin put the entire blame for the failure of the talks on Gandhi and Motilal Nehru, saying that they 'were not actuated by the spirit of peace' and added that Malaviya 'was perhaps a little more enthusiastic for the moment'.[70] The viceroy's comments show that Malaviya's assessment of British intentions were rather far-fetched. This is all the more significant because, a week later, the Congress was due to hold its 1929 session at Lahore, and different top-level nationalist leaders (including Malaviya) were to decide whether or not they favoured independence as the goal of the party.

NOTES

1. Jha, *Role of Central Legislature*, p. 209.
2. Malaviya to Lajpat Rai, 29 October 1923, in B.R. Nanda, ed., *The Collected Works of Lala Lajpat Rai* (henceforth *CWLR*), vol. V, p. 126.
3. *Leader*, 11 November 1923.
4. Wolpert, *Jinnah of Pakistan*, p. 123.
5. Legislative Assembly Debates, vol. 4, 1924, p. 531.
6. Reading to Oliver, 14 February 1924, Reading Papers, roll no. 9.
7. Reading to Oliver, 14 February 1924, Reading Papers, roll no. 9.
8. B. N. Pandey, ed., *A Centenary History of the Indian National Congress*, vol. II (New Delhi, 1985), p. 376.
9. Pandey, *A Centenary History*, p. 398.

10. Reading to Birkenhead, 24 September 1925, Reading Papers, roll no. 9.

11. Reading to Birkenhead, 24 September 1925, Reading Papers, roll no. 9.

12. Wolpert, *Jinnah of Pakistan*, p. 127.

13. M.R. Jayakar, *The Story of My Life*, vol. II, p. 261.

14. Gandhi to Motilal Nehru, 17 August 1924, G.D. Birla Papers.

15   Gandhi to G.D. Birla, 7 August 1925, in Birla, *Bapu: A Unique Association*, pp. 32–3.

16. Sitaramayya, *History of the Congress*, p. 276.

17. Sitaramayya, *History of the Congress*, p. 307.

18. Malaviya to C. Vijayaraghavachariar, 2 May 1926, C.V.R. Papers.

19. Malaviya to C. Vijayaraghavachariar, 2 May 1926, C.V.R. Papers.

20. Malaviya to C. Vijayaraghavachariar, 2 May 1926, C.V.R. Papers.

21. Malaviya to C. Vijayaraghavachariar, 6 May 1926, C.V.R. Papers.

22. Malaviya to C. Vijayaraghavachariar, 6 May 1926, C.V.R. Papers.

23. Malaviya to C. Vijayaraghavachariar, 6 May 1926, C.V.R. Papers.

24. Bhagwan Das to Motilal Nehru, 2 June 1926, Sri Prakash Papers.

25. AICC Papers 11–13 (Part I)/1926.

26. Motilal Nehru to Lala Lajpat Rai, 4 September 1926, *SWMN*, p. 296.

27. Bhagwan Das to Motilal Nehru, 2 June 1926, Sri Prakash Papers.

28. Motilal Nehru to Rangaswami Iyangar, 9 October 1926, *SWMN*, p. 155.

29. *Leader*, 15 September 1926.

30. Motilal's statement on negotiations with Malaviya, 12 September 1926, *SWMN*, vol. V, p. 484.

31. H.N. Mitra, ed., *The Indian Quarterly Register, 1926*, vol. II (Calcutta, 1926), cited in Ravinder Kumar and M.D. Sharma, *Selected Works of Motilal Nehru*, vol. V (New Delhi, 1995), pp. 65–6.

32. B.R. Nanda, *The Nehrus: Motilal and Jawaharlal* (London, 1962), p. 168.

33. Mitra, *Indian Quarterly Register, 1926*, vol. II, p. 51.

34. *Leader*, 19 April 1926.

35. Motilal Nehru to Jawaharlal Nehru, 29 July 1926, vol. V, p. 110.

36. Lajpat Rai to Malaviya, 14 October 1926, *CWLR*, vol. 10, p. 145.

37. Bhagwan Das to Motilal Nehru, 2 June 1926, AICC Papers, 11–13, Part I/1926.

38. Bhagwan Das to Motilal Nehru, 2 June 1926, AICC Papers, 11–13, Part I/1926.

39. Bhagwan Das to Motilal Nehru, 17 June 1926, AICC Papers, 11–13, Part I/1926.

40. Sri Prakash to G.D. Birla, 16 June 1926, AICC Papers, 11–13, Part I/1926.

41. Motilal Nehru to Sri Prakash, 13 June 1926, *SWMN*, vol. V, p. 69.

42. Bhagwan Das to Sri Prakash, 23 October 1926, AICC Papers, 11–13, Part I/1926.

43. Sri Prakash to Bhagwan Das, 24 December 1926, Sri Prakash Papers.
44. Sri Prakash to Jawaharlal Nehru, 26 November 1926, Sri Prakash Papers.
45. Motilal to Jawaharlal Nehru, 2 December 1926, *SWMN*, vol. V, p. 182.
46. Motilal Nehru to T.C. Goswami, 30 November 1926, *SWMN*, vol. V, p. 179.
47. Telegram from Motilal Nehru to Sitla Sahai, 25 October 1926, *SWMN*, vol. V, p. 186.
48. Motilal to Jawaharlal Nehru, 2 December 1926, *SWMN*, vol. V, pp. 132–3.
49. Malaviya to G.D. Birla, 17 December 1926, G.D. Birla Papers.
50. Sitaramayya, *History of the Congress*, p. 361.
51. Motilal Nehru to Jawaharlal Nehru, 6 January 1927, *SWMN*, vol. V, p. 194.
52. Motilal Nehru to Jawaharlal Nehru, 30 December 1926, *SWJN*, vol. V, p. 193.
53. Nanda, *Motilal Nehru*, p. 172.
54. Motilal Nehru to Gandhi, 6 May 1927, *SWMN*, p. 245.
55. *Hindustan Times*, 27 November 1927.
56. G.D. Birla to Gandhi, 8 December 1927, G.D. Birla Papers.
57. Jha, *Role of Central Legislature*, p. 212.
58. Motilal to M.S. Aney, 24 March 1927, *SWMN*, vol. V, p. 231.
59. Motilal Nehru to Jawaharlal Nehru, 30 March 1927, *SWMN*, vol. V, p. 235.
60. Motilal Nehru to Purushottamdas Thakurdas, *CWMN*, vol. V, p. 363.
61. Motilal Nehru to Gandhi, 20 October 1928, *CWMG*, vol. 27, p. 233.
62. Motilal Nehru to Gandhi, 14 August 1928, Motilal Nehru Papers.
63. Lajpat Rai to Motilal Nehru, 28 October 1928, *CWLR*, p. 251.
64. M.B. Lal, *Mahamana Madan Mohan Malaviya* (Varanasi, 1978), p. 445.
65. Sitaramayya, *History of the Congress*, p. 331.
66. Nanda, *Motilal Nehru*, p. 205.
67. Malaviya to Irwin, 12 January 1929, Halifax Papers.
68. Hailey to Irwin, 7 October 1929, Halifax Papers, roll I.
69. Goschen to Irwin, 8 October 1929, Halifax Papers, roll I.
70. Irwin to Malaviya, 24 December 1929, Halifax Papers, no. 498, roll 10.

9   The Civil Disobedience Movement

The transformation of the Congress was clearly reflected in its Lahore session of 1929 as it resolved that 'the word Swaraj in Art. I of the Congress constitution shall mean Complete Independence', desired that 'all Congressmen will henceforth devote their exclusive attention to the attainment of complete Independence for India...', and authorized the All India Congress Committee 'whenever it deems fit, to launch a programme of Civil Disobedience'.[1] The proccedings and the executions of the Lahore session were guided by Gandhi. The main resolution on 'purna swaraj' (complete independence), quoted above, was moved by him. He had to push through the resolution in the midst of pressures from the right wing and the irreconcilable left wing. Malaviya voiced his opposition against the resolution, asking for the All Parties Conference to reconvene and for the Congress to accept the demand for the round table conference. Malaviya was one of the leaders (along with M.A. Ansari and Sarojini Naidu among others) who considered the decision regarding complete independence to be a mistake. Aney, Kelkar, and Satyamurti favoured council entry and the liberals were advocates of dominion status. The official historian of the Congress points out that 'the Lahore session was as strenuous a session as it was critical ... the attempt was to behead the main resolution or amputate its limbs and thus truncate it altogether' and adds that 'in all these differences the common bond was common antipathies not community of sympathies, convictions or programme [sic]'.[2] Gandhi mildly set aside the objections raised by Malaviya and several other Congress leaders by saying, 'We have got our duties to perform.'[3] Neither the programme of the forthcoming struggle nor any firm date for the beginning of the movement was announced at the Lahore Congress session, reflecting the dilemma of the Congress with regard to the actual form of struggle against the government.

MALAVIYA'S RESIGNATION FROM THE CWC

On the day the decision of the Congress goal of complete independence was taken at Lahore, Malaviya sent the following formal communication to Jawaharlal Nehru who was now the president of the Congress:

> As I do not agree with the resolution passed by the Congress yesterday, relating to its policy and programme I think it is due to the Congress and myself that I should not continue to be a member of its Working Committee. I, therefore, respectfully tender my resignation from the Committee.[4]

There were a few other resignations including that of M.A. Ansari, Aney, Kelkar, Bhagwan Das, and Khaliquzzaman. Each of them had their own reasons for dissociating themselves from the main Congress resolution.

The new CWC met on 2 January 1930 to take steps to implement the decisions of the Lahore Congress. It focused its immediate attention on such members of the councils who had not responded to its call to resign, asked them to respond forthwith, and desired that they should refrain from participating in the functioning of the provincial as well as the central legislatures. Malaviya did not resign his seat in the Legislative Assembly. He was still nursing the hope of some positive results from the proposed round table conference.

DISENCHANTMENT FROM ASSEMBLY POLITICS

It is against this backdrop that the sixth session of the third Legislative Assembly started in Delhi in January 1930. Twenty-seven members of the assembly resigned their seats in response to the Congress' call. The Swarajist opposition block had, therefore, disappeared from the assembly and its place was taken by the Nationalist Party under Malaviya's leadership. The composition of the House clearly promised a 'tranquil' session.[5] But this tranquility was often disturbed by Malaviya's interruptions.

On 10 March 1930, Malaviya sought adjourment in the assembly to discuss the arrest and conviction of Sardar Vallabhbhai Patel while he was scheduled to address a public meeting in a village in Gujrat. This was a forewarning of the government's intention of embarking upon repressive measures against the supporters of the Salt Satyagraha. Malaviya castigated the government on the ground that Patel was arrested before he had made a speech and thus had not breached the law. Malaviya received little support from the Independents who largely remained neutral, while the Muslim members of the assembly voted with the government.[6]

Malaviya's total disappointment with the assembly came soon after. The government brought forward the Cotton Textile Industry (Protection) Bill in the middle of March proposing to impose 20 per cent duty on import of cotton piece goods from all countries, except England, giving it, in effect, 5 per cent Imperical Preference. Malaviya, Kunzru, M.R. Jayakar, G.D. Birla, and others were opposed to the principle of Imperical Preference. Malaviya formally proposed an amendment to the official bill asking for equal duty on imported cotton goods irrespective of the country of their origin.[7] When his amendment did not pass, Malaviya was greatly disappointed and came to the conclusion that it was time to quit the assembly. It his letter of resignation dated 2 April 1930, addressed to the viceroy, Malaviya recounted his past association with the legislature and his eagerness to work for reforms in the hope that they would be put in practice in the spirit they were framed. He criticized the presence of a solid bloc of 40 official and nominated members in an assembly of 140 at the beck and call of the government to support any measure of its choice and finally added:

> I have, therefore, been driven to the conclusion that I must no longer, by remaining a member of the Assembly, continue to lend my support to a constitution under which so atrocious a wrong can be perpetrated upon my people. It will be my earnest and prayerful endeavour to devote all my time and effort to see that this system is replaced, as early as possible, by a system worthy of the name of the Government.[8]

MALAVIYA'S DECISION TO JOIN THE MOVEMENT

Malaviya's decision to quit the Legislative Assembly was a well-calculated move. His disenchantment with the council politics was now complete. He realized that it was futile to hope for any satisfactory arrangement of the political future of India with the support of the government. Hence the natural choice before him was to participate in the civil disobedience movement and he had this choice very much in his mind when he decided to opt out of the assembly. By now, Malaviya was fully convinced that Gandhi's appraisal of the political situation was much more realistic than his own. He could foresee that Gandhi's assessment of the British motives was correct and sound, and lost no time in dedicating himself wholeheartedly to the movement. Malaviya's decision, taken at this time, was much different from that of the non-cooperation days. He was prepared to make amends in 1930 as he was witnessing the tremendous upsurge of people across the country and was convinced that it was wiser to move with the wave than against it.

The comment of the official historian of the Congress on Malaviya's decision to join the civil disobedience campaign that 'it was providential that help should have come to the Congress from unexpected quarters' signifies that not many Congressmen expected such a move from him. The author further writes: 'At this time, however, Malaviyaji's position was that he would not resile from Civil Disobedence but that he did not endorse Independence.'[9] This estimate of Malaviya's position in the Congress was largely correct since he was still a votary of keeping India's ties with Britain intact. He saw no contradiction in not subscribing to the Congress goal of 'purna swaraj' and still devoting himself completely to the civil disobedience movement.

There was an obvious relief in the Congress camp following Malaviya's announcement of joining the civil disobedience movement. Welcoming his stand, Motilal Nehru wrote to Malaviya saying that 'the country needs your single-minded devotion and participation in the real fight for freedom outside sham legislatures',[10] hoped that he 'would devote his energy to the popular work that awaits him', and desired that Malaviya would remain 'firm' in his participation in the compaign.[11]

Malaviya's active involvement with the civil disobedience movement coincided with the start of the Salt Satyagraha launched by Gandhi at the end of his historic Dandi March on 6 April 1930. Gandhi's call to deliberately defy the Salt Law was popularized throughout the length and breadth of the country. The satyagraha continued for the next two months and was nominally continued thereafter in a sporadic manner.

Gandhi had foreseen such a situation at the very beginning of the campaign. His 'final message' on 11 March was that 'suitable measures may be adopted' by the Congress committees and he specifically laid down that 'liquor and foreign cloth can be picketed'.[12] When the apex body of the Congress decided to widen the scope of the movement in the middle of May, it was acting upon Gandhi's wishes. The strategy of the Congress was now modified. It began to pay less attention to the sale and manufacture of contraband salt and decided to concentrate increasingly on the boycott campaigns and related efforts. The CWC called upon the Congress bodies 'to carry on intensive propaganda for the boycott of foreign cloth and to organize the picketing of shops dealing in foreign cloth'.[13] The Congress reposed its faith in these principles throughout the eventful year.

Malaviya chose to concentrate on the campaign to boycott foreign cloth believing that this was the best weapon in India's armoury. He undertook extensive tours to Amritsar, Kanpur, Allahabd, Calcutta, and Bombay, addressed various public meetings, got in touch with local merchants, and impressed upon them not to sell foreign cloth. Detailed official reports of Malaviya's visits, his movements, and utterances give us a clear picture of the manner in which he led the movement. The district magistrate of Amritsar conceded that up to the middle of June 1930 there was 'no unpleasant incident' from any part of the city. He accepted that 'the picketing has so far been done by peaceful persuasion and prospective purchasers are induced to refrain from buying foreign cloth.' The Punjab governor also noted that 'there have been no reports of intimidation'.[14] It was a great tribute to Malaviya that the government officials acknowledged in their confidential reports that the local merchants were willing partners in the boycott campaigns.

Malaviya's intention of visiting Calcutta during the last week of April led to considerable consultations between the provincial government and the Government of India. The Bengal administration was specifically informed that the viceroy was 'very reluctant to see Pandit Malaviya prosecuted' and asked that 'no special order should be served on Pandit Malaviya and that no prosecution without previous reference should be started for any seditious speeches'.[15] Clearly the viceroy did not desire to offend Malaviya at this juncture. On his part, Malaviya was equally cautious not to give any opportunity to the provincial government to intervene. He successfully persuaded the

Marwari merchants of the city to respond to the directions of the Congress. There was considerable discussion at this point of time on the question of whether or not the merchants should be permitted to sell the foreign cloth that was lying in stock. Malaviya was prepared to allow the merchants to sell their existing stocks of foreign cloth in return for promises from them not to import or order foreign cloth for a specified period. Malaviya's suggestion was not accepted by the CWC.[16] It firmly rejected any plea for concession to the merchants even for a short period. The discussions in the CWC indictated again that Malaviya was slowly losing hold in the decision-making process of the Congress.

POPULAR UPRISING IN PESHAWAR

The popular uprising in Peshawar, the capital of the sensitive North-West Frontier Province that lay on the border, alarmed the British. The arrest of Badshah Khan and a number of other leaders led to a massive upsurge in Peshawar with crowds confronting armoured cars and defying intensive firing by the army for three hours.[17] According to the official estimate, 30 protesters were killed while unofficial estimates ranged from 200 to 250. A platoon of Garwal Rifles refused to open fire on the Paktoons. The British army was able to restore order in Peshawar ten days later and a reign of terror was unleashed in the area.[18] These brutal killings at Peshawar led to a wave of protests in several towns including Allahabad. Malaviya decided to undertake a journey to Peshawar to make an on-the-spot assessment of the situation and boost the morale of Badshah Khan and his associates who had boldly faced British brutalities. The Punjab government, however, did not permit Malaviya to go beyond Rawalpindi. He addressed a huge public meeting at Rawalpindi, highlighing the refusal of the soldiers of Garwal Rifles to fire at the innocent crowd that had gathered on the fateful day at Peshawar. The Punjab government considered Malaviya's speech objectionable on the ground that it could cause disaffection among the police and troops. In the exchange of correspondence that followed, the Government of India advised the provincial government not to proceed against Malaviya as it would 'certainly alienate from Government a considerable body of moderate Hindu opinion in the Punjab'.[19]

Faced with increasing defiance from the entire nation, the government lost little time in showing its repressive face in the middle of 1930. Following the rapidly deteriorating situation at Peshawar, it decided to use new weapons of repression besides the old ones. On 29 April the Press Ordinance was promulgated to curb anti-government exhortations. On 4 May, Gandhi was arrested before he could proceed to Dharsana to continue his defiance of salt laws. There was a massive wave of protest in several parts of the country against Gandhi's arrest. Two additional ordinances, namely the Prevention of Intimidation Ordinance and the Unlawful Instigation Ordinance, were issued on 30 May to counteract Congress propaganda efforts. The provincial governments were authorized to declare the Congress activities unlawful and were given extensive powers to curb Congress activities. They were also permitted to imprison Congress leaders as and when deemed necessary. The provincial governments were further permitted to initiate measures disallowing the Congress to stage any processions, meetings, or demonstrations.[20]

MALAVIYA'S ARREST

By now the Civil Disobedience had entered a critical phase and Malaviya realized that the time for making a fateful choice had come. He plunged into the nationalist struggle by writing the following letter to the acting Congress President, Vallabhbhai Patel:

> By declaring the Working Committee of the Congress an illegal body the Government is putting the final stone in its edifice of repression.... The only fitting reply I can give to Government is to place my services at the disposal of the country by becoming a member of the Congress Working Committee. Whenever you consider it fit call upon me.[21]

Malaviya's letter was in line with his earlier speech in the Legislative Assembly during which he said, 'Who would go to the Round Table Conference if Mahatma Gandhi is in prison?' Thus, he had already expressed his doubts regarding the wisdom of discussions on constitutional reforms in the first round table conference in Gandhi's absence. The only other alternative course before him was to participate in the movement with greater vigour even at the risk of going to jail.

Malaviya reached Bombay on 30 July to attend the officially banned CWC meeting being held in the city. Two days later, Malaviya and Patel led a large procession in the city to observe Tilak's death anniversary. The local authorities soon banned the procession by imposing Section 144 of the Criminal Procedure Code and resorted to a lathi-charge to disperse the procession. Several Congress leaders, including Malaviya and Patel, were arrested for a short period and later released.[22] Meanwhile, Malaviya moved to Delhi to take part in the next CWC meeting knowing very well that since such a meeting had been declared illegal by the Delhi administration and that he could be arrested any time for the defiance of this order. However, it did not deter him from visiting Delhi according to his original plans. Malaviya was arrested on 27 August along with all other members of the CWC, sentenced to six months imprisonment, and lodged in Naini Jail from 28 August to 14 December 1930.[23] His jail term was later reduced on health grounds.

PICKETING AT THE BHU

In its efforts to further widen the scope and intensity of the civil disobedience movement, the Congress announced on 27 June:

> The time has arrived when students of Indian Colleges should take their full share in the movement for national freedom and directs all Provincial Committees to call upon such students within their respective juristication to place their services at the disposal of the Congress in such a manner and to such an extent including complete suspension of their studies as the exigencies of the national movement may require.[24]

On the instructions of the United Provinces Congress Committee, the Varanasi City Congress Committee organized picketing at the Banaras Hindu University. This adversely affected the teaching work in the university for its new academic session that was to begin in July 1930. Malaviya faced considerable difficulty in coming to terms with the local Congress leaders. For quite some time, his attempt was to work out an amicable solution with their cooperation allowing normal teaching work in the university to continue and yet giving opportunity to such students who wanted to devote themselves to the nationalist struggle to move out of the campus. In an effort to find a solution, he addressed the students of the university in the presence of the Congress picketers and announced that

> those students who felt it their duty to take part in the present national movement were free to go but those who wanted to pursue their studies should not be obstructed in their work.[25]

He desired that the university students should be allowed to choose between pursuing their studies at the university or to move out of it and engage themselves in the nationalist struggle.

Malaviya later sought the help of the senior local Congress leader Bhagwan Das, to persuade the Congress volunteers to suspend picketing at the university. In spite of his efforts, the picketers continued their coercive tactics causing considerable hardships to students and teachers of the university for two months. Finally, Malaviya secured the help of the acting president of the Congress, Sardar Vallabhbhai Patel, and, after his intervention, the Congress volunteers withdrew from the university in August 1930.[26]

CRISIS BEFORE THE BANARAS HINDU UNIVERSITY

Malaviya's commitment to maintain calm within the university and his anxiety that the teaching work be carried on within the campus without any outside intervention was, however, not appreciated by the government. It insisted that political activity within the university be disallowed and its teachers and students be totally debarred from engaging themselves in the nationalist struggle. The provincial government painted a grim picture of the growing political undercurrents in the university:

> Apart from the Vice-chancellor whose political activities are well known it is clear that some ten professors and other members of the Univeristy staff have been closely connected with the Civil Disobedience Movement and have taken part in inducing the students to interest themselves in taking up political and anti-Government propaganda.[27]

Another complaint the provincial government had was that the revolutionaries were active in the university:

> It is also clear that during recent years students in the University have either themselves been members of, or have been closely connected with members of various revolutionary parties engaged in the cult of violence.[28]

The provincial government came down heavily on Malaviya's role in the proceedings:

> Its life and soul, its hero and idol, Pandit Madan Mohan Malaviya, himself acting all the time as its foremost firebrand was directly responsible for encouraging political activities in the University.[29]

The official reports of Malaviya's active involvement in the nation-alist campaign were warning signals to the provincial government, for there was growing fear that the example set by him was likely to encourage the staff and students of the university to follow in his footsteps. The provincial Criminal Investigation Department (CID) became active and prepared a detailed report of the various political activities of the University teachers and students in order to show that the university administration was ineffective.

Acting upon the confidential reports regarding the affairs of the university, the Government of India directed the university to imme-diately implement the following instructions:

1. That the University should dispense with the services of the profes-sors and other members of the staff who have taken an active part in political agitation directed against the authority of Government.
2. That the students who have been convicted of offences connected with the civil disobedience movement and those who openly defied the law should be expelled.
3. That a rule should be made that all students of the University should sever their connection with the Youth League.[30]

To put further pressure on the university, the Government of India resolved to withhold payment of the first instalment of its annual grant payable in 1930. Even though he was lodged in the Naini jail from August to December 1930, Malaviya was in constant touch with Pro-Vice-Chancellor A.B. Druva and gave detailed guidelines to him with regard to the future course of action to be followed by the university.[31] Malaviya took a firm stand to withstand the government's pressure tac-tics. He refused to promise any action against university teachers and students on the basis of accusations made against them by the govern-ment and insisted that the university should have complete autonomy to manage its own affairs. He was totally unwilling to bow down to the dictates of the government, was not unnerved by the suspension of the financial grant to the university, and was prepared to face the consequences arising out of these circumstances.[32]

The university took its own time in preparing a cautious reply to the communication received from the Government of India. Echoing Malaviya's views on the role of the university during the ongoing nationalist struggle, the pro-vice-chancellor argued that 'the experi-ence in this country as well as in other countries unmistakeably shows that in times of political stress and storm it is hardly possible that young men will remain absolutely cold and unresponsive to outside influences'.[33] It was stated further that 'it was hardly to be expected that teachers and students of the University should remain unaffected by the present national movement.'[34] The pro-vice-chancellor submitted that only two teachers of the unviersity took active part in the movement and they had already tendered their resignation to the university. As to the role of the students, the pro-vice-chancellor pointed out that many of them had left the university due to different reasons and, as such, there was no record of their movements outside the campus.

Before the end of the year, the crisis before the university blew over because of the intervention by the British government. The secretary of state advised the viceroy to release Malaviya forthwith. He explained that 'after a conversation with Prime Minister and Sapru yesterday the Prime Minister authorized me to telegraph to you saying he thought on the whole it would be better if Malaviya was unconditionally released.'[35] Malaviya was accordingly set free on 23 December 1930 before the completion of his jail term.

The events at the university moved swiftly after Malaviya's release. The Government of India and the provincial government softened their opposition to the university and sent senior officers to sort out outstanding issues with Malaviya, promising to release overdue grants to the university. By February 1931, the financial grants that were held up so far were released, giving considerable relief to Malaviya.

Gandhi fully endorsed Malaviya's stand in a public speech saying that 'the Hindu University would have lost its grants but for the fearlessness and readiness for sacrifice of Pandit Madan Mohan Malaviya' and further added that 'Malaviya was determined that the University should go without the grant rather than any teacher or student who served the country be penalized for that service'.[36]

GANDHI–IRWIN PACT

By the time Malaviya was released from jail, there were clear signs that the civil disobedience movement was on the decline. The Congress was coming around to the belief that the capacity of the masses to 'make sacrifices was not unlimited'.[37] In this broad context, the viceroy initiated measures to open a dialogue with the Congress, ordered the release of the members of the CWC, issued a statement withdrawing the ban imposed on its meetings, and impressed upon the provincial governors the need for creating a peaceful atmosphere. Obviously the viceroy was exploring avenues to peace, which he tried to prepare after the close of the first session of the Round Table Conference, wherein the strength of the Congress and its entitlement to speak for a vast majority of the Indian people was stated and endorsed by speaker after speaker. C.Y. Chintamani deplored that the British system of administration, 'which can be maintained only by casting into jail such noble beings as Mahatma Gandhi and Madan Mohan Malaviya is a doomed system'.[38]

Much depended on Gandhi's willingness to negotiate at this stage. He did not reject the viceroy's overtures out of hand because he felt that there was a sense of fatigue among the people. Ideologically also, 'Gandhi was no different from the Moderates in his basic strategy of negotiating with the British for concessions'.[39] This helped the liberal leaders play an important role in persuading Gandhi to open dialogue with the government. The upshot of the discussions was Gandhi's decision to seek an interview with the viceroy who was, perhaps, waiting for such a call. In response to Gandhi's letter of 14 February, the viceroy conveyed his consent by telegram on 16 February. Gandhi left for Delhi on the same day to enter into 'the very delicate conversations' with the viceroy, which continued up to 5 March.

Malaviya was with Gandhi throughout the period of negotiations with Lord Irwin. It is on record that during these top-level discussions, Gandhi held continous discussions with the members of the CWC and Malaviya. The latter extended full support to Gandhi's efforts and was available in Delhi for the purpose, helping Gandhi sort out various issues that emerged during the talks. According to the Gandhi–Irwin Pact signed on 5 March 1931, the Congress agreed to 'discontinue' the civil disobedience movement and 'take part in the second session of the Round Table Conference'.[40] It was announced that further discussions on the scheme of constitutional reforms would take place on the basis of the statement made by the British prime minister.

The pact or settlement was the main point of discussion in the Karachi session of the Congress held during the last week of March 1931. The debate on the provisions of the pact was prolonged and even acrimonious. The younger leaders of the Congress, led by Jawaharlal

Nehru and Subhash Chandra Bose, were highly critical of the settlement and voiced their opposition openly against it. But they did not
carry the struggle in the session beyond voicing their opposition. It
was, however, Gandhi's responsibility to explain his position and he did
his best to win over the radicals. A few weeks later, it was decided to
appoint Gandhi as the sole spokesman of the Congress in the forthcoming Second Round Table Conference.

NON-INCLUSION OF MALAVIYA IN THE CWC

Malaviya's exclusion from the CWC in the Karachi Congress session
of 1931 invited considerable criticism among his supporters. Since he
was excluded from the committee for the second year in a row, there
were several queries regarding the rationale behind such a step. As the
list of names was drawn up by Gandhi in consultation with the present
and past presidents of the Congress, he took upon himself to explain
as to why this decision was taken. In a public statement, Gandhi
explained that Malaviya was 'deliberately' kept out of the CWC as it
was thought that 'being subjected to the Committee's discipline might
prove embarrassing to him' and added that such an arrangement would
give him 'freedom of action' while, at the same time, keep him available
for 'advice' in his capacity as the past president of the Congress.[41]

It soon became clear that Malaviya's exclusion from the CWC was
no routine matter. It was a well-thought out decision taken by the
newly emerging leadership of the party after the Lahore session. They
had not taken kindly to Malaviya's resignation from the CWC and
deliberately planned to keep him out of the high-level deliberations
of the Congress. The next few months were to confirm Malaviya's
weakening hold over the party.

As Malaviya 'still wished to give the Empire a chance',[42] his visit to
London was likely to help Gandhi find a solution to the complex questions relating to constitutional changes in India. Gandhi's participation
in the Second Round Table Conference, however, remained uncertain
until the last moment as serious differences emerged between the
Congress Party and certain provincial governments over the harsh measures undertaken against the peasants after the March settlement. Since
Irwin's term as viceroy had ended in April and Willingdon had taken
over his place, the Congress was keen to find out whether the new

viceroy was committed to the understanding reached earlier between his predecessor and Gandhi. The Congress had its own doubts about the willingness of the new viceroy to abide by the terms of the March settlement. Malaviya stepped in at this juncture and played the role of a mediator between Gandhi and the new viceroy. He spent a good deal of time in the summer months at Simla and had several meetings with Willingdon. He was also busy in finding a way out of the differences between Gandhi and the provincial governments. Ultimately, a 'second settlement' was agreed upon between Gandhi and the viceroy.

This gave 'intense relief' to the new viceroy, Willingdon, who thought that Gandhi was 'amenable and anxious to help with a real desire to work out a satisfactory constitution'. The viceroy was hopeful that Gandhi 'will be a help and not hindrance' during discussions in the Second Round Table Conference.[43] The viceroy's view paved the way for Gandhi's departure to London together with Malaviya and Sarojini Naidu. Gandhi remarked that he was going to London 'alone, yet not alone'[44] as Malaviya and Sarojini Naidu were attending the Second Round Table Conference 'with the consent of the Congress' and 'because of their independent status', not 'over the head of the Congress'.[45]

DELIBERATIONS IN THE SECOND ROUND TABLE CONFERENCE

That Gandhi, Malaviya, Sarojini Naidu, and prominent liberal leaders should find the deliberations of the Second Round Table Conference frustrating from beginning to end was hardly surprising. Their attempts to raise the constitutional dialogue at an altogether new level foundered on the rocks of imperialist manoeuvres and sectarian intransigence. The delegates to the conference were so chosen as to ensure that every religious and communitarian cleavage in the social fabric of India would manifest itself and thwart any national consensus which might threaten imperial hegemony over India. Thus, the communal issues became more important than the main question of constitutional changes for which the conference was actually called.

In his opening speech at the Second Round Table Conference on 15 September 1931 Malaviya expressed the hope that 'we should be able to arrive at a settlement among ourselves'. He further elaborated:

It is inconceivable to my mind that the future constitution of a great country like India should be blocked by a small question like that of satisfying minorities. I call it a small question because I hope that it is a question which can be settled, which is not incapable of solution and I hope when our discussions have proceeded further we shall find some solution which will enable us to go forward with the building of the Constitution.[46]

At this time, Malaviya's perception of the communal problem was in no way different from most of the other nationalist leaders, including Gandhi, who were keen that the question be solved by the representatives of various communities themselves rather than by the intervention of imperial masters or their representatives. Gandhi openly stated that the Indian delegates had not been invited from six thousand miles away to London to settle the communal question and thus to sidetrack its energies to the 'secondary' issues.[47] Both Gandhi and Malaviya felt that various communities had been led to place an undue emphasis on the communal question as a condition precedent to constitutional advance.[48]

During the first and the second meeting of the Minorities Committee held on 28 September and 1 October 1931, Gandhi emphasized that he would not agree to separate electorates or reservation being conceded to any community other than Muslims and Sikhs to whom the privilege had been extended in the past. He also rejected the suggestion that the communal problem be decided by British arbitration. This irked the Muslim delegates who were apprehensive that nothing was likely to be gained by the conference because of the deep differences on the communal question between the representatives of different communities, social groups, and political parties that had assembled at London. Gandhi's insistence on Ansari's presence at the conference further alienated the Muslim delegates while his other statements frightened almost all other Hindu and Sikh leaders.[49]

In a very significant letter from London, Devdas Gandhi gave a first-hand account of his assessment of the communal situation at the end of the second meeting of the Minorities Committee:

The whole discussion was sordid ... Babu was pained beyond measure. The opposition was worse than expected. He has no heart at the work of the Minorities Committee where MacDonald is as supercilious and patronising as ever. In spite of this he has agreed to the Muslim request that he should call together representatives of various groups in order to discuss the whole communal question.... He feels that the communal question is being brought deliberately to the forefront and magnified by the Government because they did not to want to part with power.[50]

With the appointment of a minorities subcommittee under the chairmanship of Gandhi in the first week of October 1931, the issue of communal representation came to the forefront. Gandhi concentrated on effecting a deal with the Muslim representatives and openly informed Dr B.R. Ambedkar and the leaders of small minorities that they did not need any special representation and the Congress did not contemplate any for them.

Gandhi wrote in early October that 'it is quite correct that I have personally said that I would give a blank cheque to the Musalmans regarding their demands' and made similar assertions in his talks with Hindu leaders as well.[51] Gandhi concentrated on effecting a deal with the Muslim representatives. Up to the end of October, he continued to have informal talks with them in the hope that they would support the Congress programme and not line up with the small minorities.

While writing from London, Devdas Gandhi expressed the hope that Malaviya would stand by Gandhi: 'I must say that Malaviyaji is much more inclined than before to accept Bapu's advice of complete surrender but the orthodox Hindu section seems to him to be holding in readiness to denounce any settlement that may possibly be arrived at between the Congress and the Muslims.'[52] Expressing similar views about Malaviya, Mooje stated:

His heart is sound, but he has no fixity and there is no knowing what he will do in the end. I fear he will not have the courage to refuse compliance with Mahatmaji's request.[53]

He repeated the same view during his stay in London: 'Pandit Malaviya has no courage to oppose Mahatmaji in the open conference. I will be isolated. But I will not hesitate to oppose him.'[54]

By the middle of October 1931, Malaviya began to have second thoughts regarding his plans to extend full support to Gandhi. He was alarmed by Gandhi's frequent assertions that Hindus should give a 'blank cheque' to Muslims and concede to their demands. Like other Hindu and Sikh leaders, Malaviya feared that Gandhi was ready to offer undue concessions to Muslims and thereby weaken the position of Hindus and Sikhs in the Muslim-majority provinces of Punjab and Bengal. During the crucial stage of negotiations relating to the communal problem, he preferred to remain silent rather than coming out in open support of Gandhi. He appeared to be more in the company of the Mahasabha leaders rather than standing firmly with Gandhi. Malaviya faced considerable criticism later for taking such a position at the Second Round Table Conference.[55]

THE SECOND PHASE OF THE CIVIL DISOBEDIENCE MOVEMENT

While Gandhi was away in London, Viceroy Willingdon reversed the conciliatory policy of his predecessor as exhibited at the signing of the Gandhi–Irwin Pact and formulated his own strategy of launching a hard and immediate blow against any attempt to revive the nationalist struggle. The promulgation of 'Emergency Power Ordinances' in the last few months of 1931 in UP, Bengal, and the North-West Frontier Province were just examples of what was to come a little later.[56]

Meanwhile the failure of the Second Round Table Conference cast its shadow on Indian politics. Events moved swiftly on unexpected lines soon after Gandhi's return to India on 28 December 1931. When he attempted to initiate telegraphic correspondence with the viceroy, the latter's reply was cool and discouraging. Even Gandhi's request for an interview was granted by the viceroy under conditions Gandhi could not agree on. On 31 December 1931 the Congress announced the resumption of the civil disobedience movement with the same objectives as had been adopted in the earlier phase of the struggle.

The Government of India launched its preemptive strike by arresting Gandhi, Sardar Patel, and several other prominent Congress leaders on 4 January 1932. It further strengthened itself on the same day with four more ordinances—the Emergency Powers ordinance, the Unlawful Instigation ordinance, the Unlawful Association ordinance, and the Prevention of Molestation and Boycotting ordinance. These ordinances gave the most far-reaching powers to the magistrates and police officers. Civil liberty ceased to exist and both person and property could be seized by authorities at their will. It was a declaration of siege for the whole of India. The government acted with lightning speed in applying its carefully planned repression. Within a week, various top Congress leaders of different provinces were behind bars.

Even though the Congress was not fully prepared for the renewal of the campaign, the popular response was massive. The Congress fought valiantly and, within the first four months, over eighty thousand satyagrahis (those who practice the policy of satyagraha) were jailed and lakhs took to picketing of shops that sold liquor and foreign cloth. People defied the restrictions imposed by the government in large numbers. Demonstrations, celebrations of national days, and other forms of protest were the order of the day.

Reaching India on 14 January 1932, about a fortnight after Gandhi's arrival in the country, Malaviya was one of the first to give vent to his feelings of frustration generated by the savagery of the government's early response to the resumption of the civil disobedience movement. On 29 January, he sent to the viceroy a virulent denunciation of his refusal to see Gandhi, 'the greatest Indian living ... adored by countless millions of India [sic] and widely respected in all parts of India' and pointed out that the viceroy's 'refusal of an interview was a flagrant departure from the path of conciliation laid out through the Delhi Pact'.[57] Malaviya was soon to understand that the viceroy had deliberately avoided meeting the Mahatma because he wanted to give out the clear message that the 'path of conciliation' had been abondoned and that the government would go all out to suppress the nationalist struggle.

Paying handsome tribute to Malaviya's active role during the second phase of the civil disobedience movement, the official historian of the Congress writes: 'He never spared himself and was ever busy issuing statements exposing the high-handed action of the authorities, ever encouraging and inspiring Congress workers by his indomitable will and phenomenal energy.'[58] The official version was that Malaviya was 'in effect the main directing force of the Congress.' It was reported that 'though Kitchlew was nominally the President of the Congress Malaviya presided over the Congress policy'.[59] The commissioner of Kumaun division noted that 'even apart of the influence of Gandhi as a Mahatma [sic] the fact that Madan Mohan Malaviya has gone over to the extreme action is a matter of great weight.'[60] The Secretary, Home Department of the Government of India, recorded that 'Malaviya was holding frequent meetings with such Congress leaders as are available ... is stirring or attempting to stir up feelings against Government and the police'.[61] Even though the provincial governments were often nervous at the time of Malaviya's visits to various cities and suggested strong action against him, the Government of India did not allow them to put Malaviya behind bars and allowed him to carry on his activities.

PRESIDENTSHIP OF THE EMERGENCY SESSION OF THE CONGRESS IN 1932

Malaviya decided to intensify the nationalist struggle by engineering the emergency session of the Congress in Delhi in 24 April 1932. It was the brain-child of Sarojini Naidu, then Acting President of the Congress, who approached Malaviya to preside over the session. Gandhi thought it was a 'good idea that the Congress should hold its session even in this year of repression. Of course it will lead to nothing though if Malaviyaji and a few others are arrested that will be all the good.'[62] Malaviya was served with an official order prohibiting his and his associates' entry into Delhi on 22 April at the Jamuna bridge entrance. Having disobeyed the order, Malaviya was arrested and taken to the central jail in a car. In spite of the police vigilance and the arrests of delegates at various points in the city, about 500 delegates gathered at the clock tower at Chandni Chawk and elected their own officiating president. The printed resolutions of the Congress Subjects Committee were read out and adopted. The session lasted only for a short while. By the time the police arrived, the session was over. Certain arrests were made and prosecutions were launched against others. Malaviya was released after a week. The whole incident showed how deeply the Congress was rooted in the minds of the people and how futile the endeavour of the British government to crush the civil disobedience movement was. Thus Malaviya was entirely successful in popularizing the nationalist message among the people.

Malaviya's next move was to issue a public statement on 2 May giving an account of different repressive measures adopted by the government during the early months of the movement. He sent hundreds of copies of the statement for distribution in England and other countries so as to enlighten the public in those places about the atrocities set in motion by the Government of India. He made a pointed reference to the following actions of the government to prove his point:

1. The lot of the political prisoners was miserable in the extreme, with a very small sprinkling of Congressmen placed in 'A' and 'B' classes and more than ninety-five per cent put in the 'C' class. This was a complete reversal of the categorization of political prisoners from what was followed in 1930. Evidently, the official purpose was to make the life of participants in the nationalist struggle as miserable as possible.

2. Heavy fines, running often to four figures, were imposed to overall well-to-do people and often their properties were auctioned at throw-away prices.

3. Reports of at least 102 cases of lathi-charges, firing, and house searches indicated that the overall effort was to terrorize the people.

Referring to the positive features of the civil disobedience movement, Malaviya claimed that the 'Muslims and the non-Congressmen had sympathised with its objects', gave a long list of non-Congressmen who condemned the actions of Government', and pointed out that the 'participation of women was a distinguishing feature of the movement'.[63] His all-out effort was to highlight the success of the campaign in spite of the efforts made by the government to put it down by coercive measures.

VISIT OF THE INDIAN LEAGUE DELEGATION

Meanwhile, Malaviya was keen that an authoritative, independent, and impartial inquiry be made regarding the reign of terror being perpetrated by the British authorities in India. With this end in view, he got in touch with the London branch of the Indian League. Its chairman, Miss Slande, wrote in June 1932: 'Panditji is in correspondence with London regarding a deputation which the India League is planning to send out to India. It will be an important thing. Panditji wanted me to give suggestions as to what they should see.'[64]

Malaviya remitted a sum of five hundred pounds to England to meet the expenses of the deputation of the India League, which comprised three Labour-party members of the British parliament, besides V.K. Krishna Menon, to visit the country. The delegation was in India from 17 August to 7 November 1932. It went to every province in order to get an insight into the various repressive measures adopted by the government to crush the movement. The report of the delegation is a very valuable record of the acts of terrorism perpetrated by the government in 1932. It was collected with scrupulous care and accepted after careful scrutiny of the evidence collected. It is seldom that such an account of a complicated and extensive civil turmoil in a vast country like India is available for the purpose of ascertaining the truth. The report of the India League delegation corroborated the account of the atrocities committed by different provincial governments in suppressing the movement.

Malaviya was constantly on the move throughout the year, busy organizing the *swadeshi* (of one's own country) programmes, picketing of liquor shops, and no-rent campaigns, and visited different cities to carry forward propaganda efforts to popularize these programmes of the civil disobedience movement.

PRESIDING OVER THE 1933 EMERGENCY CONGRESS SESSION

Recognizing Malaviya's role in the civil disobedience movement, the Congress again called upon him to preside over the emergency session at Calcutta on 1 April 1933. When the district collector of Benaras served Malaviya an order prohibiting him from undertaking the journey to Calcutta, the latter announced his determination to defy it. He left for Calcutta by train on 31 March. The provincial government spared no efforts to prevent the holding of the Congress session. Malaviya was not allowed to reach Calcutta and was arrested at Asansol, an intermediate station. With him were arrested Mrs Motilal Nehru, Dr Syed Mahmud, and the office bearers of the Reception Committee. Nearly a thousand delegates were arrested before their journey or on the way to Calcutta. Almost 1,200 delegates succeeded in reaching the city and, in spite of the ban imposed by the provincial government, met at the place selected for the session. The police were soon upon the scene and lathis rained on the peaceful assembly of Congressmen. The session, however, continued for a short time and was addressed by the working president, Mrs Nellie Sengupta. At least eight resolutions were adopted at the session in spite of all the brutalities perpetrated by the police.

Malaviya issued a long statement giving out the details of brutal police assaults on the delegates.[65] His presidential address was also released to the press for wider circulation. Malaviya implored 'all Hindus and Musalmans, Sikhs, Christians and Parsees and all other countrymen to sink communal differences and to establish political unity among all sections of the people and invited them to 'prepare a constitution which shall give India real independence'.[66] The session has been described 'as a most extraordinary one'.[67]

THE UNITY CONFERENCE

Towards the end of September 1932, Malaviya made efforts to revive negotiations between the Hindus and Muslims with a view to bringing about an agreement and substituting it for the Communal Award, which was announced by the British Prime Minister at the concluding session of the Second Round Table Conference. He took the lead in urging the Muslims to reconsider their attitude on the communal question. He met Shaukat Ali in order to discuss with him the question of communal unity so as to secure 'a permanent honourable agreement between the two communities'.[68] The nationalist Muslim leaders, including M.A. Ansari and Khaliquzzaman, gave their full support to Malaviya's endeavours. The Muslim League was also prepared to cooperate with the proposed conference. However, the Muslim leaders in Punjab and Bengal expressed their strong disapproval of the summoning of the conference and refrained from attending it.

Notwithstanding the opposition of a section of Muslims, the Unity Conference met in Allahabad on 3 November and continued its deliberations for three weeks. Among the delegates were 63 Hindus, 39 Muslims, 11 Sikhs, and 8 Indian Christians. Since the Communal Award could be modified by mutual consent, Malaviya had a challenging task to find a solution to the claims and counterclaims of Hindus and Muslims. It was due to his efforts that Hindus agreed to waive their opposition to the provision for Muslim majority in the legislatures of Punjab and Bengal. It was decided that in Bengal, the Muslims would get 51 per cent of the seats and the Hindus and others would get 44.7 per cent. In Punjab also, the percentage of Muslim seats remained the same, Sikhs were given 20 per cent and the Hindus got 27 per cent. The Unity Conference also arrived at an agreement on the question of the separation of Sindh with certain conditions. The resolution stated that 'Sindh be constituted into a separate province enjoying the same measure of autonomy as other provinces with safeguards to minorities similar to those agreed to in the case of other provinces.'[69] In return, the Muslims agreed to surrender the right of separate electorates and the percentage of seats in the Central Legislature.

In the mean time, discordant notes came pouring in. A section of the Bengal Muslims declined to give up separate electorate while another section condemned the Allahabad agreement as wholly inadequate. Various Muslim leaders of Punjab also raised their voice against the decisions of the conference. Malaviya's visit to Calcutta did not bear fruit as the representatives of the European community refused to see him.

While Malaviya was still busy finding a solution to the conflicting demands of the various communities of Bengal and Punjab, the news of the special Communal Award reached India. Samuel Hoare, the secretary of state for India, announced in London the British government's decision to concede to Muslims one-third of British-India seats in the Central Legislature with a separate electorate. The Unity Conference had agreed to 32 per cent with a joint electorate. The statement of the British government sealed the fate of the Unity Conference. Any hope of the success of the Allahabad Unity Conference soon faded.

The Unity Conference is a positive proof of Malaviya's sincere effort for Hindu–Muslim unity. Tagore wrote to Malaviya, 'Your efforts have had a perceptibly wholesome effect on other communities and we feel grateful for the lead you have given to our country in its present crisis.'[70]

POONA PACT

On 17 August 1932 the British prime minister announced his scheme of minority representation known as the Communal Award whereby the depressed classes were given separate electorates along with the additional right of contesting seats in general constituencies. Thus the British prime minister gave a double vote to the depressed classes for their own separate constituencies as well as for the general constituencies. Gandhi, who was then a prisoner in Yarvada Jail, saw it as a well-calculated move to neutralize the weightage of the Hindus by driving a wedge between them and the untouchables. Gandhi had already announced at the Second Round Table Conference that he would resist with his life the grant of separate electorates to the depressed classes. He consistently argued that the injection of the poison of separate electorates was calculated to divide the Hindu community without doing any good to the depressed classes. On 13 September, the newspapers carried the sensational announcement that Gandhi would embark on a fast unto death as a protest against the grant of separate electorates to the depressed classes. The news shook India from one end to the other.

Reacting to Gandhi's decision, the top national leaders joined together to find a way out to avert the impending tragedy. Malaviya immediately issued a statement summoning a conference of Hindu leaders to hammer out an agreement:

> I honestly believe that there is enough patriotism and devotion to religion among us to help us to arrive at an agreement which will satisfy the reasonable desire of the depressed classes to take their proper share in public life of India without putting them in a separate pen segregating them from the rest of the community.[71]

The conference proposed by Malaviya met at Bombay and Poona (present day Pune). It was attended by T.B. Sapru, M.R. Jayakar, C. Rajagopalachari, N.C. Kelkar, Rajendra Prasad, Moonje, B.R. Ambedkar, M.C. Rajah, and others. After long and protracted negotiations, an agreement was arrived at which is known as the Poona Pact. Under this agreement, the leaders of the depressed classes, led by Dr B.R. Ambedkar, abandoned their demand for separate electorates. The pact doubled the representation of depressed classes in the provincial legislatures and revised the electoral system. Malaviya and all other leaders present at the conference signed the pact. Gandhi was in constant touch with leaders about the deliberations at Poona and had approved the provisions of the pact. The British government accepted the Poona Pact and Gandhi ended his fast on 26 September. Malaviya's efforts in bringing about the Poona Pact were widely recognized and appreciated.

TEMPLE ENTRY BILL

While still lodged in Yarvada Jail, Gandhi threw his entire weight in favour of Ranga Iyer's Temple Entry Bill introduced in the Legislative Assembly in February 1933. Gandhi argued that the government was 'morally bound to give such assistance as may be necessary' to the depressed classes in the observance of the Poona pact and should, therefore, 'facilitate the progress and passage of the bill'.[72] Gandhi impressed upon the Government of India that the bill be placed immediately before the assembly and the law be enacted as early as possible.[73]

The Government of India was, however, not convinced. The home member of the viceroy's council observed:

> We cannot agree to the Bill being rushed through without proper consideration in the country. It has never been explained why there should be such a great haste in this matter while all other practical questions affecting the welfare of the depressed classes are being neglected.... We have no wish to obstruct consideration but the question must be fully examined and adequate time given for opinions to be formed and expressed.[74]

The Government of India was cautious from the very beginning. It had allowed the introduction of the bill in the legislature and was prepared to move further only after the public opinion in the country was unanimously in its favour.

The government announced that it had no intention of 'rushing through the bill, that the question should be properly ventilated and subjected to fullest discussion ... enforcing balance evenly between those supporting the measure and those who were opposed to it'.[75] In this broad context, the government decided to allow consideration of the bill like any other ordinary bill and was not inclined to act swiftly as was desired by Gandhi.

Sharp differences soon came to the surface between Gandhi and Malaviya on the former's insistence with regard to early and swift passage of the Temple Entry Bill. Malaviya was totally opposed to legislative interference in socio-religious issues. He made his fundamental objection known to Gandhi in the following words:

> I am opposed to any interference of our legislatures, particularly as they are constituted at present, in any of our religious or socio-religious matters. I am even more strongly opposed to such interference direct or indirect, in the management of our temples and I am grieved to find that not only have you blessed Mr. Ranga Iyer's Bill, but you are pressing that it should be passed without being circulated to elicit public opinion. I believe this is oppressing the hearts of many among those who love you and desire not to differ from you.[76]

Disillusioned and hurt by Gandhi's open support to the demand of rushing through the bill in the Central Legislature, Malaviya contended that those who were opposed to the passage of the bill should be allowed to state their objections:

> I do not see any justification for the view that a bill of such a delicate character should be rushed through the legislature without the ordinary procedure prescribed for the bills being followed.[77]

Malaviya firmly opposed Gandhi's proposal that the bill could be adopted in the Legislative Assembly by following any extraordinary procedure in the following words:

> I am convinced that the propaganda to rush the bills through the legislature has been a wrong move. I hope that Gandhiji may yet agree that the bills should be circulated for opinion. That will give us time to formulate proposals calculated to bring about an understanding between the two sections of the community.[78]

In August 1934, the Central Assembly finally took up the Temple Entry Bill for consideration. It was opposed from many quarters on different grounds. Explaining the official attitude, the home member said that the government was opposed to it as a matter of principle and on the ground that the measure was impracticable. The bill was finally withdrawn by Ranga Iyer. Commenting on the 'ill-fated measure', Gandhi wrote: 'The Temple Entry Bill is gone. The Sanatanists too are now jubilant. We must not mind their joy.'[79] Later, in a public speech at Varanasi in July 1934, Malaviya referred to his disagreement with Gandhi on the Temple Entry Bill and emphasized that a socio-religious question should be decided in accordance with the injunctions of the Shastras and not by legislation.

SUPPORT TO THE ANTI-UNTOUCHABILITY CAMPAIGN

Gandhi's non-stop campaign against untouchability, in which he was engaged from November 1933 to August 1934, was a significant socio-historical event in India. It represented a great social turmoil in which different segments of society reacted for or against Gandhi's very unconventional proposals with great passion, indifference, or suspicion. Known as the Harijan campaign, it manifested all the contradictions of the Hindu society.[80] Attempts were made during the 1911 census to place the Hindus and the untouchables separately. Malaviya warned the Hindus that the government wanted to weaken them by encouraging separatist tendencies. He attempted to get the verdict of orthodox learned pandits in favour of the removal of disabilities of the untouchables and was aware that the path of persuasion was weary.

In his programme of the anti-untouchability campaign, Gandhi and Malaviya worked together as they had almost similar ideas and shared a two-fold strategy. While they preached their message of atonement to the caste Hindus and exhorted them to extend their embrace to their hitherto untouchable brothers—the members of the scheduled castes—their message was to become conscious and acquire health, education, and dignity with their own efforts and unite and organize till the rest of the society treated them with the respect due to them. Malaviya was convinced that the Shastras enjoined the untouchables, as a matter of right, to enter temples and enjoy all other rights with full dignity in society. He convened several meetings of Sanatanis and the supporters of Varnashram Swarajya Sangh in order to impress upon them the urgent need to welcome the scheduled castes to the broader fold of Hindu society. The orthodox section was, however, not much convinced and thought that Malaviya was too radical in his approach.

In this broad context, it can be explained why Gandhi had to face opposition from the orthodox sections of society during his Harijan tour in Varanasi and a few other places. On 31 July 1934, there was a public meeting at Central Hindu School in which 'the Sanatan Dharmis had intended to offer opposition and obstruction'.[81] Both Gandhi and Malaviya worked out the strategy to face the situation. They offered the representatives of Satananis fifteen minutes at the meeting in which 'to put forward the orthodox point of view' and, therefore, no demonstration was made. Gandhi then explained his views on untouchability and no opposition was voiced in the meeting. He was followed by Pandit Deo Naik Acharya who spoke clearly and forcibly 'until he spoilt any effect he might have made by undue verbosity and was eventually shouted down'.[82] Malaviya, who was occupying the dais with Gandhi, spoke next and extended full support to his pleadings. In his long speech, Malaviya paid rich tributes to the untouchables for their devotion to Ram and Krishna, their unflinching attachment to the principles of the Hindu religion, and their brave

resistance to the efforts of Muslims and the Christians to detach them
from Hinduism.[83] In the period following the Poona Pact, Malaviya
had realized the urgent need of bringing this underprivileged section
closer to the Hindu society.

NOTES

1   Zaidi and Zaidi, *Encyclopedia of the Indian National Congress*, p. 417.
2   Sitaramayya, *History of the Congress*, p. 610.
3   *CWMG*, no. 42, pp. 330–5.
4   Malaviya to Jawaharlal Nehru, 1 January 1930, AICC Papers, G115/1930.
5   J.A. Coatman, *India in 1929–30* (Calcutta, 1931), p. 9.
6   Legislative Assembly Debates, vol. I, 1930, p. 132.
7   Legislative Assembly Debates, vol. I, 1930, p. 1522.
8   *Leader*, 9 April 1930.
9   Sitaramayya, *History of the Congress*, p. 471.
10 Motilal Nehru to Malaviya, 12 April 1930, *SWMN*, vol.VI, p. 131.
11 Gandhi's notes, 10 April 1930, *CWMG*, vol. 43, p. 222.
12 Gandhi's speech at Daman, 11 March 1930, *CWMG*, vol. 43, p. 47.
13 Zaidi and Zaidi, *Encyclopedia of the Indian National Congress*, pp. 31–7.
14 AICC Papers, file no. G150/1930.
15 Home Poll, file no. 499/1930.
16 AICC Papers, file no. G151/1930.
17 Judith M. Brown, *Gandhi and Civil Disobedience* (Cambridge, 1977), pp. 109–10.
18 AICC Papers, G156.
19 Home Poll, Proceedings, file no. 204/1930.
20 Home Poll, Proceedings, file no. 257/V, 1930.
21 Malaviya to Vallabhbhai Patel, 5 July 1930, AICC Papers (supplement) 35/1930.
22 Home Poll, Proceedings, 14 December 1930.
23 Home Poll, Proceedings, 14 December 1930.
24 Resolution adopted at the CWC meeting in Allahabad, 27 June 1930, AICC Papers (supplement) 35/1930.
25 A.B. Druva to Sardar Vallabhbhai Patel, 28 July 1930, AICC Papers 150/1930–31.
26 A.B. Druva to Sardar Vallabhbhai Patel, 28 July 1930, AICC Papers 150/1930–31.
27 Letter from the Government of the United Provinces, 22 September 1930, Home Poll, Proceedings, no. 141/1930.

28   Letter from the Government of the United Provinces, 22 September 1930, Home Poll, Proceedings, no. 141/1930.

29   Divisional Commissioner, Varanasi, to Chief Secretary, Government of the United Provinces, 26 September 1930, UPSA, file no. 127/1930.

30   Frank Noyce, Secretary to Government of India, to A.B. Druva, Pro-Vice-Chancellor, 30 September 1930; Dar and Somskandan, *History of Banaras Hindu University*, p. 617.

31   *Leader*, 25 September 1930.

32   *Leader*, 25 September 1930.

33   A.B. Druva to the Secretary of Education, Government of India, 15 November 1930, UPSA, file no. 127/1930.

34   A.B. Druva to the Secretary of Education, Government of India, 15 November 1930, UPSA, file no. 127/1930.

35   Telegram from W. Benn, Secretary of State for India, to Irwin, 15 December 1930, Halifax Papers, roll 3, no. 47.

36   Gandhi's speech at Gujrat Vidyapeeth, 11 April 1931, *CWMG*, p. 407.

37   Chandra, *India's Struggle for Independence*, p. 510.

38   Proceedings of the Indian Round Table Conferences, September to December 1931, Parliamentary Papers 1931–32, pp. 142–56.

39   S. Gopal, *Jawaharlal Nehru: A Biography, Volume I: 1881–1947*, Part I (Bombay, 1976), p. 150.

40   *CWMG*, vol. 45, p. 247.

41   Gandhi's statement, 16 April 1931, *CWMG*, pp. 8–10.

42   Telegram from Gandhi to Irwin, 20 July 1931, Halifax Papers.

43   Templewood Collection, 28 August 1931, roll 2.

44   Gandhi's statement, 28 August 1931, *CWMG*, vol. 47, pp. 366–7.

45   Gandhi to R.B. Gregg, 29 September 1931, *CWMG*, vol. 48, p. 90.

46   *Leader*, 18 September 1931.

47   Nanda, *Mahatma Gandhi*, p. 322.

48   Nanda, *Mahatma Gandhi*, pp. 322–3.

49   Brown, *Gandhi and Civil Disobedience*, pp. 246–7.

50   Devdas Gandhi to Jawaharlal Nehru, 2 October 1931, Jawaharlal Nehru Papers.

51   Devdas Gandhi to Jawaharlal Nehru, 2 October 1931, Jawaharlal Nehru Papers.

52   Devdas Gandhi to Jawaharlal Nehru, 2 October 1931, Jawaharlal Nehru Papers.

53   Moonje to Pandurang, 30 September 1930, B.S. Moonje Papers, roll no. 9.

54   Moonje to Kelkar, 24 September 1931, B.S. Moonje Papers.

55   *Leader*, 18 October 1931.

56   Brown, *Gandhi and Civil Disobedience*, pp. 265–7.

57   Telegram from Malaviya to Willingdon, 30 January 1932, Halifax Papers.

58   Sitaramayya, *History of the Congress*, p. 895.

59   Home Poll, Proceedings, file no. 12/24/1932.

60   Home Poll, Proceedings, 24 December 1932, file no. 12/24/1932.

61   Note by Maurice Hallet, Home Secretary, Government of India, Home Poll, Proceedings, file no. 14/28/1932.

62   Mahadeva Desai's diary, 28 March 1932, cited in N.D. Parikh, *Day to Day with Gandhi, in Six Volumes* (Varanasi, 1968).

63   Home Poll, Proceedings, file no. 3/13/1933.

64   Majumdar, *History of the Freedom Movement in India*, vol. III, pp. 461–3.

65   Malaviya's statement, 'What Happened at Calcutta', 9 April 1933, Home Poll, Proceedings, file no. 3/13/1933.

66   Malaviya's presidential address, Home Poll, Proceedings, 4-III/1933.

67   Sitarammayya, *History of the Congress*, p. 934.

68   *Leader*, 10 October 1932.

69   *Hindustan Times*, 31 December 1932.

70   *The Hindustan Times*, 30 December 1932.

71   *Leader*, 15 September 1932.

72   Gandhi to Personal Assistant to the Viceroy, 13 February 1933, Home Poll, 50/II/1933.

73   Gandhi to Secretary, Home Department, 19 February 1933, Home Poll, 50/II/1933.

74   Home Member's note, 6 February 1933, Home Poll, 50/II/1933.

75   Telegram from Secretary of State to Government of India, 12 January 1933, Home Poll, 50/II/1933.

76   Malaviya to Gandhi, 8 January 1933, G.D. Birla Papers.

77   Malaviya to G.D. Birla, 18 February 1933, G.D. Birla Papers.

78   Malaviya to G.D. Birla, 18 February 1933, G.D. Birla Papers.

79   Tendulkar, *Mahatma*, vol.V, p. 136.

80   B. Ray, *Gandhi's Campaign Against Untouchability* (New Delhi, 1996), p. 14.

81   Report from the Chief Secretary, UP, to the Government of India, 4 August 1934, file no. 10R/469, NMML.

82   Report from the Chief Secretary, UP, to the Government of India, 4 August 1934, file no. 10R/469, NMML.

83   *Aaj*, 2 August 1934.

10 Communal Award and After

With Gandhi's release on 8 May 1933, hopes had been aroused of an honourable settlement between the Congress and the government, leading to the withdrawal of the civil disobedience movement. Soon after his release, Gandhi issued an appeal asking the Government of India 'to take advantage of this suspension and uncondionally discharge all civil resisters' and asserted that 'if there is will on the part of the Government a modus vivendi can be found'.[1] While Gandhi was convalescing after his fast, leading Congressmen including Malaviya, who were not in jail, assembled at his bedside in Poona to take stock of the political situation. The discussions showed that most Congress leaders felt that it was the right time to withdraw the civil disobedience movement. However, opinions differed on the manner and terms of withdrawal. Malaviya was opposed to the unconditional withdrawal of the movement in view of the unbending attitude of the government. He favoured an honourable setlement with the government.[2] Gandhi was authorized to explore possibilities of peace and contact the viceroy. The latter's reply, however, was disappointing, and he showed no inclination to open negotiations with Gandhi.

Undaunted by the viceroy's open rebuff, Malaviya came forward with the novel suggestion of issuing an appeal to the British prime minister asking him to 'induce the Government of India to adopt the correct attitude'. He proposed to rope in fifty to hundred non-political dignitaries of the country, get their signatures, and despatch such a representation to the British prime minister. C.Y. Chintamani, the editor of the *Leader*, was given the responsibility to coordinate efforts. G.D. Birla was asked to hand over Malaviya's message to Rabindranath Tagore.[3]

Such an effort, however, fell through as no consensus could be arrived at on the wisdom of seeking the British prime minister's intervention over the head of the viceroy.

REVIVAL OF THE SWARAJ PARTY

Discussions with Congress leaders in the early months of 1934 convinced Gandhi that the country was fatigued and in no mood to continue the movement. According to his advice, the CWC, at its meeting held in Patna on 18 May 1934, suspended the Civil Disobedience campaign.

Realizing that a change in Congress policy was the need of the hour, a Congress Leaders' Conference met in Delhi and favoured the revival of the Swaraj Party. Malaviya and several other leaders attended the meeting with the sole object of contesting elections to the Legislative Assembly due to be held that year. A small deputation was sent to Gandhi to explain the general trend of discussion at the conference and to seek his blessings. Gandhi had been opposed to the participation of the Congress in the councils during the 1920s. But recent experience revealed to him that a number of Congressmen found the councils useful for self-expression. He wrote:

> I have made an independent study of the Council-entry question. It appears to me that there will always be a party within the Congress wedded to the idea of Council-entry. The reins of the Congress should be in the hands of that group and that group alone needs the name of the Congress, I have accepted that for all time.[4]

Gandhi welcomed the revival of the Swaraj Party in the AICC meeting held at Patna in May 1934. Soon after, the Swarajists met at Ranchi and adopted a revised constitution. While the Swarajists were unanimous in condemning the White Paper, they pleaded that the time for consideration or rejection of the mode and proportion of representation as contained in the Communal Award would arrive when they met in the Constituent Assembly. The revival of the Swaraj Party with Gandhi's blessings and its policy of escapism on Communal Award forced Malaviya to join issue with the Swarajists. Reacting sharply to the wisdom of forming the Swaraj Party and its stand on the Communal Award, Malaviya contended that 'if Communal Award stands, every class and creed in the country will be organised under it as a separate political community to scramble for its own interests in the Legislature in disregard of people as a whole. The atmosphere will forbid the growth of mutual confidence.'[5] Therefore, he asked the Congress to boldly declare that there was no need of a constitution which was not based on joint electorate. Writing to Gandhi, G.D. Birla wrote:

> Since Dr. Ansari, Bhulabhai and Dr. Roy have announced the formation of the Swarajya Party Pandit Malaviya seems to be very upset. He is not quite sure what attitude he would take at the time of election. You know he holds strong views about the Communal Award.... All that Panditji wants is that the newly formed Swaraj Party should not show any attachment to the Communal Award.[6]

In his reply Gandhi had the following to say:

> The Award affair is very difficult indeed. Something is possible if Muslims accept the way out suggested by me. Even if they do not do so the path is not straight enough. I am afraid however, that the Swarajists will not like it. I do not find the atmoshpere faouarable for the success of Hindu–Muslim–Sikh unity work.[7]

Malaviya's main worry was that the Congress was not announcing its official stand on recent constitutional proposals and the Communal Award because 'almost everywhere[,] it was disgustingly carrying on a domestic war in its own ranks'.[8] It was divided on various issues and 'local factions, ideological camps, opponents and adherents to Communal Award all wanted to control the proposed electioneering machine and prevent their opponents from so doing'.[9] In such a political situation the Congress was unprepared to chalk out any clear-cut policy as desired by Malaviya.

CONGRESS STAND ON THE COMMUNAL AWARD

When the CWC met at Bombay on 17–18 June 1934, fundamental differences came to surface between Malaviya and M.S. Aney, the Berar Responsivist leader who had been a consistent supporter of Malaviya's stand on the Communal Award, on the one hand and the majority of its members on the other. In spite of the objections voiced by Malaviya and Aney, the Congress announced its decision in a resolution, which stated: 'The Congress claims to represent equally all communities composing the Indian Nation and, therefore, in view of the division of opinion, can neither accept nor reject the Communal Award.'[10] The committee did not even permit any freedom of conscience on the issue of the Communal Award.

The Congress realized that any further controversy on Hindu–Muslim unity would jeopardize the anti-imperialist struggle of the Indian people. In order to convince Malaviya, Gandhi wrote:

> I have given my opinion that there is no escape from the Communal Award if we are to secure Musalman's cooperation.[11]

The committee took care to see that it did not incur the displeasure of the Muslim community who, independent of party affiliation, had welcomed the award and the recognition of separate electorates on which the award was, in principle, founded. The working committee did not reject it. It also did not accept the award for that would have antogonized the Hindus. When the resolution was adopted in spite of their objections, both Malaviya and Aney tendered their resignation. They were, however, persuaded to reconsider their move till a final verdict was announced later.

The discussions with Malaviya and Aney were renewed at the Banaras meeting of the CWC from 27 to 30 July. Gandhi was very keen to persuade the committee to explore a workable formula which would appeal to Malaviya. Short of abandoning its fundamental attitude of non-acceptance and non-rejection of the Communal Award, the committee explored all avenues for discovering a 'via media' with a view to retain Malaviya and Aney's cooperation. In view of the points made by them relating to the deep and long-standing conviction of some leading Congressmen with regard to the question of electorates, Gandhi offered a compromise formula providing for an exception being made in the case of those among otherwise eligible candidates who had conscientious objection to the Committee's resolution on the Communal Award. Gandhi's formula was not found adequate by Malaviya and Aney. In view of this, Gandhi resigned the presidentship of the Congress Parliamentary Board and Malaviya and Aney resigned from the CWC and declared their intention to form a separate party.

G.D. Birla had informed Gandhi well in advance about Malaviya's 'strong views' on the Communal Award and his intention to form a new party:

There is a danger of another party being formed under the leadership of Pandit Malaviya if the situation is not handled tactfully and in time.... But I think it is possible to reconcile Panditji's views with that of Swaraj Party if it gives freedom to its members to fight against the Communal Award in its own way. If this is not done it is likely to cause a serious split among the nationalist Hindus, a thing to be avoided.[12]

It was unfortunate that in spite of Gandhi's best efforts, the Communal Award proved to be the 'bitterest source of division' between the Congress and Malaviya.[13]

MALAVIYA'S DECISION TO FLOAT A NEW PARTY

In his long letter of resignation, Malaviya reiterated his earlier views on the Communal Award and contended that to maintain neutrality merely because there were differences of opinion on this issue was bad in policy and contrary to Congress tradition of opposing the wrongs and injustices and of advocating what it thought to be just, right, or necessary in national interest. He argued further that the Communal Award would not lapse with the lapse of the White Paper and if it was allowed to stand unchallenged, its provisions might be incorporated in the Bill which might be brought in place of the White Paper. Malaviya was against giving the wrong impression that the Award had been accepted by the Congress to the Hindus as well as Muslims.[14]

In a letter addressed to 'Mahatma Gandhi and the members of the Working Committee', Malaviya and Aney wrote:

We are convinced that the decision of the Working Committee defining the attitude of the Congress on the Communal Award involves a wide departure from the policy of the Congress in the matter of separate and joint electorates, is anti-national and is calculated to block the way of the establishment of Swaraj or responsible government in India.

The two leaders went a step further by informing the Congress High Command:

We desire to inform our Congress fellow-workers of the programme we propose to follow in view of the decision of the Working Committee. We shall be glad to meet you and other Congressmen who may be in Banaras for this purpose at the Vidyapeeth today or tomorrow at any time that may be convenient to Mahatma Gandhi.[15]

Malaviya made it a point at the very outset, to convince Gandhi and the 'fellow Congress Workers' that his proposal regarding the formation of a new party was not in any way aimed against the Congress and that he was keenly looking forward to work in collaboration with it.

Those present in the meeting held in Kashi Vidyapeeth on 31 July endorsed Malaviya's decision and authorized him to take the necessary steps towards organizing a new party. Invitations were soon issued to 700 persons to meet in Calcutta on 18 August, for the inauguration of the new party. Malaviya explained:

> Owing to the regrettable difference which has arisen between the CWC and Mr. Aney and me on the question of the attitude of the Congress towards the Communal Award, it has been decided to form a new political party under the name of the Nationalist Party, to work for the rejection of the White Paper proposals as a whole i.e. including those contained in the so-called 'Communal Award'. A conference of nationalists who agree with the objects of the party will be held at Calcutta on the 18th instant.[16]

Malaviya's choice of Calcutta for the inaugural session of the Nationlist Party was significant as the bitterest opposition against the Communal Award came from the Hindus of Bengal. The award was particularly disadvantageous to them and they appeared determined to resist it. The Nationlist Party's campaign had moved the Bengali Hindu notables. Rabindranath Tagore, for instance, approved of the agitation and was pained at the failure of the Congress High Command to organize an all-India agitation against the award. Writing to Malaviya on the eve of the inaugural session, Tagore asserted that 'it was impossible to win Swaraj on the basis of separate or communal representation'.[17] In trying to revoke the decision, the Hindu notables sent a memorial to the secretary of state. The memorial, representing remarkable unity among the Bengali Hindu notables, defended the opposition of the award on the ground of the 'enormously predominant role that Hindus have played under British rule in the intellectual, cultural political, professional and commercial life of the province'.[18]

Subhash Bose completely rejected the award. To him, it was not an award but 'a lesser evil than the partition of Bengal'. He argued that 'instead of transferring power to the Indians, this imperial device divides India still further so that the effect of the meagre constitutional reforms may be neutralised'. In Bose's view, the High Command's refusal to sanction agitation against the award was 'dictated by the desire to placate Dr. Ansari and the nationalist Muslims'.[19] Since the nationalist Muslims consistently condemned the communal electorate, 'how could they give up opposition against the Award?'[20] Bose's elder brother, Sarat Chandra, soon demonstrated that he was willing to go to battle with Gandhi and the High Command.[21]

There was an 'ambivalence' in Malaviya's politics[22] as he retained a foothold both in the Congress and the Mahasabha throughout the 1920s and, to a large extent, followed the same course in the post-civil-disobedience period. While he could follow such a policy without much opposition from the Congress in the earlier period, the same could not be possible after 1934. This was forseen by G.D. Birla who gave his analysis to Gandhi in the following words:

> About the communal question Panditji is sailing between the Congress and the Mahasabha. He agrees with none. He would like to have an amicable settlement and yet is not prepared to reasonably satisfy the Mahamedans. At present he insists that Communal Award should be wrecked which of course is an impossible job.[23]

G.D. Birla did not mince words in cautioning Malaviya against his plans of floating a new party:

> It is very unfortunate that on such critical occasions you take a rather uncompromising attitude. I feel you are going to deal a staggering blow to the cause of solidarity.... And the Hindu Mahasabha crowd whom you are going to include in your party is, I am sure, not out to help. The very people with whom you were reluctant to work with a few months back are now becoming personagrata with you. It is a pity that at times you lend yourself to exploitation.[24]

After the receipt of a copy of this letter, Gandhi commented that 'it was certainly strongly worded but quite necessary',[25] indicating his approval of Birla's criticism of Malaviya's plans of action. Gandhi was well aware of the fact that, for the first time, G.D. Birla 'was standing against Malaviya'[26] and yet, he did not discourage Birla from following such a course.

RELATIONS BETWEEN THE NATIONALIST
PARTY AND THE CONGRESS

Aware of such criticisms of his tie-up with the Hindu Mahasabha, Malaviya took upon himself to clear the air at the time of the establishment of the Nationalist Party. In a manifesto issued on this occasion, he isisted that 'the object of the Nationalist Party is the same as that of the Indian National Congress' and further stated:

> As between the candidates set up by the Congress Parliamentary Board and those set up by the Nationalist Party the only difference will be that while both will generally press and fight for the same political programme the former will be compelled by the decision of the Working Committee to remain neutral regarding the Communal Award while the latter i.e. the members of the Nationalist Party will oppose it tooth and nail.[27]

Malaviya attempted to explain that the Nationalist Party shall be a 'source of strength' to the Congress:

> The Nationalist Party in the Assembly will be a source of strength and support to the Congress Parliamentary Party in the fight for Swaraj. In choosing between the two, therefore, the voters in effect will only have to decide whether they will vote for the programme of the Congress party plus neutrality towards the Communal Award or for the same programme plus opposition to the award.[28]

The manifesto of the new party emphasized that it aimed at voicing its opposition against the 'attitude of neutrality which the Working Committee of the Congress adopted towards the Communal Award'[29] and this was the only issue on which the Nationalist Party and the Congress differed. Malaviya further promised to work with the Congress after the election in the Legislative Assembly.

Malaviya's speeches during the inaugural session of the Nationalist Party were along the lines laid down in the manifesto discussed earlier. He was at pains to explain the need for a new party and asked how his step could be unjustified 'if Dr. Ansari and his friends were justified in forming a party within the Congress'. Malaviya repeatedly pointed out that the objective of his party and that of the Congress were in no way different as both desired to win swaraj as early as possible. He stated that the Communal Award was a very important question and the Congress should not turn a blind eye to it. Expressing full faith in the principle of a joint electorate, he said that any other form of election would spell doom for the country. He pointed out that the Communal Award was the 'gift' from the British government and was not evolved by Muslims. He argued that it was time that different communities should sit together and evolve a solution to the problem. His speeches were in no way against any political party or community and he still hoped that it was possible to find a solution to the main question.

Even after the formal announcement of the establishment of the Nationalist Party, Malaviya continued to emphasize his loyalty to the Congress and was always on the lookout to arrive at some understanding with the party before the forthcoming November elections. In a public speech at Nagpur on 10 September, he stressed that it was beyond his imagination to work against the Congress. Recounting his association with it for the previous fifty years, he argued that his fight was not against the Congress but against the CWC.[30]

In several speeches delivered at Calcutta in the middle of September, Malaviya asserted that it was impossible to win swaraj on the basis of separate electorates as this would encourage various major communities of the country to work in different directions. He pointed out that the separate electorate was not demanded by the Muslims. It was introduced by the British to strengthen their imperial domination over the country.[31] While delivering lectures in a few other cities of Bengal, Malaviya explained the long history of the electoral system of the country and the continuous efforts made by the British to divide the people on the basis of separate electorates. Tracing the long-standing Congress position in favour of joint electorates, Malaviya wondered how it reversed its position and agreed to accept the Communal Award.[32]

Gandhi still thought that a workable compromise between the Congress and Malaviya was possible. With this end in view he encouraged Malaviya to come forward with his proposals. This was in line with the stand he had taken earlier at Banaras. But the other Congress leaders, such as Vallabhbhai Patel and Rajendra Prasad, were prepared to negotiate with Malaviya more with a desire to impose their own terms rather than acting upon Malaviya's proposals. They were not agreeable to Malaviya's proposal of allowing freedom to the Congress legislators to vote according to their conscience. Nor did they agree to Malaviya's request for leaving out one or two seats in each province to the Nationalist Party. Under these circumstances, the CWC meeting of 10 September 1934 proved disappointing to Malaviya[33] who had specially been invited for discussions at Wardha. He could see for himself at Wardha that Gandhi could not be of any help to him.

The Congress soon decided to define its stand with respect to the 'coming elections', urged all provincial and other subordinate Congress organizations to regard it as their duty to help the Congress Parliamentary Borad in its election activities, and stressed that it was not open to them to support any other party or candidate opposed to the official policy of the Congress. It further asked every Congressman to support the Congress candidates in the forthcoming elections.[34] Now that the Congress saw that assembly elections were around the corner, it hardened its stand announcing that it expected full support from every Congressman and made it amply clear that it proposed to enter the election arena on its own terms and not with the support of the Nationalist Party. Even though the Congress resolution did not name Malaviya's party, the reference to it was understood by everyone. It is strange that Malaviya did not see the writing on the wall. During the Congress session at Bombay on 28 October, he did not hesitate to speak against the officially sponsored resolution on the Communal Award. This led to considerable bitterness between him and Rajendra Prasad who was presiding over the session. The latter wrote later that Malaviya's supporters threatened him on this occasion.[35]

As a keen observer of the political scene, M.R. Jayakar pointed out the contradictions in Malaviya's stand in the following words: 'A party cannot remain in the Congress and then agitate against it taking advantage of its name, prestige and popularity.'[36] Malaviya could not visualize this on the eve of assembly elections. Even after the formal establishment of the Nationalist Party in late August, he continued to pronounce his links with the Congress and looked forward to arriving at a compromise with it over the next two months. It was only after the annual Congress session of October 1934 that Malaviya could finally realize that the Congress had chosen to enter the election arena alone and was not interested in coming to terms with the Nationalist Party. He had been in a diffident mood for a long time, which adversely affected the prospects of his party. He only had a month at his disposal to prapare for the coming elections and select the party candidates. For instance, it would be interesting to explain how the candidature of Krishna Kant Malaviya was announced. Almost a month earlier, he had openly referred to his predicament in his editorial in *Abhudaya*. Krishna Kant Malaviya was then the president of the Allahabad City Congress Committee which wanted him to fight the elections on a Congress ticket from the Banaras–Gorakhpur assembly constituency. At the same time, Malaviya desired that his nephew, Krishna Kant, should fight for the same seat as the Nationalist Party candidate, but Kant was not enthusiastic. However, he was ultimately prevailed upon to fight the election from the Banaras–Gorakhpur constituency as a Nationalist Party candidate and this announcement was made on 1 October.[37] However, due to some technical problem his candidature was officially disallowed and his adversary, Ishwar Saran, was declared elected on the Congress ticket. Krishna Kant later filed an election petition on the basis of which Ishwar Saran's election was declared null and void and Krishna Kant Malaviya was declared elected unopposed on the Nationalist Party ticket.[38]

Malaviya went round to as many provinces as possible, delivering lectures and addressing various election meetings in which he asked the voters to exercise their franchise in favour of candidates who were opposed to the Communal Award. The Nationlist Party, however, could not put forward an impressive show. It had limited resources, fewer leaders, and lacked organizational strength. Besides, it was subjected to scurrilous propaganda at the hands of the Congress press. Several meetings organized by Malaviya's supporters were disturbed by the rival groups and a few of them ended in fiasco.

The election results were disappointing to Malaviya. The Nationalist Party won eleven seats. Most of the successful candidates of the party belonged to Bengal. The performance of the party was not impressive in Bihar, UP, and Punjab. The Hindu Mahasabha could secure only one seat, which was won by Bhai Parmanand in Lahore. The Congress tally was forty-four and its overall performance was impressive.

LINKS WITH THE HINDU MAHASABHA

Up to 1930, Malaviya retained a foothold both in the Congress as well as in the Mahasabha and attempted, all along, to bring the two parties as close to each other as possible. While he was fairly successful in this venture, the developments that followed later made his task not only difficult but also challenging. This was largely because, from this time onwards, the two parties started moving on different lines, adopted newer strategies, and began to follow hard lines on different political issues. In this changed political scenario. It took Malaviya a fair amount of tightrope-walking to convince the Congress as well as the Mahasabha leadership about his real intentions.

With regard to Malaviya's role in the Mahasabha, Jawaharlal Nehru rightly made a distinction between the strategy adopted by the Hindu Mahasabha up to 1930 and 'the new developments' that followed thereafter in the following words:

> He [Malaviya] had not much to do with it lately and it almost seemed that the new aggressive leaders of the Mahasabha had pushed him out. So long as he had been one of the leading spirits, the Mahasabha, in spite of its communalism, had not been politically reactionary. But latterly this new development has become very patent and I felt sure that Malaviyaji could not have anything to do with it and must have disapproved of it.[39]

Earlier in November 1933 Jawaharlal Nehru's address to the students of the Banaras Hindu University turned out to be a great source of embarrassment to Malaviya as the visitor utilized the occasion to launch a frontal attack on the Hindu Mahasabha.[40] In language that even Gandhi regarded as 'too fierce', Nehru condemned the Mahasabha for its reactionary and anti-national policy of cooperation with the government and support of vested interests.[41] Nehru realized later on that 'it was not in the best of taste to criticize the Hindu Mahasabha at a meeting presided over by Malaviyaji who had long been one of its pillars'.[42]

Since the immediate reason for Nehru's provocation was the information passed on to him that certain very objectionable resolutions on the communal relations had been adopted by the Hindu Mahasabha and the Arya Kumar Sabha at their Ajmer sessions, Malaviya immediately took it upon himself to clear the air and despatched to him a complete and authentic version of the actual resolutions passed at the session. His effort was to convince Nehru that no such communal resolutions had been passed at Ajmer and that the latter based his remarks on some incorrect information wrongly conveyed to him. Malaviya stated:

It appeared from your remarks that it was a resolution like that before your mind when you spoke as strongly as you did against the Hindu Mahasabha and the Arya Kumar Sabha. But it is clear now that neither of these Sabhas passed any such resolution.[43]

Writing further, he expected that 'in view of the big fight that lies before us you do not desire unnecessarily to antagonise a large section of the Hindu community against you'.[44] While still nursing hopes of a possible tie-up between the Congress and the Hindu Mahasabha in the struggle for freedom, Malaviya attempted to impress upon Nehru the importance of keeping the link intact. When Nehru informed Malaviya that he intended to issue a public statement on the Mahasabha, the latter got alarmed and hastened to write to Nehru again, putting forward 'certain facts' before him. Explaining the Mahasabha's role, Malaviya pointed out in the earlier part of the letter that:

> If you see the resolutions of the Hindu Mahasabha during the last many years, you will find that it has, as a body, all along opposed separate communal electorates and reservations and has consistently advocated joint electorates without reservations.[45]

Malaviya further added:

> The Hindu Mahasabha has in this respect taken up an attitude which is nationalistic and in line with the attitude of the Congress. It is only fair that you should give credit to the Mahasabha for this fact while you are perfectly entitled to express your condemnation of the view of those Punjab Hindu leaders and organizations which, you say, have advocated the 'deplorable anti-national attitude' of calling for Anglo-Hindu unity meaning thereby a cooperation with British Imperialism in the hope of getting a few crumbs and who have neutralized to some extent the tremendous gains of the last few years.[46]

Conceding that Nehru's criticism of the stand taken by certain Mahasabha leaders was largely correct, Malaviya finally advised him to express his views cautiously:

> I am anxious that while expressing your disapproval of what you consider to be hurtful to national interests you should so express yourself that, as far as possible, you should not alienate but carry with you the support of all nationalist Hindus who have carried on or supported the national fight for freedom during the last fifty years.[47]

Malaviya's letters were very much in Jawaharlal Nehru's mind when he issued a long statement on 'Hindu and Muslim Communalism' on 27 November 1933. Nehru began with an expression of regret and apology for 'a hoax in regard to the alleged resolution of Hindu Mahasabha and Arya Kumar Sabha'.[48] However he was 'unrepentant' with regard to his criticism of the Hindu Mahasabha and asserted that 'the activities of Hindu communal organizations, including the Mahasabha, have been communal, anti-national and reactionary'.[49] Referring indirectly to Malaviya's advice, Nehru explained his position in the following words:

> I have been warned by friends whose opinion I value that my attitude towards communal organizations will result in antagonizing many people against me. This is indeed probable. I have no desire to antagonize any countryman of mine for we are in the midst of a mighty struggle against a powerful opponent.[50]

Malaviya's letters to Nehru reflect his keen desire to work as a link between the Congress and the Mahasabha. He went all out to plead the Mahasabha's case to Nehru so that the bridge between the two parties was kept intact. It was indeed tragic that during the next few years Malaviya could neither bring round the Mahasabha to his line of thinking nor convince the newly emerging Congress leadership of the need for keeping closer contacts with the Mahasabha.

Malaviya's resignation from the Congress Parliamentary Board and his announcement of the formation of the Congress Nationalist Party encouraged the Mahasabha leaders to bring him more fully into their fold. B.S. Moonje, the secretary of the Mahasabha, rushed to Banaras on 31 July 1934 and stayed with Malaviya for a week in an effort to explore the chances of closer cooperation between the Nationalist Party and the Mahasabha in the forthcoming assembly elections. The newspapers reporting about Moonje's visit were, however, not very hopeful of the success of his mission.[51] This did not dishearten the Mahasabha leaders and they asked their party colleagues to get ready to extend full support to Malaviya. Moonje observed that 'at the Conference we will have to announce formally that the Mahasabha wholeheartedly cooperate with the Nationalist Party of Malaviya'. He got in touch with M.S. Aney who had also resigned from the Congress along with Malaviya and suggested that 'this party as well as the Hindu Mahasabha can render most useful service to the country by acting as a buffer between the Congress and the Muslim League'.[52] Ganpat Rai, the general secretary of the Mahasabha, urged Malaviya to 'realize the urgent need of the common name of the "Hindu party" for the Hindus outside the Congress in all the provinces of India'.[53]

While offering these suggestions to Malaviya, the Mahasabha leaders were well aware of the former's strong links with the Congress. B.S. Moonje pointed out:

> He [Malaviya] is of the Congress mentality, first drive out the English by cooperating with the Muslims and then consider the respective position of the two communities. It is difficult for him to give up his long association with the Congress.[54]

The general secretary of the Mahasabha was equally aware of the closer links between Malaviya, the Congress, and Gandhi:

> The manifesto of Pandit Malaviya is out and it appears that he would organize a party but on account of his commitment with Gandhi he would not set up any candidate against the Congress Parliamentary Board candidates. But the Hindu Mahasabha cannot afford to do that.[55]

In addition to the Mahasabha, the Justice Party of Madras also came forward to extend support to the Nationalist Party and conveyed its intention in this regard to Malaviya through the president of the Hindu Mahasabha, Bhai Parmanand.[56]

Malaviya was, however, not impressed by the offer of support conveyed to him by the Mahasabha or any other party. He firmly laid down that the membership of the Nationalist Party would be open to only those who owed allegiance to the Congress and were its members. M.R. Jayakar was disappointed by Malaviya's decision 'to restrict the operation of their Party in the narrow way he has done and left many of his friends outside who will not easily forget their exclusion'.[57] Jayakar was referring, in particular, to Malaviya's refusal to enrol Bhai Parmanand as a member of the Nationalist Party because of the latter's refusal to join the Congress.

Malaviya not only put up only Congressmen as candidates on behalf of the Nationalist Party for the assembly elections but also impressed upon the Mahasabha not to fight the elections on its own.[58] Malaviya's suggestion was not acceptable to certain leaders of the Mahasabha who thought that this was the right opportunity to assert themselves. The secretary of the Mahasabha observed:

Of course, there would be cases where the Nationalist Party may hesitate
to risk their relations with Congress and Mahatmaji and we would have
to assert for the rights of the Hindus through the Hindu Mahasabha.[59]

Differences between Malaviya and a section of the Mahasabha were,
however, not confined to electoral strategy alone. They had fundamental disagreements with regard to reaching out to Muslims. While
Malaviya strongly supported efforts to arrive at some understanding
with the Muslims, tried continuously to enter into a dialogue with
leading Muslim leaders from 1932 to 1934, and was all along prepared
to evolve a compromise formula acceptable to them, the Mahasabha
was not prepared to negotiate with them on equal terms. The newly
emerging Mahasabha leaders did not share Malaviya's vision. They
were openly hostile to Muslims, talked of the 'Muslim peril'[60] and
thought that any proposal to open dialogue with Muslims was a sign
of weakness. Voicing their views, Moonje expressed his disappointment
in the following words:

> As for Pandit Malaviya I cannot rely on him. He will be a handicap
> to us. He is prepared to swallow the whole award if Muslims agree to
> some kind of joint electorate. We cannot pay such a heavy price for
> joint electorate. But he will, in his own anxiety, to make up quarrel with
> Muslims [*sic*].[61]

Malaviya's perception of the Muslims[62] did not appeal to B.S. Moonje.
He, therefore, asked:

> How Mahasabha would carry struggle against Muslims and Govern-
> ment against such a weak kind of personality. He is the gretest [*sic*] man
> amongst as but has no backbone.... I cannot rely on him when a kind of
> civil war has been imposed on us by Muslims. With him as our leader in
> the war his only 'mantra' is be meak [*sic*] and surrender to the Muslim
> demands.[63]

The secretary of the Hindu Mahasabha went to the extent of asking
Malaviya, 'Would you, therefore, realize the urgent need of the common name of "Hindu Party" for the Hindus outside the Congress in all
the provinces of India?'[64] He could not appreciate Malaviya's anxiety
of keeping his links with the Congress intact even after the formation
of a new party. Ganpat Rai pleaded for an independent line of action
and desired that the Hindu Mahasabha should make its presence felt at
the time of the assembly elections. He wrote:

We must pool our strength under their—Malaviya–Aney—leadership. Of course there would be cases where Nationalist Party may hesitate to risk their relations with the Congress and Mahatmaji and we would have to assert for the rights of the Hindus through the Hindu Mahasabha.[65]

The correspondence of Moonje, Ganpat Rai, and Bhai Parmanand, to name only a few prominent Mahasabha leaders, show that from the beginning they looked to the assembly elections as a great opportunity for the Mahasabha largely because the constituencies were divided into Muhammadan and non-Muhammadan categories. In the latter constituencies, the Hindus were the voters and the Mahasabha saw this as an opportunity to assert itself. But the Mahasabha leaders could not appreciate Malaviya's 'Congress mentality' and his advice to the Mahasabha leaders to keep away from electoral politics. Moonje, time and again, criticized Malaviya and wrote that he could 'not see eye to eye with him on matters relating to Mahasabha'.[66] Bhai Parmanand received the shock of his life when Malaviya made it a point to open the doors of his party only to Congressmen. Since Bhai Parmanand was opposed to Malaviya's precondition, the latter did not allow him to fight the elections on a Nationalist Party ticket. He fought the election on Mahasabha ticket from Lahore, won the election, and sought to take revenge during the next year leading to further division in the Mahasabha camp. Moonje lost the election in spite of his repeated claims of being a great defender of Hindu interests. Most of the Mahasabha leaders took a keen interest in the assembly elections thus reflecting their political ambitions.

The available evidence shows that Malaviya was either unaware of the political ambitions of the Mahasabha leaders or he deliberately ignored their views in order to keep them in good humour as he needed their help in carrying on the battle against the Communal Award. During the next two years, he faced several challenges in his efforts to keep his links with the Mahasabha and the Congress intact.

POST-ASSEMBLY-ELECTION SCENARIO

After the assembly elections, the Congress High Command not only reiterated its earlier policy towards the Communal Award but also defended it by referring to the fact that the Congress Party's victory in all general seats in Madras, Orissa, UP, and the Central Provinces 'conclusively proved that the Congress had the support of the vast majority of the Hindu electorate'.[67] It conveniently downplayed the Congress failure in Bengal and Punjab. Soon after, Rajendra Prasad, the Congress president, and Jinnah met in long sessions on 28 and 31 January 1935. Rajendra Prasad put forward a formula which included joint electorates and reservation of seats on a population basis with freedom for minorities to contest more seats, the franchise being so arranged as to reflect the proportion of various communities in the electorate. Jinnah's proposals for substituting the award were unacceptable to the Nationalist Party. Malaviya, as its leader, insisted that 'till the Hindus of Bengal get their share, in proportion, they are not going to endorse the outcome of the talks'.[68] G.D. Birla noted that 'Pandit Malaviyaji, I fear, will not be helpful, as usual' and added 'He [Malaviya] neither agrees with the rank communalists nor with the Jinnah–Rajendra Prasad formula. He has given me a number of suggestions but it is no use discussing them since I know that Jinnah is not prepared to go beyond the formula.'[69] Birla was regularly in touch with Gandhi and kept him informed about the Rajendra Prasad–Jinnah talks. When Rajendra Prasad sought Gandhi's help in winning over Malaviya, the latter acknowledged that 'to bring round Malaviyaji appears to be a difficult proposition but he would put up no opposition if Sikhs could be persuaded. There is no occasion now for my writing to him though I shall do so if that is your wish. Ghanshyamdas is enough. After the others have agreed even Jamnalalji can go to Panditji.'[70]

The entire exercise proved abortive. Though the Congress High Command was in favour of a settlement, the Muslim leadership did not agree to abandon separate electorates and Jinnah failed to persuade his colleagues to do so.

Not content with the Congress moves, Malaviya organized an all-India anti–Communal Award Conference in Delhi on 23 February 1935 to demonstrate that the Hindus were not ready to support any scheme as long as the Award prevailed. Moving the main resolution on this occasion, Malaviya was careful not to speak a single word against the utterences of the Muslim leaders. The award, he said, would not help any community except the Europeans, and it would not allow the tree of self-government to grow. The conference resolved to appoint a committee to organize a country-wide agitation against the award and to send a deputation to London headed by Malaviya.[71] Malaviya's journey to London, however, could not materialize because of his illness. But his agitation against the award continued.

While protesting against the Communal Award, Malaviya received the greatest support from Bengal Congressmen who thought that the central leaders cared little about their problems. At an all-Bengal Hindu Conference organized at Calcutta early in 1935, Tushar Kanti Ghose, editor of the *Amrita Bazar Patrika*, gave voice to the 'bhadralok' opinion when he declared that 'the educated Hindus of Bengal had built the Indian National Congress. They had always obeyed its mandate.... What a pity that the very Congress failed to do anything for Bengal at the time of crisis.'[72] The High Command's alleged betrayal of Bengal's interests made it legitimate for many Bengal Congress leaders to defy the central leaders. Both, the Bengal Congress and the Nationalist Party, were upset. In a telegram to the Congress president, the secretary of the Nationalist Party described the former's formula as 'nothing but selling Bengal to Muslims'.[73]

Malaviya's stubborn resistance to the Communal Award brought forth criticism from both the Congress and non-Congress circles and led to unnecessary tension between the two major communities. It appears that in carrying on his crusade against the Communal Award, Malaviya lost sight of the potentialities of the existing political situation that could be exploited to the detriment of the national cause. He incurred the hostility of several Congress leaders including Rajendra Prasad and Sardar Patel.

MALAVIYA'S OUSTER FROM THE *HINDUSTAN TIMES*

Another fallout of Malaviya's vigorous campaign against the Communal Award was his ouster from the management of the English newspaper, the *Hindustan Times*. Since 1927, Malaviya was controlling the newspapers with the financial support of G.D. Birla. There was an impression that the newspaper was airing out his views in its editorials, articles, and occasional writings. G.D. Birla watched the reports in the newspaper with deep misgivings and a tug of war ensued between him and Malaviya with regard to the reports about the Communal Award presented in the newspaper. Since the middle of 1934, Birla set his eyes

on keeping Malaviya out of the management of the paper and decided
to take over control of it himself. Birla gave out full details to Gandhi:

> Panditji every day pressed the point about the policy of the Hindustan
> Times and went to the extent of saying that I should leave the paper
> entirely in his hand. I could not accept his suggestions because it was
> not a question of merely my resignation.... So I definitely said 'No' and
> suggested that the matter be put before the directors and the sharehold-
> ers. This distressed Panditji very much for some time but eventually he
> agreed to have a non-committal policy. So the Hindustan Times will
> now make no comment either against or in favour of Panditji. I thought
> that was the best under the circumstances. I did not like to shock him
> by putting him out of the Board.[74]

Thus the differences between them had come to such a point that
Birla used his financial control of the paper to his advantage and almost
compelled Malaviya to keep his hands off the paper that the latter had
established, nursed, and guided for several years. Thus, Malaviya lost the
sympathy and support of one his close associates on the question of the
Communal Award.

ESTRANGENMENT BETWEEN MALAVIYA AND THE MAHASABHA

Despite the unity in the campaign against the Communal Award
between the Mahasabha and Malaviya, dissensions came to the surface
over the question of electing the president for the Kanpur session of
the Mahasabha in April 1935.[75] Malaviya's candidature was opposed by
Bhai Parmanand who nursed a grievance against the former for denying his entry to the Congress Nationalist Party and for insisting on the
keeping his party within the Congress fold. Bhai Parmanand, Ganpat
Rai, and a section of the Mahasabha openly announced their faith in
the Hindu *rashtra* (nation). Their main plank was to oppose Muslim
demands tooth and nail. Thus, strong ideological differences came to
the fore within the Hindu Mahasabha. Malaviya was totally opposed to
these objectives and, therefore, a tug of war began between his supporters and the followers of Bhai Parmanand and others. Malaviya did not
attend this Mahasabha session and, in his absence, several resolutions
were adopted at Kanpur reflecting the new ideological stance of the
party. The tone and content of several resolutions were anti-Muslim

and they were held responsible for communal riots. The Congress was criticized for its stand on the Communal Award.[76]

At the next annual session of the Mahasabha held in December 1935 at Poona, Malaviya's influence was clearly visible. As president of the session, he made a strong plea in favour of Hindu–Muslim unity by asserting that 'the flame of nationalism has got to be lighted in the hearts of all Indians and unity between communities, castes and creeds must be its effects'. Malaviya regretted 'the present situation as regards relations between Hindus and Muslims of India'[77] and recounted the circumstances that led to the failure of unity talks between him and Maulana Shaukat Ali at Allahabad. At the UP Hindu Sabha Conference held in Agra in April 1936, Malaviya reiterated his faith in Hindu–Muslim unity:

> The Hindu and Muslims have to live together in this country. We work together in thousands of ways. We have the walls of our houses side by side and live together and yet there is no trouble—when we fight there is trouble. It is the duty of all of us to promote unity.'[78]

Such utterances by Malaviya from the Mahasabha platform were unpalatable to its sectarian leaders like Bhai Parmanand and Ganpat Rai. They ultimately prepared themselves to bypass Malaviya at the Lahore session of the Mahasabha. The session was shifted from UP to Punjab without consulting or even informing Malaviya. His re-nomination for the post of president of the Mahasabha was opposed by Ganpat Rai on the ground that he was a 'spent force'.[79] Malaviya, foreseeing trouble, wisely decided to stay away from the 1936 session of the Mahasabha. The Reception Committee of the Lahore session refused to admit the UP delegation consisting of Malaviya's men and his son Radhakant, as delegates and offered them admission only as visitors, which they refused. The treatment meted out to this delegation was a pointer to the events that followed. The estrangement between Malaviya and the Mahasabha was now complete.

As the relations between the Hindu Mahasabha and the Congress deteriorated further in the lead up to the 1937 elections, Malaviya was left with no other option but to move closer to the latter. He fought for Hindu interests, not for the Hindu rashtra, and continued to work for Hindu–Muslim unity. Malaviya's speeches from the Mahasabha platform, quoted earlier, amply demonstrate his faith in Hindu–Muslim unity.

NOTES

1   Gandhi's statement, 8 May 1933, *CWMG*.

2   Malaviya to G.D. Birla, 15 May 1933, G.D. Birla Papers; Birla, *Bapu: A Unique Assocation*, pp. 307–8.

3   G.D. Birla to Rabindranath Tagore, 18 April 1933, in Birla, *Bapu: A Unique Assocation*, pp. 335–7.

4   Gandhi to G.D. Birla, 20 April 1934, in G.D. Birla, *In the Shadow of the Mahatma* (Bombay, 1968), p. 128.

5   *Hindustan Times*, 9 May 1934.

6   G.B. Birla to Gandhi, 14 April 1934, inBirla, *In the Shadow of the Mahatma*, p. 127.

7   Gandhi to G.D. Birla, 15 April 1934, in Birla, *In the Shadow of the Mahatma*, p. 127.

8   T.B. Sapru to Polak, 13 August 1934, Sapru Papers, series II.

9   Brown, *Gandhi and Civil Disobedience*, p. 376.

10   Sitaramayya, *History of the Congress*, p. 965.

11   Gandhi to Malaviya, 16 April 1934, Syed Mahmud Papers.

12   G.D. Birla to Gandhi, 14 April 1934, in Birla, *In the Shadow of the Mahatma*, p. 127.

13   Brown, *Gandhi and Civil Disobedience*, p. 377.

14   Malaviya's letter to the Congress Working Committee, *Hindustan Times*, 29 July 1934.

15   Malaviya and M.S. Aney to Mahatma Gandhi and Members of the Congress Working Committee, 30 July 1934, AICC Papers G-34/1934.

16   Malaviya to B.S. Moonje, 8 August 1934, B.S. Moonje Papers.

17   *Abhudaya*, 27 August 1934.

18   *Amrita Bazar Patrika*, 16 April 1934.

19   M.V. Sharma, *The Right Man in the Right Place: Subhash Chandra Bose* (Lahore, 1938), p. 98.

20   Bose, *Indian Struggle*, pp. 290–1.

21   Leonard A. Gordon, *Brothers ggainst the Raj* (New Delhi, 2000), p. 229.

22   Salil Misra, *A Narrative of Communal Politics* (New Delhi, 2001),   p. 292.

23   G.D. Birla to Gandhi, 14 April 1934, in Birla, *In the Shadow of the Mahatma*, p. 127.

24   G.D. Birla to Malaviya, 15 August 1934, G.D. Birla Papers.

25   Mahadev Desai to G.D. Birla, 18 August 1934, G.D. Birla Papers.

26   Mahadev Desai to G.D. Birla, 18 August 1934, G.D. Birla Papers.

27   Malaviya's Manifesto of the Nationalist Party, 18 August 1934, B.S. Moonje Papers, file no. 37/1934(II).

28   Malaviya's Manifesto of the Nationalist Party, 18 August 1934, B.S. Moonje Papers, file no. 37/1934(II).

29 Malaviya's Manifesto of the Nationalist Party, 18 August 1934, B.S. Moonje Papers, file no. 37/1934(II).

30 *Abhudaya*, 17 September 1934.

31 *Abhudaya*, 24 September 1934.

32 *Abhudaya*, 8 October 1934.

33 *Abhudaya*, 17 September 1934.

34 Sitaramayya, *History of the Congress*, pp. 569–70.

35 Prasad, *Autobiography*, p. 393.

36 M.R. Jayakar to Moonje, 21 September 1934, B.S. Moonje Papers, 37/1934.

37 *Abhudaya*, 3 October 1934.

38 Reeves, Graham, and Goodman, *Handbook to Elections in Uttar Pradesh*, p. 381.

39 Jawaharlal Nehru, *An Autobiography*, pp. 458–9.

40 Jawaharlal Nehru's speech at Banaras Hindu University, 13 November 1933, *SWJN*, pp. 157–8.

41 Gopal, *Jawaharlal Nehru*, vol. I, p. 182.

42 Jawaharlal Nehru, *Toward Freedom* (New Delhi, 1995), p. 288.

43 Malaviya to Jawaharlal Nehru, 25 November 1933, Jawaharlal Nehru Papers.

44 Malaviya to Jawaharlal Nehru, 25 November 1933, Jawaharlal Nehru Papers.

45 Malaviya to Jawaharlal Nehru, 26 November 1933, Jawaharlal Papers.

46 Malaviya to Jawaharlal Nehru, 26 November 1933, Jawaharlal Papers.

47 Malaviya to Jawaharlal Nehru, 26 November 1933, Jawaharlal Papers.

48 Malaviya to Jawaharlal Nehru, 26 November 1933, Jawaharlal Papers.

49 Jawaharlal Nehru's statement, 27 November 1933, *SWJN*, vol. VI, pp. 161–71.

50 Jawaharlal Nehru's statement, 27 November 1933, *SWJN*, vol. VI, pp. 161–71.

51 *Abhudaya*, 4 August 1934.

52 Moonje to M.S. Aney, 5 August 1934, B.S. Moonje Papers.

53 Ganapat Rai to Malaviya, 1 August 1934, V.D. Savarkar Papers.

54 B.S. Moonje to J.K. Birla, 19 May 1934, B.S. Moonje Papers, roll no. 10.

55 Ganapat Rai to B.S. Moonje, 8 August 1934, Hindu Mahasabha Papers.

56 Ganpat Rai to Malaviya, 29 August 1934, B.S. Moonje Papers.

57 M.R. Jayakar to B.S. Moonje, 21 September 1934, B.S. Moonje Papers.

58 *Hindustan Times*, 6 May 1934.

59 Ganpat Rai to B.S. Moonje, 9 May 1934, B.S. Moonje Papers.

60 B.S. Moonje to C. Vijayaraghavachariar, 25 August 1934, B.S. Moonje Papers.

61   Moonje to J.K. Birla, 19 May, 1934, B.S. Moonje Papers, roll no. 10.

62   Moonje to J.K. Birla, 19 May, 1934, B.S. Moonje Papers, roll no. 10.

63   Moonje to J.K. Birla, 10 May 19324, B.S. Moonje Papers, roll no. 10.

64   Ganpat Rai to Malaviya, 1 August 1935, V.D. Savarkar Papers, roll no. 3.

65   Ganpat Rai to Malaviya, 9 August 1934, B.S. Moonje Papers.

66   Moonje to J.K. Birla, 19 May 1934, B.S. Moonje Papers, roll no. 10.

67   Rajendra Prasad's diary notes, AICC Papers, G-65/1935.

68   Rajendra Prasad's diary notes, AICC Papers, G-65/1935.

69   G.D. Birla to Gandhi, 15 February 1935, in Birla, *In the Shadow of the Mahatma*, p. 136.

70   Gandhi to Rajendra Prasad, 28 February 1935, in Rajendra Prasad, *Correspondence and Select Documents*, edited by Valmiki Chaudhury, vol. I (New Delhi, 1985), p. 8.

71   Mitra, *Indian Annual Register, 1935*, vol. I, p. 314.

72   Mitra, *Indian Annual Register, 1935*, vol. I, p. 12.

73   Indra Narayan Sen to Rajendra Prasad, 15 February 1935, Rajendra Prasad Papers.

74   G.D. Birla to Gandhi, 25 February 1935, in Birla, *In the Shadow of the Mahatma*, p. 136.

75   Ralhan, *Hindu Mahasabha*, p. 107.

76   Misra, *Narrative of Communal Politics*, p. 293.

77   Ralhan, *Hindu Mahasabha*, vol. I, p. 313.

78   Malaviya's speech, 18 April 1936, in Mitra, *Indian Annual Register, 1936*, part I, p. 212.

79   Ganpat Rai to R.G. Bhinday, 24 July 1936, V.D. Savarkar Papers, roll no. 3.

11 The Last Phase

At the Lucknow session of the Congress, Jawaharlal Nehru described the Indian Reforms Act as a 'charter of slavery' and the Congress rejected the new constitution 'in entirety'. The Congress went on to assert that 'independence cannot be achieved through the legislatures'.[1] However, the Congress decided to contest the elections for the provincial legislative assemblies partly because it considered it unwise to leave the field clear to anti-national elements and partly because there was a powerful wing within the Congress which saw possibilities of constructive work in the provinces within the limited framework of the act of 1935.[2]

NEHRU SEEKS MALAVIYA'S COOPERATION

Both the Congress and the Nationalist Party were anxious to avoid a direct clash at the time of these elections and realized the need for arriving at an understanding with each other as early as possible. A firm denunciation of the Communal Award by the Congress in April 1936 stating that 'the rejection of the Government of India Act of 1935 involves rejection of the Communal Award which is wholly unacceptable being inconsistent with independence and the principle of democracy'[3] created a most favourable atmosphere for an electoral understanding between the Nationalist Party and the Congress. With this end in view, Jawaharlal Nehru, the Congress president, set the ball rolling in April 1936 by seeking Malaviya's help in bringing about 'cooperation' between the Congress and the Nationalist Party. In a very significant letter, he explained the Congress position to Malaviya by writing:

So far as the Congress is concerned, as some of us told you and other friends, we are prepared to go a long way to bring about this accommodation provided, of course, this is based on an anti-imperialist policy and on Independence.[4]

Jawaharlal Nehru 'was willing to cooperate with anybody, irrespective of ideology, who was opposed to imperialism'. Nehru's general indifference to communal issues and his belief that they would be submerged once the emphasis was shifted to economic matters affecting the common people enabled him to ignore the communal tinge in organizations that were otherwise opposed to the British.[5] This was reflected in his letter to Malaviya referenced below:

> The communal decision by itself cannot obviously be made the sole basis for any action as it is the by product of the political situation.... Concentration on the communal decision with no clear outlook in regard to wider political issues can have no meaning and can only result in perpetuating that very communal decision which we object to.[6]

On his part, Nehru desired to know 'what the Nationalist Party proposes to do in regard to these wider political issues as well as the narrower issue of communal decision', sought Malaviya's help in clearing up the situation so that they might all know where they stood, and pleaded, 'We should of course try to agree as far as possible, but even if we cannot agree let us exactly know where we differ.'[7]

Over the next two months, there was an exchange of letters between Nehru and Malaviya, and the two leaders met at Mussoorie on at least two occasions. Nehru later issued a statement to the press giving out the details of his negotiations with Malaviya:

> The communal decision was of course discussed but we spent far more time over other and, what I considered, more vital matters affecting our freedom struggle. These matters form the background of our whole struggle and it seems to me that clarity in regard to them is essential. The communal decision and its consequences are important but they are after all offshoots of the main problem, not the main problem itself. Both of us started with the fixed premise that in our freedom struggle all of us should make every effort to bring together all the forces that are anti-imperialist and are working for Indian freedom.[8]

Jawaharlal Nehru frankly admitted that the communal question 'has undoubtedly been an element of discord amongst us' and desired that 'it is for us to end or at least to minimise this discord'. He offered the following solution for this vexing issue:

> I feel that the question can ultimately be settled satisfactorily only by mutual goodwill between the communities and in a spirit of accommodation as well as consideration of the true interests of the masses whether Hindu, Muslim, Sikh, Christian or others.[9]

Nehru further added: 'This, I believe, is fundamentally the Congress policy. This, I think, [is] in its essence the outlook of the Nationalist Party. The gap between the two is more imaginary than real and is based more on certain past incidents than on present circumstances.' He emphasized that 'we are not out for just an electoral arrangement but for a more fundamental tackling of the problems and for this I seek a wider basis of goodwill'.[10]

THE CWC IN FAVOUR OF A LIMITED PACT

At its meeting held in June 1936, the CWC welcomed the 'desire for cooperation expressed by Malaviyaji and some of his colleagues' and expressed the hope that it would be possible to 'find ways and means to ensure such cooperation in the nationalist struggle against imperialism.'[11] At a subsequent meeting, the committee announced a categorical rejection of the Communal Award and thereby removed the main cause of Malaviya's grievance against the Congress. Malaviya was impressed by the Congress election manifesto, which prepared the ground for his collaboration with the Congress in the elections.

In an effort to forge a grand anti-imperial alliance, Jawaharlal Nehru found Malaviya a willing partner in the middle of 1936 and his admission that the gap between the two was more imaginary than real is ample testimony to the fact that Malaviya was entirely willing to work with the Congress. Nehru insisted that the communal question was not the main problem but the offshoot of the main issue of the struggle for freedom and was entirely willing to work with the Nationalist Party.

In spite of Nehru's efforts, no formal alliance was reached at the all-India level between the Congress and the Nationalist Party as some of the vocal and influential members of the CWC did not see eye to eye with his proposal of cooperation between the Congress and Malaviya at the time of elections. Perhaps there was a lurking fear of Malaviya's motives and Mahasabha links in their minds. In such a situation, only a limited agreement confined only to UP was formalized between the Congress and Malaviya's Nationalist Party through the efforts of Rafi Ahmad Kidwai. According the terms of the agreement, the Congress kept aside twenty seats to which Malaviya's nominees could be elected. These nominees of the Nationalist Party were given full freedom to choose their own line with regard to the Communal Award and allied matters. When this agreement, proposed by Rafi Ahmad Kidwai, was put forward for the approval of the CWC, some of its members expressed their displeasure at the terms offered and approved the agreement with considerable reluctance.[12] Since the Congress–Nationalist Party agreement was confined to UP and no formal alliance could be reached at the all-India level, Malaviya and his associates thought that they were obliged to cooperate fully with the Congress in UP but free to act independently in other provinces. This led to considerable misunderstanding between Malaviya and the Congress at the later stage.

MALAVIYA'S ELECTION PROPAGANDA

It is against this background that Malaviya undertook extensive propaganda for the candidates of both, his party and those of the Congress. He said openly during the election tours that he was making no distinction between the candidates set up by the Nationalist Party and the Congress and asserted that he was a friend of both. He made every effort to convince the electorate that Hindu interests were perfectly safe in the hands of the Congress and refuted the allegation that the Congress was anti-religion or anti-Hindu.[13] Achyut S. Patwardhan, a member of the CWC, acknowledging Malaviya's role during the elections, observed:

> He [Malaviyaji] has rendered great service to us in counteracting Hindu Mahasabha propaganda at certain times and the general assurances to Hindu sentiment which his support to the Congress secures are factors which cannot be easily ignored.[14]

Malaviya's election speeches revealed the depth of this allegiance to the Congress. To him, the Congress was 'like a mother after whom he ran as a child runs after the mother'.[15] He asserted that his differences with the the party on certain issues did not come in conflict with his allegiance to it. During the course of the election campaign, Malaviya addressed scores of election meetings in various cities and small towns calling upon the electorates to vote for the Congress and the Nationalist Party as these parties were working together for India's independence.

He exhorted the people not to follow the lead of communal organizations. He concluded his election tour with visits to the eastern districts of the UP, Basti, Gorakhpur, Deoria, and Allahabad. Various local newspapers published detailed reports of his visits to these places and reported that large crowds assembled to hear him in rural areas.[16]

NEHRU 'DISTRESSED'

While the election process began smoothly in January 1937 with the close cooperation between the Congress and the Nationalist Party in UP, Malaviya's election tour in Punjab led to considerable bitterness between the two parties and its leaders. It had its origin in the pre-election negotiations between them. Malaviya felt bound to work with the Congress in UP alone and considered himself free to act independently in other provinces. Acting upon such an interpretation, Malaviya decided to support Shanno Devi and Keshoram's candidature for the Punjab Assembly and oppose the Congress candidates. Jawaharlal Nehru, the Congress president, was 'much distressed' at the development and conveyed his discomfiture to Malaviya:

> I am faced with the clear position that Sannodevi and Keshoram are opposing Congress nominees and you are openly supporting them. What am I to do about this? I am getting large number of letters of protest and enquiry as to what steps we should take in the matter. I do not know what to say in reply. Your general and particular support of many Congress candidates has been of great value to us. Even apart from this the feeling that we have you on our side has been a great consolation to us. But how am I to distinguish between you with all my regard for you and others who have acted similarly? I have no answer to that question and it seems to me that some answer must be given. Hence my distress.[17]

REPRESENTATIONS AGAINST MALAVIYA

Jawaharlal Nehru sought Malaviya's 'advice' in the matter and informed him that he was getting in touch with the members of the CWC as this was a question of considerable and general importance.[18] Only a month previously, the CWC had framed rules under which disciplinary action could be taken against those involved in anti-party activities. Referring to these rules, certain representations were made against Malaviya demanding disciplinary action against him.

RESPONSE OF CWC MEMBERS

Only four members of the CWC responded to Nehru's letter dated 26 January 1937 (referred to above). While Abul Kalam Azad favoured disciplinary action against Malaviya, the other two CWC members, Vallabhbhai Patel and Achyut Patwardhan, did not approve any such move. Patel wrote: 'The case of Pt. Malaviyaji is difficult to deal with. He puts us in a very embarrassing position. Apart from his age and past services our reverence and regard for him are so great that it is difficult to take any drastic action against him.' Patel therefore suggested that:

> a polite request to him [Malaviya] to desist from the embarrassing activ-ities would serve the purpose particularly at this stage when the Lahore elections, in which his attitude was inexcusable, are over. It is true oth-ers naturally blame us for not taking action against him. A mild warning in his case will be a sufficient reply to such people.[19]

Another member of the CWC, recounting the support extended by Malaviya during the elections, wrote: 'Personally I should consider it advisable to leave the matter where it is ... within a week or so the unfortunate circumstances would terminate automatically.'[20] Bhulabhai Desai's letter was on similar lines:

> With reference to certain anti-Congress activities of Pt. Madan Mohan Malaviya it is a matter for regret that he should allow himself to be swayed by personal attachments of early days to certain non-Congress individuals. My own personal feeling is that we should address a letter to him calling his attention to this inconsistent and self-contradictory at-titude and expressing the hope that in future he will stand by the Con-gress unreservedly because that is his most recent attitude as expressed in his conduct and latest acts and doings.[21]

NEHRU'S VIEW ON REPRESENTATIONS

On receipt of these replies from the CWC members, Nehru felt considerably relieved. His own opinion on this delicate issue was not much different from the views expressed by Vallabhbhai Patel and Patwardhan. Nehru stated:

> Malaviyaji has been acting in a self-contradictory manner. On the one hand he has supported the two anti-Congress candidates in the Punjab and on the other hand Malaviyaji has given his unstinted support to Congress candidates in the U.P. as also in the Punjab and elsewhere. In

spite of bad health he has toured widely in support of our candidates. In some instances he has suppressed his own inclinations such as in the case of C.Y. Chintamani whom he would have liked to support but becasue of the Congress opposition he remained silent. In the U.P. he has cooperated fully with the Congress.[22]

Even though Nehru appreciated Malaviya's 'unstinted support' during the elections in UP, he did not share the latter's view that he was free to carry on election propaganda elsewhere according to his choice. Much of the misunderstanding emerged from Malaviya's strategy during the elections, particularly in Punjab. His intervention in Punjab was disliked by Nehru as well as by various other leaders of the Congress. It had its origin in the ambiguous relationship between the Congress and the Nationalist Party and the earlier refusal of the CWC to work out a formal electoral alliance with Malaviya. However, it added to Malaviya's discomfiture and gave an opportunity to certain Congress leaders of UP and others to make representations to Nehru to initiate disciplinary action against him. The tragedy of the situation was that Nehru was quick to act and did nothing to discourage those Congressmen who were opposed to Malaviya's line of action. At same time he was in a quandary:

> What possible action can we take against him? He is not a member of any of our executive committees except the A.I.C.C. of which he is an ex-officio member as ex-president. To debar him from ordinary membership seems to me an extreme step which seems to me undesirable.[23]

By this time Nehru had come to understand that the CWC resolution of December 1936 stipulating disciplinary action against erring Congressmen was being either misrepresented or misused by the presidents of certain provincial Congress Committees. He, therefore, laid down that all such actions should come into effect only after due consideration of the CWC. Wisdom finally prevailed and the CWC ultimately decided not to proceed further against Malaviya.[24]

MALAVIYA DESCRIBED AS AN 'OUTSIDER'

This unnecessary and unfortunate controversy revealed that by this time Malaviya had lost much of his earlier prestige in the Congress. As president of the Congress, Jawaharlal Nehru made no bones about it. He recorded that 'in effect he has been more an associate of the Congress than an active member'.[25] Obviously, Nehru was treating Malaviya more

as the founder president of the Nationalist Party than a Congress stal-
wart. Nehru was far more forthright a fornight later stating that:

> one can hardly consider Malaviyaji as a part of Congress organization.
> He happens be an Ex-President but otherwise he comes to us from
> outside offering the cooperation of another camp.[26]

It is really strange that Nehru voiced such views about Malaviya
in the post-election period and gave prompt attention to representations made against him. There is no evidence that he expressed any
displeasure against such a trend and allowed groupism to grow within
the Congress. Even after appreciating Malaviya's role during elections
in UP, he was not prepared to permit him to act independently in
Punjab. In any case, his opinion that Malaviya was an 'associate' of the
Congress and not 'a part of it' came as a rude shock to many. There was
an impression that Malaviya's 'magnanimity was not fully reciprocated
by the Congress'.[27] His cooperation with the Congress during the
election campaign was easily forgotten and 'he was treated with gross
discourtesy'.[28] This was particularly tragic since Malaviya had not only
carried out election propaganda in favour of the Congress but had also
invited considerable criticism of his erstwhile Mahasabha associates.
Commenting upon Malaviya's role, Raja Ram Pal Singh wrote: 'His
right leg is in the Congress, though not much wanted there, his left leg
in the Hindu Sabha, his head in the Hindu University and his heart
everywhere and therefore nowhere.'[29] Malaviya had already severed
links with the Mahasabha in the hope of winning Congress favour. At
this juncture, the opinion of the Congress president that Malaviya was
an 'outsider' was a gross injustice to him, particularly at the fag end of
his long and illustrious career in the Congress.

A VICTIM OF ELECTORAL POLITICS

More than anyone else, Jawaharlal Nehru was well aware that there
was 'a regular conspiracy in higher Congress circles' and 'all-India
politics during the last five years has been too dirty'.[30] If this was
the state of affairs before the elections, one could easily imagine
the impact of the electoral politics in UP and elsewhere. Obviously,
Malaviya fell victim to groupings within the Congress. His only
mistake was that he failed to forsee that several new and ambitious
leaders were on the lookout to consolidate their position within the

party by any means, fair or foul. Such leaders did not hesitate to make representations against Malaviya and voiced their grievances against him during the elections and after. In fact there were signs of a simmering anti-Malaviya campaign as is evident from Sampurnanand's complaint against him. Sampurnanand made a representation against Malaviya to Nehru accusing the former of not issuing an appeal of support in his favour on the eve of election in the Banaras constituency as he had done for the other two Congress candidates. His grievance was that 'this behaviour on his part added materially to our anxieties and our expenses'. Without citing any convincing evidence in support of his accusation, Sampurnanand appealed to the Congress president to take action against Malaviya saying, 'I personally do not see why people in his position should go scot free when humbler fry are being penalised.'[31] As a known supporter of the anti-Malaviya lobby of Banaras, Sampurnanand was unnecessarily airing his grievance against Malaviya after winning the election. This was a clear case of 'a hardening on party lines within the Congress ... an atmosphere of suspicion and bitterness and conflict', as noted by Nehru himself.[32]

RETIREMENT

Old age and failing health ultimately led Malaviya to virtually retire from active politics in 1937 and resign from the post of vice-chancellor of the Banaras Hindu University two years later. For the rest of his life, he maintained a keen interest in public life. He was at Delhi while important negotiations regarding India's independence were underway in 1942 and showed keen interest in the course of events in the Banaras Hindu University during the same year. The pre-partition riots of 1946 caused him severe mental anguish and he made anxious enquires from all those who met him. Various eminent persons have, in their statements, recorded Malaviya's keen interest in public life till he breathed his last in 1946.

NOTES

1   B. Shiva Rao, *The Framing of India's Constitution: Select Documents*, vol. I, p. 80.
2   Nanda, *Mahatma Gandhi*, p. 385.
3   Nanda, *Mahatma Gandhi,* p. 96.

4   Jawaharlal Nehru to Malaviya, 20 April 1936, *SWJN*, pp. 359–60.

5   Gopal, *Jawaharlal Nehru*, vol. I, pp. 208–9.

6   Jawaharlal Nehru to Malaviya, 20 April 1936, *SWJN*, pp. 359–60.

7   Jawaharlal Nehru to Malaviya, 20 April 1936, *SWJN*, pp. 359–60.

8   Jawaharlal Nehru to Malaviya, 20 April 1936, *SWJN*, pp. 365–6.

9   Jawaharlal Nehru to Malaviya, 20 April 1936, *SWJN*, pp. 365–6.

10   Nehru's statement for the press, 22 June 1936, *SWJN*, vol. VI, pp. 365–6.

11   AICC Papers, file no. 246/1936, Congress bulletin no. 3 of 1936, 14 August 1936.

12   *Hindustan Times*, 7 September 1936.

13   *Hindustan Times*, 25 January 1937.

14   Achyut S. Patwardhan to Jawaharlal Nehru, 4 February 1937, AICC Papers, E-17/1937.

15   *Hindustan Times*, 31 October 1936.

16   *Swadesh*, 20, 24, and 25 January 1937.

17   Jawaharlal Nehru to Malaviya, 26 January 1937, AICC Papers, E-17/1937.

18   Jawaharlal Nehru to Malaviya, 26 January 1937, AICC Papers, E-17/1937.

19   Vallabhbhai Patel to Nehru, 31 January 1937, AICC Papers E-17/1937.

20   Achyut S. Patwardhan to Jawaharlal Nehru, 4 February 1937, AICC Papers E-17/1937.

21   Bhulabhai Desai to Jawaharlal Nehru, 22 February 1937, AICC Papers E-17/1937.

22   Jawaharlal Nehru to Members of CWC, 7 February 1937, AICC Papers E-17/1937.

23   Jawaharlal Nehru to Members of CWC, 7 February 1937, AICC Papers E-17/1937.

24   Jawaharlal Nehru to Members of CWC, 7 February 1937, AICC Papers E-17/1937.

25   Jawaharlal Nehru to Members of CWC, 7 February 1937, AICC Papers E-17/1937.

26   Jawaharlal Nehru to Sampurnanand, 23 February 1937, AICC Papers, E-20/1937.

27   Parmanand, *Mahamana Madan Mohan Malaviya*, vol. II, p. 962.

28   Parmanand, *Mahamana Madan Mohan Malaviya*, vol. II, p. 963.

29   *Leader*, 25 September 1936.

30   Jawaharlal Nehru to Sarat Chandra Bose, 26 July 1936, *SWJN*, vol. VII, pp. 368–89.

31   Sampurnanand to Nehru, 21 February 1937, AICC Papers, E-20/1937.

32   Jawaharlal Nehru, *An Autobiography*, p. 600.

Conclusion

Taking Madan Mohan Malaviya as its focus, this work has been an investigation into the nature of India's struggle for freedom. Tracing his role and actions in public life, it has addressed questions such as whether Malaviya's career generated certain changes in Indian nationalist politics and, if so, in what direction and how. It has analysed the various stages of Malaviya's leadership and his ability to wield and retain authority. Overall, this book has sought to prove that, rather than being a restraining influence on the nationalist struggle, Malaviya laid a solid foundation for the uplift of the nation through his faith in constitutional politics, efforts to improve education, and activities in the socio-cultural realm.

The study of such an all-India figure as Malaviya demanded a two-pronged analysis—of the potential leader, his personal drives, career aspirations and the qualifications for a particular style of political activity, and the needs of various sections of society that he could satisfy. This work on Malaviya has, therefore, investigated a particular example of continental leadership. It has shown how far he could remain effective and what challenges he faced in the changing political environment.

The nature of Malaviya's leadership could conveniently be studied in three different periods: (a) from 1886 to 1919, (b) from 1919 to 1928, and (c) from 1929 to 1937. While in the first of these phases his voice prevailed in the Congress, in the second, Gandhi posed new challenges before him, and, in the third, there were clear signs that he was gradually losing hold over the party. A contemporary historian of the Congress points out that

the patriarch of the Congress ... who made his maiden speech in
Calcutta Congress in 1886 continues with unbroken and unabating
passion to serve the National Institution, now as a humble worker and
now as a leader, now as a whole hogger and now as a great protector,
now as an opponent of Non-Cooperation and Civil Disobedience and
now as a true Satyagrahi and civil resister in British Jails.

He further adds:

Panditji is one man who has had the courage to be alone in what he
considered to be right. At one time he was on the crest of a wave of
popularity, at another he was listened to with indifference on the Congress platform. He never yielded to current forces either by sheer inertia
or by fear of popular reprobation.[1]

Malaviya's ascent to a position of prominence was achieved in the
context of the quickening pulse of politics in the country. The Indian
National Congress in the late nineteenth century was the organized
political expression of the educated and professional classes. At the provincial level, its vigour depended entirely on the local leaders and the
extent to which they were organized for political action. In the United
Provinces, Congressmen coordinated their efforts through regional
and local committees that promoted the annual national Congresses
and local campaigns on public issues. The capital of UP was Allahabad
and much of the leadership of the Congress came from the city. The
local political milieu of Allahabad played an important part in shaping
Malaviya's awareness.[2]

The entry of a young Malaviya into nationalist politics was as dramatic as it was distinctive. The reports of the early Congress sessions
written by A.O. Hume bear eloquent testimony to Malaviya's role
in these sessions. These reports indicate that the young Malaviya had
learnt well the lesson of presenting his arguments in a persuasive and
convincing manner, imbibed the Congress ideology and programme,
and conveniently emerged as a prominent leader of northern India.

The assumption that British rule in India rested upon liberal principles
and that the statesmen who controlled the destiny of the British empire
would respond positively to the growth of national consciousness in the
country went a long way towards shaping the attitudes of leaders like
Malaviya. The moderate strategy to which he subscribed rested upon
far too flattering an appreciation of the strength of liberal principles
or the intentions of liberal statesmen within the British government.

Malaviya voiced these liberal sentiments almost continuously in every Congress session attended by him. Besides, he made a powerful plea for improving the lot of the peasantry, referred to the deteriorating economic condition of the people, and demanded remedial measures for overcoming recurring famines in the country. By 1897, there were signs of frustration and impatience in his speeches with regard to the economic policies that were followed by the government.

By the first decade of the twentieth century, Malaviya prominently belonged to the very select group of the Congress Party that was referred to as 'the inner circle', 'the caucus', or the 'oligarchy', which actually governed and guided the organization.[3] Malaviya's authority, as well as of those belonging to this top-level body of the Congress, was personal and informal arising mainly out of his quality of leadership, organizational ability, social status, and dedication to the party.

Malaviya's sympathies and his stand at the Surat Congress can best be explained with the help of the articles that he wrote in his newly started Hindi weekly journal, *Abhudaya*. He held the Extremists responsible for converting the Congress from a 'deliberative body' into a 'Kurukshetra', deplored the abuses hurled at the Congress old guards by the extremist leaders, and termed their speeches as the 'height of impertinence'. He did not hesitate in placing the entire blame for the Surat split on the Extremists, especially Tilak.[4] Malaviya believed that the constitutional method was the only hope for the Congress. He was in full agreement with the top Moderate leaders' strategy of keeping the Extremists out of the Congress, redefining the Congress creed, and reassuring the British rulers that the party was a loyalist organization.[5] In April 1908, Malaviya participated in the Allahabad Convention that adopted a rigid and elaborate constitution and incorporated the Congress 'creed' defined earlier at Surat.[6]

By the time Malaviya was asked to preside over the Congress session at Lahore in 1909, the confusion and chaos in the Moderate camp had grown enormously. In a letter to Wedderburn on 24 September, Gokhale wrote that the national movement 'appears to be going to pieces throwing us back on Provincialism ... the situation is further complicated by the fierce antagonism between Hindus and Mohammedans ... the relations between the two communities are the worst'.[7] In view of the growing opposition to Ferozeshah Mehta's nomination to the presidency, he thought it best to step down only a fortnight before the Congress was due to meet at Lahore. To avert any further crisis, Congressmen in both Punjab and Bengal immediately agreed to request Malaviya to take over the august office. The situation in which the choice fell to Malaviya speaks of the eminent position he had come to occupy by this time.

Malaviya was the first Congress leader from UP to preside over the Congress session in 1909. Presiding over the session at Lahore, he voiced his deep commitment to constitutional politics and liberal principles and expressed his faith in the British connection, which he hoped and desired would continue for the 'advantage of Indians'. A large part of his extempore address was devoted to the examination of the Reform Act of 1909. Malaviya fiercely opposed the separate electorates and weighted representation accorded to the Muslims.[8]

Malaviya proved to be an effective and seasoned parliamentarian and successfully fought the British on their own ground. Through his well-reasoned arguments on the floor of the Provincial Legislature from 1903 to 1910 and the Imperial Legislative Council from 1910 to 1930, he aroused the national conscience against imperial oppression. In March 1910, one of the most reactionary measures in the recent history of India, the Press Bill, was introduced. It was an attempt to muzzle the press as it vested wide powers to the executive to control the writings in the press. It was a strange spectacle in the Central Legislature when Gokhale supported the official measure and Malaviya went all out to condemn the bill and attack its provisions. He showed exemplary courage in responding to the call of the freedom of the press. Malaviya opposed the Seditious Meetings Bill in the same year, arguing that such a 'draconian' law would give wide powers to the executive that would be free to abuse it.[9]

With the publication of the Montford Report in July 1918, markedly different opinions were voiced by the Congress leaders. To sort out their differences, a Special Congress session was held in Bombay. Malaviya played the role of a peacemaker in this session, appealing to the Moderates to work with the Congress unitedly. He prevailed upon everyone to work out a common strategy towards the proposals of constitutional reforms. In recognition of this unifying role, Malaviya was chosen to preside over the Delhi session in 1918. That he was taking over the presidency of the Congress for the second time within a decade was a clear recognition of his dominant position in the party.

In his presidential address, Malaviya demanded that the principle of self-determination be applied to India and desired that the proposed constitutional measure be so framed as to contain specific provisions for the introduction of full responsible government in the provinces.

When Gandhi gave a call for the non-cooperation movement, Malaviya was not convinced that such a form of struggle against the Raj was either necessary or practicable. The AICC meeting of May 1920, held at Banaras, decided that the final decision in this regard would be taken at the Special Congress session to be held later. Malaviya fully endorsed the decision and appealed to Gandhi both privately and publicly not to resort to non-cooperation till the Congress had pronounced upon it. In spite of the appeal of the 'Dharmatma', as Gandhi described Malaviya, the former launched the non-cooperation struggle on 1 August 1920[10] on his own, and did not wait for the Special Congress session. Thus the two leaders started drifting apart from the very beginning of the non-cooperation campaign.

The sequence of events from the Special Congress session of September 1920 and the wide variety of evidence available in this regard convincingly show that if Gandhi could ultimately have his way it was because he had come for the session fully prepared while the old guards of the Congress, like Malaviya, were uncertain and sceptical about their stand. Expressing this view, a contemporary observer noted that 'Malaviya could not overcome his dubiousity about Gandhi and his Satyagrah'.[11] When the resolution on the non-cooperation movement was adopted against Malaviya's wishes, he did not mince words in expressing his opposition to the new strategy and declared his resolve to pursue ' course of action different from that adopted by the Congress'.[12]

Malaviya was the only prominent leader who opposed the non-cooperation resolution and the new creed of the Congress at the Nagpur session held in December 1920, and did not succumb to Gandhi's pressure in the way C.R. Das, Lajpat Rai, and several other leaders did.

From this time onwards, Malaviya kept himself away from the non-cooperation movement, did not participate in it, and yet maintained close interest in the struggle as well as in the role played by various leaders. Instead of challenging Gandhi, he often had close links with him all through the campaign and, on several occasions, advised him on his relationship with the government.

The Moderate strategy and the old style of politics to which Malaviya subscribed at this juncture, however, came to the fore during the Prince of Wales' visit to India in November–December 1921. The country witnessed the strange spectacle of Malaviya welcoming the prince at the Banaras Hindu University and honouring him with a DLitt degree while not only the city of Banaras but almost every city in the country the prince visited greeted him with total boycott. Malaviya's action cannot be easily defended. It showed that he was completely out of touch with the intensity and depth of the feelings of the people against the British Raj and was attempting to downplay the success of the non-cooperation movement. It brought no credit to Malaviya.

Malaviya earnestly desired to build a bridge of understanding with the government that would ensure the elevation of India to the standing of a self-governing nation and heavily relied on the viceroy in achieving this political goal. In a confidential letter to the secretary of state, Montagu, the viceroy reported in July 1921 that Malaviya had stressed that 'a firm enunciation of British policy on Swaraj was the need of the hour'.[13] Montagu's response that 'it is really astonishing to me that intelligent persons like Malaviya can still harp on the ambition to have a definite time limit announced for Swaraj'[14] demonstrates the wide gap between the views of the British statesmen and the expectation of Malaviya on the crucial issue of swaraj.

Late in December 1929, the focus of the political scene shifted to Lahore where Malaviya's leadership was tried in a different kind of Congress session. He opposed the main resolution defining complete independence as the goal of the Congress. He was equally against the programme of the boycott of the Central Legislative Assembly. Gandhi mildly set aside Malaviya's objections with the remark that 'we have got our duty to perform'. On the day after the Lahore session, Malaviya resigned from the membership of the CWC, informing the president that he did 'not agree with the resolution passed by the Congress yesterday relating to its policy and programme'.[15] There were a few other resignations including that of M.A. Ansari, Aney, Kelkar, Bhagwan Das, and Khaliquzzaman. Malaviya's resignation was prompted by his disappointment and despair over the Congress declaration of severance of ties with the British government, which he thought was an unwise step. His considered view was that such a step was impractical and

unnecessary. The ultimate result of his intervention was that he began
to lose much of his prominent position in the Congress. Malaviya did
not figure in the list of 'dictators' who were to assume supreme powers
of the Congress during the crucial months of 1930.

Gandhi's decision to initiate the civil disobedience movement
through the Dandi March and the popular response it evoked caught
Malaviya's imagination to such an extent that he plunged into the
fray without any further loss of time. He now realized that Gandhi's
appraisal of the political situation was much more realistic than
the optimistic view that he had formerly taken of British motives.
Malaviya was on Gandhi's side throughout the period of struggle and
for peaceful negotiations during the civil disobedience movement. No
assessment of Malaviya's involvement in the nationalist struggle will be
complete without evaluating his active role from 1930 to 1934.

When Gandhi left for London to attend the Second Round Table
Conference at the close of August 1930, there was optimism in official
circles. The viceroy expressed 'intense relief' that Gandhi would be
'amenable and anxious for help ... with a keen desire to work out
a satisfactory constitution'.[16] At this juncture, Gandhi felt 'alone, yet
not alone' as Malaviya and Sarojini Naidu were also accompanying
him to attend the conference 'because of their independent status',
'with the consent of the Congress', and not 'over the head of the
Congress'. Recognizing Malaviya's unique position in Indian politics,
the Government of India had invited him to take part in the London
conference. However, such a nomination was made with full concur-
rence of Gandhi.[17] Even though Malaviya was assigned an independent
status at the conference, his constant effort was to strengthen Gandhi's
hands. A close associate of Malaviya wrote from London that he 'will
not have the courage to refuse compliance of Mahatma's request'.[18]

Malaviya decided to intensify the nationalist struggle by engineering an emergency session of the Congress in Delhi in April 1932. It was
the brainchild of Sarojini Naidu who, as acting president, approached
Malaviya to preside over the session. The local government prohibited the session, turned away many political leaders who planned to
attend the session, and arrested Malaviya en route to Delhi. In spite
of all these odds, the emergency session was held for a short spell and
turned out to be a symbolic gesture of protest.[19] In a public statement,
Malaviya gave an account of the repressive measures up to the time

of the session and arranged for its distribution all over the country as well as in England. By this time, the official view that Malaviya was 'in effect the main directing force of the Congress'[20] gained ground. Recognizing Malaviya's role during the renewed civil disobedience campaign, he was called upon yet again to preside over another emergency session of the Congress held in Calcutta on 1 April 1933. The enthusiasm and the spirit of resistance manifested on the occasion was by no means less than that displayed at Delhi during the previous year. More than two thousand delegates were elected from different parts of the country of whom about a thousand were arrested before their start or during the journey. Malaviya and Jawaharlal Nehru's widowed mother were detained before they reached Calcutta and, yet, the session was held in spite of all the efforts made by the provincial government to prevent it. A few days later, Malaviya issued a long statement giving out the details of brutal police assaults on the delegates attending the session. In his presidential address, released to the press, Malaviya implored 'all Hindus, Musalmans, Sikhs and Christians to sink communal differences and establish political unity' and invited them 'to prepare a constitution which shall give India real independence'.[21] Subhash Chandra Bose later commended 'the response made by the country to the Congress appeal in 1932 and 1933'.[22] Historians have, however, paid scant attention to these two Congress sessions and to Malaviya's attempts to activate the second phase of the civil disobedience movement.

Malaviya's misjudgement of the changing political situation during the final stages of the electoral politics of 1936–37 ultimately placed him in a peculiarly awkward situation when representations were made to the Congress president for taking disciplinary action against him for opposing official Congress candidates and supporting their rivals in Punjab. The consideration given to these representations by the Congress president and the CWC came as a surprise to many and there was an impression that Malaviya was treated with 'gross discourtesy'. This gave the impression that the Congress was no longer a 'platform' from which different voices and opinions could be expressed. Malaviya was, therefore, forced to realize that he was out of tune with the newly emerging trends in the Congress. He decided to step down from active politics in 1937 and also resigned from the post of vice-chancellor of the Banaras Hindu University two years later.

The gamut of Malaviya's public life, covering well over fifty years, was wide enough to include political, social, educational, and religious activities, and he had a personality that enabled him to play a prominent role in all of them with equal felicity.

That the young Madan Mohan Malaviya grew up in Allahabad was a fact of considerable importance since the city provided the setting in which he could realize his full potential, first in the socio-cultural activities of the city and the province and next as a distinguished leader in the cause of India's freedom. The crystallization of communal identities in UP, establishment of institutions of local self-government, creation of centres of higher education, and the development of a new consciousness of cultural and religious heritage contributed to radical change in the political climate of the city of Allahabad and the province as a whole in the closing decades of the nineteenth century.[23] It is in the examination of the distinctive social, cultural, and political milieu of Allahabad and the region that we find the answer to the emergence of Malaviya's distinctive style of politics in the early decades of the Congress.

A decisive step demanding the substitution of Hindi in the Devanagri script for Urdu in Persian script, then in use in law courts and revenue records, was taken by Malaviya in 1897 when he published a detailed and exhaustive memorandum entitled 'Court Characters and Primary Education in N.W. Provinces and Oudh'.[24] This well-written, persuasive, and thoroughly documented memorial was presented to the lieutenant governor of the province by a deputation consisting of the rajas of Manda, Ayodhya, and Awagarh, along with Sundar Lal and Malaviya. The deputationists succeeded in establishing the case for Hindi and the provincial government announced its decision in April 1900, according to which a large part of their demands was accepted. The government permitted the introduction of Hindi in law courts in addition to the use of Urdu. The concession, limited in scope, was enthusiastically welcomed by the supporters of Hindi and they gave full credit to Malaviya for his skill and persuasion. From this time onwards, Malaviya increasingly put forward the view that no nation could come into being without the development of Indian national language (*rashtrabhasha*) and directed his energies to install Hindi as the national language of the country.[25]

Malaviya's tireless efforts to establish and promote the Banaras Hindu University were oriented towards strengthening and improving

the Hindu community materially, physically, and intellectually so that
it could reverse a perceived sense of decline and ultimately assume its
rightful place in the hierarchy of races and nations. This was clearly
reflected in 1905, in the prospectus Malaviya put forward for the
establishment of the Hindu university. The prospectus began with an
analysis of the then-prevailing Indian situation, contained Malaviya's
refutation of the thesis that Hinduism hampered modern development,
and his assertion that traditional values were necessary for modern
civilization.[26] Malaviya published his 'Revised Scheme' for the proposed university in July 1911, reflecting the broad terms on which
Mrs Besant and the maharaja of Darbhanga were prepared to work
unitedly with him. Malaviya's revised scheme meant considerable concessions to the wishes of the Government of India. Since the promoters
of the Banaras Hindu University were willing to accept all the directions of the government and since Malaviya gave them full support
in this direction, there were no further difficulties in negotiating the
terms and conditions under which the university was to be established.
Within a few years, Malaviya was able to win over the confidence of
the viceroy as well as his colleagues.

Winning over the favour of the government was important to
Malaviya for another reason. The ruling chiefs were not prepared
to help Malaviya in raising funds for the university without the
Government of India's consent. When Malaviya approached the maharajas of Bikaner, Darbhanga, and Banaras, they informed him in no
uncertain terms that they would come forward to help in his venture
only after the government of India's approval. The official correspondence clearly indicates that the viceroy and his advisers held the key
with them, encouraged the ruling chiefs to play leading role in establishing the university, and attempted to drive Malaviya into a corner.
However, Malaviya's persuasive nature and impressive personality and
reasonableness ultimately brought round both the representatives of
the Government of India and the ruling chiefs. More than anything
else, his tireless fundraising campaigns all over the country from 1911
to 1913 and the overwhelming response extended to him convinced
everyone that the Hindu masses were with him in the establishment of
the university at Banaras.

The passage of the Hindu University Bill in October 1915 was a
great victory for Malaviya. As a member of the Supreme Legislative

Council, he promised that the proposed university 'will promote broad liberation of mind and a religious spirit which will promote brotherly feeling between man and man'. The foundation-stone-laying ceremony was inaugurated at Banaras in February 1916 by the viceroy who was full of praise 'for the arrangements that were perfect', 'the wonderful success for the whole function', and 'the enthusiastic gathering assembled on the occasion'.[27] The tenor of the viceroy's letter regarding the university and its founder was in complete contrast to the misgivings voiced by him earlier in 1911.

Malaviya has not always been identified with positive and courageous aspects of Indian nationalism but rather with the negative and destructive aspects of religious fanaticism and bigotry. Some scholars have considered Malaviya's efforts to promote Hindu interests as being at variance with the higher purpose of national regeneration. His religious revivalism is often blamed for fostering communal identity in opposition to national identity. It has been pointed out that 'Malaviya's revivalism ... led almost inevitably to communal conflict'.[28] He is held responsible for raising 'the cry of Hinduism in Danger'.[29] Such accusations, to say the least, are far-fetched, for Malaviya never thought of using or supporting any such slogans. In a similar vein, it has been said that 'Hindu communal propaganda was an important part of Malaviya's offensive'[30] and, in this regard, special mention has been made about the controversy surrounding the playing of music in front of mosques at Allahabad. Such writers have depended entirely upon the biased and prejudiced version of the local officials and have not cared to examine various other important archival sources. In its official account of these occurances, the UP government pointed out: 'The Pandit though undoubtedly a strong protagonist of Hinduism has ordinarily been careful, at the time, to preach the cause of Hindu–Muslim unity. He has not personally been prominent in Hindu–Muslim disputes in Allahabad.'[31] Similarly, the assessment of the governor of UP was that 'Malaviya has, in fact, avoided than courted the role of an inflammatory apostle of Hinduism in the United Provinces'.[32] These extracts are self-explanatory and convincingly show that Malaviya had no role to play in the communal build-up at Allahabad.

During this period, Gandhi came out openly in favour of Malaviya, expressing his firm view that wining over his suppport towards the cause of Hindu–Muslim unity was the need of the hour. In a public statement, Gandhi stated that he 'could never believe that Malaviyaji was the enemy of Muhammadans and a block in the way of Hindu–Muslim unity'[33] and warned the Khilafat leaders that 'the reviling of Pandit Malaviya would not bring them near the solution'.[34] Sumit Sarkar raises the question as to why 'Gandhi himself never broke with him'.[35] Gandhi maintained the best of relations with Malaviya during these years as well as in later decades, largely because of his inherent faith in Malaviya's intentions.

In this context, it is necessary to analyse Malaviya's association with the Hindu Mahasabha up to 1930 and his disenchantment with it thereafter. In the earlier period, Malaviya was fairly successful in retaining a foothold in both the parties. After the Belgaun Mahasabha session of 1924, he expressed his satisfaction that 'all the prominent Hindu leaders have come round to the opinion that with the Congress movement there must be the Hindu Mahasabha movement'[36] and emphasized that 'the Hindu Mahasabha was never brought into existence as a communal organization to fight against any community'.[37] Close links with the Congress and a broad religious outlook were the two major planks which guided Malaviya through all along his relations with the Mahasabha.

The early 1930s opened up new challenges. Malaviya raised a storm of protest against the neutral stand taken by the Congress on the Communal Award, formed a new party called the Nationalist Party in late 1934, and fought the assembly elections against the Congress with the support of the Mahasabha. This proved to be a turning point as Malaviya did not leave the newly emerging Mahasabha leadership in any doubt that his loyalty to the Congress was still intact and that he would not allow it to exploit the situation. Having failed to persuade Malaviya to follow the Mahasabha line, it turned completely against him during 1934–36. They had fundamental differences with regard to reaching out to Muslims.[38] While Malaviya supported efforts to arrive at some understanding with the Muslims during the Unity Conference at Allahabad in September 1932 and was prepared to evolve a compromise formula acceptable to them, the Mahasabha did not share his vision. To clear the air Malaviya reiterated from the Hindu Mahasabha platform in December 1935 that 'the flame of nationalism has to be lighted in the hearts of all Indians and unity between communities, castes and creeds must be its effects'. Malaviya's speeches were in complete contrast to the views of the newly emerging Mahasabha leadership and they soon parted company with him.

In such a political situation, the Congress met Malaviya half-way to effect a compromise. The ball was set rolling by Jawaharlal Nehru. Under his leadership, the Congress denounced the Communal Award and declared that it was unacceptable. This created a most favourable atmosphere for an electoral understanding between the Nationalist Party and the Congress. Though such an understanding was confined to UP, it paved the way for a working alliance between Malaviya and the Congress leadership for the 1937 provincial elections in other provinces as well.

It is worth mentioning here that Jawaharlal Nehru was fully aware of the 'bourgeois-modern-inspiration' that animated Malaviya. As a contemporary observer of the political changes, it would be appropriate to quote his assessment of Malaviya in his autobiography published in the mid-1930s. He wrote:

The sole changes he desires, and desires passionately, is the complete elimination of foreign control in India. The political training and reading of his youth still influence his mind greatly and he looks upon this dynamic, revolutionary post-War world of the twentieth century with the spectacles of the semi-static nineteenth of T.H. Green and John Stuart Mill and Gladstone and Morley with a three or four thousand year background of Hindu culture and sociology.'[39]

Nehru provides us a glimpse into the secular inspirations of Hindu nationalism. According to him, Malaviya's Hindu baggage was of Hindu culture and sociology.[40] He was one among the Hindu nationalists who was inspired by the secular modern ideas of leading European thinkers.

NOTES

1 Sitaramayya, *History of the Congress*, pp. 169–71.
2 Bayly, *Local Roots of Indian Politics*, p. 152.
3 Ananda Charlu, 'The Indian National Congress: A Suggestive Report', *Hindustan Review*, July–August 1903, p. 20.
4 *Abhudaya*, 10 January, 1908.
5 H.W. Nevinson, *New Spirit in India* (Delhi, 1975 [Indian reprint]), pp. 233–7.
6 *Leader*, 24 April 1908.
7 G.K. Gokhale to Wedderburn, 24 September 1909, Gokhale Papers.

8   Report of the Twenty-fifth Indian National Congress, 1909, pp. 42–9.

9   Jha, *Role of the Central Legislature*, pp. 22–3.

10   Gandhi to Malaviya, 15 July 1920, *CWMG*, no. 18, p. 121.

11   M.R. Jayakar, *Story of My Life*, vol. I, p. 575.

12   *CWMG*, no. 18, p. 121.

13   Reading to Montagu, 9 June 1921, Reading Papers, no. 10.

14   Montagu to Reading, 6 July 1921, Reading Papers, no. 10.

15   Malaviya to Jawaharlal Nehru, 1 January 1930, AICC Papers, G-115/1929.

16   Willingdon to Hoare, 28 August 1931, Templewood Collection.

17   Telegram from Gandhi to Irwin, 20 July 1931, Halifax Papers, no. 146.

18   B.S. Moonje to Pandurang, 28 November 1931, B.S. Moonje Papers.

19   AICC Papers, no. 15/1932.

20   Harry Haig's note, 22 September 1932, Home Poll, Proceedings, 5/18/1932.

21   Malaviya statement, 'What Happened at Calcutta', 9 April 1933, Home Poll, Proceedings, 3 December 1933.

22   Bose, *Indian Struggle*, p. 36.

23   Tiwari, *Mahamana Madan Mohan Malaviya*.

24   M.M. Malaviya, *Court Characters and Primary Education in the N.W. Provinces* (Allahabad, 1897), pp. 1–96.

25   *Bharat Jiwan*, 27 January 1901.

26   Dar and Somskandan, *History of the Benaras Hindu University*, pp. 49–74.

27   Hardinge to Butler, 10 February 1916, Butler Collection.

28   Paul Brass, *Factional Politics in an Indian State: The Congress Party in Uttar Pradesh* (London, 1961), p. 20.

29   Pandey, *Ascendancy of the Congress*, p. 203.

30   Pandey, *Ascendancy of the Congress*, p. 118; David Page, *Prelude to Partition: The Indian Muslims and the Imperial System of Control* (Oxford, 1982), pp. 56–9.

31   W. Marris to Irwin, 12 August 1926, Halifax Papers, no. 216.

32   S. O'Donnell to Irwin, 10 August 1926, Halifax Papers, no. 44.

33   Speech at Khilafat Conference, Amritsar, 6 December 1924, *CWMG*, vol. 25, p. 402.

34   Speech at Khilafat Conference, Amritsar, 6 December 1924, *CWMG*, vol. 25, p. 402.

35   Sumit Sarkar, *Modern India*, p. 236.

36   Malaviya to C. Vijayaraghavachariar, 30 December 1924, C.V.R. Papers.

37   *Pratap*, 24 February 1926.

38   Salil Misra, *Narrative of Communal Politics*, p. 294.

39   Jawaharlal Nehru, *An Autobiography*, p. 157.

40   Aditya Nigam, *The Crisis of Secular Nationalism* (New Delhi: Oxford University Press, 2006), pp. 70–3.

Select Bibliography

GOVERNMENT RECORDS (UNPUBLISHED)

National Archives of India (NAI), New Delhi

Director of Criminal Intelligence, Weekly Reports, 1905–20.

Fortnightly Reports, United Provinces, 1920–37.

Proceedings and Files of the Education Department, Government of India, 1905–20.

Proceedings and Files of the Government of India, Home Department, Political Branch, 1894–1937.

Selections from Vernacular Newspapers of the North-western Provinces and Oudh, 1885–1901, Allahabad.

Uttar Pradesh State Archives, Lucknow

Proceedings and Files of the Government of UP General Administration: Education, Police, and Judicial (Criminal) Departments, 1905–36.

Criminal Investigation Department, Lucknow

Police Abstracts of Intelligence, UP, Weekly Reports on Political Affairs, 1920–37.

ORGANIZATIONAL RECORDS

All India Congress Committee Papers, NMML, New Delhi, 1920–37.

All India Hindu Mahasabha Papers, NMML, New Delhi, 1936–37.

United Provinces Congress Committee Papers, NMML, New Delhi, 1926–37.

PRIVATE PAPERS

B.S. Moonje Papers (NMML, New Delhi)
Chelmsford Papers (NAI, New Delhi)
Halifax Papers (NAI)
Hardinge Papers (NAI, New Delhi)
Harcourt Butler Papers (NAI)
H.G. Haig Papers (NMML, New Delhi)
James Meston Papers (NAI, New Delhi)
Jawaharlal Nehru Papers (NMML)
Khaperde Papers
Motilal Nehru Papers (NMML)
M.R. Jayakar Papers (NAI, New Delhi)
M.S. Aney Papers (NMML, New Delhi)
Proscribed Publications (NAI)
Rajendra Prasad Papers (NMML)
Reading Papers (NAI)
Sita Ram Papers (NAI)
Sri Prakash Papers (NMML)
Syed Mahmud Papers (NMML)
T.B. Sapru Papers (NAI, New Delhi)
Templewood Papers (NAI)
V.S.S. Sastri Papers (NMML)

NEWSPAPERS AND JOURNALS

Aaj (Varanasi), 1920–37
Abhudaya (Allahabad), 1907–37.
Bharat Jiwan (Varanasi) 1885–1925.
Hindi Pradeep (Allahabad), 1878–1910.
Hindustan Times (New Delhi), 1928–36.
Leader (Allahabad), 1909–34.
Matwala (Mirzapur) 1916–26.
Pratap (Kanpur), 1909–30.
Samaya (Jaunpur), 1920–47.
Shakti (Almorah), 1918–32.
Swadesh (Gorakhpur), 1920–30.
Vartaman (Kanpur), 1920–34.

PUBLISHED RECORDS

Collected Works of Mahatma Gandhi. Publications Division, Government of
India, New Delhi, vols 1–36.

Dhanki, J.S., ed. *Perspectives of National Movement: Select Correspondence of Lala Lajpat Rai.* New Delhi, 1996.

Kumar, Ravinder and D.N. Panigrahi, eds. *Selected Works of Motilal Nehru,* vols I and II. New Delhi, 1982 and 1984.

Kumar, Ravinder and H.D. Sharma, eds. *Selected Works of Motilal Nehru,* vols III to VI. New Delhi, 1986–93.

Mitra, H.N. *Indian Annual Register 1920–1937.* Calcutta, 1920–37.

Nanda, B.R., ed. *Selected Works of Govinda Ballabh Pant,* vols I to IX. New Delhi.

———. *The Collected Works of Lala Lajpat Rai,* vols I to X. New Delhi, 2008–11.

Pandey, B.N., ed. *Indian National Movement 1885–1945: Select Documents.* New Delhi, 1979.

Reeves, P.D., B.D. Graham, and J.M. Goodman. *A Handbook to Elections in Uttar Pradesh.* New Delhi, 1975.

S. Gopal, ed. *Selected Works of Jawaharlal Nehru,* vols I to X. New Delhi.

Zaidi, A.M. and S.G. Zaidi, eds. *The Encyclopaedia of the Indian National Congress,* vols 1–28. New Delhi.

BIOGRAPHIES ON MADAN MOHAN MALAVIYA

Akkad, B.J. *Malaviyaji.* Bombay, 1948.

Bakshi, S.R. *Madan Mohan Malaviya.* New Delhi, 1991.

Chaturvedi, S. *Malaviya and Hindi Journalism.* Allahabad, 1988.

Gupta, S.L. *Pandit Madan Mohan Malaviya: A Socio-Political Study.* Allahabad, 1978.

Gajrani S. and S. Ram, eds. *Pandit Madan Mohan Malaviya.* Delhi, 2009.

Parmanand. *Mahamana Madan Mohan Malaviya,* vols I and II. Varanasi, 1985.

Sundram, V.A. *Mahamana Malaviya.* Varanasi, 1948.

Dhruva, A.B., ed. *Malaviya Commemoration Volume.* Banaras Hindu University, 1932.

Singh, N.L. *Mahamana Malaviya Birth Centenary Commemoration Volume.* Varanasi, 1965.

MALAVIYA'S TRACTS AND PAMPHLETS

A Criticism of Chelmsford Report. Allahabad, 1918.

Badrinath Temple. Allahabad, 1924.

Court Characters and Primary Education in N.W. Provinces and Oudh. Allahabad: Indian Press, 1897. *Cable on Indian Situation.* New Delhi, 1932.

Draft Report of the Committee of Unity Conference. Allahabad, 1932.

Delhi Congress, An Appeal for Unity. Allahabad: Leader Press, 1918.

Searching Questions upon Mortial Law in the Punjab. Lahore: Pelican Press, 1919.
Statutory Commission. New Delhi, 1928.

SECONDARY SOURCES

A Bridge of Words: Selected Correspondence of G.D. Birla. Calcutta, 1994.
Amin, Shahid. *Event, Metaphor and Memory: Chauri Chaura 1922–1992.* Delhi, 1995.
Bayly, C.A. *Rulers, Townsmen and Bazars.* Delhi, 1992.
————. *The Local Roots of Indian Politics, Allahabad, 1880–1920.* Oxford, 1975.
Birla, G.D. *Bapu: A Unique Association,* vols I to IV. Bombay, 1977.
Bose, Subhash Chandra. *The Indian Struggle 1920–1942.* Calcutta, 1964.
Brass, Paul R. *Language, Rreligion and Politics in North India.* London, 1974.
Brown, Judith M. *Gandhi and Civil Disobedience.* Cambridge, 1977.
————. *Gandhi's Rise to Power: Indian Politics 1915–1922.* Cambridge, 1972.
Chandra, Bipan. *Communalism in Modern India.* New Delhi, 1984.
————. *India's Struggle for Independence.* New Delhi, 1989.
————. *Nationalism and Colonialism in Modern India.* New Delhi, 1979.
Dalmia, Vasudha. *The Nationalization of Hindu Traditions: Bhartendu Harishchandra and Nineteenth Century Banaras.* Delhi, 1996.
Damodaran, A.K. *Jawaharlal Nehru: Communicator and Democratic Leader.* New Delhi, 1997.
Dar, S.L. and S. Somaskandan. *History of the Banaras Hindu University.* Banaras, 1966.
Das, Durga. *India: From Curzon to Nehru and After.* London, 1969.
Desai, A.R. *Social Background of Indian Nationalism.* Bombay, 1979.
Dixit, Prabha. *Communalism: A Struggle for Power.* New Delhi, 1972.
Frietag, Sandria, B. *Collective Action and Community: Public Arenas and the Emergence of Comunalism in North India.* Delhi, 1990.
————. *Culture and Power in Banaras: Community, Performance and Environment 1800–1980.* Delhi, 1989.
Gopal, Ram. *Indian Muslims: A Political History, 1958–1947.* Bombay, 1959.
Gopal, S. *Jawaharlal Nehru: A Biography, Volume 1, 1881–1947.* Bombay, 1959.
————. *Radhakrishnan A Biography.* Bombay, 1989.
Gordon, Leonard A. *Brothers against the Raj.* New Delhi, 2000.
Gould, Harold. *Grass Root Politics in India: A Century of Political Evolution in Fyzabad District.* New Delhi, 1994.
Graham, Bruce. *Hindu Nationalism and Indian Politics: The Origins and Development of the Bharatiya Jana Sangh.* Cambridge, 1993.
Guha, Ranjit, ed. *Subaltern Studies,* vol. 1. New Delhi, 1982.
Hardy Peter. *The Muslims of Modern India.* Cambridge, 1972.

Hasan, M. *Nationalism and Communal Politics in India 1916–28.* New Delhi, 1978.

Indraparakash. *Hindu Mahasabha: Its Contribution to Indian Politics.* Delhi, 1966.

———. *Where We Differ.* Delhi, 1947.

Jaffrelot, Christophe. *The Hindu Nationalist Movement and Indian Politics, 1925 to the 1990s: Strategies of Identity Building, Implementation and Mobilisation (With Special Reference to Central India).* New Delhi, 1996.

Jain, A.P. *Rafi Ahmad Kidwai: A Memoir of His Life and Times.* Bombay, 1965.

Kaura, Uma. *Muslims and Indian Nationalism.* New Delhi, 1977.

Khaliquzzaman, Choudhry. *Pathway to Pakistan.* Lahore, 1991.

King, C.R. *One Language Two Scripts.* New Delhi, 1996.

Kudaisiya, M.N. *The Life and Times of G.D. Birla.* Delhi, 2003.

Low, D.A., ed. *Congress and the Raj: Facets of the Indian Struggle.* London, 1977.

———. *Soundings in Modern South Asian History.* London, 1968.

Majumdar, R.C. *History of the Freedom Movement in India.* Calcutta, 1964.

Malaviya, Madan Mohan. *Speeches and Writings of Pandit Madan Mohan Malaviya.* Madras: G.A. Nateson & Co., 1920.

Mehta, A. and A. Patwardhan. *Communal Triangle in India.* Allahabad, 1944.

Menon, Visalakshi. *Indian Women and Nationalism: the U.P. Story.* New Delhi, 2003.

Misra, B.B. *The Indian Political Parties: An Historical Analysis of Political Behaviour up to 1947.* Delhi, 1976.

Misra, Salil. *A Narrative of Communal Politics: Uttar Pradesh 1937–39.* New Delhi, 2001.

Moore, R.J. *The Crisis of Indian Unity.* Delhi, 1974.

Nanda, B.R. *Gokhale, Gandhi and Nehrus: A Study in Indian Nationalism.* London, 1974.

———. *Mahatma Gandhi.* Oxford, 1958.

———. *The Nehrus.* London, 1962.

Nehru, J. *An Autobiography.* New Delhi, 1980.

Page, David. *Prelude to Partition: The Indian Muslims and the Imperial System of Control.* Oxford, 1982.

Pande, B.N., ed. *A Centenary History of the Indian National Congress,* vols 1–3. New Delhi, 1985.

Pandey, Gyanendra. *Construction of Communalism in Colonial North India.* New Delhi, 2000.

———. *The Ascendancy of the Congress in Uttar Pradesh, 1926–34: A Study in Imperfect Mobilisation.* Oxford, 1977.

Panikkar, K.N. *Culture, Ideology, Hegemony: Intellectuals and Social Consciousness in Colonial India.* New Delhi, 1995.

Prasad, B. *Hindu–Muslim Questions.* Allahabad, 1941.

Prasad, R. *India Divided*. Bombay, 1946.

Ralhan, O.P., ed. *Hindu Mahasabha*, vols I and II. New Delhi, 1997.

Reeves, P.D. *Landlords and Government in Uttar Pradesh:A Study of Their Relations until Zamindari Abolition*. Oxford, 1993.

Robinson, Francis. *Separatism among Indian Muslims: The Politics of the United Provinces Muslims, 1860–1923*. Oxford, 1993.

Sampurnanand. *Memories and Reflections*. Bombay, 1982.

Sitaramayya, Pattabhi. *The History of the Indian National Congress*. Bombay, 1935.

Speeches of Pandit Madan Mohan Malviya, Madras: Ganesh & Co., 1919.

Wadhwa, R.L. *Hindu Mahasabha*. New Delhi, 1999.

Wolpert, S.A. *Tilak and Gokhale*. Delhi, 1961.

Index

217; diversity within, 2; establishment of, 3; inquiry report of, 106–8; and Communal Award, 253–5; as political organization, 3; for rebels as 'New Party', 16; special session at Bombay, 95. *See also* Congress sessions

Congress sessions, 7–10, 17–21, 33–6, 95–7, 107–8, 114–16, 119–20, 131, 144–6, 148–9, 202, 211, 241, 260, 287–90; Allahabad, 7–9, 144; Banaras, 17–18; Calcutta, 5, 18; Delhi, 97; Gauhati, 211–12; at Kanpur and after, 202; Karachi, 233; Lahore, 221; Madras, 7; Nagpur, 19, 119–21; Malaviya's presidentship of, 97–9, 103, 281; Surat, 20–1, 287

Congress Subjects Committee, 31, 239

Congress Working Committee (CWC), 136, 172, 222, 225–8, 232–3, 252–4, 256, 259, 277–81, 290, 292; in favour of Limited Pact, 277–8; non-inclusion of Malaviya in, 233–4; Malaviya's resignation from, 222; resolution of December (1936), 281

Congress–League Pact of 1916, 145. *See also* Lucknow Pact

cow sacrifice, 181

cow-protection movement, 5

Daily Express, and Malaviya's 'moving appeal', 151

Dandi March (1930), 224, 291

Das, Bhagwan, 47, 63, 66, 77–8, 117, 205, 209–10, 222, 229, 290

Das, C.R., 106–8, 120, 128–31, 152, 199, 289; resolution of, 107

Das, Govind, 47, 77

Defence of India Act, 31, 90
denominational universities, 53–4
Desai, Bhulabhai, 280
Desai, Mahadeva, 172
dominion status, 199, 216–18, 221; Annie Besant for, 159
Dubey, Anandi Prasad, 155–6, 230
Dussehra celebrations, 177
Dwarkadas, Jamnadas, 128–9

elections: of 1923, 197–8, 208–11; of November 1926, 204; propaganda on, 278–9
electoral politics, 154, 267, 282; of 1936–37, 292; Malaviya as victim of, 282–3
Emergency Power Ordinances, 237
Extremists, 16–18, 20–1, 32–3, 36, 43, 93, 95–6, 287

First World War, 97, 99
forcible conversions, 147, 165, 172
fundraising campaigns, 49–50, 52, 61

Gandhi, 74–5, 101–2, 108, 112–20, 122–3, 127–31, 133–7, 166–8, 217–18, 224, 227, 231–5, 237–8, 244–7, 251–5, 291; anti-untouchability campaign of, 247; Malaviya's appeal to, 129; arrest at Sabarmati Ashram, 137; at Bombay, 135; call of boycott of education, 117–19; call for civil disobedience campaign, 134–8; call for non-cooperation movement, 289; campaign against untouchability, 246; and Congress to Khilafat movement, 146; Harijan tour in Varanasi, 247; on Hindu–Muslim question, 169; lecture, 74–5;

procession, 180, 182, (*see also* riots in Allahabad); representations against, 279; Residential Hindu University, 40; retirement, 283; and round table conference, 129, 131–2; on Rowlatt Bills, 100; and Sapru, 218; for self-government, 90, 98, 214; with Shiva Prasad Gupta, 51; in subcommittee of Banaras Hindu Society, 66; Sundar Lal and, 60, 71; for *swaraj*, 123–4; on Swaraj Party, 208; teaching career, 4–5; on Temple Entry Bill, 246; and untouchables, 247; to Vallabhbhai Patel, 227; on Vernacular Press Act, 29; and Wacha, 96; Wedderburn to, 89; and W. Marris, 191

Malaviya, Radhakant, 271

Marris, Sir W., 172, 183, 191

Marwari merchants, 226

Medina, 151

Mehta, P.M., 21

Meston, James, 36, 66–7, 70, 86, 89

Mill, John Stuart, 297

Minorities Committee (1931), 235

Minto, Lord, 22, 92, 144

Misra, Gokaran Nath, 49, 66

Moderates, 17–22, 26, 32, 34, 36, 91, 93–6, 120, 198, 232, 288; reunion of Extremists and, 32–3. *See also* Extremists

Mohammedan University, 50, 54, 57; Mohammedan Education Conference for, 44

Mohammedans, 24–5, 171, 184–6, 287; separate electorates for, 24–5

Mohsin-ul-Mulk, 13

Montagu, Edwin, 90–3, 106–7, 123–5, 137, 290; letter to, 123

Montagu–Malaviya talks, 91–2

Montford Report (Montagu–Chemsford report) on constitutional reforms, 93–4, 967, 288

Moonje, B.S., 152, 156–7, 187–8, 203, 207, 211, 244, 264–7

Moplah uprising, 146–8, 164–5

Morley, John, 22–3, 25, 297

Morley–Minto Reform Act of 1909, 22–4

mosques controversy, music before, 172–8. *See also* Ramlila celebration, Allahabad

Muddiman Committee, 200

Muddiman, Alexander, 200

Muhammedan Educational Conference, Nagpur, 45

Muir College of Allahabad, 3–4

Muslim League, 34–6, 88, 112, 147, 215, 242, 265

Muslim university, 45, 50, 53–5; establishment of, 45, 54; Foundation Committee for, 45; to lay foundation, 49; movement for, 46

Mussoorie, Malaviya's meeting with Nehru at, 276

North-Western Provinces and Oudh, 11, 293

Nagri Pracharni Sabha, 11, 143

Nagri resolution, 13

Naidu, Sarojini, 203, 206, 221, 234, 239, 291

National Convention at Surat, 21

National Liberal League, 96

Nationalism, 1, 22, 99, 158, 162, 173, 205, 271, 296

Nationalist Party, 201, 212, 214, 222, 255–61, 264–70, 275–9, 281–2, 296–7; formation of, 199; relations between Congress and, 258–61

About the Author

Jagannath Prasad Misra, formerly Professor and Head, Department of History, Banaras Hindu University, Varanasi, India, had a long teaching career at Kanpur, Pilani, and Varanasi. His published works include *The Administration of India under Lord Lansdowne* (1975), *Aadhunik Bharat Ka Itihas* (2003), *Madan Mohan Malviya* (1987), and *Swadhinta Aandolan* (1995). He has published a number of papers on various aspects of India's struggle for freedom.